P9-DBT-383

Augsburg Commentary on the New Testament

JOHN

Robert Kysar

Augsburg Publishing House

Minneapolis, Minnesota

AUGSBURG COMMENTARY ON THE NEW TESTAMENT
John

Copyright © 1986 Augsburg Publishing House

All rights reserved. Except for brief quotations in critical articles or reviews, no part of this book may be reproduced in any manner without prior written permission from the publisher. Write to: Permissions, Augsburg Publishing House, 426 S. Fifth St., Box 1209, Minneapolis MN 55440.

Scripture quotations are from the Revised Standard Version of the Bible, copyright 1946, 1952, and 1971 by the Division of Christian Education of the National Council of Churches.

Library of Congress Cataloging-in-Publication Data

Kysar, Robert.
  JOHN

   (Augsburg commentary on the New Testament)
   Bibliography: p.
   1. Bible. N.T. John—Commentaries. I. Title.
II. Series.
BS2615.3.K97   1986   226'.507   85-26736
ISBN 0-8066-8860-2

Manufactured in the U.S.A.   APH 10-9018

1   2   3   4   5   6   7   8   9   0   1   2   3   4   5   6   7   8   9

To the students in my courses on the Gospel of John
at the Lutheran Theological Seminaries
of Philadelphia and Gettysburg
who have taught me so much about this gospel.

CONTENTS

FOREWORD

The AUGSBURG COMMENTARY ON THE NEW TESTA-
MENT is written for laypeople, students, and pastors. Laypeople
will use it as a resource for Bible study at home and at church. Students and instructors will read it to probe the basic message of the
books of the New Testament. And pastors will find it to be a valu-
able aid for sermon and lesson preparation.

The plan of each commentary is designed to enhance its useful-
ness. The Introduction presents a topical overview of the biblical
book to be discussed and provides information on the historical
circumstances in which that book was written. It may also contain
a summary of the biblical writer's thought. In the body of the commentary, the interpreter sets forth in brief compass the meaning of
the biblical text. The procedure is to explain the text section by
section. Care has also been taken to avoid the heavy use of technical terms. Because the readers of the commentary will have their
Bibles at hand, the biblical text itself has not been printed out. In
general, the editors recommend the use of the Revised Standard
Version of the Bible.

The authors of this commentary series are professors at seminaries and universities and are themselves ordained. They have
been selected both because of their expertise and because they
worship in the same congregations as the people for whom they
are writing. In elucidating the text of Scripture, therefore, they at-

test to their belief that central to the faith and life of the church of God is the Word of God.

The Editorial Committee

Roy A. Harrisville
Luther Northwestern Theological Seminary
St. Paul, Minnesota

Jack Dean Kingsbury
Union Theological Seminary
Richmond, Virginia

Gerhard A. Krodel
Lutheran Theological Seminary
Gettysburg, Pennsylvania

ABBREVIATIONS

lQS	Manual of Discipline (Dead Sea Scroll)
ICC	International Critical Commentary
JB	Jerusalem Bible
JBL	*Journal of Biblical Literature*
LXX	The Septuagint (Greek OT)
NAB	New American Bible
NT	New Testament
NEB	New English Bible
NIV	New International Version
NTS	*New Testament Studies*
OT	Old Testament
RSV	Revised Standard Version
SBLDS	Society of Biblical Literature Dissertation Series
SNTSMS	Society of New Testament Studies Monograph Series
TEV	Today's English Version (Good News Bible)

INTRODUCTION

"John's Gospel is the one, fine, true, and chief gospel, and is far, far to be preferred over the other three and placed high above them." So wrote Luther in one of the drafts of his "Preface to the New Testament." Luther preferred John's gospel because it offered more of the words and fewer of the acts of Christ, and hence, for him at least, it was among the books which " . . . show you Christ and teach you all that is necessary and salvatory for you to know. . . . "[1] His praise of this gospel is justly deserved, if somewhat exaggerated; for indeed John's gospel presents the heart of the Christian message with clarity and force. The purpose of this commentary is simply to allow that clarity and force to reach the contemporary reader.

This introduction is intended to clarify the approach taken in the commentary itself; it is not possible in this limited space to argue for all of the positions described below. For such arguments the reader is directed to the bibliography. It must suffice here to state some of the presuppositions which undergird the commentary. Those center around three clusters of topics: First, the matter of sources, the history of the composition of the gospel, and its setting; second, the questions of date and authorship; and finally, some of the prominent theological themes.

1. Sources, Composition, and Setting

It is now widely recognized that the Fourth Gospel contains traditional materials which the evangelist used in the composition of his gospel. It is not likely that the evangelist himself was an eyewitness to the historical ministry of Jesus, but it is likely that he had access to traditions which reached far back into the earliest Christian community and that some of those traditions might have been authenticated for the evangelist by one who was an eyewitness, namely, "the beloved disciple" (21:20-24). However, the task of identifying that which might be witness to the actual historical ministry of Jesus is difficult, if not impossible. It is nonetheless certain that the evangelist had knowledge of traditions which were regarded as primitive.

In what form did those traditions reach the evangelist? Did they include the other three canonical gospels? Both questions are widely debated in contemporary scholarship. With regard to the latter, the issue of the relationship of the Fourth Gospel to the Synoptics (Matthew, Mark, and Luke) has recently entered a new phase with a revitalized argument for John's dependence on one or more of the Synoptics. This commentary, however, will suppose that there was no direct literary dependence and that similarities between John and any one of the Synoptics is best explained by the thesis that both depended on a common early Christian tradition. That thesis allows one to explain both the similarities and the differences between John and the Synoptics.

If not by way of the Synoptic Gospels, in what form did the traditions reach John? Again there is no consensus among scholars. However, a growing number contend, as I do, that among his sources was a collection of wonder stories concerning Jesus which we will call the *signs source*. This source was doubtless a missionary tract employed in the Johannine community to evangelize among the Jews. It may have contained some narrative materials beyond the simple accounts of wonder stories (e.g., the call of the disciples, 1:35-51). If it did not contain a *passion narrative*, then surely John employed another source which did. Beyond a signs source and a passion narrative, the fourth evangelist probably used a *sayings source* which preserved traditional words of Jesus, but in a peculiar way. It appears that traditional sayings of Jesus had been preserved and interpreted in a homiletical fashion. That is, sayings attributed to Jesus had been developed into homiletical bits by means of typical Jewish styles of interpretation (cf. Borgen).

Introduction

Hence, the sayings material of the Fourth Gospel is distinctively different from that of the Synoptic materials, and within that sayings material it is sometimes (but most often not) possible to isolate a short traditional saying from a broad context of interpretative comments.

Each of these sources was probably written, but beyond these, John may also have incorporated sayings and narratives which were still preserved in *oral* form. The relationship of these sources to the editorial work of the fourth evangelist is most often detected at two points in the gospel. First, the distinction between tradition (source) and the evangelist's work (redaction) is visible at points in which there appears to be a break in the flow of the narrative or discourse, such as the one found at 14:31. These breaks in continuity are in effect the "seams" which are visible in the conjunction of source and interpretation. The second point at which such seams are witnessed is in the apparent contradictions in the theology of the gospel. It is assumed in our commentary that contradictions and paradoxes within the thought of the gospel are most likely due to the interrelationship of traditional views inherited by the evangelist and his own views (or those of the Johannine community contemporaneous with him; cf. §3 below).

But the history of the birth of the Fourth Gospel as we know it today was probably a bit more complicated than the simple incorporation of certain source materials into the evangelist's structure. Such a first step was doubtless the occasion of the completion of what we might call the original gospel. There is evidence, however, that after the publication of the original gospel there were changes and additions to it which formed what might have been comparable to a "second edition" of the gospel, revised and enlarged. Chapter 21 is the most obvious example of this expansion of the original gospel. It seems that the traditions behind the gospel were used and were relevant to the community at an early stage of its history. New circumstances called for a reinterpretation of those written and oral pieces, and it was then the Fourth Gospel itself was written. However, at a still later stage the attempt was made to allow the gospel to address more directly the new situation of the community, and at this stage some (but not extensive) revisions of the gospel were made. The result is that our Fourth Gospel reflects several stages in the history of the community responsible for it and attempts to relate the kerygma to those differing situations.

Therefore, the issue of the setting of the gospel is really a kind of condensed history of a particular Christian community in the first century. The best efforts to reconstruct that history result in at least a three-stage view. At the first stage, the Johannine community constituted a part of a Jewish synagogue, i.e., the earliest Johannine Christians were Jewish Christians who believed that the Christian faith was continuous with the Jewish faith and who were content to live within the context of a Jewish community. At this first stage we may suppose that beliefs were not radically different from Jewish forms of belief. Their view of Jesus was that he was the Messiah who had come and then promised to return to fulfill the hopes of the Jews as well as the Christians.

The second stage of this history brought the split of the Christians and the Jews of the synagogue. It appears that the Johannine community experienced an expulsion from their religious home in the synagogue for at least two reasons: First, their increasingly successful missionary efforts among their colleagues in the synagogue (in part due to the signs source) began to pose a threat to the leadership of the synagogue, and an earlier emphasis on what the two groups shared in common was steadily giving way to an emphasis on the differences. Involved in this may also have been the effective missionary work of the Johannine Christians among Samaritans (cf. chap. 4). The second reason for the expulsion was the destruction of the Jerusalem temple by the Romans in A.D. 70 and the resulting crisis of faith for the Jews. The destruction of the temple brought a kind of identity crisis for the Jews—what is Judaism without a center of sacrificial worship?—and may have resulted in purging sympathizers of Jesus of Nazareth from some synogogues. (In three places in the gospel the expulsion of the Christians from the synagogue is echoed—9:22; 12:42; and 16:2.) This informal and localized expulsion of the Christians (like those remembered in the narratives of Acts, e.g., 19:8f.) was possibly later formalized and made a common practice by the Council of

Jamnia, 90–95 (cf. Martyn).[2] This expulsion had a mighty effect on the Christian community, producing a trauma of faith of major proportions. It was amid this crisis that the fourth evangelist gathered the traditions of the community and interpreted them so as to address the needs of the newly isolated community. It was then that the major themes of the gospel took shape, providing the Johannine Christians assurance and confidence in the midst of the uncertainty of their recent experience of deprivation. Furthermore, it was in the subsequent, and perhaps violent, debate with the members of the synagogue that the gospel found its setting (e.g., 16:2).

The third stage of the history of the community was close to, if not identical with, the setting for the publication of 1 John. While the crisis of the expulsion from the synagogue had been resolved and the community was an independent Christian body, there appeared some internal conflicts over the interpretation of the original gospel in general, and the proper belief and practice in particular. Moreover, relationships with other Christian communities had become important (cf. chap. 21). Certain additions to the gospel appear to address this situation.[3]

2. Date, Authorship, and Style

The task of dating the gospel has become a question of dating the stages in the history of the Johannine community and in reality has become less important for the interpretation of the document than its setting. For the most part, scholars still date the gospel in the last decade of the first century. Those who hold that the expulsion of the Johannine Christians from the synagogue was as a result of the formal decree of the Council of Jamnia must, of course, date it within a few years after that council. Since I contend that the expulsion was more likely an earlier fact, I am inclined to set the date of the writing of the original gospel around 80. The first stage of the history of the community sketched above would fall within the range of 40–70. The second stage should be dated 70–80, and the last 80–100. Without the necessity of having the Gospel of John written after the Synoptics on which it is supposed to be dependent, it seems likely the evangelist did his work perhaps a decade earlier than is most often thought.

The identity of the fourth evangelist is hopelessly lost in anonymity. We deny that he was an eyewitness of Jesus (cf. above) and that he is to be identified with the "beloved disciple." It is more likely that the evangelist (whom we shall continue to call John for the sake of convenience) writes of a revered founder of the community whose witness is the basis of the community tradition; the writer speaks of this honored figure as "the disciple whom Jesus loved." If this "beloved disciple" is not the author of the gospel, who was he? He is mentioned at least five times (13: 23; 19:26-27; 20:1-8; 21:7, 20-24) and may be the "other disciple" who is referred to twice (18:15-16 and 19:35). The evangelist clearly claims for this anonymous disciple an intimate relationship with Jesus and an equal status with Peter (even though the "beloved disciple" is not mentioned until chap. 13). While some have attempted to identify this figure with one known to us from the Gospels (most often John, son of Zebedee, or Lazarus), it seems wiser to admit the unknowable in this case. It is true that the evangelist tends to idealize this figure, but it would seem that there is an actual historical person at the root of this tradition (cf. Kysar, *Fourth Evangelist*, 86-146).

If we cannot identify the fourth evangelist, we can offer some description of him on the basis of his work (I will use the masculine pronoun to refer to the author but do not thereby exclude the possibility that the person was female): First, he was a Christian well grounded in Jewish thought and practice, and not ignorant of Hellenistic thought. He was either a very sophisticated theological thinker who was conscious of subtle differences in views or else a most inept thinker who was unaware of the contradictions of his thought. We contend that the former is true. He was also a very skilled writer and storyteller. While the Greek of the gospel is among the simplest of the NT, his use of symbolism, irony, skillful literary structure, and intentional ambiguity suggests that he was a creative and artistic writer. The style of his writing is somewhat unusual. Especially in the discourse materials we see him interweave themes in a way often foreign to our understanding of logical development. The discourse materials appear to us to move with less logic and structure than with artful associations. It has been said, with good reason, that the style of the Johannine discourses is more like a spiral than a straight line. What may appear as loosely related ideas strung together in a confusing jumble may actually be a kind of development, common in Jewish interpretation of Scripture, carefully conceived to explore every angle of a theme. The result is often a mosaic of ideas (cf. the outline below).

3. Theological Themes

Here we can only hint at some of the prominent themes that exercise a controlling power in the thought of the Fourth Gospel. Because the gospel is the result of tradition, composition, and revision we will find that the theology is not a tight, logical whole, as we might like it. Instead, there are often different positions articulated on a single theme. Therefore, before listing theological themes, it is necessary to emphasize that the thought of the gospel is always designed to speak to very concrete situations. The relevance to a specific occasion was more important to those responsible for the gospel than was consistency and unity of thought. It is fair, then, to say that the theology of John is an *applied* theology, a reflection on the content of the faith with an eye to its relationship with a specific community at a given time. We may, therefore, further characterize the thought of the gospel as "community theology" as opposed to theology done in the abstract. With these facts in mind, we may identify six themes in the gospel as especially important.

First, *the identity of Jesus* is for the gospel the single most important factor in what it means to be a Christian. To know that Jesus was from God and has ascended to God would seem to be the Christological heart of the gospel. Around that center John has built a number of Christological components, some of which are more characteristic of the tradition he incorporated than of his own reflection. In rank order from the highest, most radical claims he makes for Jesus to the "lower," less demanding assertions are these: Christ is God (1:1 and 20:28). Christ existed before creation (1:1) and before his appearance as a human (17:24 and perhaps 8:58). Christ is "I AM"—a claim for the authority of God, if not also the identity of God (6:20; 8:24). Christ is the revefaler of God (8:19; 7:16-18; and 14:21-24). Christ is a "stranger in this world" who has descended from above and will again ascend (3:13-15; 9:62; 20:17; 3:31). Christ is the Father's Son (3:35; 5:22; 6:38) and unique Son (1:18; 3:16). Christ is the special envoy of God (5:24, 30; 10:36; 11:42; 17:8). Finally, Christ is the worker of wonders (2:1-11; 6:1-14). There are other ways of summarizing John's complicated view of Christ, but these components introduce most of what we will find in the pages of the gospel. While some of the traditional titles for Christ, such as "Son of God" and "Son of man" (1:24, 49; and 5:27; 6:27), are used, they are recast within the Johannine mold, shaped around the simple title "Son" and the concept of Jesus as "sent" by the Father.

Second, although John does not present *Jesus' death* as a sacrifice for human sin, there is no doubt that the death of Jesus was for John an event which, when properly viewed in faith, brought one into a new relationship with God. The crucifixion is part of John's concept of the "ascent" of the Son back to the Father (20:17), and it is that peculiar "lifting up" of the Son which at once reveals his true identity and enthrones him as king of all humanity (3:14; 8:28; 12:32, 34). His death has power to draw humans to himself (12:32) and to give them eternal life (the Johannine equivalent of salvation). While John's view of the cross is difficult to capture in a single proposition, it seems that the cross was the ultimate expression of God's love which was the power to reorient human life (3:16; 1:12; 15:13).

Third, the whole of John's thought is suspended within a *dualistic structure* which appears to represent the two realms in which humans can live. That structure is represented symbolically with a number of themes (e.g., light and darkness, above and below), but in each case they signify, on the one hand, the life of unbelief and, on the other hand, the life of faith. Whether or not John conceived of these options as having cosmic reality, the impact on the reader is the necessity of choosing to live either in the darkness or the light. There are two possibilities for human existence—belief or unbelief. It is Christ who presents these options to humanity and who makes it possible for humanity to embrace the "light" (1:5, 9). The implication of the dualism which John surely intended was that there could be no position between the light and the darkness—it was one or the other.

The dualism of decision which is so important for the gospel raises the further issue of *the nature of faith*—the fourth theme. While there seems to be an insistence that humans must respond with belief to the revelation of the Father in the Son (6:66-70), John deprives human faith of any credit or merit in itself by equally insisting (in contradiction to what has just been said) that faith is entirely a gift—a reality brought about by the Father's work in human lives (6:44; 17:6). A further nuance in John's concept of faith encounters us when we ask how the signs of Jesus evoke faith. John says, on the one hand, that people do believe on the basis of Jesus' wondrous acts (e.g., 2:11); but, on the other hand, he insists that "seeing signs" is not the most mature grounds for faith (e.g., 4:48; 20:29). Belief, in most passages in John's gospel, has as its object a personal relationship with Jesus (e.g., 4:39); in other passages the object is the words of Jesus (e.g., 2:22) or a statement about Jesus (11:27). Beginning in John, therefore, we see the tendency toward understanding faith as a matter of proper doctrine, a tendency continued in the Johannine epistles. Faith here, however, is always a dynamic matter; it is used only as a verb and never a noun.

While John uses the concept of the *Spirit* in a way very similar to other NT writers (e.g., 3:5ff.), he advances the Christian view of the Spirit with the concept of the "Paraclete." In five passages within the section called the farewell discourses (chaps. 14–16) John sketches a creative and original view of the Spirit. The Paraclete is the successor to Jesus who brings the revelation of the Father found in Christ to the believers, reminds them of all that Jesus said, glorifies Christ, and convicts the world of unbelief (14:15-17; 14:26; 15:26-27; 16:7-11, 12-14). It is in these passages that John relates the Spirit to the Father and to the Son (although not in such a sophisticated sense as the later doctrine of the Trinity) and enlivens the way in which the Spirit may be understood as related to the community of faith amid a world of unbelief.

Because of the presence of the Paraclete in the life of the believer, the blessings of the end-time—the eschaton—are already present. At times John speaks as if that final consummation of history is still a future event conceived in terms typical of apocalyptic thought, both Jewish and Christian: The end-time will bring the coming of Christ, the resurrection of the dead, judgment, and eternal life for believers (e.g., 14:3, 18, 28; 6:39-40; 12:48, 25). Yet, at other times, all of these are spoken of as present realities in the lives of the believers (e.g., 3:18; 5:21, 24, 26). Moreover, there is also some evidence for the view that believers upon their death are taken directly to a heavenly home where they dwell immediately with God (14:2-3; 17:2-3). It is clear that John's eschatology is a complex one that bridges the distinctions of time and strongly affirms the present life of the believer. In this twofold (or threefold) eschatology we see a possible hint at how John has combined in his gospel older traditional views (future eschatology) with his own interpretation of those views (present or realized eschatology).

These six themes do little more than hint at the rich and none-too-simple views of the Fourth Gospel. Perhaps, however, they do whet the appetite of the reader for the whole banquet of thought found in this gospel.[4]

Note: When in the text of the commentary references to other passages in John's gospel are followed by "above" or "below," the reader is directed to the author's comments on them.

OUTLINE OF THE GOSPEL OF JOHN

It is sometimes argued that the structure of John as it stands to-day could not possibly be what the evangelist originally intended. Such an argument takes its force from certain points in the gospel at which it appears there is a break of some sort without sufficient transition. One example is the relationship between chap. 14, on the one hand, and chaps. 15-17, on the other. John 14:31 seems to indicate the conclusion of the discourse with the disciples and the departure to the garden where the arrest of Jesus takes place. The three chapters in between seem intrusive. Another example involves the geography of chaps. 5 and 6. In the former we are told that Jesus is in Jerusalem (v. 1); suddenly in 6:1 he is back in Galilee. Such difficulties have motivated some to suggest that the gospel has suffered a violent rearrangement from the order it originally had, or that the gospel represents the unfinished work of the author. Whatever the case may be, there is no doubt the present order presents difficulties (cf. n. 12).

Even with those difficulties, however, theories of rearrangement which seek to restore a lost order or complete the gospel as the evangelist might have intended seem very speculative and unnecessary. The order of the gospel as it stands does make some sense, even with the difficulties, and apparently the redactor did not feel constrained to improve it. The outline suggested below is an attempt to express the logic of the present order without recourse to rearrangement. The difficulties with the order most likely have resulted from (1) the use of traditional materials by the evangelist and (2) later additions to the work of the original gospel.

With all of our high regard for the skill of the evangelist, it appears that he was not always careful to cover the "seams" between his sources and his own composition. Alan Culpepper captures the truth in these words: "As a construction, the gospel is magnificent but flawed. Magnificent in its complexity, subtlety, and profundity, but oddly flawed in some of its transitions, sequences and movements" (p. 231).

I. Introduction: Beginnings (1:1-51)

    A. The Cosmic-Historical Beginning (1:1-18)
        1. The Relationship of the Word with God and His Function in Creation (1:1-5)
        2. The Distinction between the Light and Its Witness (1:6-8, 15)
        3. The Rejection and Acceptance of the Word (1:9-13)
        4. The Humanization of the Word (1:14)
        5. The Benefits of the Humanization of the Word (1:15-18)

    B. The Witness of the Baptizer (1:19-34)
        1. The Baptizer's First Witness (1:19-28)
        2. The Baptizer's Second Witness (1:29-34)

    C. The Gathering of the Disciples (1:35-51)
        1. Disciples of the Baptizer Follow Jesus and Witness to Him (1:35-42)
        2. The Calling of the Other Disciples (1:43-51)

II. Jesus Reveals Glory (2:1—12:50)

    A. Signs and Speeches (2:1—5:47)
        1. The First Sign—the Wedding at Cana (2:1-11)
        2. The Cleansing and Replacement of the Temple (2:12-25)
        3. The Nicodemus Discourse (3:1-21)
        4. The Baptizer's Third Witness (3:22-36)
           a. The Continuation of the Witness (3:22-30)
           b. An Attached Discourse (3:31-36)

2. Peter's Reinstatement and Commissioning (21:15-19)
3. The Importance and Destiny of the Beloved Disciple (21:20-24)
4. A Final Ending (21:25)[5]

COMMENTARY

Introduction: Beginnings (1:1-51)

■ The Cosmic-Historical Beginning (1:1-18)

John begins his narration of the ministry of Jesus only after first describing the cosmic origin of Jesus. This is striking when compared to the Synoptics. It pushes behind even the divine conception of Jesus told by Matthew and Luke (of which John seems to know nothing). John leaves us no room to doubt the importance of this Jesus—an importance that requires us to conceive of the "beginning." Throughout his gospel he will stress that knowing who Jesus is, so that one can properly believe in him, necessitates knowing where he is from and to where he will return (e.g., 6:42; 16:5). Jesus' origins are with God from the very beginning before creation, and it is only natural that he should return to his status with the Father after his earthly sojourn. The reader is privy to this knowledge from the first, and consequently knows what many of the characters in the plot of the gospel do not (e.g., 8:48ff.). This skillfully sets the stage for the evangelist's use of irony.

The passage, usually called the prolog, has an undeniable poetic structure which has led many to speak of it as a "hymn" or a revision of what was originally a hymn (vv. 6-8 and 15, however, are prosaic insertions). It is possible that the prolog in some form did function as a hymn in the worship life of the Johannine community, but we cannot be sure how it was employed or what its precise form was before its use here to introduce the gospel. Several other questions also arise: First, what is the relationship of this passage to the remainder of the gospel? Some see it as a later addition, perhaps from a source outside the Johannine community. One reason for this suggestion is the appearance of several non-Johannine words, e.g., "grace" (*charis*) in vv. 14, 16, and 17. On the other hand, the motifs of the prolog fit too well the proposed setting for the gospel described above in the Introduction to ascribe it to any other than the Johannine community.[6] It is more likely that the word *grace* here is from a very early creedal statement, parts of which were incorporated into the hymn. That such a creedal statement was originally a Jewish hymn to wisdom is possible but beyond proof. Second, there is the difficult question of the referents of the prolog. At what point does the passage begin to speak of the historical Jesus and his work—v. 14, v. 10, or v. 5? If v. 14, then everything before that would seem to describe the work of the Word in the created order and/or Israel's history. In the outline below I suggest that vv. 5 and 9-13 refer to the work of the Word in the history of Israel, and that vv. 14-18 refer to the historical Jesus. This explains the appearance of the first person pronoun at v. 14 ("we beheld"). The Christian community can personally witness to the presence of the Word in the historical-Jesus.

A final question regards the meaning of *logos* ("Word," applied to the preexistent Christ in 1:1, 14). In this limited space we can only suggest that it was a rich religious-philosophical word perhaps chosen for its diverse meanings and its wide use. First, it is clearly related to the "Word of the Lord" (*dabar YHWH*) in the OT where it is used of the creative power of God (Ps. 33:6; cf. Genesis 1) and the message of God for the human community (e.g., Hos. 1:1). But *logos* may also be related to Jewish concepts of wisdom (*sophia*) in the later periods of the OT and the intertestamental period. Many of the things ascribed to the *logos* in the prolog are parallel to statements made of wisdom. For example, Proverbs 8 gives wisdom a role in creation as v. 3 does to *logos*, and wisdom is said to take up her dwelling among humans in Sir. 24:8 as *logos* does in v. 14. *Logos* may then have been a Christian counterpart to wisdom and molded in the image of that Jewish motif. But in Hellenistic thought too *logos* was prominent. In Stoic thought *logos* was the reason of the universe, and parallels to the prolog can be found in the work of Heraclitus of Ephesus and elsewhere. It appears that the author of the hymn has deliberately chosen a Greek word with a full variety of associations. By doing this he implicitly claims that Christ fulfills the expectations of the whole of the human race, Gentile and Jew. The evangelist does a similar kind of thing elsewhere in the gospel, employing rich, multiple-meaning words in a creative way (e.g., "Paraclete," cf. 14: 15-17 below). We can do no more here than suggest a definition of the Johannine concept of *logos*: simply put, it represents the self-expression of God.

The prolog has four essential parts (aside from the two references to John the baptizer in vv. 6-8 and 15), each of which speaks of a period of divine revelation in the world:

1. The relation of the Word to God in the beginning, at creation (1-5).
2. The rejection and acceptance of the Word in the world and Israel's history (9-12).
3. The humanization of the Word in Jesus (14).
4. The benefits of the humanization of the Word especially in relationship to the Hebraic tradition (15-18).

The Relationship of the Word with God and His Function in Creation (1:1-5)

1-2—**In the beginning** echoes Gen. 1:1, setting the description of **the Word** in relationship with that time before time when God created the universe. **Beginning** (*archē*) should be thought of not only in temporal terms, however, for it suggests first in importance (cosmic) as well as first in time (temporal). **The Word was with God and the Word was God** speaks of the mystery of the Word, for it asserts the identity of God and his Word (**was God**, *theos ēn ho logos*) along with the suggestion of individuality—**the Word was with** (*pros*) **God**. (The absence of the definite article before **God** in **the Word was God** is not sufficient grounds to translate *theos ēn* "was divine.") The relationship is intentionally stated in a paradoxical manner. That paradoxical relationship is further stated in what John affirms about the relationship of the Father and the Son (see below). Verse 2 restates a portion of v. 1 in poetic parallelism.

3-4—Here the Word is defined as the divine agent of creation, through whom God's creative work is carried on, so that all existence depends upon the Word. But the Word is not only the source of **life** (v. 4) in a natural sense, for the meaning of life (*zōē*) here is more than existence. It is one of John's several terms for salvation and the equivalent of "eternal life" (e.g., 3:36). **Life** is the true existence of humanity, the kind of existence intended for humanity at creation. Hence, that **life** can be called **light** (*phōs*), another of John's words for the authentic life, the life of those who live in relationship with the Father as his children.

5—The dualism of the gospel is now introduced. The creative life-giving light of the Word intrudes into the darkness which represents the distortion of creation and the chaos of unbelief and alienation from God—the results of the fall. The word translated overcome (*katalambanō*) is ambiguous, for it can mean "mastered" or "comprehended" as well. Perhaps in the poetic style of the prolog all of those nuances are intended. The **darkness** of unbelief has neither understood nor mastered the Word. And yet the darkness continues even though the Word brings **light** into its midst. The revelation does not eliminate the reality of unbelief and evil.

The Distinction between the Light and Its Witness (1:6-8,15)

The flow of the prolog is interrupted here at 6-8 and again at 15. That surely suggests how important it was for John that his readers properly understand the baptizer. He is not to be confused with Christ. Perhaps the Johannine community knew of those who followed the baptizer, claiming that he was the Messiah. The community had another reason for special interest in the identity of the baptizer, for some of its members were at one time his disciples, as 1:35-39 shows. The gospel has one thing to say about the baptizer and says it several times—he is a witness to Christ, no more, no less (1:6-8, 15, 19-34; 3:22-30). Like Jesus **John** is **sent** from God (e.g., 3:17), and it is sometimes said that Jesus bears witness (e.g., 8:18). **Believe through** (*pisteusōsin di*') is an expression also used of Jesus' word (4:41) and works (14:11). So **John** is given an honored role, one which sets him in a unique position, even though he is not to be identified as Christ. Verse 15 declares that the one who came temporally second is the more important. The Greek *prōtos* (**ranks before**) may imply "first" in the sense of prior existence as well as significance.

The Rejection and Acceptance of the Word (1:9-13)

9-11—In this section attention is upon the presence and work of the Word in the history of Israel. Verse 9, a transition, presents a problem of translation. Does the phrase **coming into the world** refer to **every person** or to the **light**? As an introduction to the work of the Word in Israel, it might be best to understand v. 9 as the RSV renders it. This **true light**, as opposed to all the alleged revelations, "lights up every person," giving enlightened existence. The goal of the revelation through the Word is to enlighten every life with divine love and thereby restore a right relationship with God. Verse 10 expresses the irony of the **world's** blindness and especially Israel's blindness to the very source of its existence. As to the question whether this verse refers to the presence of the light in the created order or in Israel's history, it may be that both are implied. The light is rejected both in its form as God's presence in the created order and as the revelation in Israel's history. With this John begins his tragic commentary on the rejection of the revelation which plays such an important part throughout this gospel. Even in **his own home** (*idia*), **his own people** (*idioi*, i.e., Israel) rejected him (v. 11).

12-13—Some would say that v. 12 is the climax of the prolog, for it states the saving results of the appearance of the Word in human history.[7] To those **who** believe he gives **power** (or "authority" or "right," *exousia*) **to become children of God.** Faithful Israel knew that power which made them children of God. The Jewish origins of the Johannine Christians are evident here in what appears to be a statement of continuity between the presence and work of the Word in Israel's history and in Jesus. The revelation communicates not only insight but also **power** for a new birth (cf. 3:3). Humanity itself is impotent to become what it was destined to be and must rely entirely on a transcendent power to change. The contrast in v. 13 between **blood, flesh,** and the human **will,** on the one hand, and **of God,** on the other, is not to be taken as a dualism of flesh and spirit but simply as a Semitic way of referring to the human as opposed to the divine.

The Humanization of the Word (1:14)

This verse sets the **Word** apart from all of its antecedents in religious thought, for here the Word becomes a concrete, flesh-and-blood human. As a human now, the *logos* resides among humans as one of them. The word translated **dwelt** (*eskēnōsen*) connotes the Hebraic history in which the **glory** of Yahweh lived among the people, encamping, tabernacling, or tenting among them (cf. Exod. 33). The first person plural **we** betrays the confession of the Christian community to firsthand knowledge. The verse poses the paradox of the incarnation. On the one side, the **Word** is flesh (*sarx*) and yet, on the other, the divine **glory** (*doxa*) is perceived in him. John will say more on this paradox, but the divine nature of the Word now enfleshed as a human is still visible through the eyes of faith. **Glory** (*doxa*) is a rich word which essentially means the presence of God experienced through mighty deeds. It is God's presence the community sees in faith, a divine presence which could only be credited to the exclusive **Son from the Father.** This is the first of four times John refers to Christ not simply as the Father's Son but as the *monogenēs* ("only" or "unique," an only child) Son (cf. 1:18; 3:16, 18). The intent is to distinguish Jesus from any other claimants to divine sonship, such as attributed to the kings in the OT (e.g., Ps. 2:6-7). The prolog goes beyond identifying Christ with the Jewish Messiah who, like the king, could be called the Son of God. Now Christ is the *only* **Son of the Father.** This use of *monogenēs* may have apologetic roots, responding to protagonists who degrade Jesus' sonship by reference to Israel as the sons and daughters of God.

Full of grace (*charis*) **and truth** (*alētheia*) means the saving, life-changing power of the presence of God in Christ. **Truth** is one of

John's favorite terms for the content of the revelation and its power in humans (cf. 8:32; 14:6). But **grace** is used in John only here and in v. 17. For those who are willing to take the risk of faith, this human Jesus is one in whom can be seen the presence of God which yields all the benefits of the divine presence.

The Benefits of the Humanization of the Word (1:15-18)

16-17—Now the benefits of the presence of God are confessed with an eye toward the saving history of God in Israel. **His fulness** suggests the immeasurable richness of the revelation of God in Christ. The Greek word *plērōma* came in gnostic thought to mean the whole realm of the heavenly world. Here it is the wholeness of the divine glory in Christ. **Grace upon grace** is the best rendering of the expression which can also mean "grace instead of grace," or "grace in the place of (*anti*) grace." In Johannine usage **grace** is best understood as love, since love plays such a central role in the gospel as a whole. The sense of this verse seems to have to do with the grace of God in Israel's history and in the incarnation. Does the expression *anti* mean that the latter *replaces* the former or that together they constitute an *accumulation* of **grace?** Both possibilities can be argued to be at home in Johannine thought; but, if vv. 9-13 do indeed acknowledge the work of the Word in Israel's history, then the accumulation of grace would seem more natural at this point. Furthermore, such an interpretation implies that the act of God in Christ does not contradict, nor even replace, but fulfills the saving history of God in Israel—a view which is typical of John's attitude toward Israel. In God's saving work one good gift of love is piled upon another! The gift of God in **the Law** (Torah) is now recognized and honored. But **grace and truth** exceed the Law in importance. Here as elsewhere in the gospel Christ is seen as the legitimate fulfillment of the Torah, and those who genuinely embrace the Torah see in Christ its fulfillment (e.g., 8:39ff.).

18—This is the climax of the prolog. It begins with a common Jewish affirmation: **no one has ever seen God.** But now the invisible God is revealed in a visible manner in the revelation of Christ. Hence, Jesus can claim to be the "window" to **God**—cf. 14:9 below. The greatest gift of all is that now **the only Son, who is in the**

bosom (*kolpos*) **of the Father, he has made him known.** The impossible has been done—the very heart of God has come to self-expression in Christ. A textual variant for the word **Son** reads "God." The strongest reason for preferring the reading *God* to **Son** is the fact that it is by far the more difficult of the two. Nor is it beyond John's faith to call the Son God (unlike the majority of writers of the NT—cf. 1:1; 20:28). **Made him known** (*exēgēsato*) might more literally be translated "exegeted him" (contrast Exod. 19:11; 33:23).

With the concept of the *logos* the prolog unites the whole of God's saving activity among humans, from creation through Israel's history to the incarnation. The community affirms its faith that Christ is the final and conclusive revelation of the one true God. The point of the passage is not to make metaphysical statements about the person of Christ but to confess the results of the revelation for humanity. The focus of the Christology of the gospel is "functional," not "essentialistic" (i.e., having to do with the "nature" of Christ). Nonetheless, here the logical metaphysical conclusions of the impact of Jesus' work are hinted at (1:1). The reader is now equipped with a proper understanding of Jesus, so that the gospel story can be properly read. The prolog is a poetic hymn of praise used to "frame" the gospel story itself.

■ The Witness of the Baptizer (1:19-34)

The Baptizer's First Witness (1:19-28)

19-21—The prolog has already turned our thoughts to the historical reality of Jesus, and now John continues with a statement of the witness of the baptizer, fleshing out what is said of him in vv. 6-8, 15. Throughout the remainder of chap. 1 the identity of Jesus remains at center stage. **Who are you?** the baptizer is asked, when the question John is really interested in is who Jesus is. **The Jews** in v. 19 appears as John will often use it, namely, as a designation for the religious leaders of the time. **Priests and Levites** are perhaps specialists in the rites of purification and hence are interested in the use of baptism by **John.** The baptizer denies that he is the **Christ, Elijah,** or the **prophet.** Unlike Matthew and Mark (but not unlike Luke) John does not think of the baptizer as the figure of Elijah returned to be the forerunner of the Messiah (Matt. 11:14; Mark 9:13). **The prophet** refers to the "prophet like Moses" who was to accompany the Messiah, as some Jews believed, or who was himself the Messiah, as others seemed to have held (cf. Deut. 18: 15-18). John stresses again that the baptizer has no status except as a witness to Jesus.

22-23—In the face of his denials, the Jewish leaders ask again who the baptizer is. He responds in v. 23 in the words of Isa. 40:3, a quotation used to describe the baptizer in all of the Gospels (Matt. 3:3; Mark 1:3; Luke 3:4). Here, however, the quotation is placed on the lips of the baptizer himself and is not simply the evangelist's description of him, as is the case with the Synoptics. The original meaning of the passage was the bold proclamation of Deutero-Isaiah that God was about to act in history to free the people from their exile and lead them back to their homeland. Here too the meaning is the announcement of God's impending act of salvation.

24-28—Now it is strangely said the messengers are from **the Pharisees,** in distinction to the broader term, "the Jews," used in v. 19. Some suggest that John has linked together here two different traditions concerning the interrogation of the baptizer. It appears that the various groups of Jewish leaders of Jesus' time were meaningless to the evangelist who was writing decades later and for whom **the Pharisees** represented the whole of Judaism. If the baptizer denies being any one of the eschatological figures mentioned in v. 21, **then why are you baptizing?** The implication is that baptism was expected to be performed by those messianic figures, but we have no other evidence for this expectation, except perhaps among the Essenes of Qumran. The baptizer's answer (v. 26) minimizes the importance of water baptism and instead turns attention to the **one whom you do not know.** The Messiah, it was sometimes said, would live incognito among the people until such time as he chose to reveal himself. And again (v. 27) the baptizer relegates himself to an inferior position with regard to Christ, as 1:

6-8, 15 does. The statement is paralleled in the Synoptic Gospels in a slightly different form (e.g., Mark 1:7). The baptizer deems himself unworthy to do even that which it was forbidden to force a slave to do—remove the master's shoes. John presents the baptizer as a model of Christian witness. The witness must always minimize himself or herself in order to point unequivocally to the one to whom the witness is directed. Verse 28, it would seem, distinguishes **Bethany** from the one named in 11:1ff. There is, however, no other trace of a Bethany in Transjordan.[8] It is nonetheless unlikely that John intended some symbolic meaning rather than a simple place-name.

The Baptizer's Second Witness (1:29-34)

29—The witness of the baptizer becomes more specific now: **The Lamb of God who takes away the sin of the world.** For the most part, the Gospel of John does not view the death of Jesus in terms of sacrificial worship, and therefore this title seems out of place. Several possibilities arise. It may be that this is a fragment of sacrificial language preserved in tradition (as 1:19-51 may well be incorporated from the signs source) which the evangelist repeats without attaching a great deal of importance to it. It may also be that **the Lamb** is not intended to refer to the lamb used in sacrifices for atonement but rather to the Passover lamb, with which John does identify Christ (cf. 13:1ff. below). Whether or not the Passover lamb was viewed as expiation for sin by the Jews of the first century is uncertain. The association of the liberation of the people with Passover suggests that it is the Passover imagery John has in mind here, especially since he often employs that imagery (cf. 6:4 below).

30-32—The baptizer identifies Jesus as the one to whom he has referred earlier (vv. 15, 27), and now in v. 31 defines his baptizing as a preparation for the recognition of the Messiah. Verse 32 repeats the common Christian tradition of the descent of **the Spirit** upon Jesus at his baptism (e.g., Mark 1:10). But notice that it here is not situated at the actual baptism of Jesus. The evangelist is careful to avoid reporting John's baptism of Jesus, for he does not want in any possible way to subject Jesus to the baptizer (cf. Luke 3:21).

The descent of the Spirit upon Jesus is not entirely appropriate (certainly not necessary), given the affirmations of the prolog, but John repeats it here to stress that it is Christ who is the source of the Spirit (cf. 7:39 and 20:22 below). **Remained on him** employs John's favorite expression for relationships within the scope of the divine, namely, *menein* ("abide," e.g., 15:4ff.). Here it denotes the close and intimate tie between the Spirit and the Son (cf. 14:16 below).

33-34—The baptizer confesses openly that his knowledge of the Messiah's identity is possible only because of God's gift to him. John sometimes seems to say that it is always by God's gift that we are able to confess Christ (e.g., 6:37). **This is he who baptizes with the Holy Spirit** (v. 33) is John's way of saying two things: First (and again), the baptizer's **water** baptism is inferior to the gift Jesus brings. Second, the gift of the Spirit is for John the only baptism. While John is not opposed to the practice of Baptism, he has little to say about it (cf. 3:22; 4:2; and 3:5 below). The gift of the Spirit is for him superior to water Baptism, and it is his claim that he and his community have been "baptized" with **the Spirit**/Paraclete (e.g., 14:15-17). The tradition did affirm, however, the association of water and Spirit baptism. This is the first of only three times that John uses the expression **the Holy Spirit.** Here and in 20:22 it is used without definite articles, but at 14:26 it appears in its full form, *the* **Holy** *the* **Spirit.** In v. 34 **Son of God** is the second of the titles for Jesus which appear in this section, the first being "the Lamb of God" (v. 29). **Son of God** (*ho huios tou theou*) is one of the traditional titles for the Messiah, having its roots in the association of the Messiah with the ideal, Davidic king of Israel. John uses the title nine times (1:49; 3:18; 5:25; 10:36; 11:4, 27; 19:7; 20:31; and in this passage), most often in its traditional sense but also in connection with eschatological themes which are uniquely Johannine (e.g., 3:18; 5:25 below). For John it is a title suggestive of the intimate relationship between the Father and the Son, but he prefers the simpler title, "Son."

The baptizer's function as a witness has been performed in exemplary fashion. John will stress that witness is of vital importance and that unless one correctly attends to the witnesses to Christ, belief is hardly possible (cf. 5:30-47 below). So, while careful to relegate the baptizer to the status of only a witness, John has exalted him to a function of great significance. The witnesses enable persons to come to Christ, and that role is a privilege of the highest kind.

■ The Gathering of the Disciples (1:35-51)

Disciples of the Baptizer Follow Jesus and Witness to Him (1: 35-42)

35-37—The high honor of being a witness to Christ is now acted out with clear and successful results. The baptizer is **with two of his disciples,** repeats his witness that Jesus is **the Lamb of God,** and his **disciples** follow **Jesus.** The Synoptics tell us nothing of the followers of the baptizer, although Acts 19:1-7 may suggest that there were such. It may be that among the original members of the Johannine church there were those who had been recruited from the disciples of the baptizer, and this story preserves that memory. It may also be the case that this story is another instance of a polemic against those who persisted in believing that the baptizer was the Messiah and against whom the author speaks with nearly every mention of the baptizer. Whatever the case, John shows that the witness of the baptizer is effective in bringing **two disciples** to **Jesus.**

38-39—It is to be noted that in this section devoted to the gathering of the disciples the word **follow** (*akoloutheō*) figures prominently—vv. 37, 38, 40, and 43. John preserves the common idea that being a disciple involves **following** the master with all that that entails. Jesus asks the disciples following him, **What do you seek?** (v. 38). John will later raise the issue of the motives of those who seek **Jesus** (6:26f.), and so it is possible that the question he places on Jesus' lips here also calls for an examination of motives for discipleship. The disciples ask the rather strange question of Jesus' place of residence—strange, that is, unless one recognizes again the basic Christological motif of the gospel, namely, Jesus' origin. They address Jesus as **Rabbi** (cf. 3:2, 26; 4:31; 6:25; 9:2; 11:8), adding still a third title used of Jesus in this section and the previous one. A parenthetical comment translates the Hebrew title for the reader. It seems unlikely that John and his original readers would have needed such a translation, and so it is probably the case that such parenthetical translations (cf. 1:41; 20:16) are the work of a later redactor of the gospel. Jesus responds to their interest with the invitation, **Come and see** (v. 39). The invitation is repeated in v. 46 when Philip responds to Nathanael's skepticism. Discipleship involves two factors: First, it is a journey, an adventure, in which the disciple trusts the course of the journey to the master; hence, Jesus invites the two disciples to **come**—to undertake a pilgrimage. Second, for John, discipleship involves the opportunity for firsthand experience, and so Jesus invites the two to **see**, to learn for themselves. For John "seeing" is a means of perceiving through faith (cf. 14:9 below). Hence, the invitation is to come and follow Jesus and with the eyes of faith **see** who Jesus really is. Note that the risk of the journey (**come**) necessarily precedes the experience of seeing. Verse 39 reports that the two as yet unnamed disciples do precisely that. The time reference (**that day . . . tenth hour**) may have some symbolic meaning, but more likely it simply indicates the fact that they spent some time with their new master.

40-42—The "chain reaction" quality of witness is shown as one of the disciples, **Andrew**, enlists his brother, **Simon**. His witness to his **brother** (v. 41) is simple—**We have found the Messiah** (the fourth title in our growing list). The signs source from which John drew this story presented the rather simple and naive view that those who are open and waiting discover the identity of Jesus swiftly. **First** in v. 41 renders *prōton*, the most likely of four different readings in the manuscripts. Among the others is *prōtos*, which suggests that Andrew was the first of several to find Simon, and *prōi*, meaning an early hour of the day. Upon meeting him Jesus gives Simon his nickname, **Cephas** (v. 42), an Aramaic word meaning "rock" (cf. 21:15 below). Interestingly, **Peter** receives his name in Matt. 16:18 in response to his own confession at Caesarea Philippi, but here in association with Andrew's confession.

The Calling of the Other Disciples (1:43-51)

43-46—We are to understand that the narrative from v. 19 to this point has taken place in "Bethany beyond the Jordan" (v. 28). But now the scene shifts to **Galilee,** which illustrates the frequency with which John moves Jesus back and forth between Judea and Galilee, as compared with the Synoptics. **Bethsaida** (v. 44) was a predominantly Gentile city across the border from Galilee into Gaulanitis. It is Jesus who takes the initiative to call **Philip** with the simple command, **Follow me.** The seeming lack of realism about the story—that one would immediately respond to such a command by a stranger—is not important, for John is not so much interested in the subtleties of the narrative as he is in its meaning for discipleship. Once again there is a "chain reaction" (cf. v. 41 above) following the call to discipleship. **Philip finds Nathanael** and makes the claim that **Jesus is the one of whom Moses in the law and also the prophets wrote** (the fifth title applied to Jesus). The words have the substance of Andrew's witness in v. 41—the Messiah. Like Andrew, Philip speaks of Jesus in traditional messianic terms. He claims that the long-expected Messiah is **Jesus of Nazareth.** This is the only time John refers to Jesus with this place-name (cf. 18:5 below). **The son of Joseph** appears only here and 6:42. **Philip's** claim troubles Nathanael, for nothing of any importance is to be expected from **Nazareth.** His words are perhaps a slogan of contempt for Nazareth on the part of those in surrounding villages. To Nathanael's skepticism, Philip mimics the words of Jesus, **Come and see** (cf. v. 39 above).

47-48—What it is that **Nathanael** "sees" when he has come to Jesus is now told. Jesus greets him with the words, **Behold, an Israelite indeed, in whom is no guile.** The Greek is literally, "here is truly an Israelite." The adverb rendered **indeed** (*alēthōs*) may in this construction serve as an adjective, "a *true* Israelite" (as in TEV and NAB). This is the only appearance of the word **Israelite** in John, but it suggests a basic conviction that the "true" Israelite recognizes God's act in Christ, unlike others who claim to be children of Abraham but refuse to believe (8:32ff.). John's quarrel is not with the Hebraic tradition, but with those who refuse to see its fulfillment in Christ. This is apparently an instance of Jesus' omniscience, for **Nathanael** is amazed (v. 48a), although the precise reason for his amazement is not clear. He is even further amazed when Jesus tells him that **Jesus** saw him when he was **under the fig tree** (v. 48b). That evokes his confession of faith—v. 49. Many efforts are made to find some symbolic meaning in Nathanael's sitting under a fig tree, such as the suggestion that it is under fig trees that the rabbis taught. Better is the simpler point that Jesus overwhelms Nathanael with his wondrous knowledge, and on the basis of that Nathanael (impulsively?) believes in Jesus. John is very cautious about a faith that rests on the experiences of wondrous deeds (e.g., 4:48), even though the signs source which he used taught such an understanding of faith (e.g., 2:11). The response of Jesus to the confession of Nathanael (vv. 50-51) implies that Nathanael's faith has only begun to grow, and greater maturity awaits him. Nathanael is the only one of the disciples named in this section who is not mentioned in the various lists of disciples found in Matt. 10:1-16; Mark 3:13-19; Luke 6:12-16; and Acts 1:13.

49-51—Nathanael's confession, **Rabbi, you are the Son of God! You are the King of Israel!** repeats the second and adds a sixth title in vv. 19-51. It echoes the words of the baptizer in v. 34. The two titles are essentially synonymous. **The Son of God** (cf. v. 34 above) is **the King of Israel.** Once again Jesus is addressed in traditional messianic language. In v. 50 Jesus marvels at the impulsive faith of Nathanael, and promises him that he will **see greater things than these.** It is not the wondrous signs to which Jesus refers here, although Nathanael will witness them. The **greater things** have to do with the understanding of Jesus' identity and his revelation of the Father. This is suggested by v. 51 and the rather strange promise that Nathanael and the others **will see heaven opened, and the angels of God ascending and descending upon the Son of man.** This descriptive metaphor recalls the dream experience of Jacob (Gen. 28:12ff.) but looks forward to the unveiling of the intimacy of the Father-Son relationship. What Nathanael will marvel at is less the mighty works of this Jesus than his identity; for in him the heavenly and earthly realms come in touch with one another, and he is the conduit through which the divine reality is expressed in this world. But more specifically, this strange figure of the **angels**

ascending and descending may be an allusion to the cross. It is the cross for John where Jesus is finally glorified by the Father. The contact with the heavenly realm symbolized in the **angels** occurs most especially in the cross. Nathanael's faith based on the wondrous knowledge of Jesus finds its maturity in the discovery of the identity of Jesus in the cross.[9]

In v. 51 the reader encounters the first of the uses of the double "amen" formula translated **truly, truly.** This is a unique expression found only in the Gospel of John. Whereas the single *amēn* is used to introduce sayings of Jesus in the Synoptic Gospels (e.g., Matt. 5: 18 and Mark 14:30), the double *amēn* is without biblical precedent. There is, however, some evidence of it in the Qumran literature where it is found in liturgical passages (1QS 1:20; 2:10, 18; 10:1-17). John employs the expression 25 times. The effect of the doubling of the *amēn* is to reinforce the importance of the saying that follows. It has the effect of suggesting the speaker's solemn oath to what he or she is about to say. In the Johannine tradition it may have been attached to logia (sayings) of a very primitive origin (cf. Lindars, 48).

Son of man completes and climaxes the series of titles for Christ used in vv. 19-51. A total of seven different titles appears: "Lamb of God," "Son of God," "Rabbi," "Messiah," "him of whom Moses in the law and also the prophets wrote," "King of Israel," and **"Son of man."** Each describes the perception of others as to the nature of Jesus (except the last, which is attributed to Jesus himself). Jesus refuses none of them, even though for the most part they represent traditional messianic titles. It is significant, however, that Jesus' own title concludes the list—**Son of man.** This is a traditional Christian title and one that appears frequently on the lips of Jesus in the Synoptics (e.g., Mark 8:29-31). The title is found 13 times in the Fourth Gospel and is used most often in conjunction with the crucifixion (e.g., 3:14; 8:28) and the benefits of Christ's revelation (6:26, 53), but also with eschatological themes (5:27; 9:39). John preserves this traditional title and the claim that it is used most often by Jesus (e.g., 5:27), although the Johannine Jesus far prefers the title "Son." Here John suggests that all of the previous titles stand in the shadow of this one. If the other titles tend to emphasize the glory of Jesus' messiahship in traditional terms, **Son of man** implies that messiahship involves the reality of the cross. There can be no theology of glory, even for John, that does not embrace a theology of the cross.

The section 1:35-51 is an artistic blend of the themes of discipleship and Christology. It still lacks the full flavor of John's own unique Christology (due in part to the fact that it was probably part of the signs source, cf. Introduction §1), but it nonetheless demonstrates a Johannine emphasis that discipleship roots in the correct perception of the identity of Jesus.

Jesus Reveals Glory (2:1—12:50)

▪ Signs and Speeches (2:1—5:47)

Chapter 2 begins the narration of the public ministry of Jesus after the preparation for that ministry has been completed in chap. 1. Further, the gospel seems to divide itself between chaps. 12 and 13, the first section narrating the public ministry of Jesus and the second the private teaching of the disciples and the passion story. The first is often called the "book of signs" and the second the "book of glory." In the first half of the gospel Jesus *reveals* the glory mentioned in 1:14, while in the second, he himself is glorified by God—he *receives* glory. Within chaps. 2–12 there are four sections moving steadily toward the inevitable conflict with the religious establishment and unbelief. The first of those sections narrates a series of wondrous works ("signs") and conversations-discourses. This is the foundation of Jesus' ministry and sets the direction which the following chapters take.

The First Sign—the Wedding at Cana (2:1-11)

1-2—The time reference of v. 1 is sometimes taken symbolically and associated with the resurrection on the third day, but such speculation seems unnecessary. John's time references seldom have clear symbolic significance, and it appears in this case that it may well have come from his signs source. The first two verses set up the persons to be involved in the subsequent story— Jesus, his disciples, and his mother. (The mother of Jesus, however, is never called Mary in this gospel; cf. 19:25 below.) As to the disciples, they are seldom called the Twelve (but cf. 6:67 and 20:24), and their identity is never specified beyond the five mentioned in chap. 1. Generally, the word **disciple** (*mathētēs*) in John means only a "believer," and there is little interest in defining a circle of more intimate followers.

3-4a—The story is told with characteristically Johannine brevity. The **wine** supply is depleted, and **Jesus** is informed of this by his **mother.** Jesus' response in v. 4 seems harsh. To address one's mother with the simple vocative, **woman** (*gunai*), seems abrupt, although we find the same word used in 19:26 when Jesus speaks to his mother from the cross (cf. 4:21). Moreover, there are numerous instances in the Synoptic Gospels of Jesus' use of the expression (e.g., Luke 13:12; Matt. 15:28), almost enough to say that it is represented as Jesus' normal way of addressing a woman. But its use to address his mother suggests a certain reserve or aloofness as if to disavow any authority she might have over him. The expression translated **What have you to do with me?** tends to confirm that detachment. The Greek literally reads, "What to me and to you?" (*ti emoi kai soi*). It may be a Semitic expression to suggest "the matter has nothing to do with us." Certainly it declares a separation from the matter at hand with considerable sharpness (cf. instances in the Synoptics when the words are used by demons to address Jesus—Mark 1:24; Matt. 8:29; Luke 8:28). Jesus here declares his freedom from any kind of human manipulation. He will not be controlled by his mother's or any human's desire. The Johannine Christ stands free of all human power, except as he wills to be subject to that power, as is the case in the passion narrative. He is a divine king whose sovereignty places him beyond human control. It is sometimes a pattern in Johannine stories of Jesus' encounter with human need first to rebuke the one asking for help, only to go on to fulfill the request (cf. 4:48ff. and 11:3ff.). That pattern is evident here.

4b—But there is a further response to his mother's implicit request: **"My hour has not yet come."** Jesus speaks frequently of his **hour** (*hōra*) as a way of referring to the crucifixion (e.g., 7:30; 8:20; 12:23, 27; 13:1; 17:1). He speaks of his hour as not yet come, and then, finally, of its arrival. It refers to that decisive time when in the crucifixion and resurrection he is glorified by the Father. Here the sense is that this is not the moment for his glory to become known and followers must await that time.

5—**His mother** seems to confirm her faith in Jesus' ability to fulfill the human need of the time. It is pointless to speculate about her reasons for trusting Jesus. Suffice it to say that she expresses at least a minimal confidence in her son's ability to perform wondrous acts. She is not a featured character in John's drama, but she does appear at the foot of the cross to hear her son commission the beloved disciple to care for her. There she may be presented as a symbol of the family of the church; but here she does not play a symbolic role (cf. 19:25-27 below).

6—The **six stone jars** are, however, of symbolic importance. Their function at the wedding was to supply **water** for the Jewish practice of washing before and after a meal. Their construction of **stone,** as opposed to earthenware, assured their purity (Lev. 21: 29f.). Their number may symbolize the incompleteness of the Hebraic-Jewish tradition, **six** being one short of the complete number, seven; however, such an interpretation may be pushing John's symbolism too far. Their capacity suggests the enormity of the wonder about to be performed. While John narrates fewer wonder stories than his canonical colleagues, each of his is remarkable by virtue of the extent of the wonder (e.g., the blind man of chap. 9 has been blind from birth; in chap. 11 Lazarus has been dead for three days). It is not necessary to assign the quantity of **water** in the jars a symbolic value. It is clear, however, that the jars and their contents represent the Hebraic-Jewish tradition and the revelation it embraces.

7-10—Jesus takes command of the situation and orders that the jars be filled with **water** to the **brim** and then some taken to the **steward.** The latter (*architriklinos*) would appear to be the "head waiter," doubtless a guest overseeing the occasion. When in v. 9 he **tasted** the **water now** changed to **wine,** he marveled at its quality. His words to **the bridegroom** are half amazement and half humor (v. 10). Whether he accurately states a common practice in serving **wine,** we do not know. John's only interest at this point is to stress that the quantity of wine is not only generous but the quality superb as well. It may well be that the **steward's** remark is a tiny joke John offers his readers.

The marvelous transformation of the water into wine is teeming with meaning. It must first be acknowledged that the excessive quantity of the wine calls to mind the hopeful imaginings of the abundance provided by the messianic age (e.g., Jer. 33:6; Isa. 60: 5). In Christ that promised day has arrived and all the abundance of God's blessings is poured out on the people. Their depleted resources are filled to the brim with God's grace (1:16). But there are still further meanings to be explored. The wine represents the fulfillment of the Hebraic-Jewish tradition with the revelation of God in Christ. The water for purification is transformed into the wine, which is God's gracious offering of himself in Christ. The message of 1:17 is communicated here in symbolic form. John on several occasions narrates a wondrous act only to transform the wonder into a symbolic story with a deeper message (e.g., chap. 9 where the healing of the physical ailment becomes a story of spiritual blindness and sight), and he has done the same here.

11—This may be the conclusion of the story as John found it in his signs source. (The second sign is mentioned in 4:54). It is not peculiar to John to speak of the wondrous acts as signs (sēmeia); the Synoptics and Acts employ the word in such a fashion (e.g., Matt. 12:38; Mark 8:12; Luke 23:8; Acts 2:43). Acts of wonder and power are understood as signs of the authority of the doer, and as such they legitimatize the actor's claims for himself or herself. The other gospels generally represent Jesus as taking a dim view of signs, and the word stands for a misconception of the role of marvelous deeds (much as in 4:48), although Acts uses the word in a positive way (e.g., 2:22). John's signs source supposed that Jesus' wonders were persuasive evidence of his divine authority and therefore evoked faith. So, we are told, does this wondrous transformation of water into wine. The pattern is sign, which manifested glory (doxa), which in turn occasioned belief on the part of the disciples who witnessed the act. The evangelist will show us that it is more complicated than that (cf. 20:29 below). In addition to qualifying the simplistic view of signs in his source and often giving the narratives symbolic value, John understands the signs as ambiguous events which point to the identity of Jesus only for those who dare to comprehend them in faith (in this case the disciples). Only on the condition of faith do they reveal Christ's glory. The result is a circular view: signs presuppose faith, yet they produce it.

The Cleansing and Replacement of the Temple (2:12-25)

12—This is a transitional passage likely associated with the signs source. The geographical description is possible but hardly the shortest route. This is one of several indications in the gospel that **Capernaum** was home for Jesus (cf. 6:17, 24, 59), as is the case in the Synoptics (e.g., Mark 2:1). Jesus' **brothers** (*adelphoi*) are mentioned here and in 7:3-10 and would appear to mean blood brothers. However, 20:17 uses the expression in the sense of believers.

13—The occasion is the first of three journeys to **Jerusalem** reported by John and the first of three **Passovers** (cf. 6:4 and 11:55). The reference is a deliberate effort to locate the narrative within the context of the formative Jewish celebration of the exodus. The cleansing of the temple is a narrative John shares with the Synoptics (Matt. 21:12-13; Mark 11:15-17; Luke 19:45-46). His account, however, has some peculiar features—the **Passover** setting (v. 13), the "sheep and oxen" (v. 14), the fashioning of a "whip" (v. 15), the slightly different wording of Jesus' statement (v. 16), and the allusion to Ps. 69:9 (v. 17), plus the words attributed to Jesus in v. 19. The most significant difference, however, is the setting for the act early in the ministry of Jesus rather than during his last week, as the Synoptics have it (cf. below).

14-17—Jesus drives out of the outer courts of **the temple** (*hieron*, the whole structure; cf. v. 19) those who made their living selling animals for sacrifice and changing Roman coinage into Jewish for the payment of the temple taxes. The use of the **whip** (*phragellion*, v. 15) is occasioned by John's inclusion of the larger animals (**sheep and oxen**) among those driven out. The command of Jesus in v. 16 differs from the Synoptic reports where it is a citation of Isa. 56:7 and/or Jer. 7:11, but the expression **My Father's house a house of trade** resembles the Lukan words in 2:49. It is typical Johannine use of **Father** (*patros*) for God. Either the Johannine tradition of these words has shed its similarities with the OT citation, or else the Synoptic tradition molded the words to resemble the citation. The contrast of the two **houses** for different purposes suggests a criticism of the temple cult. Now in v. 17 another citation from the OT is found in place of the one at v. 16: **Zeal for thy house will consume me** (Ps. 69:9). In Psalm 69 the speaker understands that his suffering is due to his commitment to the temple; here the expression is interpreted messianically, as other parts of Psalm 69 were taken by the early Christians (cf. Mark 15:36). The Greek text of this psalm probably read "consume me" and the Johannine tradition has made it a future tense (**will consume me,** *kataphagetai me*) to make clear the reference to the cross. **That it was written** (*hoti gegrammenon estin*) is a standard formula to introduce scriptural citations (e.g., Matt. 4:4; Mark 1:2; Rom. 3:4). **His disciples remembered** indicates that John believes the ministry of Jesus was understood only after the crucifixion-resurrection and the gift of the Spirit-Paraclete (cf. 2:22 and 12:16). (The Paraclete is said to remind believers of Jesus' words—14:26.) The commitment of Jesus to the purification and fulfillment of the Hebraic-Jewish tradition will lead to his eventual death.

18-19—Now begins the dialog with the Jews over Jesus' bold act. John with regularity uses simply **the Jews** (*hoi Ioudaioi*) to refer to the religious leaders of the time (e.g., 19:31), and here it clearly means those responsible for the temple. They demand a **sign** which will demonstrate Jesus' authority for such a brash act (cf. Mark 11:27f.). The request for a sign as evidence for belief typifies unbelief or at least immature faith (e.g., 4:48; 6:2, 14, 30), because often in John the word of Jesus alone is grounds for true belief (5:24). In response to the request Jesus speaks of his death and resurrection—the only true sign (v. 19). **Destroy** (*luein*) and **raise up** (*egeirein*) are words used of a building, but the latter is the verb often employed for the resurrection (Matt. 26:32; Acts 13:37). Contrast the saying in Mark 14:58 where the verb more exclusively has to do with buildings—*oikodomeō*. John is here playing on the double meaning of ambiguous words, as he loves to do (cf. 3:3 below). **In three days** is a variation on the creed-like formula of the early gospel message (cf. Matt. 27:63; Mark 8:31; often, "on the third day"—Matt. 16:21; Luke 18:33) referring to the resurrection of Christ. **Temple** (*naos*) refers more specifically to the inner temple, the sanctuary, as opposed to the word used in v. 14 (*hieron*). This saying, attributed here to **Jesus,** is found on the lips of false witnesses in the religious trial in the Synoptics (Mark 14:58; Matt. 26:61), as well as on the lips of mockers at the foot of the cross (Mark 15:29; Matt. 27:40). One can only speculate as to how it is the Johannine tradition preserved as an authentic word of Jesus what the Synoptic tradition ascribed to the conspiracy against him. It may well be, however, that the Johannine tradition preserves a primitive form of a resurrection prediction which then became associated with the temple narrative. Could it be that the Synoptic tradition attributed it to opponents for apologetic reasons?

20-22—Not surprisingly the leaders take the words of Jesus literally to refer to the physical structure and marvel that he claims to be able to rebuild what **has taken forty-six years to build.** Their response represents the first instance of a common Johannine literary technique. Words of Jesus spoken of a spiritual or intangible reality are misunderstood by hearers (usually unbelievers) to refer to a physical reality (cf. 3:4 below). At the time of the destruction of Herod's temple by Romans in 70 C.E. the building was still unfinished. Our best knowledge is that the construction was begun in 20 B.C.E. which would date the words of the leaders (v. 20) at about 27 C.E. Obviously, the leaders have no idea of the meaning of Jesus' words, but then neither do the **disciples** until after the resurrection (v. 22); and John has to make the point clear to his readers (v. 21). Again (as in v. 17) it is said that the **disciples remembered that he had said this,** no doubt led by the Spirit-Paraclete. But what is **the Scripture the disciples believed** in addition to **the word which Jesus had spoken** (v. 22)? It may be a reference back to v. 17, but more likely it is the belief that the OT in general foresaw the resurrection of Jesus and the declaration of his righteousness (cf. 1 Cor. 15:4 where the creedal statement includes "in accordance with the scriptures"; note also the general reference to Scripture in John 20:9).

What the religious leaders could never understand and what the disciples understood only after the resurrection is that the Father's Son now replaces the temple as the locus of the divine in the world. What the temple has been in the Hebraic-Jewish tradition Christ himself is for the Christian community. In the context of the celebration of God's liberation of the people from slavery in Egypt Christ not only cleanses the temple but provides for its replacement. By his death at the hands of the religious establishment and his resurrection he becomes the focal point of God's presence on earth, even as God's presence was once centered in the temple. The reason for John's positioning the temple narrative at this early juncture is that its message is central to John's apologetic for the superseding of Judaism in Christ. This replacement is one of the central points John hoped to communicate in his gospel. The presence of God in the world is no longer to be identified with a *place* but now with a *person.*

23-25—A transition to the Nicodemus story is provided by suggesting that faith based on marvelous works alone is not to be trusted. In Jerusalem Jesus is most often met with unbelief, as we will see. Here the belief is of a shallow form aroused only by **the signs which he did.** "**Signs** faith" must give way to an authentic trust of Jesus' person founded on his word and not his wondrous acts. John's Jesus, however, knows the inner being of humans and hence is not fooled by the pretenses of genuine faith. Christ is in need of no information about humans, for he knows them already (v. 25).

The Nicodemus Discourse (3:1-21)

1—Those who believe for the wrong reasons in 2:23-25 lead the reader to one who does not yet believe, but who is searching, because he too is impressed by the signs Jesus has done (v. 2). **Nicodemus** is a character unique to this gospel and is mentioned only at two other places beyond the present passage (7:50 and 19:39). Whatever impression one gains from this passage, Nicodemus appears as a sympathizer, if not a full believer, in the other passages. He is called **a Pharisee, a ruler of the Jews,** which may suggest that he was a member of the ruling body, the Sanhedrin, although the sole reference to that body in the gospel does not mention Nicodemus (11:47). Nicodemus for John represents a learned Jew and one whose intentions are sincere, even if his faith is inadequate. Furthermore, Nicodemus may mirror those Jews of the local synagogue of the evangelist's time who are sympathetic with the Christians but lack the courage to confess their faith openly, i.e., "closet believers."

2—Nicodemus comes to Jesus out of the darkness of **night,** implying that Nicodemus belongs to that realm of darkness and unbelief which does not comprehend the light (1:5). He honors Jesus as a **Rabbi** and a **teacher come from God,** but in terms of John's view of Christ such titles fail to penetrate the identity of the revealer. The affirmation that **God is with** Jesus ironically contrasts to Jesus' true identity, the Father's unique Son. The **signs** done by Jesus are not sufficient grounds for belief in him in any full sense. Signs arouse curiosity but not mature faith.

3—Jesus moves the discussion immediately to a level of importance. (He is in control of this conversation as he is in all such discussions in the gospel.) The reference here and in v. 5 to the **kingdom of God** (*tēn basileian tou theou*) are the only uses of the expression in the gospel, in sharp contrast to its frequent appearance in the Synoptics ("Kingdom of Heaven" in Matthew). John will customarily employ other terms to refer to what the Synoptics mean by the kingdom of God, e.g., life and eternal life. The Johannine tradition apparently reinterpreted the metaphor of the kingdom (which perhaps originated with Jesus himself) into its own categories, ones more meaningful to the community and ones which lack political overtones (cf. 18:36 below). One enters the kingdom, Jesus goes on to say, only if she or he is **born again.** The word translated **again** (*anōthen*) also means "from above," an example of John's fondness for words with multiple meanings. Hence, the birth of which Jesus speaks is a new, spiritual birth which originates from "above," that is from the divine realm (as opposed to the human, unbelieving realm of the "below"). The rebirth of which Jesus speaks is a matter of being given a new origin, an origin from God; for one's origin determines one's being, in Johannine thought. For **truly, truly** cf. 1:51 above.

4-7—**Nicodemus,** of course, entirely misunderstands Jesus and asks how it is possible for an **old** person to **be born**—another instance in which human blindness causes one to fail to comprehend the revelation of God before one's very eyes. Nicodemus thinks in terms of the repetition of the human origin (physical, tangible), while Jesus has in mind another sort of origin (spiritual, intangible). This is an instance of the common motif of misunderstanding employed by the evangelist (cf. 2:20 above and 4:9-15 below) as a literary device to further the conversation and as a theological statement of the deprivation of the human condition. Verse 5 repeats the necessity of the new birth from above but this time describes it as a birth **of water and the Spirit** (*ex hudatos kai pneumatos*). This "reorientation" is accomplished by divine power and not human will, even as believers are made children of God by divine and not human power (1:12). **Water** in this gospel is most often the symbol for the Spirit (7:38-39) and the revelation of God in Christ (4:14). Whether John intended an allusion to Baptism is difficult to say, given the sparse discussion of Baptism in the gospel. More likely is that **water** here stands for the truth revealed in Christ, and later interpreters justifiably identified it with Baptism. There is also some slim textual evidence that **water and** was a later addition to the passage (vg^{ms}, Or^{pt}) which would further suggest that the baptismal interpretation was the result of later reflection (cf. n. 20). Verse 6 further emphasizes the divine nature of this new birth, and the contrast of the **flesh** (*sarx*) and **spirit** (*pneuma*) here is not to be taken as a moral dualism but only a contrast of the divine and the human. It is the divine origin compared with the human origin. If Nicodemus understood this distinction of origins, he would **not marvel** at the words of Jesus.

8-10—The rebirth is accomplished only by the divine **Spirit,** and now that **Spirit** is described in a metaphor of sorts. The word translated **wind** is *pneuma* and means **spirit** as well—another instance of Johannine use of words with double meanings. Hence in describing the mystery of the wind and its freedom to come and go, the verse also speaks of the mystery and freedom of the **Spirit.** John's play on the word *pneuma* leads him to say that **so it is with . . . born of the Spirit,** i.e., their rebirth is mysteriously accomplished by a free, divine power beyond them. **Nicodemus** is still puzzled, expresses his bewilderment, and with that disappears from the scene (v. 9). Verse 10 emphasizes the blindness of the religious leadership, for John wants to contrast others with the inability of Nicodemus to grasp the truth (cf. chap. 4).

11-12—The plural pronoun **we** (expressed in no less than four verbs) suggests that the community speaks now in place of the words of Jesus. The community proclaims its **witness** with certainty, because it speaks out of firsthand experience; but its witness goes unheeded. The conversation has now shifted to the time of the evangelist, and the other party in the dialog are the Jews of the local synagogue. In v. 12, however, the singular pronoun is once again used. What are the **earthly things** (*ta epigeia*) which have not been believed? The logical connection back to the rebirth discussion is hardly clear, but perhaps we should understand **earthly things** to mean the acts of the Spirit in this world, so that the rebirth is in that sense an earthly thing. The **heavenly things** (*ta epourania*) have to do with the descent and ascent of the Son which is the subject of the next verse. If the human experience of the Spirit is beyond our understanding, how then shall we be able to understand the advent of Christ from the heavenly realm?

13—This verse is clearly spoken from the perspective of the evangelist, for it assumes that Jesus has already ascended (*anabebēken*). It denies all mythologies of revered persons who ascended into heaven, and speaks of the divine origin and destiny of Jesus (cf. 2 Kings 2). An important Christological theme of the gospel is the descent and ascent of the Son (cf. 6:62; 20:17). The variant reading "who is in heaven" once again makes it clear that the statement is the church's confession. **The Son of man** (cf. 1:51 above) is associated in Jewish messianic thought with the heavenly figure descending to earth (cf. Dan. 7:14; 1 Enoch 70:2; 71:1). The verse makes absolute Jesus' claim to divine authority.

14-15—The thought of v. 13 is continued in only a very loose way. Numbers 29:1ff. tells how **Moses** raised up a bronze **serpent** on a pole, and the people who gazed upon it were healed of the bites of poisonous snakes. The comparison with Jesus' crucifixion is that those who look upon **the Son of man . . . lifted up** will be cured of spiritual poison. The use of the OT story is strange but not unusual typological interpretation. **Lifted up** (*hypsoō*) is one of John's several expressions for the crucifixion (cf. 8:28; 12:33-34). The word was used of crucifixions but also of the exaltation of a king, the enthronement of a ruler. John's play on the word hints at his understanding of the cross—Christ's crucifixion is his enthronement as king. **Must** (*dei*) suggests the determination of the divine plan for Jesus (cf. Mark 8:31). All of this is for the purpose of eternal life (zōē aiōnios, v. 15). This expression in John is a frequent way of identifying the benefits of Christ's revelation and means the authentic life lived in relationship with the Father (cf. 1:4 above). It refers not only to life beyond death but also to the quality of the life of faith (cf. 5:24).

16-18—Verse 16 expands the meaning of the cross for John. The Father's Son is given (edōken) out of love and to express the divine caring. Eternal life ties this verse with the previous one. World (kosmos) is often used in a pejorative way in John to speak of the realm of unbelief (e.g., 17:14; 9:39; 12:31) and is synonymous in such cases with "darkness." If its negative sense is intended here, it underscores the quality and extent of God's love for the fallen world. There is little in this gospel concerning the destiny of unbelievers, but here the word perish (apolētai) stands as the opposite of eternal life. To perish is to live apart from God and to experience the consequences of that separation. Verse 16 may well be the key to understanding John's view of the cross: In the cross the supreme expression of God's love is enthroned as king of all. Verses 16-17 employ another of John's favorite Christological themes, namely, the Son is sent by the Father (e.g., 5:37; 6:44; 7:16). The purpose of his mission is not condemnation (krinō, to judge or decide) but salvation. Here and at 12:47 the purpose of Christ's mission is not judgment but salvation; still, at 5:30; 8:16 and 26 it is said Jesus does judge. The point is that judgment is not the goal of the revelation, although it invariably results. Saved (sōthē) means brought to eternal life. Verse 18 explains that judgment is the consequence of one's decision to believe or not to believe. To fail to believe is to be judged in the sense of being condemned; to believe is to pass beyond judgment. John almost always uses krinō in its negative sense of condemnation, as the RSV translates it here (but not at other passages, e.g., 5:30). But the associated meaning of krinō, to decide, is prominent also, for to decide is to be judged by one's own choice. The concept of judgment is the first instance of John's present (or realized) eschatology— the view that the realities usually associated with the last days (the end of history) are already present. In this case, judgment usually linked with the end-times is a phenomenon of the present moment when one responds to the revelation of God in Christ. **Name** is a Semitic way of speaking of the person, i.e., Christ. On **only Son of God** cf. above at 1:14 and 1:34.

19-21—Verse 19 issues the sobering judgment that humanity is condemned for its preference for the **darkness** even when the **light** is in the world. John is profoundly realistic regarding the depravity of humanity. **Deeds** (*erga*) give expression to the true nature of a person; and when those acts cannot stand in the **light**, it demonstrates the person's **love** of the **darkness**. A person of the darkness does not want his or her deeds **exposed** (*elenchthē*, literally "reproved"—v. 20). Behavior which is **true** (*alētheia*) is behavior consistent with the truth of the revelation, and such behavior is done within the environment of the divine (v. 21). This conclusion concerning darkness may be an implicit judgment of Nicodemus who came under the cover of darkness to see Jesus (v. 2).

The so-called Nicodemus discourse after v. 12 becomes a string of loosely related sayings linked with one another by key words, e.g., "judgment" in vv. 17 and 18. Such a flow of thoughts is typical of Johannine discourses (cf. 6:32-40). What distinguishes this passage is its display of prominent theological themes in the gospel. If there is a common thread, it might be found in the possibilities made available to humanity as a result of Christ. Those new possibilities mean that God has provided a way by which humans can be rescued from their plight, alienated from their Creator and their true identity (light). Such a rescue is like a new birth which can only be effected by divine power and commences new and authentic life. It is a new birth entirely beyond human control and manipulation and entirely in the hands of God. One of John's rich contributions to the early Christian view of the Spirit is that *"pneuma* life" which results from a faith reception of God's offer of love in Christ.

The Baptizer's Third Witness (3:22-36)

The Continuation of the Witness (3:22-30)

22—Suddenly, the baptizer reappears in the narrative to continue and complete his witness to Jesus. There is little connection between this short section and what comes before and after, and some interpreters would rearrange this piece to have it related to the baptizer's witness in chap. 1. The last previous geographical note the evangelist gave us is in 2:23 which states that **Jesus** is in Jerusalem. Now we are told he is in the **land of Judea.** John seems little concerned with geographical movement. Verse 22b is no less confusing. The **them** would seem to refer to the **disciples.** It is only in John that we are told **Jesus** himself actually **baptized** (cf. v. 26); but this statement is soon corrected in 4:2 with the parenthetical observation that only the **disciples** did the baptizing, and **Jesus baptized** no one. A possible explanation of these verses is that John uses his source at this point without careful regard for its fitting the context. This accounts for the geographical difficulty as well as the contradiction concerning Jesus' practice of baptism. It may be that one of John's traditions preserved the fact that Jesus practiced baptism and another denied it. Possibly a tradition associated with the former followers of the baptizer who became Christians claimed that Jesus took up the baptizer's use of baptism (cf. n. 20).

23-24—The precise location of **Aenon near Salim** is debated, but was likely in Samaria midway between Judea and Galilee in the Jordan valley where there are ample springs. The popularity of the baptizer's ministry is affirmed in the Synoptics as well as here (cf. Mark 1:5). Verse 24 indicates that John's tradition contained the fact of the baptizer's arrest, if not death, as related in the Synoptics (Matt. 4:12; Mark 1:14; Luke 3:20; cf. Matt. 14:1-12; Mark 6:14-29; Luke 9:7-9). But John is alone in narrating a concurrent ministry of the baptizer and Jesus, since the Synoptics claim that Jesus' ministry began only after the baptizer's arrest. This is still another hint at some degree of competition between the followers of the baptizer and the earliest Christians (cf. 1:35-37 above; also Bultmann, pp. 17-18, 108, 167-168).

25-26—The dispute over **purifying** (*katharismos*) is not specified and its relation to the concern over Jesus (v. 26) is not clear. Perhaps the issue is the use of water, since the baptizer's use of water differed markedly from Jewish purification rites. A **Jew** is the only use of the singular in the gospel, and a variant reading which has "Jews" is more consistent with Johannine usage. The concern of **John's disciples** with Jesus' baptism again informs us of a competitive relationship between the two groups. Here again, as in v. 22, Jesus is **baptizing.** The popularity of the Jesus movement, stated in **all are going to him,** is mentioned again in 11:48 and implied in 6:1-15.

27-30—This comprises the baptizer's last witness to Jesus. The sense of v. 27 is that those coming to Jesus have been given over to him by divine powers, and the thought is similar to this gospel's claim that belief in Jesus involves a divine act within the lives of believers (e.g., 6:44; 17:6). Implicit too is that the role of the baptizer is divinely ordained. Verse 28 alludes back to 1:19f. in which the baptizer has denied any special office except that of a witness to Christ. He does claim here that he has been **sent** (*apestalmenos,* cf. 1:6), a word John uses also for Jesus' mission (e.g., v. 16). Only here does the baptizer use the title **Christ** (*ho Christos*) for Jesus, although he has earlier clearly identified him as the Messiah in other terms (1:34). The baptizer now uses a metaphor for his relationship with Jesus (v. 29). He is like the "best man" in a wedding party, standing back to give the place of honor to the **bridegroom,** delighting in the bridegroom's happy **voice,** and finding his joy in the happiness of the couple. Whether or not the metaphor intends to call to mind the symbol of the people of Israel as the **bride** of God (e.g., Hos. 2:21) is not clear. The inference, however, is that Jesus is now the **bridegroom** of the people of God (cf. Mark 2:19-20; Rev. 18:23). Verse 30 effectively concludes the baptizer's view of himself as the witness. His place in the plan of salvation is now nearly complete, and he will slip off the stage to give Jesus his central place. Again **must** (*dei*) is used to express the divine plan of humanity's salvation (cf. 3:14 above). Like a model of witness, the baptizer points to another without drawing attention to himself (cf. Matt. 11:11; Luke 7:28).

An Attached Discourse (3:31-36)

31-33—Some would try to understand vv. 31-36 as the continuation of the words of the baptizer, but the RSV is correct in ending the quotation of the baptizer with the conclusion of v. 30. Verses 31-36 seem to be an unattached discourse inserted at this point because of the appropriateness of the distinction between one **from above** and one **of the earth** for Jesus and the baptizer. It also fits the context insofar as the theme of witness is continued. Verses 27-30 speak of the baptizer's witness and vv. 31-33 of Jesus' witness (v. 32) and that of the believers (v. 33). It is best to assume the evangelist is the speaker in vv. 31-36. Verse 31 employs a variation of the usual Johannine dualistic opposition of **above** (*anōthen*) and below with **earth** (*tēs gēs*) here functioning in place of "below." **Heaven** (*ouranos*) is used in parallelism with **above** at the end of the verse. The point is to stress Jesus' origin in the divine realm and hence the authority of his words. **Above all** (*epanō pantōn*) may refer to space but here indicates absolute sovereignty. **Of the earth** (*ek tēs gēs*) is literally "out of the earth" and defines the origin of the human (and in this case, perhaps, the baptizer). **Earth** does not carry the pejorative sense of "world" and means only the realm of the human. Verse 32a argues that Jesus' witness to the divine truth is firsthand, for **he has seen and heard it**. One who has read the prolog understands John's meaning. Verse 32b is the sober recognition that the **testimony** of Jesus is rejected. The Johannine community had experienced the bitter rejection of their evangelistic efforts and understood the rejection of the historical Jesus as a precedent for that experience. But there are some who accept the revelation, and they vouch for the truth it brings to them. **Seal** (*sphragizō*) is used at 6:27 of God's accreditation, but here of the affirmation of the believer. **That God is true** means that the revelation has **God** as its content and that **God** is **true** to his word as it is expressed in Christ. As with the witness of the baptizer above, the believer witnesses to Christ by affirming the truth of the revelation.

34-36—Verse 34 doubtless refers to Jesus (and not the baptizer). The envoy does not come speaking his own **words** (*hrēmata*) but those of the one who **has sent** him and by implication carries the authority of his master. That Jesus' **words** are his Father's is a frequent theme in this gospel (e.g., 14:24). **It is not by measure** (*ou . . . ek metrou*) denotes the unbounded gift of the **Spirit** in Jesus. The one who **gives the Spirit** here is most likely the Father, for the subject is Jesus' authority. (Both Jesus and God are said to give the Spirit—14:16 and 15:26.) Jesus' words are God's because Jesus is filled with God's Spirit (cf. 1:32 above). The most prominent Christological motif of the gospel—the Father-Son relationship—appears in v. 35. That the "pneumatic" Christology of v. 34 (Jesus is filled with the Spirit) could appear side by side with the **Son** Christology is typical of the way in which John incorporates a variety of modes of Christological thought without thought to their logical consistency. The relationship of the **Father** and the **Son** is one of intimacy and **love.** The two motifs mentioned here are common to the relationship: **The Father loves the Son** (e.g., 5:20; 10:17; 15:9) and **has given all things** to the Son (e.g., 13:3 and 16:15). The latter indicates that the functions and roles usually reserved exclusively for God are assigned to Christ (e.g., 5:20, 27). The intimacy of the relationship, therefore, is not simply metaphysical speculation, for it means that for all practical purposes Jesus acts for God. (On the relationship of the **Father** and the **Son** cf. esp. 10:30 and 14:28.) Verse 36 speaks of the results of this relationship. **Believes in** (*eis*), the most common expression for faith, suggests that faith is a personal relationship with Christ himself and implies trust and commitment. **Has eternal life** is another example of John's realized eschatology—the one who **believes** already possesses the quality of **life** which will reach beyond the grave. It is not that he or she has only the *promise* of **eternal life.** This is the most common of the several results of faith for John. The opposite of faith is disobedience, and hence believing is obeying the command of God in Christ. The command, however, is not an ethical injunction but a demand that Christ be trusted and believed. Disobedience means that **life** in the sense of full, authentic existence is lost. (**Life** functions here as an abbreviation for **eternal life.**) The failure to believe leads inescapably to an existence which is distorted and inauthentic. This is the only use in John of **the wrath** (*orgē*) **of God,** and John tells us little of what it entails. Here **wrath of God rests upon him** is parallel to and synonymous with **shall not see life**. Hence, the result of unbelief is **the wrath of God** which means the failure to live as life was intended to be. The condemnation begins with this life and is not a punishment beyond death (which John never describes), even as **eternal life** is the immediate consequence of faith. The verb **rests** is literally "remains" (*menein*), one of John's favorite words to describe the relationship of the believer with Christ. Here it means that the unbeliever lives within the context of a broken, alienated relationship with God.

Within vv. 31-36 we see a progression of thought from the authority of Jesus and his relationship with the Father (vv. 31, 32a, 34-35), to the acceptance and rejection of him (vv. 32b, 33), and finally to the consequences of rejecting and accepting him (v. 36). This passage is in a sense a miniature digest of the whole message of the gospel. Like the message of the entire gospel, this passage expresses the conviction that human existence and destiny hinge upon what God has done in Christ and the response to that act. The human response necessitates knowing the true identity of Jesus and trusting one's life to him.

The Faith of the Samaritans (4:1-42)

In the prior three sections (2:1-11; 2:13-22; and 3:1-21, excluding 3:22-36 which is a kind of interlude) John has driven relentlessly at the theme that the revelation of Christ necessitates a radical transformation of the established religion. While he emphasizes again and again that Christ is the fulfillment of the Jewish and OT traditions, John nonetheless claims that the fulfillment is accomplished in a way difficult for the established religion to accept. This theme is due in large part to the setting for the gospel, which involved the Johannine Christians in a hostile debate with the Jews of the local synagogue from which the church had recently been expelled. John hammers at that point again in the present passage in which heretical, half-breed Samaritans, disdained by the Jews, come to believe in Jesus. The contrast of the simple Samaritan woman and her enthusiastic faith with the puzzled uncertainty of the learned Jew, Nicodemus, cannot have been unintentional on the part of the evangelist. She emerges from this narrative as a model for Christian faith and witness.

1-3—**The Lord** is one textual reading while another equally strong reading has "Jesus." While neither word functions in the sentence without difficulty, the latter is preferable. Jesus' popularity had come to the attention of **the Pharisees,** and that motivates **Jesus** to leave **Judea** and return to **Galilee** (v. 3). John often uses "the Jews" where **Pharisees** are meant, but for him the distinction was probably not important, since **the Pharisees** were the dominant group after the destruction of the temple in 70 C.E. Here we are to understand an implicit danger for Jesus in the Pharisees' knowledge of his popularity. This is the beginning of the steadily mounting hostility of Jesus' opponents. Verse 1 is clearly another assertion of the superiority of the Messiah to his witness, the baptizer (cf. 1:26-27; 3:28-30). Verse 2 is the correction of 3:22, 26, most likely inserted by the evangelist into his source, for he would not have wanted to suggest that Jesus in any way imitated the baptizer. Beyond this verse and the implications of 3:22, 26 we are told nothing of the practice of baptism by either Jesus or his disciples, which suggests that it was not a prominent note in either John's source(s) or John's own community (cf. n. 20).

4-6—**He had to pass through Samaria** is not geographically correct, and so divine necessity seems the intended meaning. (*Edei* is the imperfect of *dei*, which is elsewhere used to convey divine determination, e.g., 3:30.) In v. 5 **Sychar** is described as **near the field that Jacob gave to his son Joseph.** No such village is known, and so it has been proposed that "Shechem" is the site or else "Askar," an extant village about one-half mile north of **Jacob's** well. Gen. 33:19; 48:22 and Josh. 24:32 are the basis for the mention of the field, although the well itself is not mentioned in the OT. Verse 6 begins by setting the conversation which is about to ensue within the context of the patriarchs of the Hebrew people. **Jesus is wearied.** The high Christology of the gospel is tempered on several occasions with reminders of the genuine humanity of Jesus (e.g., 19:28). The time notation of **the sixth hour** (about noon) makes for a difficulty with the woman's arrival to get water, for the women of the village would not usually come in the heat of the day to draw their supply of water. That the woman comes at this hour to avoid others because of her notoriety as a sinner seems speculative and makes more of the inference of the woman's immorality than John does! The evangelist again includes a time notation which he does not exploit for symbolic purposes.

7-9—Jesus requests a drink of the woman. This casual request becomes the basis of the symbolism to follow. Verse 8 is a clumsy insertion to account for the absence of the disciples and set up their return later (v. 27). It may be an indication that John is composing the narrative on the basis of a story in his sources and that the role of the disciples at the end is one of his several additions. However, the entire narrative shows numerous signs of John's style. The amazement of the woman that Jesus would speak to her, much less ask a drink, is realistic as we are told in the later half of the verse. Jesus violates custom on two points by asking the woman for water: First, conversations with a strange woman were frowned upon by the rabbis (cf. v. 27); second, and more serious, contact with Samaritan women ran the risk of contracting impurity, since such women were regarded by the Jews as impure, as if they were constantly in a state of menstruation (cf. Lev. 15:19). Verse 9b may be a later addition to the gospel, and we cannot be sure that it is an accurate statement of conditions in either Jesus' or John's day, although in the second century it would have been appropriate. Historical subtleties aside, Jesus is pictured here as one who disregarded established customs in favor of contact with all people (cf. Synoptic representations, e.g., Mark 2:15ff.).

10-12—Jesus takes the initiative to move the conversation to the topic of his identity and the gift he has to offer the woman, ignoring the reservations she has just stated. The combination here of the gift of God and who it is that is speaking is important, for it shows the relationship between the identity of Jesus and the gift of the revelation in Christ. That gift is now called living water (hydōr zōn), which also means "flowing water." But Jesus uses the expression to identify the rich offer which God gives to humans in Christ—the gift of true life. Living water may also refer to the Spirit given through Christ (cf. 7:38-39) but the two meanings are nearly synonymous. Verse 11 demonstrates that the woman has understood Jesus' words to refer to the flowing waters of the well and wonders how Jesus could draw the **water** without an implement. This is John's typical use of misunderstanding as a means of suggesting the blindness of the world to God's revelation in Christ (cf. 3:4). The woman has taken Jesus' words literally to refer to the physical reality of water, while his words speak of a spiritual reality. Verse 12 is perfect Johannine irony. The woman is indignant at what she takes to be Jesus' impertinence and asks, **Are you greater than our father Jacob?** The reader smiles, for it is clear to all but the woman in the scene that, yes, of course, Jesus is far greater than Jacob and all the figures of ancient Israel. The statement about **Jacob** and **his sons and his cattle** is not documented in the OT but perhaps represents a popular tale associated with the well.

13-15—Jesus continues his discussion of the spiritual **water.** It is a water that quenches the human **thirst** for fullness and truth, as opposed to the **water** of the well. The contrast is more, however, than physical and spiritual water, for it is an implicit contrast between the revelation of God in Israel's history (to such as Jacob) and the revelation in Christ. There is an incompleteness to the former—**every one who drinks of this water will thirst again**—which only the latter can fulfill. It quenches **thirst,** but it also becomes in the human a source of **eternal life.** The gift of God fills the whole being of the human and runs over. The revelation penetrates every part of human existence and brings authentic existence. The **living water** is the gift; **eternal life** is the result of the gift. But the woman's mind is still trapped within the tangible, physical realm (v. 15), and she thinks that here is an offer of her own personal supply of endless water so that she would never have to carry water again! Understandably, she is eager for this convenience, but Jesus has in mind a gift of greater importance than any modern convenience.

At this point we can see the way John has employed the technique of misunderstanding throughout the discussion. Jesus begins with a reference to physical water to which the woman responds appropriately (vv. 7, 9). Then Jesus shifts the referent of his words to the spiritual water of life (v. 10) which the woman understands in terms of physical water (vv. 11-12). Jesus continues his discussion of the water of salvation (vv. 13-14) only to have the woman once again read his words as speaking of the water of the well (v. 15). John's subtle point is that humans are captured within the realm of the physical, material world which makes it difficult for them to grasp the revelation offered in Christ. For the evangelist this is part of the all-pervasive blindness of human sin.

16-19—Jesus is in control of the conversation, and he shifts the subject slightly so that the woman's need for the spiritual and not the physical water might be demonstrated. Jesus knows her situation, and so in asking that she **call** her **husband** he knows what the woman must say. The purpose of Jesus' comments is not to embarrass or accuse the woman; her sin (if it is such, and that is not entirely clear) is not the central feature of the conversation. The purpose rather is to open the discussion to a level of honesty so that it can become clear who the woman is and who Jesus is. It is not absolutely necessary that we interpret the woman's situation as sinful, since we are not told of the occasions for her numerous remarriages (i.e., perhaps each had died, and she had remarried legally). It is Jesus' extraordinary knowledge of the woman's life that is the important point in the passage. The woman's marvel at Jesus' knowledge reminds us of Nathanael (1:49), but she concludes that Jesus is a **prophet** (v. 19). **Sir** (*kyrie*) does not carry the Christological import of "Lord" here. It is difficult to say whether John intended us to take **prophet** (*prophētēs*) at this point in the general sense of one who demonstrates extraordinary powers, or in the more strict sense of *the* messianic prophet-like-Moses (Deut. 18:15; 34:10-12) which was the model by which the Samaritans understood their messiah, *Taheb* (see v. 25 below).[10] It is more likely that John attributes to her only a sense of Jesus' marvelous knowledge by which she has only begun to grasp his identity. About the use of **husband** (*andras*) some suggest that the woman's **husbands** signify the Samaritan religion, for the Hebrew word would be *Baal*, "lord." The Samaritans were accused of worshiping five gods as a result of Assyrian influence (2 Kings 17:24-31). The numerous lords and the present illegal lord would be symbolic of the heresy of the Samaritans. While we must always be alert to pick up John's symbolism, there is nothing in the text

2:1—5:47   *John*

which would require a symbolic meaning here, and the simpler interpretation seems the better.

20-22—The woman now attempts to distance herself from this man of wondrous knowledge by raising one of the points of dispute between Jews and Samaritans—the **place of worship.** In opposition to the concentration of worship in the temple at **Jerusalem,** the Samaritans claimed that the proper site was their own temple on Mt. Gerizim (cf. 2 Kings 17:28-41) even though the building itself was destroyed by John Hyrcanus, the Jewish Hasmonean king, in 128 B.C.E. Her excursus into points of difference between this stranger and herself does not work, however, and Jesus abruptly moves the discussion to the new age (v. 21; for **woman** cf. 2:4 above). **Believe me** (*pisteue moi,* cf. 8:45; 10:37) has the force of stressing the truth of what Jesus is about to speak. **The hour is coming** (*erchetai hōra*) is a way of speaking of the imminent eschatological transformation of human worship, which Jesus says in v. 23 has already come. The worship practices of both the Jews and Samaritans and their petty differences will be rendered insignificant in that promised time. Verse 22 is difficult in some ways, for here we find the Johannine Jesus speaking as a Jew and claiming that Judaism is the source of **salvation** and has a knowledge superior to that of the Samaritans. In spite of John's polemic against Judaism, he continues to represent the fact that Jesus lived as a Jew. **Salvation is from the Jews** may seem strange in this gospel, but it is an acknowledgment on John's part that God's saving act is done among the Jews and in the context of Jewish history and tradition. The Johannine Christian community honored its roots in Judaism even in their schism from the synagogue. Verse 22 may, however, be from John's source and be another instance of his retaining something in his tradition about which he might have reservations.

23-24—The statement of v. 22 is also set against the transformation of the religions by eschatological events. That time is not only **coming** but **now is** (*nyn estin*), an affirmation of Johannine realized eschatology. **True** (*alēthinoi*) **worshipers** will now **worship in spirit and in truth** (*alētheia*), meaning that the revelation in Christ creates new possibilities for worship. To **worship in spirit**

and in truth is to worship in the context of the gift of God in Christ. **Spirit** (*pneuma*) more likely stands for the divine presence than the human spirit; hence, the point does not have to do with sincerity in worship but the relationship with God out of which believers offer their worship. It is this kind of worship in full knowledge of the **Father** that God wants. The title **Father** suggests an entirely new relationship with the God who is now worshiped. Verse 24 repeats the point of v. 23, prefacing it with the assertion that **God is spirit**. The spirit in the context of which true worship takes place is none other than God himself. This is not an attempt to describe God but to affirm the way in which God deals with humanity and the relationship God has with believers as a result of the revelation.

25-26—The **woman** musters all her understanding of her religion to respond to this marvelous traveler, and she gives expression to the messianic hope that **all things** will be revealed in the last day. The Samaritan concept of **Messiah** was not that of a descendent of David but the return of a prophet-like-Moses (hence their title *Taheb*, "one who returns"). Verse 26 is the long-awaited revelation of Jesus' identity to this woman; it is the denouement of the conversation: **I . . . am he.** Again John seems unconcerned about the nuance of messianic thought with which Jesus identifies himself. For he understands that Jesus encompasses the whole range of messianic expectations, even that of the Samaritans. However, Jesus responds to the woman with the mysterious and powerful **I am** (*egō eimi*), the first of a number of occurrences of this expression in John. In other cases, the use of this expression is intended to suggest divine authority for Jesus through what might be an allusion to the divine name of God in Exod. 3:14 and the Greek rendering of passages in Deutero-Isaiah in which God is made to speak of himself as *anī hū* ("I, he," e.g., 43:25; cf. the discussion of the absolute use of the expression without a predicate, below at 8:24 and 28). Whether it is intended to carry such lofty authority here is not certain but seems possible, since it is an epiphany scene in which Jesus' true identity is revealed. It is the identity of the thirsty traveler (of which the woman had no knowledge) which had made her incapable of understanding his strange offer of "living water" (vv. 10-15). Now that identity is manifested, and the nature of the gift he offered, as well as his fulfillment of her messianic hopes, are made clear.

27-30—Now comes a shift in the scene. The **disciples** enter the stage, and the woman exits (v. 28). The reason for the disciples' absence up to this point is in order that they might return to marvel that Jesus was talking with **a woman**. But they lack the courage to ask what it is Jesus is seeking and why he is **talking with her**. The shock of his talking with a woman is greater than the fact that the woman is a Samaritan only because John has highlighted the latter already in v. 9. Their reluctance to ask Jesus their questions is similar to 16:5 and 21:12. Is it their awe of his identity that makes them reserved? Before the conversation with the disciples can take place, John tells us of the actions of the woman (vv. 28-30). She departs in such haste that she leaves behind her **water jar** (symbols of a life in "darkness"?) in order that she might share her new discovery with those of her village. Her witness to them is a delightful bit of enthusiastic exaggeration: **A man who told me *all* that I ever did!** Her faith is not yet mature, for she is still uncertain that he is the Messiah, but sure enough to want her friends to encounter him. Verse 30 suggests the response to her witness, which is underway while the conversation with the disciples takes place in vv. 31-38.

31-34—These verses are a kind of interlude in the narrative, appropriate in the sense that the story concerns in part the value of Christian witness and the importance of evangelistic mission. First, however, the **disciples** are concerned that Jesus **eat** (v. 31); and, when he responds with the fact that as the Father's Son he has spiritual **food to eat,** they are entirely puzzled. With another instance of Johannine misunderstanding even the disciples miss what it is Jesus is talking about (v. 33—cf. 16:17-18). John introduces the statement of the mission of the disciples to evangelize with a declaration of Jesus' own mission, for the Christian mission in the world is modeled on Jesus' own mission. **Jesus** sends his followers (v. 38) even as he is **sent** (*pempsantos*, cf. 20:21 below). That which nourishes Jesus is performing his mission. His strength comes from his relationship with the one **who sent** him. **To do the**

will of him who sent me and to accomplish his work are synonymous in meaning. The first is an often-repeated theme on the lips
of Jesus in this gospel (e.g., 5:30; 6:38), emphasizing the single-
mindedness of the one sent from the Father. Him who sent me is
a common title for God in John (e.g., 8:16; 9:4). The second
phrase has a wider perspective, namely, the whole of God's saving
activities in the world. Accomplish is the RSV rendering of *tel-
eiōsō*, which might better be translated here "complete" or "fulfill." God's work (*ergon*) is his tireless efforts, stretching over the
whole of Israel's history, to overcome the alienation effected by
human sin. Jesus can speak of his entire ministry as his work given
to him by the Father. His work is then God's work. It is that effort
which is brought to a conclusion in Jesus' death (cf. 19:30).

35-38—Attention shifts to the missionary task of the community of believers more properly. Verses 35-38 are an independent
saying on mission inserted here because of the successful conver-
sion of the Samaritans (cf. vv. 41-42 below). We have no evidence
that the saying cited in v. 35 was a common one. The point is that
normally there is intervening time between planting and harvest;
but that time for growth and maturing is eliminated in the process
of harvesting the results of Jesus' ministry. In this case the time of
ripeness comes with the appearance of the Son. While the immediate context suggests that Jesus is speaking of the ripeness of the
faith of the Samaritans, the point is the commissioning of the community of believers generally to be about the task of reaping the
results of the work of Christ. (It is superfluous to try to figure on
the basis of this verse the time of the narrative; such is far from
John's mind.) Verse 36 states that those who follow to reap the
benefits of Jesus' mission receive their reward in the joy they share
with God and Christ. The fruit (*karpon*) for eternal life is the benefits for humanity of the Son's work. Even though the joy of the
reaper is shared with the sower, there is a proper function for
each, suggesting that Christian evangelism is always a reaping of
the results of God's act in Christ (the sowing). This proverb is attested in ancient sources in various forms (cf. Barrett, p. 242). The
eschatological day of reaping stands in relationship to all who have
labored to sow (v. 38). In this case, the picture is expanded, so that

those who **have labored** are all the instruments of God's saving activity in the past. The believers **have entered into their labor** in the sense of working at the will of God for humanity, even as many before them have. This little discourse on Christian mission makes a number of salient points: First, the believer stands in the wake of God's final act in Christ, benefiting from the power of that event. Second, the believer joins hands with those who have labored for the restoration of humanity—those figures of Israel's history, but also God himself!

39-42—The story of the faith of the **Samaritans** is resumed now in v. 39 but with the clear implication that their coming to Christ exemplifies the point of the intervening discourse. The **Samaritans come and believe in him because of the woman's testimony.** As immature and as inadequate as her faith may have been (and John surely views it that way), her witness has been most effective. While John will be critical of faith that lacks depth and insight into Jesus' identity and which is based on experience of marvelous works (v. 42), here he stresses that such faith has powerful results when it is shared with others. Still, such faith based on the witness of others must move on to a firsthand experience—belief in Jesus' word (v. 41). Verse 40 suggests a prolonged ministry in the area of Samaria. And as a result of it, **more believed** (v. 41). Belief in the **word** (*logos*) of Christ is for John more mature and authentic than faith in his works. In v. 42 John closes the scene with the fact that the secondhand experience of the villagers through the woman's witness is replaced with a firsthand experience. For the Johannine community such firsthand experience with the word of Jesus himself is not limited to the contemporaries of the historical Jesus, for the Spirit-Paraclete makes his word directly accessible in a firsthand way for those who seek it (cf. 14:26; 16:13). This unusual and surprising narrative concludes with still another surprise: Jesus is confessed as **Savior of the world** (*ho sōtēr tou kosmou*). This is the sole use of such a title in John, although he occasionally employs the concept of salvation (3:17; 5:34; 10:9; 12:47). To the Samaritans alone is given the privilege of this title. In Johannine parlance, if we should understand the title in this context, Christ is the one who rescues the realm of disbelief and distortion (the **world**) from itself. It is again evident that John is indebted to a source which probably included this unique title.

This is a remarkable section in several ways. First, it is the sole account of a ministry of Jesus among the Samaritans. (Luke even suggests that such a mission was aborted [9:52ff.] and Matthew has Jesus forbid the disciples to go among Samaritans during their mission [10:5].) It must therefore represent an experience of the Johannine Christians in which Samaritans were converted and included in the community. The narrative may also represent a tradition concerning Jesus' own ministry to a Samaritan village, but of that we can be less sure. Regardless of its historical roots, John preserves it because it contains an important tradition for his community. He clearly uses it in contrast with the Jews who refuse to believe, but it is also one of the clearest references to mission in this gospel. Of the several possible hints at a kind of universalism in John (cf. 12:32 and 10:16) this is surely a powerful one, especially if it is true, as I believe it is, that the Johannine community had its roots in Jewish Christianity. Jesus is one who offers the revelation of the Father to all persons!

Second, it is another narrative in which John sketches a range of Christological views climaxing in a high title (cf. 1:35-51 and 9:1-38). In this case, the titles vary from the innocent "sir" (*kyrie*, v. 11) with no religious significance to "prophet" in v. 19 and the "Messiah" (vv. 25, 30) and finally the "Savior of the world" in v. 42. John surely intends for us to see in this progression a gradually clearer insight into Jesus' true identity concluding with an assessment of his function as Savior. Moreover, this progression is another instance of John's broad Christology— a view of Christ which encompasses a wide variety of titles and concepts.

Finally, this narrative furthers the sketch John draws of the role of witness in the mission of Christ in the world. He has presented the baptizer as a model of witness, and he now portrays another model—a Samaritan woman whose faith has only begun to blossom. John often honors the role of women as disciples (e.g., Mary Magdalene, 20:1-2, 11-18), but here he also honors the power of a faith which is yet immature. Witness to such a faith has results far beyond itself. With this narrative he invites Christians to put aside timidity and reluctance and to share their stories of faith, however minimal they may be!

The Healing of the Royal Official's Son (4:43-54)

43-45—This is a transitional passage, the primary purpose of which is to move Jesus from Samaria to **Galilee,** the setting for the healing story of vv. 46-54. Verse 44 is the Johannine report of the Synoptic saying found in Matt. 13:57, Mark 6:4, and Luke 4:24. In each case in the Synoptics the saying refers to Jesus' rejection in his home country of Galilee, and in John it echoes 1:11. The difficulty is, however, determining to what region the Johannine saying refers. Arguments are made that in this gospel it is Judea which is **his own country, and Jesus** returns to **Galilee** because of his rejection in Judea. But the Galilean roots of Jesus are relatively clear in John (1:46; 7:40-42, 52; 19:19), although in each case the home of Jesus is described by others, most often opponents. On the other hand, the saying seems to make little sense here if it refers to Galilee, for Jesus is said to be on his way to that region. Notwithstanding, others have argued that the region referred to is Galilee, and the rejection he experiences is that the Galileans' faith is based solely on his signs (vv. 45 and 48). Neither explanation is entirely satisfactory. It may be that the reference to an isolated and unattached saying is inserted here in order to prepare the reader for the fact that the faith of the Galileans will not be mature, true faith. It is given its place here by the evangelist as he moves into the subsequent story which is from his signs source and reflects John's dim view of faith based on signs. Verse 45 confirms the fact that the welcome he receives by Galileans is occasioned by **all that he had done in Jerusalem** (cf. 6:26)—". . .a superficial welcome based on enthusiasm for miracles is no real *honor*" (Brown, vol. l, p. 187). The proverb of v. 44 expresses the fact that familiarity fogs one's vision of the true character of a person.

46-48—The second of the wonder stories of this gospel is now told. This passage is often compared to the healing of the slave of the centurion at Capernaum found in Matt. 8:5-13 and Luke 7:1-

10. Suffice it to say that the Synoptic story lacks the healing at extreme distance, and the Johannine story lacks the explicit praise of the faith of a non-Israelite. It is probable, however, that the two different forms represent a single tradition which has been reshaped in two or more different communities. Verse 46 prepares the reader for the wonder to be narrated by recalling that **Cana was where he had made the water into wine. Capernaum,** located on the northwestern side of the Sea of Galilee, is the apparent home of Jesus according to Matt. 4:13 and Mark 2:1. It is also the site of numerous other narratives (e.g., Mark 1:21-28; Matt. 17:24-27). In John's gospel it is named also in connection with two other incidents (2:12 and 6:17, 24, 59). **Official** (*basilikos*) can mean either "one of royal blood" or "one in the service of royalty." If this man is to be identified with the centurion of the Synoptic accounts, he was likely a Gentile in the service of Herod Antipas. If that is not the case, the most we can say is that he was a representative of royalty of some sort. John might well want us to think of him as a Gentile, so that his faith, like that of the Samaritans, contrasts with the failure of Jews to believe. Verse 47 suggests the initial confidence of the official in Jesus and the urgency of the situation. Verse 48 is **Jesus'** rebuke of the man and his request. Jesus chides him for believing only because of **signs and wonders.** The latter (*teras*) is the only occurrence of this word in the gospel; neither is it common in the Synoptics, although it is frequent in Acts (e.g., 2:22, 43). Jesus' rebuke of one who requests a healing is not uncommon (e.g., Mark 7:27) and is comparable to Jesus' response to his mother in 2:4. Some even find a pattern in the Johannine wonder stories which often includes something like a rebuke (cf. 11:4). But more to the point, this verse expresses John's suspicion of "signs faith" (cf. 2:23-24). It has been suggested that this verse stands out in the story like an editorial insertion made in a narrative drawn for the most part from the signs source, and there is good reason to embrace that view. The signs source was probably a collection of wonder stories which sought to evoke faith in Jesus by narrating his wonders.

49-50—Verse 49 is the simple plea of a distraught father which expresses compassion for his **child** (*paidion,* "young child"). Perhaps we are to understand that this expression of compassion stirs Jesus to respond favorably to the father's request. In v. 50 **Jesus** orders the healing without going to the **man's** home—an instance of the extreme marvel of the healings of Jesus in this gospel. **Go, your son will live** (literally, "lives") reflects Elijah's words in 1 Kings 17:23. "Lives" (*zē*) is used to mean "healed," possibly because Hebrew has no word for "recovered" and hence used "lives" in this sense. The official **believed the word that Jesus spoke.** Now it appears that he believes without the benefit of knowing that the sign is accomplished and that speaks favorably for his faith, given the perspective of the evangelist. But the expression *pisteuein* with the dative is not yet here the personal trust John uses more frequently to describe true faith (*pisteuein eis*). Still, the contrast of "signs faith" and "word faith" is surely intentional.

51-53—The healing is here confirmed, a common conclusion for healing stories in the Gospels (e.g., Mark 5:42). Even the exact **hour** of the healing corresponds to **Jesus'** words. In v. 53 we are told that the official **and all his household believed.** (For the coming to faith of whole families cf. Acts 11:14; 16:15, 31; and 18:8.) **Believed** (*episteusen*) is used here in the absolute without an object and means that the official and his family fully believed. The story has taken us through three different kinds of faith: First, faith based solely upon signs (v. 48); second, belief in Jesus' word (v. 50); and, third, absolute faith in a Christian sense (v. 51). It is possible that John means for us to understand this progression of faith as a paradigm of the emergence of genuine belief and perhaps even the necessary steps toward mature Christian conviction. It is in this way that John reconciles his own view of faith with the more simplistic view of his signs source. The most authentic kind of faith in the view of the evangelist, however, is that which believes "without seeing" (described in 20:29). For Jesus' life-giving acts see chap. 11 below.

54—This is the second instance of "numbered signs" in the gospel (cf. 2:11). Between the two passages we have other signs mentioned (2:23), but this healing is only the second recorded in **Galilee.** It is the appearance of these "numbered signs" that has given some scholars a clue to the use of a signs source behind this gospel, and reconstructions of that source sometimes claim to find seven signs in John which may have come from the source (in addition to the two mentioned, 5:1-9; 6:1-13; 6:16-21; 9:1-7; and 11:1-54).

The healing of the royal official's son is perhaps another example of a faith response to Jesus from one other than an adherent of the established religion. Both of John's descriptions of exemplary faith are of those other than Jews, and we cannot help but see this as a further condemnation of the established religion. John is saying too that faith comes from those we may least expect to have the potential for believing. God's gift of a faithful response to the revelation is offered to *all*, and it is often the least likely recipient who embraces it! But faith is a process, never a simple possession, as this narrative demonstrates so very well.

The Sabbath Healing of the Man with the 38-Year Illness (5:1-18)

1—On the question of the transposition of chaps. 5 and 6 see n. 12. **After this** is John's loose tying of this with the previous narrative (cf. 3:22). The precise **feast** is not named, and the best manuscripts omit the definite article, meaning **a feast**. The evangelist has little interest in the occasion except as a means of getting **Jesus** to **Jerusalem.** If it was an obligatory pilgrimage to Jerusalem for the Galilean Jews, it would have been Passover, Pentecost, or Tabernacles. While John sometimes seems to use the symbolic significance of Passover (e.g., 6:4), it is curious that he has no such interest in this unspecified feast.

2-5—The Greek of v. 2 is difficult, for there seems to be a word missing. It is a question of whether pool is qualified by **called** or by **sheep.** That is, either "near the sheep _____ there is a pool called . . ." or "near the sheep pool there is a _____ called . . . ." The RSV opts for the former, supplying the word **gate** to the text. Likewise, the textual witnesses for **Bethzatha** vary considerably. Nonetheless, a strong candidate for the location of the pool has been discovered—a pool that had five colonades, hence John's **five porticoes.** This discovery near St. Anne's church **in Jerusalem** has justifiably reopened the issue of John's preservation of historically accurate materials. It is indeed the case that this gospel may contain fragments of primitive tradition, and it need not be dismissed in favor of the Synoptics as a source of historical knowledge concerning Jesus. This should not blind us, however, to the thorough redactional reinterpretation of those traditions and the methodological difficulty of isolating primitive traditions. Verse 3a indicates that the pool was regarded as having some healing benefits (cf. v. 7). Verses 3b-4 are clearly a later addition, according to nearly all textual critics. Verse 5 identifies one of the ailing persons at the pool as having **been ill for thirty-eight years.** The longevity of his illness is described in order that we might understand the magnitude of Jesus' healing. The exact nature of his illness is not mentioned, but v. 7 would seem to suggest at least partial paralysis.

6-9—The healing is told with economy. The narrator mentions again the fact of **Jesus'** marvelous knowledge, so that his act in no way is determined by human desire. One requirement seems implied, however: **Do you want to be healed?** The power of the revelation is available to humanity, but its appropriation requires a sense of need. Verse 7 is more than likely the reason for the textual gloss in vv. 3b-4, for the response of the ill **man** indicates that **when the water is troubled** it has healing powers. Doubtless the pool was fed by periodic rushes of water from a stream. Such influxes were believed to have a healing power for a short time or for only a limited number of persons. The healing is accomplished by the simple command of Jesus (v. 8). The words are parallel to those used in Mark 2:11 in the healing of the paralytic. This has given some interpreters evidence of John's use of the Markan story, but more likely there was interchange between the two healings in the preliterary period of the tradition. **Pallet** (*krabattos*) is a mattress used by the poor, and is the word used both in this story and in Mark 2:4ff. (Its only other occurrence in the NT is in Mark 6:55.) Jesus does not aid the man by helping him into the pool at the proper time, but by the intercession of an entirely new healing power available only through Christ. Its results are instantaneous (**at once**—*eutheōs*) and effective, for the man exhibits his cure by obeying Jesus (v. 9). His actions are typical of the healing stories in which the effectiveness of the cure is publicly demonstrated. The healing story has all of the characteristics of the Synoptic healings and betrays the form by which such stories were transmitted orally (cf. Dodd, *Historical Tradition*, pp. 174-180). While John has repeated the story in its traditional form, he will now proceed freely to interpret it from his own perspective.

10-13—Only at the conclusion of v. 9 are we told that all this takes place on **the sabbath.** The query of **the Jews** (v. 10) indicates that Johannine interpretation is in power at this point in the narrative, for obviously it is the Pharisees who would be concerned about such matters. Carrying a mattress would constitute one form of labor, according to the laws of the Mishnah (e.g., *Shabbath* 7:2 and 18:3). Healings in the Synoptics are attacked several times on the basis of Jesus' violation of the Sabbath regulations(e.g., Mark 3:1-6). The man attempts to escape any guilt by passing the blame on to **the man who healed me,** thus implicating Jesus. The man's responses here and in v. 15 are to be compared to the blind man in chap. 9. The religious leaders want the identity of the healer (v. 12), but the man does not know who Jesus is (v. 13). He has no sense of gratitude, even enough to motivate him to learn the name of his healer. Just why the **crowd** causes **Jesus** to leave the scene is not clear, but we might suppose that Jesus is not looking for the kind of fame which would arise as a result of his marvelous healing, even as he avoids popular enthusiasm for the feeding of the multitude (6:15). The repetition of the command, **Take up your pallet and walk,** in vv. 8, 11, and 12 is a feature of the oral transmission of the narrative preserved even as John begins to impose his meaning on the tale (notice its repetition in Mark 2:9, 11).

14—The scene shifts to **the temple** (more precisely, "temple courts," *hieros*). What importance, if any, the location has is not clear; nor is it clear why the man and Jesus should be there. Perhaps the injunction that the man should **sin no more** is set in the temple to suggest that the reorientation called for in Christ is both institutional and personal. Jesus' command, **Sin no more, that nothing worse befall you,** has been understood as a reflection of the prominent Jewish view (arising from the OT) that sin and illness are related. Healing by the forgiveness of sin is not an uncommon Synoptic theme and is a feature of the story in Mark 2 (esp. v. 5) and suggests the popular view that sin causes illness (cf. 1 Cor. 11:30). That might well be taken to be the meaning of Jesus' words in v. 14, if it were not for the fact that the man is about to demonstrate a sin of larger consequence in v. 15. It is clear that, while he is healed of his illness, he still suffers an illness of the spirit which is reflected in his lack of gratitude and his betrayal of Jesus to the authorities. The more important cure—coming to faith in Christ—is not achieved here (again, compare him with the blind man of chap. 9). Therefore, Jesus' words refer to that deeper sin of which he is guilty and are not necessarily an indication that Jesus or John embraced the view that illness results from wrongdoing. John 9:3 may indicate the author's rejection of the simplicity of that view.

15—The **man** immediately finds the authorities and informs them of the identity of the healer. With this ungrateful act the man leaves the scene. Those who benefit from **Jesus'** wondrous works are not necessarily brought to faith. The marvelous signs do not accomplish faith even in those who are beneficiaries of the wonder. John once again shows his reservations about the signs. In chap. 9 he will assert that the road to faith extends far beyond the effects of Jesus' grand deeds.

16-18—The healed man is responsible for the fact that the authorities **persecuted Jesus.** The precise charge against Jesus, however, is not specified. Was it due to the healing itself (i.e., the labor of the healing which could have been delayed until after **the sabbath**), or to Jesus' command that the man violate the Sabbath by carrying his mattress? Jesus defends himself in v. 17 by appeal to the Father-Son relationship. Since the Father is active even on the Sabbath, so must Jesus be. Contrast this defense for Sabbath work with that attributed to Jesus in the Synoptics, where the appeal is to Torah (e.g., Mark 2:25). Here, however, Jesus responds by reference to his authority as the **Father's** Son. Christology supersedes the Torah and its interpretation (cf. 7:22-23 below). His response only intensifies the efforts of the authorities to **kill him** (v. 18). This is the first we have heard of a death plot against Jesus, and it arises abruptly. John will refer to it again and again from this point on in order to enhance the inevitability of the destiny of Jesus at the hands of the established religion. Verse 18b raises certain problems. The authorities are motivated for two reasons, we are told: The violation of the Sabbath and Jesus' claim that he is **equal with God** (*ton theon ison*). The latter is due to the fact that Jesus **called God his own Father** (*patera idion elegen*). It does not appear to have been blasphemous to speak of God as Father. Still, the expression **his own Father** might mean Jesus claims God to be his Father in a special way (i.e., the equivalent of "only Son"); this may rely on the tradition that Jesus used the very personal form of Father, *Abba*, in addressing God.[11] The suggestion that Jesus could act as God acts on the Sabbath is the clearer basis of the charge that he claimed equality with God. On the other hand, it may also be that John's sense of irony is at work here. Jesus has said nothing that claims an equality with God, and the authorities have read that into his words. The irony is that Jesus *is* indeed an equal to the Father, something the readers know but the authorities do not. John is fond of having the leaders speak the truth without their being fully conscious of what it is they are saying (cf. 11:48-52 below). The words of the authorities are doubtless the words of the opponents of the Johannine community and reflect the centrality of Christology in that controversy.

The healing itself is of little consequence in John's view, if it does not lead to the accurate perception of the identity of the healer. His interpretation of the healing in vv. 10-18 shows that the central issue for him is the person of the healer, not the wonder itself. The sign is ambiguous, and neither the healed man nor the religious authorities perceive it with the eyes of faith. Even the wondrous power of the *logos* in flesh is not an unambiguous manifestation of God to those unwilling to dare the response of faith.

Father's Activity and the Son's (5:19-30)

19-20—Verse 18 provides the basis for the discourse in vv. 19-30, and the link of the discourse with the healing story is found only in those words of v. 18. **Jesus said to them** provides a transition between the offended leaders and the discourse proper. Once again, truly, truly introduces a Christological claim and the seriousness with which John takes these words (cf. 1:51 above). Verse 19 asserts the **Son's** subservient role to the **Father,** which may be intended as a direct contradiction to the claim that Jesus makes himself equal to God (v. 18). The sonship Christology of this gospel, for the most part, places Christ in a subordinate position to the Father (cf. 14:28), and we should not expect it to give expression to the Christological position of the later church. The emphasis of v. 19 is that what the Son does reflects the activities of God and is not to be construed as Jesus' own will (except as that will is one with the Father's). **What he sees the Father doing** recalls 1:18 and the fact that only the Son in preexistence has seen God. The Son's actions are imitations of the Father's actions. The Son carries the authority of the Father in his acts. Verse 20 further describes the Father-Son relationship: **For the Father loves the Son.** For the same point see 3:35; 10:17; 15:9; 17:23, 24, 26. The word for **love** is *philein* and this is the only time it is used of the Father-Son relationship. *Agapein* is the more common verb used in the passages cited. However, there appears to be no distinction between the two words in John. **For** (*gar*) implies that the reason the Father shows the Son all that he does is his love of the Son. The intimacy of the relationship and the preexistent status of the Son is behind the phrase **shows him all that he himself is doing.** Some have seen in the background of these verses what was originally a parable of the Father-Son relationship based on the association between the master and the apprentice. That may well be the case but is beyond demonstration. In **greater works than these** the **these** (*toutōn*) refers to the signs (and the healing in vv. 1-9 in particular?). The meaning (as in the case of this phrase in 1:51) is that the glorification of the Son by the Father which reveals their relationship will dim the **marvel** (*thaumazō*) of the signs. If the signs give life in the physical sense, Christ will give life in the sense of salvation in his glorification. At 7:21 Jesus again speaks of the astonishment of the people at his wonders. **Marvel** is intended to express the response to the physical signs and to say that it is to be exceeded by the wonder of Jesus' identity and his saving work.

The impact of vv. 19-20 is that in Christ God acts authoritatively. What God is expected to do, Jesus does. Consequently, how one responds to Jesus is one's response to God. "All these different phrases, that the Son does or says what he has seen or heard with the Father, give expression to the same idea, namely, that this is *the Revealer in whom we encounter God himself speaking and acting*" (Bultmann, p. 253). This is the basis of John's Christology—the Father and the Son function as a single unity. The remainder of the discourse explores that truth with special regard for the eschatological acts of God, i.e., those things it is supposed God will do at the last day.

21-23—As we expect God to give life in the resurrection of the dead, Christ **gives life to whom he will.** The resurrection life is already present in the gift of life from **the Son.** John's realized or present eschatology begins this section concerned with eschatological gifts, although future eschatology will likewise be affirmed (cf. vv. 28-29). The gift of **life** is an expression of Christ's absolute freedom made possible by the fact that his **will** and that of **the Father** are identical. The **life** given by the **Son** is the eschatological life. Verse 22 shifts the topic to another eschatological theme— **judgment.** Jewish eschatology held that God would act as the judge of all humans at the last day, just as he would bring their resurrection from the grave, but now it is claimed that God has placed that role in the hands of the Son (cf. the discussion of judgment above at 3:17-19). In facing Christ, then, one is facing his or her judge. **Honor** (*timaō*) has the sense of "placing a high value on a person." John uses the word on two other occasions, once to speak of Jesus' honoring the Father (8:49) and once to speak of God's honoring those who serve Jesus (12:26). The *functional unity* of the Father and Son is the point of v. 23. Since Jesus will function as judge in the last day, he is to be regarded as one would regard God. It is likely that John's own community struggled with the Jews of the local synagogue who did **not honor the Son** and believed that thereby they did **honor the Father. Who sent him** invokes another Christological theme which enforces the Father-Son relationship. Just as the Son is to be regarded as one would the Father, so the official envoy **sent** by the **Father** is to be treated as one would treat the sender. The official agent commissioned by a king carried the authority of the king. So is Christ the official agent of the Father (cf. 3:17 above). John uses two words, *pempein* and *apostellein*, interchangeably for the mission of the Son: here it is the latter but in 3:17 the former.

24—The thought moves to the gift of **eternal life,** repeating the theme of v. 21. The gift depends upon hearing (*akouō*) and believing (*pisteuō*), two frequent verbs in John but found only here in combination. However, reception of the revelation is often said to involve hearing Jesus' words (e.g., 8:43, 47; 12:47; 18:37). As is the case with seeing, to hear Jesus often has the meaning of correctly discerning the revelation and in those cases has to do with a "spiritual" discernment nearly interchangeable with belief (e.g., Jesus **hears** the Father, 8:40, and it is believers who truly hear Jesus, 18:37). The word is incarnated in a human who must be perceived with faith in order for the divine glory to be known (1:14). **Hears my word** (*logos*) is coupled with **believes him who sent me** in a synonymous parallelism, for to **hear** truly the **word** of the envoy is to **believe** the sender. It is unusual for John to speak of believing God. Much more frequent are the statements of belief in Jesus. John 12:24 and 14:1 would suggest that believing in Jesus is the equivalent of believing (in) God. To those who believe, the eschatological gifts are given in the present. **Has eternal life** indicates that the quality of existence bestowed by the revealer takes its beginnings in this earthly life and not alone in the life beyond the grave. The point of v. 21b is repeated here. The believer to whom eternal life is given is not judged (used in the Johannine sense of "condemned"). **Judgment** (*krisis*) takes place in the moment of decision for or against Christ, and by grasping the revelation in faith the believer has thereby received God's blessing and **has passed from death to life.** With overtones of Pauline thought, **death** (*thanatos*) is the way of existence dominated by an alienation from God, and **life** (*zōē*) is the authentic quality of living in a relationship of love with the Father.

25-27—The theme we have just heard is repeated but now in the symbolism of resurrection. **The hour is coming and now is** (cf. 4:23) refers to that final day of the eschaton which is already realized in the presence of Christ. (That **hour** is used, rather than "day," is peculiarly Johannine and derived from Jesus' own **hour;**

cf. 1 John 2:18.) With God's act in Christ the time distinction between the future and the present is bridged. To **hear** is again the equivalent of believe (cf. v. 24), and as in the previous verse **dead** refers to those trapped in the realm of unbelief. The **voice** (*tēs phōnēs*) of the Son of God has power to bring life and healing (cf. 5:8 and 11:43) and is the powerful *logos* of God by which creation is effected now within the historical realm in the human Jesus. Verse 26 repeats the theme of v. 21. **Life within himself** means the source of life. The power of the Son, however, is dependent upon the power of the **Father. Son of man** (*huios anthrōpou*) is used here in its primitive Christian sense of the eschatological agent of God—a meaning rooted in Dan. 7:13. This is the single appearance of the title in John without the definite articles (*the* Son of *the* man). The difference, however, is merely a matter of the author's preference at the moment, although the anarthrous form may reflect a pre-titular version of the expression. This verse and v. 25 show what appears to be John's use of three titles—**Son, Son of God,** and **Son of man**—without significant variety of meaning.

28-30—Verses 21-27 have spoken of the present reality of the eschatological events in Jesus, but now those same events are spoken of as future realities. Verse 28 confirms the eschatological promise of a future resurrection at the end-time. **Do not marvel at this** is ambiguous, for it can either be a connective with v. 27 or a reference to what is about to be said in v. 28. The latter appears the more likely. The phrase found in v. 25 (**the hour is coming** and now is) is repeated, but without "and now is." The focus of thought is on the future. The meaning of death at this point is physical, as the use of tombs indicates, but for John both the physical and spiritual meanings are equally important (on **voice** cf. v. 25 above). Jewish eschatological thought sometimes expressed a view of the resurrection which assumed that only the righteous would be raised, but at other times held to a general resurrection of all. The latter is in view here, as v. 29 demonstrates. The contrast of **the resurrection of life** (*anastasin zōēs*) and **the resurrection of judgment** (*anastasin kriseōs*) again reflects the peculiarly Johannine use of **judgment** in the negative sense of condemnation (cf. Dan. 12:2). The reward of **good** and the punishment of **evil** is the inescapable meaning and does not differ from other NT affirmations of this point (e.g., Matt. 25:31-46 and Rom. 2:6-8). However, in Johannine thought **good** is done only by believing and **evil** is always the consequence of unbelief (e.g., 15:1-10). It is instructive that again John has nothing to say about the fate of evil except that it will be judged to be such. Verse 30 functions as a transition from this discourse into verses 31-47 and does little more than repeat the theme of the unity of function between the Father and Son. Again the role of the Son as the agent of the Father is stressed; and because their **wills** are the same, the Son acts for God, and his actions are just because of that unity of **wills**. **On my own authority** is literally "from myself" (*ap' emautou*).

Verses 19-30 comprise an interesting discourse. Its central theme is the oneness of the Father and Son in action, but that theme is focused on eschatological events. Of the Father-Son relationship we are told (1) the Son does not act on his own but always imitates the Father (vv. 19, 30); (2) the Father loves the Son (v. 20); (3) the Father reveals himself to the Son (v. 20b); (4) the Father gives to the Son the power of resurrection and life (vv. 21, 26) and the authority of judgment (vv. 22, 26); and (5) to honor the Son is to honor the Father (v.27). The eschatological discussion in vv. 24-29 is, however, independent of the previous verses and the conclusion in v. 30. It shifts from the title Son to the Son of God (v. 25) and Son of man (v. 27). It may be that John himself has made the connection between vv. 19-23 and 24-29. More remarkable is the double vision of vv. 24-29. While vv. 24-27 affirm the *present* reality of the eschatological events, vv. 28-29 declare their *future* reality. John intends a kind of both-and emphasis in eschatology by placing the two views back to back. It is possible that his tradition contained the futuristic theme, and he affirms that view by repeating it. But alongside of it he lays his own interpretation of eschatology, namely, the insistence that those events are already real in one's encounter with Christ. The activity of the Spirit-Paraclete transposes the future into the present, but without denying the continued reality of the future. The key to John's dual eschatology lies in his concept of the work of the Spirit and in his concept of time, i.e., the convergence of past, present, and future in the revelation in Christ.

The Witnesses for Jesus and the Accusation of Unbelief (5:31-47)

The tone of the Fourth Gospel is consistently that of a trial. One senses that Jesus is on trial and that John is the attorney for the defense. This is nowhere more clear than in 5:31-47 in which Jesus is made to speak of the witnesses on his behalf. It is continuous with the defense of Jesus' actions in the previous section but now has a broader focus.

31-32—The legal decision that one cannot **witness** (*martyreō*) to oneself is reflected in v. 31 (cf. Deut. 19:15). This is contradicted by 8:14 where Jesus claims that his unique origin makes his self-witness reliable. Here we have further evidence that John did not carefully revise all of his traditional materials so as to eliminate all contradiction. **True** (*alēthēs*) here and below has the sense of "proof" or "reliability" but also reflects the Johannine connotation of truth as the revelation of God. Verse 32 begins the discussion of a number of witnesses on behalf of Jesus. The first is **another** (*allos*) who is God, and to this **witness** the discussion returns in v. 37. **I know** may be intended to suggest that the **witness** of God on behalf of Jesus is known only to him and is beyond the scope of human confirmation. The hearers cannot directly know the witness of God except as it appears in the witness of others. Hence, it is appropriate that the string of witnesses begin with the one who is the source of truth. Comparison between Jesus' defense in this passage and God's self-defense against false gods in the OT (e.g., Isa. 42:8; 43:8-13; 44:6-23) has sometimes been made—and with good cause.

33-35—Now begins the parade of the additional witnesses, the first being **John,** the baptizer. The religious leaders themselves sought his **witness** (cf. 1:19-27). **Has borne witness** translates the perfect tense of the verb *martyreō*, meaning an action in the past which continues in the present. But here is the irony (v. 34): The source of the truth about Jesus is not in any human being. Jesus needs no such human witness, and the baptizer's witness is referred to only for the sake of Jesus' opponents that they **may be saved** (*sōthēte*) in the sense of rescued from their blindness to the truth. The baptizer is a **lamp** (*lychnos*, a small portable light), not the light itself (1:8), but nonetheless an instrument by which the light was disseminated. The latter half of v. 35 suggests that there was an enthusiastic but short-lived reception of the ministry of the baptizer; indeed Josephus testifies that such was the case (*Ant.* 18.2).

36-38—As true as the baptizer's casting of the light might have been, Jesus has a witness far **greater**—his **works. Works** (*erga*) refers not alone to the signs but to the task of revealing **the Father** and being the light. Of the **works** Jesus says three things: (1) They are given to him by **the Father.** (2) They are what Jesus is **doing,** hence giving specific meaning to his activity. (3) They **bear witness that the Father has** sent him. (On the accomplishment of the **works** see 4:34 above.) The **testimony** (*martyria*) of his **works** demonstrates the decisive fact about Jesus, namely, his origin and his commission. But the **witness** of the **Father** in v. 37 is less clear. It refers back to the testimony of "another" in v. 32, but beyond that what witness of the Father does John intend? Possibly the witness of the Father is known in Jesus' works or in the Scriptures which are to be discussed in v. 39. More likely we should understand this witness to be the active presence of God in the lives of the believers, confirming the truth of the revelation in Christ. It is the self-authenticating witness known only to the community of believers through the activity of the Spirit-Paraclete. The unbelieving opponents have no access to this witness, for they **have never heard** God's word nor **seen** his **form.** Such an accusation against the religious leaders would be severe, for their tradition claimed God had been **heard** (Deut. 4:12, 15) and **seen** (Exod. 19:11, against 1:18 above). John is here denying that those who reject Jesus have truly embraced the OT tradition. By virtue of their refusal to **believe** in Jesus they demonstrate that God's word does not abide **in them** (v. 38). On **abiding** (*menein*) see 15:1-10 below.

39-40—The strong accusation continues as Jesus claims that **the scriptures** are also a **witness** to him. Although the leaders **search the scriptures** they fail to see that Jesus is the one of whom the sacred writings speak. **Search** (*eraunaō*) may be intended here as the technical word used in rabbinic circles for the study of **scriptures.** The controversy of the Christians and the Jews of John's own day is reflected in this fundamentally different view of the OT. For both, however, the **scriptures** give access to **eternal life.** Verse 40 charges that the refusal to believe in Jesus is purposive and premeditated. **To come to me** (*elthein pros me*) is a Johannine synonym for belief (e.g., 6:35, 37). **Life** is the abbreviation of eternal life.

41-44—Having itemized four witnesses for Jesus—the baptizer, Jesus' own works, the Father, and the Scriptures—the discourse moves to the more general theme of unbelief and rejection. Verse 41 claims that the **glory** (*doxa*) Jesus has is from God and does not depend upon whether or not humans accept him. Jesus' knowledge of the interior life of humans is affirmed again in v. 42. **The love of God** is ambiguous in the Greek as it is in the RSV. Here it doubtless means human love for God rather than God's love for humans. The implication is that one who truly loves God believes in Jesus. Verse 43 carries the further consequences of the absence of that love. They will accept one who **comes in his own name** but not Jesus, who comes in the **Father's name.** In the Hebraic sense of **name** (Gk., *onoma*) the phrase means that one comes with the character and identity of the one named. That Jesus has **come in my Father's name** is another way of saying that the Father has sent him or that he is the Father's Son. The **another** who **comes in his own name** (*en tō onomati tō idiō*) is probably not meant to refer exclusively to a specific figure or to the false messiahs but as a reference to the general blindness of the religious leaders. Verse 44 continues to hammer away at the same point. If they do not **seek the glory** (in the sense of "praise") **that comes from the only God,** they cannot believe, just as they cannot if they have no love of God. One's general direction and orientation determine (among other things) whether one is capable of belief. John's assessment of the human condition forces him to accentuate the reality of unbelief. The human choice is between the light and the darkness, between the glory of humans and the **glory** of **God. Only** (*monos*) **God** is also used in 17:3.

45-57—The polemic quality of the passage builds to a climax in v. 45. In 8:39ff. John will have Jesus claim that the unbelieving Jews are not children of Abraham at all. Here he asserts that the very one whom they follow, **Moses,** is their accuser. The thought is similar to that of vv. 39-40. This turns the popular speculation about Moses as the intercessor on behalf of the people upside down, making him one who convicts them of their failure to believe. Jesus is not the accuser, just as he is not the judge (cf. 8:15); human unbelief is its own judge. The unbelieving leaders have the unenviable position to have transformed the one on **whom you set your hope** into one who will be their accuser. Verse 46 makes inescapable the tie between belief in Jesus and Moses. Belief in the latter leads to belief in the former. **For he wrote of me** refers to the Torah in general and not to specific passages. Still, "the prophet-like-Moses" (Deut. 18:15, 18) has special importance for John, as would appear to be the case in 6:14 and 7:40. In v. 47 **writings** (*grammasin*) and **words** (*hrēmasin*) are intended to parallel one another. Belief in the written word is deemed easier than belief in the oral word; so if the leaders cannot **believe** Moses, they will not be able to believe Jesus. The parallel may also express the Johannine conviction that the Christians embrace both the written law of Moses and the oral tradition about Jesus.

This discourse (vv. 31-47) stresses the conviction of the evangelist that Christianity is a continuation of God's work in the OT, even though those who embrace the OT do not always correctly understand it. If he seems unduly harsh in his handling of the Jewish opponents of Jesus, it is due to his immersion in the controversy of his own day with the local synagogue. His own Jewish roots are betrayed in the firmness of his claim that truth is witnessed to in the OT; his Christian commitments are clear from the fact that he presupposes that the OT in general refers to Christ. He uses few specific passages to document that presupposition. The thrust of this discourse is that human unbelief is culpable and that the several witnesses to the truth of Christ should suffice to bring one to faith. But also implied is the fact that human depravity makes it nearly impossible for some to believe. Still, John does believe that Christ has power to draw all humans to himself (12:32).

Taken as whole, this first general section, 2:1—5:47, of the first part of the gospel narrates a number of stories shot through with Jesus' divine power to act and to understand. Coupled with those narratives are a number of discourses which invariably work at the disclosure of the true identity of Jesus. But more, this section defines the basic opposition between Jesus and the religious establishment of his day (and John's). The stage is being set for the acceleration of that opposition to tragic proportions. The reader now knows the meaning of the prolog and just how radical is the strangeness of the revelation in the world and most clearly among those who are, by society's definition, "religious."

■ Earthly and Heavenly Food (6:1-71)

The second section of the first half of the gospel continues the prominent themes of the first division—the marvel of Jesus' power, the exploration of his identity, and the growing opposition to him. The difference is only the intensity of chap. 6. In one sense this chapter is the hinge between 2:1—5:47 and 7:1—10:42. It is a pivot point because of the radicality of Jesus' claims for himself and the ever-widening gulf between him and his opponents. This chapter puts to rest any hopes of a popular and successful ministry and states the enormity of unbelief. From the end of this chapter the conclusion of John's gospel is clear. The power and intent of unbelief with regard to Jesus is now explicitly described. Humanity can hardly comprehend, much less appropriate, the revelation.[12]

The Feeding of the Multitude (6:1-15)

It is clear that in this narrative John employs a tradition related to but not identical with the Synoptic traditions (Matt. 14:13-21; Mark 6:30-44; 8:1-10; and Luke 9:10-17). Mark's two accounts of the feeding of multitudes show already that the tradition concerning this tale had taken several forms. John's access to that tale is through still another form, preserved and shaped by his own community. The unique features of his story which are most important are: The Passover setting (v. 4), the roles of Philip (v. 7), Andrew (v. 8), and the boy along with the details concerning his lunch (v. 9), the use of "when he had given thanks" (*eucharistēsas*, v. 11b),

Jesus' (rather than the disciples') distribution of the loaves and fishes (v. 11a), and the conclusion of the scene in vv. 14-15. (For an exhaustive comparison of the accounts cf. Brown, vol. 2, pp. 236-250.) There is little to show that John has used one or more of the Synoptic accounts as the basis of his story and a great deal more to suggest that an independent tradition forms that basis.

1-4—The Greek lists two names after **the Sea of**, the first **Galilee** and the second **Tiberias.** The second name was used after Herod Antipas constructed the city of Tiberias on the west shore of the sea (ca. 25 C.E.). The best guess is that John intended **other side** to designate the eastern shore, as is suggested by v. 17. The **multitude** mentioned in v. 2 and the subsequent narratives of the chapter is the only indication in John of a popular Galilean following. **Because they saw the signs.** . .is John's signal that the motives of the crowd are rather shallow (cf. v. 26). The exact **signs** to which this sentence refers are not clear. The last wonder done in Galilee is in 4:43-54. John probably took v. 2 from his source, which may have included mention in general of many **signs,** and he did not intend the verse to have a specific reference in his narrative. **The mountain** mentioned in v. 3 seems to have no symbolic importance (unlike its counterpart in Matthew, e.g., 5:1). **His disciples** have not been mentioned in the narrative since chap. 4. The mention of **the Passover** in v. 4 seems to suggest symbolic value, since each of the three Passovers mentioned in this gospel (2:13; 13:1; and here) appear at crucial points. The use of wilderness wandering motifs later in the discourse (e.g., vv. 30ff.) shows that the Passover setting is important to John. In the discourse materials he will exploit the relationship between Jesus and the manna from heaven; here he wants to suggest that Jesus' feeding of the multitude is symbolic of his freeing them from their captivity in darkness and nourishing them, just as the Passover freed them of their bondage in Egypt and just as they had been nourished by God in the desert. Taken as a whole, John's use of the Passover as a setting for the ministry of Jesus stresses that in the Christ-revelation the formative event of Israel's history is completed and fulfilled.

5-9—It is significant that the Johannine **Jesus** takes the initiative in posing the problem for the disciples, as opposed to the Synoptic accounts in which the disciples raise the question (e.g., Mark 6:35-36). The nourishment of his people comes at the initiative of God, even before their need is expressed (cf. Numbers 11). Verse 6 is the standard Johannine note reminding us of the absolute knowledge of Christ and the certainty of his intentions. The word translated **test** (*peirazō*) is used only here in the gospel (but once in the later narrative 7:53—8:11, namely, 8:6). Elsewhere its sense is either negative (to tempt or to demand proof, e.g., Matt. 16:1) or more positive (to give opportunity to show faith, e.g., Heb. 11:17). **Philip's** degree of trust is being tested, which raises to the forefront the matter of faith. The function of Philip's response in v. 7 is to show the enormity of Jesus' wonder, more bread than could be purchased with the equivalent of 200 daily wages! But it also shows that Philip's vision is limited to worldly sources of **bread.** Verses 8-9 are unique features of the Johannine narrative, adding touches of reality to the story, and may indicate the greater development of John's tradition. (In some cases the longer a story was transmitted orally, the greater the number of details that were added.) Both Philip and **Andrew** offer statements of the extent of the human need. The little boy (the Greek is *paidarion*, meaning the smallest of children) and his tiny lunch pose dramatic contrast with the abundance of food produced by Jesus' act. The story of Elisha's feeding of a hundred people in 2 Kings 4:42-44 may be in mind with the mention of the **barley loaves.** Jesus' act exceeds that of the prophet.

10-13—The scene has been set by the statement of the immensity of human need. **Jesus** assumes command of the situation, and the anticipation of the wonder is emphasized in the use of the number 5000. In v. 11 **Jesus** serves as the host at the meal, giving **thanks** and distributing the food. Not only does Jesus take the initiative in the act (cf. v. 5) but he himself gives the bread and **fish** to the people. He is pictured as the giver of the essential nourishment of humanity, acting as a typical Jewish host. Whether or not a eucharistic meaning is intended by the evangelist is often debated. The features which might suggest eucharistic symbolism are the facts that Jesus gives thanks (*eucharisteō*) and himself distributes the food. While it is possible that the Johannine community interpreted the feeding story in the light of the Eucharist, there is insufficient evidence to say that this was John's intent. It is enough to emphasize that Jesus is hosting the occasion at which the radical need of humanity is fulfilled. Verses 11b-13 are designed to stress the abundance of the gift given through Christ— the people eat as much as they want and even then there are **twelve baskets** filled with the leftovers. ". . .After all have been satisfied there is more left over than there was at the beginning" (Bultmann, p. 213). There is some evidence that the gathering of the leftovers was a common custom at a Jewish meal, but it is here to emphasize the extravagance of the wonder. **Twelve baskets** is not likely symbolic, for John seldom employs the number 12 for its symbolic value (e.g., he refers only four times to the inner circle of disciples as the Twelve—6:67, 70, 71; 20:24). The tradition passed on to John, however, may have originally intended that the number show fulfillment of the role of the ancient tribes of Israel.

14-15—The effect of the marvelous act on the people is described and functions as the public confirmation so often found at the conclusion of miracle stories. It is said that they **saw the sign** (*idontes. . .sēmeion*), but in v. 26 Jesus accuses the crowd of having not seen **signs**. The difference lies in the distinction between the role of the signs in John's source and his own view of the matter. Here the sense is only that they are impressed by the marvelous quality of Jesus' act. In v. 26 the sense is that through the wondrous act the people have not discerned the true nature of the person of Jesus. They are so impressed with Jesus that they think he is **the prophet who is to come into the world** (*ho prophētēs ho erchomenos eis ton kosmon*), an apparent reference to the concept of the messiah as a prophet-like figure, since v. 15 seems to equate this title with the role of king. The prophet-like-Moses (Deut. 18:15, 18) was merged in some messianic speculation with the Messiah himself (cf. 1:21f. above). The intent to make **Jesus king** is an ill-founded enthusiasm of the moment which has no value for John, given his view of Christ. The motivation of the crowd is made clear in v. 26. John's Jesus will have none of this and flees from the crowd. This kind of political kingship stands in contrast to the true kingship of Jesus (cf. 18:36). **Perceiving** (*gnous*, "knowing") may be a kind of supernatural knowledge on the part of Jesus (v. 15). **Jesus withdrew again to the mountain** may indicate that this conclusion is John's own construction; he pays little attention to the fact that the scene had already taken place on the mountain (v. 3). John is not interested in the theme of Jesus' own piety, so it is unlikely that **by himself** has to do with his personal relationship with God (which is so intimate that it does not even need the benefit of privacy). It suggests, on the other hand, Jesus' disengagement of himself entirely from all popular political movements.

Taken as a whole, the Johannine multiplication of the loaves and fishes teaches the reader that Jesus is the giver of divine nourishment. The crass miracle has little significance for John, except as it may symbolize a more profound spiritual gift. The OT overtones and the Passover setting clearly introduce the theme of the later discourses, which has to do with Jesus' exceeding the gifts of the prophets of Jewish tradition. As the giver of life, Jesus gives more than has been known in the past.

The Walking on the Water and the Wondrous Landing (6:16-21)

Again the Johannine narrative has Synoptic parallels (Matt. 14: 22-33 and Mark 6:45-52). What immediately strikes one in comparing this account with the Synoptic records is the simplicity and economy of John's narrative. Whether that means that John's form of the story is more primitive than the Synoptics' is hard to say, since neither abbreviation nor elaboration is always a clue to the process of oral transmission.[13] John employs a tradition related to, but independent of, the Synoptic tradition.

16-18—The narrator exhibits little interest in the transition from the feeding story to this narrative, and it may be that they were already connected in the source John used as they are in Mark (6:30-52). Verse 16 introduces the theme of darkness (**evening**) which is deliberate Johannine symbolism, suggesting that the **disciples** are immersed in the darkness of the world. It is there Jesus comes to meet them. John is not concerned for the moment with the dismissal of the crowd (cf. Matt. 14:22 and Mark 6:45). On **Capernaum** cf. 2:12 and 4:46 above. The realistic concerns for the trip in v. 17 fade in importance to the theological meaning of the episode. Now the disciples are totally in the dark. **And Jesus had not yet come to them** anticipates the marvel soon to occur and emphasizes the absence of Jesus. Verse 18 adds to the plight of the disciples—now they are in the midst of a storm. The situation is pictured in such a way as to describe the human condition deprived of a revelation from God and mired in the misunderstanding of faithlessness.

19-20—Into their deprived situation comes hope. They see **Jesus** coming to them. Their position **three or four miles** (25 or 30 stadia) would put them approximately midway across **the sea**, which is seven miles at its widest point. **Walking on** (*epi*) **the sea** can also be rendered "by the sea," but it is clear John intends the act to be miraculous. That the scene is a theophanic experience, the manifestation of the divine on the plane of history, is clear from the fright (*phobeō*, to be terrified) attributed to the disciples. This is the only use of this verb in John and nowhere else are the disciples **frightened** by the appearance of Jesus (although cf. 21: 12). That may indicate two things: First, John is using his signs source here and employing the description found in it. Second, this is a unique experience of beholding the awesome presence of the divine Son. The words of Jesus in v. 20 confirm the awful nature of the experience. **It is I** is the unfortunate translation of the startling expression "I Am" (*egō eimi*) without the predicate, although possibly the predicate is implied as the RSV takes it. Its meaning is to identify the speaker with God himself. Some would argue that, in cases such as this, the sense of the "I Am" is no more than an emphatic self-identification not to be equated with the solemn declaration of divinity in those cases where there is neither an explicit nor implicit predicate (8:24, 28, 58; 13:19). Two things suggest that at v. 20 it has its deeper meaning. First, the same form of the expression with the implied predicate "**he**" is found at 18:5-6, where at its utterance the guards fall back and to the ground—an obvious indication that the words carry the force of divine authority. Second, the setting of the expression here is certainly a theophany and, even without the "I Am" statement, Jesus reveals his divine power in the event (cf. 4:26 above and 8:24, 28 below).[14] It may be, however, that John plays with the double meaning of this expression, intending the more profound meaning in the disguise of a simple **it is I** (cf. Brown, vol. 2, p. 534). **Do not be afraid** (*phobeisthe*) speaks to the terror of the disciples mentioned in v. 19 and brings to mind Jer. 1:8. Jesus' presence quiets the turmoil of human despair.

21—The transformation of the disciples' condition by the presence of Jesus is completed. **They were glad** (*ēthelon*) is better translated "they were willing," without specifying whether or not Jesus was actually taken into the boat. The point of v. 21a is the eagerness on the part of the disciples to receive Jesus, and v. 21b represents the resolution of the disciples' plight by a wondrous landing—**immediately** (*eutheōs*). The sudden cessation of the winds in the accounts of Mark (6:51) and Matthew (14:32) is paled by the immediate arrival of the boat at its destination. Again John's tendency (or that of his source) is to heighten the wondrous quality of the story. The account ends abruptly without an interpretation, unless we are to look for its interpretation in the discourse materials to follow.

This "double sign" is clearly a manifestation of Jesus' divinity—his power to overcome the physical elements, but also human darkness and fear. By virtue of that meaning, the story fits appropriately between the sign of the feeding and the Christological discourses in the remainder of the chapter. Whether or not its meaning lies also in the context of the Passover (v. 4) and the discussion of the feeding of the people of Israel in the wilderness (vv. 31ff.) is less clear. Should we take the walking on the sea and the wondrous landing as the fulfillment in Christ of the passage through the Sea of Reeds (Exodus 14)? On the one hand, such a reading of the narrative stretches the explicit evidence for such. On the other hand, John may have sandwiched this double sign between the feeding and the bread of life discourse precisely because he wanted to convey that meaning (even though it likely did not have that meaning in his source— regardless of whether the feeding and the sea miracle were linked there as they were in the Synoptic tradition). The most that can be said is that finding exodus motifs in 6:16-21 harmonizes with its context, although John may not consciously have sought to evoke that interpretation.

The Bread of Life Discourses—Dialog with the Crowd (6:22-34)

The discourse section of the chapter, which is John's interpretation of the sign of the feeding, begins with v. 22 and continues through v. 71. It is comprised of three sections—vv. 22-34, 35-50, 51-59—plus the conclusion in vv. 60-71. The sections are closely tied to one another, although the main body of the discourse, vv. 35-50 and 51-59, gives evidence of being duplicates. The introduction to the discourse, which sets the stage and the tone of what follows, is a dialog between Jesus and the crowd (vv. 22-34).

22-24—For John this is a rather lengthy transition and a confusing one as well. It may be that it demonstrates the efforts of a later editor and even later scribes to clear up a difficult passage. The intent is to say that **the people** surmise that **Jesus** has by some unknown means joined his **disciples** on the opposite (western?) side of the lake, and they set out to find him. The Greek is not clear and several textual variants witness to efforts to provide some greater clarity (e.g., after **boat** a variety of witnesses try to clarify that this is the vessel in which the **disciples** had departed). **On the next day** is a general and imprecise link with vv. 16-21 (cf. John's use of the same phrase in 1:29, 35, 44; 12:12). Verse 23 is a parenthetical comment to explain how the crowd was able to follow the disciples; but it poses more serious problems. Is it the crowd of 5000 men plus others who experienced the feeding (v. 10) that makes the journey? Are we to imagine such a large number of boats? **The Lord had given thanks** is missing in important textual witnesses and would appear to be a scribal addition. (John rarely uses *kyrios*, Lord, in this way.) Whether Tiberias is intended as the location of the feeding is not clear. Verse 24 does no more than try to summarize the meaning of vv. 22-23. This extraordinarily confusing passage may have originated from John's efforts to mend together passages from his signs source with vv. 25-34 (which are possibly composed from another source).

25-26—**On the other side of the sea** presumably means at Capernaum on the northwestern side. **Rabbi** is a frequent title used of Jesus both by those who do not believe in him (e.g., 3:2) and those who do (e.g., 4:31). **When did you come here?** in the Greek is an ambiguous question which asks both "when did you come?" and "how long have you been here?" (*pote hōde gegonas*). It is possible, but not clearly the case, that John here intends a subtle theological reference to Jesus' origin. Verse 26 is a rebuke of a shallow faith based on the material benefits of the sign of the feeding. Jesus ignores their question and introduces his statement with the solemn **truly, truly,** which signals a declaration of divine authority. The people seek him in order to benefit from his miraculous power, and not because they **saw signs.** Here seeing signs is used to mean a faith perception of Jesus' wondrous acts which goes beyond the wonder itself to a faith in the actor. (Contrast this with 4:48 and cf. comments there.) Verse 26 may reflect the point of view of the signs source which was not as critical of belief based on signs as the evangelist was. But it also poses the importance of the question of the motive for seeking Jesus (cf. 1:38 above).

27—This introduces the theme of the bread of life discourse itself. **The food** (*brōsis*) **which perishes** sets the sign of the feeding in proper perspective. While such food is important, there is a food of greater importance. **The food which endures to eternal life** is the revelation and its benefits. **Endures** translates one of John's favorite words for the relationship of the believer with Christ and God, *menein.* The sense, therefore, is that in this imperishable **food** one knows the **life** of the new age, the authentic existence. The **food** is none other than Jesus himself, as we will learn in v. 35. **Perishes** (*apollymi*) is a word John uses on two other occasions to contrast with **eternal life** (3:16; 10:28). One is urged to **labor** for this life-giving nourishment, and the word *ergazomai* is used (translated elsewhere as "work," e.g., 5:17; 9:4). But the invitation to work for this food is radically qualified by the statement that **eternal life** is given to the believer by **the Son of man.** There is a dual aspect of the gift of eternal life. It is always a gift and not an achievement, and yet it is a gift which must be sought by humans (cf. 5:6 above). **Eternal life** is the eschatological gift which will be given, but in v. 32b is already present in Christ. **Son of man** is a title frequently associated with eschatological matters (cf. 1:51 above). **Seal** (*sphragizein*) is the stamp of accreditation, God's authorization of the **Son** (cf. 3:31 above). Did John think of this divine authorization as a certain event in the life of Jesus? Some have proposed that it is the descent of the Spirit on Jesus mentioned in 1:33, but in Johannine thought such an authorization would likely refer to the glorification of the Son in the crucifixion-resurrection. **God the Father** is an emphatic expression for John and underlines the fact of the divine stamp of approval; John would normally use only **Father**.

28-29—The question of the people in v. 28 does not clearly follow from Jesus' words, unless it is in response to the command to labor for the spiritual food. The RSV loses the association of the question with Jesus' command by translating the verb *ergazomai* **doing** instead of "labor." While the verb in the previous verse has the sense of "work for," here it means "to perform." The RSV also loses the wordplay in the Greek which literally is "to work the works of God" (*ergazometha ta erga tou theou*). **The works of God** refers to that which God desires humans to do in the plan of salvation. John thinks of the question of the crowd as a sincere inquiry, but still it misses the importance of Jesus' statement that one is but to seek the gift of eternal life. The people would have Jesus reduce the matter to a simple formula of action by which humans could insure their destinies. But John's **Jesus** will have none of that, and in v. 29 displaces all such mechanistic formulae with the invitation to **believe**. There is really only one "work" that matters, and that is faith. One must be careful not to impose upon Johannine thought the faith/works distinction we find in Paul. John is able to say that belief is a work—a human act— but an act which is made possible only by the gift of the Son. To believe is a work, but no one believes except as the Father enables her or him to believe (v. 44). Furthermore, the present (subjunctive) of the verb (*pisteuēte*) suggests an ongoing act, and the expression **believe in** (*eis*) denotes a personal trust (and hence not a single act but a process). John never uses the noun, faith (*pistis*), but always the verb, believe, suggesting that it is an ongoing process. For **whom he sent** cf. 5:23 and 3:17 above.

30-31—The result of Jesus' declaration concerning himself is the people's request for a **sign**. There is some evidence that the Jews believed the Messiah would do wonders which would demonstrate his identity, but such a view was denied by some of the rabbis (cf. Schnackenburg, vol 2, pp. 39-40). The request is for some proof of the truth of Jesus' words which would eliminate the risk of believing him. It must be a sign that can be seen. The use of the word **work** is continued (*ergazē*), extending the theme from v. 27. The request is like that found in 2:18 (cf. above) and parallels the incident recorded in Mark 8:11-12 (cf. Matt. 16:1f. and Luke 11:29-30). Their request shows that they have not properly understood the feeding (v. 26). In v. 31 the reason for the request is explained. The people have heard Jesus' remarks about food and want a sign from him like the feeding of Israel in the wilderness (Exodus 16). It may also be that their words echo a belief that with the coming of the Messiah the ancient giving of manna would be duplicated with the gift of an eschatological bread (cf. 2 Apoc. Bar. 29:8; for other references to this idea cf. Barrett, p. 288). They seek a clear messianic act which would provide assurance of the truth of Jesus' claim. The scripture cited in v. 31b is not an exact rendering of any known passage. It may be a paraphrasing of Ps. 78:24, or the combination of that and Exod. 16:4 or Neh. 9:15. Such paraphrasings seem to have been a midrashic technique used by rabbis of the first century. The source John is using may have been a Christian homily which used such rabbinic methods (cf. Borgen).

32-33—**Jesus'** response follows the scripture quoted by the people. It is **not Moses** but the **Father** who gave the manna; and the Father continues to give the spiritual nourishment (**gives**). And what he **gives** is **the true bread from heaven.** These revelatory words (**truly, truly**) follow the midrashic interpretative practice and ready the hearers for the fact that Jesus is the **true bread.** The point is that this act of God in Israel's history is now fulfilled and continued in the present work of God. The first clause of the sentence may be understood as denying either that **Moses gave** the **bread** or that it was **bread from heaven** that **Moses gave.** The choices are not exclusive of one another, but the former seems more likely in this context. The sense is further complicated by the fact that the Jews sometimes spoke of the Torah as bread (cf. Prov. 9:5). If that usage is in mind here, we have a contrast between the Torah and Jesus. It is entirely possible that John has both in mind and uses the passage as a response to Jewish opponents of his own day. **True** (*alēthinon*) is one of John's frequent words for the revelation of God in Christ (e.g., 1:9; 15:1), and the sense is less that the manna from **heaven** during the desert period was false than that the **bread** which is the revelation in Christ is superior. Some polemic intent is implied in the use of **true,** since the evangelist is concerned to argue against the charge that Christ is not a **true** revelation of God. Verse 33 makes clear that the **true bread** is that which results in genuine **life.** The Greek is ambiguous as to whether it is **bread** *that* or *who* **comes down from heaven,** but the use of the expression **come down** (*katabainō*) elsewhere in reference to Christ surely implies that the descending Son is the **bread of God** for humanity (cf. 6:38, 41, 42, and 3:13). The identification of the bread with Christ (v. 35) is anticipated here. **Gives life to the world** recalls 1:4 and echoes the intent of God's act in Christ as it is expressed in 3:16. **The world** (*kosmos*), which so often in John denotes the realm of unbelief, can be enlivened by the divine gift of bread.

34—The response of the crowd is typical Johannine misunderstanding, for they think he is speaking of a physical **bread** descended from above and want a goodly supply of it (cf. 4:15 above). They do not yet understand that Jesus himself is the bread and think that the wondrous feeding is something that can be repeated on a regular basis.

This section, which is really the front porch of the bread of life discourse, introduces the theme to be expanded in the following verses. It anticipates the grand claim that Jesus himself is the bread, while portraying the crowd as sincere but incorrectly oriented. Their questions and requests (vv. 25, 28, 30, and 34) exemplify for John the nearsightedness of humanity, seeing only that which is immediate and material.

The Bread of Life—Discourse I (6:35-50)

35—The first discourse properly begins with the grand **I am** declaration, which makes explicit what is hinted at again and again in vv. 25-34. Verse 35 is the first of seven declarations of the **I am** with the predicate nominative: Bread of life (6:35), light of the world (8:12; 9:15), door of the sheep (10:7, 9), good shepherd (10:11, 14), resurrection and the life (11:15), the way, the truth, and the life (14:6), and true vine (15:1, 5). In each of these the **I am** (*egō eimi*) is used to identify with a metaphor what it is Christ does for humanity (e.g., Jesus is to humanity what light is to darkness). The metaphor in each case breaks through the limitations of language to say that which is nearly inexplicable. Bultmann contends that each of these is what he calls a "recognition formula" which is the equivalent of saying "I am he" (pp. 225-226). Behind each lurks a polemic purpose which seeks to support the Christian claim over against other false claims. Such a purpose arose from the situation of John's church in relationship with the Jewish synagogue. (For **I am** without the predicate cf. 6:20 above and 8:24f. below.) **The bread of life** (*ho artos tēs zōēs*) stands now in the place of the "bread from heaven" and captures the function of the divine bread expressed in v. 33. The concept of food and drink as symbols for religious truth is an ancient one and arises from the metaphorical association of ordinary food and physical life with religious truth and spiritual life. In the discourse it is a dramatic symbol for the revelation which occurs in the Christ event. All of the previous associations of bread with religious phenomena (e.g., bread and wisdom, Prov. 9:5) are encompassed with the claim of **Jesus** to be the **bread of life.**

It is not likely that in the first discourse the bread was meant to evoke eucharistic meanings (but cf. vv. 51-59 below). Jesus has dramatically corrected the misunderstandings and nearsightedness of the crowd with his identification with the bread of life. The remaining clauses of v. 35 comprise a synonymous parallelism in which **he who comes to me** means **he who believes in me.** The use of **hunger** and **thirst** is to suggest that the deepest, most elemental needs of humanity find their fulfillment in Christ. **Hunger** and **thirst** stand for that incompleteness of humanity apart from its

Creator, the emptiness of existence without God. One cannot help but compare this statement (and 4:14a) with the words attributed to wisdom in Sir. 24:21: "Those who eat me will hunger for more, and those who drink me will thirst for more."

36-37—Verse 36 is troublesome for two reasons. First, it is uncertain to what previous statement of Jesus this verse alludes. A similar kind of problem is found elsewhere when Jesus refers to his own words (e.g., 6:65; 10:25, 36; 11:40). Verse 26 offers the best possible referent in this case. The second problem is a textual one: **Me** (*me*) is absent from some manuscripts. Without the **me** the sentence would make more sense in this context. **You have seen and yet do not believe.** But some think the textual evidence necessitates retaining the **me** as the more difficult reading. In this case, however, it is likely that the **me** should be omitted, so that the thought of the sentence relates to what has come before. They have **seen** signs, and yet they still **do not believe.** "The sign of the loaves quickened the appetite but not faith" (Barrett, p. 293). After the revelation of the "I am" saying, attention returns to the reality of the people's unbelief. Verse 37 views that unbelief in a different way. Verse 36 holds the people responsible for their unbelief, while v. 37 suggests that belief is the work of the Father and not the act of the human. The believers are given to Jesus (*ho didōsin moi*), which may suggest that an individual's faith is God's responsibility, especially when this verse is seen in the light of v. 44. When this thought is placed side by side with v. 36, however, it appears that the evangelist intends to say that a faith response to Jesus presupposes God's work in making such an act possible, while humans remain responsible for unbelief (below at 12:32 the question of universalism must be considered). The neuter, **all** (*pan*) **that the Father gives** (and in v. 39), is unusual (cf. v. 40) and may imply that the collective aspect of the group of believers is emphasized. **Come to me** is contrasted with **not cast out.** The promise that Jesus does **not cast out** (*ekbalō exō)* is a subtle contrast to the Christians' experience of being expelled from the synagogue, which is alluded to in John 9:34—where the same verb is used (*ekballō*). Jesus is faithful to the **Father's** will and turns away no one whom **the Father gives** (cf. v. 44 below).

38-40—The implication of v. 37 that Jesus is faithful to the **Father's** will is now pursued. As the bread of life, Jesus has **come down from heaven**, even as the bread of heaven discussed in vv. 32f. **Come down** (*katabebēka*) is one-half of the important Christological concept that the Son descends from above and ascends (*anabainō*) once again (cf. 3:13; 6:62; 20:17). In his earthly ministry the Johannine Jesus is a foreigner in this world whose origin and destiny are in the heavenly realm. The oneness of will is emphasized again (cf. 5:19f. above). Verse 39 newly states that this unity of wills centers in God's redemptive plan—that **nothing** (*pan*) handed over to the Son should be lost. The picture is that of a community of believers formed by the **Father** and entrusted to the Son. **Raise it up at the last day** is a reference to the resurrection at the end of history. John can speak both of the future resurrection and the resurrection present in the life of the believer (cf. 5:24-29 above). Here it is the resurrection only of the believers that is mentioned; in 5:28 the reference is to a general resurrection. Jewish apocalyptic schemes sometimes include only the former, sometimes the latter. Note that again the collective neuter is used, **raise it** (*auto*). The divine **will** is centered upon giving humanity **eternal life**, as v. 40 states. Here Jesus begins speaking in the third person (**Son . . . him**) and then switches back again to the first person (**I will**), perhaps indicating that the discourse is made up in part of independent sayings, some of which are attributed to Jesus and some of which are about Jesus. To **see** (*theōreō*) here means to see with faith or to perceive the true meaning and identity of Jesus. Such vision is based on physical seeing but goes beyond it to perceive only what can be known by faith (cf. 11:45; 9:39 and the related seeing of the Father by the Son, 5:19). This kind of seeing is akin to the seeing of signs at a deeper level (cf. 26) and the seeing mentioned in v. 36. (*Horaō* and *theōreō* are used interchangeably for this faith seeing.) Therefore, seeing **the Son** and believing **in him** (*eis auton*) are synonymous. Believing, hearing, seeing, and knowing are all closely related in Johannine usage (cf. Kysar, *John*, pp. 73-79). **And I will raise him up at the last day** appears again and becomes something of a refrain throughout this part of the discourse, appearing in vv. 39, 40, 44, and 54. The impact stresses that the **Son** who is the bread of life holds the power of life in himself (cf. 11:24 below).

41-42—Misunderstanding and objection punctuate the discourse, appearing in v. 41 for the first time. This is the first instance of the use of the term **the Jews** to designate the crowd and apply to Galileans. It exemplifies John's tendency to generalize unbelief in this one label— a tendency rooted in the controversy with the Jews of his own day. **Murmured** is the same word used in the LXX for the grumbling of the people of Israel in the wilderness (Exod. 16:2, 8f.). The verb *goggyzō* is used again in vv. 43 and 61. John is suggesting that the scene of the rebellious people in the desert is being played out again on the occasion of the giving of the bread of life. This is still further evidence of the importance of the Passover/exodus setting for the chapter. It is Jesus' solemn "I am" saying which occasions this discontent. But their misunderstanding is explained in v. 42. They think they know Jesus' origins in his parents and hence cannot believe that he has **come down from heaven** (cf. 1:38, 46 above). His earthly roots blind them to his divine origin. But this is typical Johannine misunderstanding in the sense that the crowd views the statements of **Jesus** in a literal, materialistic manner, while his meaning is found in the realm of the spiritual. Similar objections to Jesus are stated in the Synoptics (Mark 6:3; Matt. 13:55; Luke 4:22). Jesus is called the **son of Joseph** in John only here and 1:45.

43-44—Jesus responds, and it is important that he commands them only to cease their complaining (cf. Exodus 16) and does not argue the point. (This is the usual response to misunderstanding in Johannine style.) The divine origin of Jesus is either believed or denied, and there is no argument which proves the object of faith. Verse 44 picks up the theme of God's participation in the act of believing from vv. 37 and 39 but states it more radically. In the face of unbelief Jesus asserts that faith is possible only by virtue of the **Father's** power to attract persons to himself. (Parallel ideas may be expressed in the LXX rendering of Jer. 31:3 and Hos. 11:4, plus some rabbinic sources; cf. Barrett, p. 295.) Again we have the tension between the human responsibility for faith expressed in v. 40 and the divine initiative in the process of believing stated here and vv. 37, 39, and 65. Unbelief is overcome and faith made possible only by the intervention of God. That intervention is spoken of here as a magnetic force which pulls humans to God. The verb **draws** (*helkō*) is used in John in its metaphorical sense only here and in 12:32, where Christ's crucifixion is said to draw all persons to himself. John appreciates the mystery of the process of believing, recognizing that human will is essential but impotent without the power of God. The refrain concerning the resurrection **at the last day** appears again.

45-46—An unusual formula for a citation of Scripture appears in v. 45—**the prophets.** It may be part of the interpretative method employed by John or his source which at certain points introduces secondary citations of Scripture in the discussion of the central citation (cf. Borgen). The citation seems to be a loose rendering of Isa. 54:13. The universalism of the passage—**they shall all**—balances the implicit election mentioned in v. 44. Again the inclusive **all** (*pas, pantes*) is an invitation to believe. **Heard and learned from the Father** is to understand God's redemptive intention. Hearing is used here metaphorically much the way seeing is used in v. 40. Hearing is a dimension of the act of faith by which one discerns the truth of the revelation (cf. 5:24; 8:43, and the Son's hearing of the Father, 8:26). To know God's redemptive will can only result in believing in the Son. By implication those who profess to know God but do not believe in the Son do not really hear and learn from God. Verse 46 avoids a misunderstanding. God has not been seen (cf. 1:18 above) except by the preexistent Son (but contrast Exod. 24:10). John's argument is circular: To come to God you must come to Christ, but to come to Christ you must know God. The conclusion is that only God's power can initiate faith. **He has seen the Father** illustrates the way John presses the word **seeing** into use in a trans-sensual way (cf. v. 40 above).

47-48—Verse 47 introduces a new theme in the discourse, but not new to this gospel (cf. 5:24). Some manuscripts insert "in me" (*eis me*) after **believes,** and that is certainly the intended meaning. In the midst of the affirmations of the future resurrection encountered again and again in the discourse (vv. 39, 40, 44, 54) stands the declaration of the present reality of **eternal life.** That reality is stated in a similar way in vv. 40a, 51, 54, and 58 (cf. 50b). Verse 48 reiterates the central theme of the discourse.

49-50—Now we return to the topic discussed in vv. 25-34, namely, the superiority of the **bread** of life in Christ to **the manna** given to the people of Israel. The manna sustained physical life but could not prevent death; the bread which is Christ sustains spiritual life even beyond death. **Your fathers** suggests a fracture between Jesus and the people befitting not Jesus' own time but that of the evangelist. The statement mixes two meanings of death. In the first (**your fathers. . .died,** *apethanon*), physical death is meant; in the second (**eat of it and not die,** *apothanē*), a spiritual death is in view (v. 50). Surely John did not want to deny the reality of physical death for the believer (cf. 11:25-26 below).

This first of the two discourses proper (vv. 35-50 and 51-59) has carefully exposed the meaning of the revelatory "I am" declaration in v. 35 and, if P. Borgen is correct, everything after v. 31 is a kind of exegesis of the passage quoted there. This much is clear: the discourse intends to claim that Jesus is God's offer of salvation to humanity and by faith in him (and all that the believing process involves) humanity is given an opportunity to embrace a new and authentic existence.

The Bread of Life—Discourse II (6:51-59)

51—The second discourse, vv. 51-59, repeats the essential message of vv. 35-50 but in an offensively radical way. It begins at v. 51 with the restatement of the "I am" saying found in v. 35 (with **living bread** instead instead of bread of life—not an important distinction) combined with an identification with the expression used in the introduction to the discourse, v. 33, **which came down from heaven.** What is new is found in the last clause: **The bread . . . is my flesh. For the life of the world** (*hyper tēs tou kosmou zōēs*) suggests the meaning of the death of Christ; some find here an allusion to a sacrificial understanding of the cross akin to 1 Cor. 11:24. Such a view, however, does not find prominence in John's Gospel. The sense is like that of 3:15-16. The wording **the life of the world** is unique in the NT. The possibility of an allusion to a sacrificial view of atonement and the uniqueness of this phrasing may be indications that this part of the discourse is a later addition to the chapter. The identification of the **bread** with Jesus' **flesh** (*sarx*) introduces one of the main features of the second discourse. (As to its eucharistic meaning, see below.)

52—It is that identification with his **flesh** that causes the second objection from the crowd. The translation **disputed** is perhaps too weak, and the TEV rendering, "an angry argument," is better. The verb *machesthai* means "to fight" and is used here figuratively. It may recall the discontent of the people of Israel when they lacked water (Exod. 17:1f.). If so, this **dispute** parallels the desert scene, as the "murmuring" at vv. 41 and 60 do. Again the crowd takes the words of Jesus literally and hence cannot find any sense in his statement. The response of Jesus in the remainder of the discourse is predictably a further and more radical statement of his claim.

53—The formula **truly, truly** is an indication of a divine truth and the offensiveness of Jesus' words is sharpened. To **eat his flesh** is now added **drink his blood.** For many the expansion to include the blood demonstrates beyond any doubt that the Christian Eucharist is the subject under discussion. On a more basic level, however, **flesh** and **blood** is a Hebraic way of speaking of the whole person and describing the earthly character of human life (cf. 1:13 and Matt. 16:17). The basic thought is that the whole of the revelation of Christ must be taken in, even the fact of its historicity in the man Jesus. It is proposed, too, that John (or a later redactor) is attacking a docetic group within the church which denied the **flesh** and **blood** quality of the Eucharist as well as the incarnation (cf. Schnackenburg, vol. 2, p. 61). The other expansion in this verse is the use of the title **Son of man.** The traditional association of this title with Jesus' suffering is appropriate here, since he suffers as a **flesh** and **blood** human. The death of Jesus may then be intended here as well as v. 51. **Unless you . . . you have no life in you** is striking in its absoluteness and its exclusiveness. Whether the polemic is against Jews of John's day or docetists of a later time, the opportunity of life is found only in an incorporation of the whole human revelation of God.

54-56—Verse 54 repeats the thought of v. 53 almost exactly with only the addition of the eschatological refrain referring to the resurrection (cf. vv. 39, 40, 44). But the verb for eating is changed. In v. 53 *phagomai* is used, in v. 54 *trōgein.* The latter word was used for the eating of animals and (according to some) the noisy, audible eating of humans. Hence, the new verb may mean "munching" or "gnawing"—a still more scandalous way of expressing the theme. Verse 55 speaks of **food . . . and drink indeed,** the sense being that Christ's revelation is reliable as a source of life. A further way of stating the benefits of Jesus' **flesh and blood** revelation comes in v. 56. There results a reciprocal relationship of intimacy between the eater/drinker and Christ. **Abides in** translates the verb *menein,* which for John describes the presence of the divine with the human so that a personal and special relationship results (cf. 15:1f. below).

57-59—The channel through which life, the genuine existence intended by God for humans, is given is the human Jesus. It is God who is the source of life, and the regenerative life begins with him. **The living Father** is an unusual formulation and is the Johannine version of the "living God" (e.g., Jer. 10:10); but the meaning is that **the Father** is the source of life. The Son lives out of the grace of the Father and is subordinate to him. Because of the relationship of the Father and the Son, life is available to humans through the Son. **Because of** (*dia*) can mean here either "by means of" or "for the sake of," but the former seems more fitting. John 5:21 is comparable in meaning to this verse. As the second discourse began with only eating (v. 51) to which drinking is added (v. 53), so now it concludes with reference to eating alone. Verse 58 summarizes the thought of the two discourses, repeating v. 49 (although here it is **the fathers** as opposed to "your fathers" in v. 49) and affirming the promise of life in the revelation. Verse 59 comes as something of a surprise because we had not been told this was the setting in the introduction to the discourse (cf. v. 25). Jesus' teaching in the synagogue at Capernaum is noted in the Synoptics (e.g., Luke 7:5 and Mark 6:1-6).

Having discussed this second discourse wthout explicit reference to the eucharistic overtones of the language, we must ask whether it is an exposition of the meaning of the sacrament. Most interpreters would agree that it is. The use of the word "flesh" (*sarx*) instead of "body" (*soma*), as we find it in the accounts of the institution of the meal (esp. 1 Cor. 11:24), presents no real problem. It is entirely possible that the original Aramaic might have been rendered either way in Greek. It is further possible that the Johannine community preserved the tradition with the word **flesh** rather than *body*. What is more problematic is the absence of clear eucharistic allusions elsewhere in the gospel. Why would there be no account of the institution of the Eucharist if the Johannine community practiced the sacrament? Some supposed that a tradition of the institution has been transposed from its original setting in the last night before Jesus' death to this centralized location at the heart of his ministry (e.g., Brown, vol. 1, pp. 287-291). The proposed reasons for such a transposition are not entirely convincing. Still others argue that this second form of the bread of life discourse is the addition of a later editor to the original gospel which had no sacramental references at all (e.g., Bultmann, pp. 234-237). Yet there is little or nothing outside of this passage to indicate that the evangelist was antisacramental. The least difficult solution to this quandary is to hold that the Johannine community was not opposed to the sacrament but neither did it attribute much, if any, significance to it. Only after the expulsion of the community from the synagogue and its more extensive relationship with other churches did the sacrament emerge as an important part of the Johannine community's life. Some time after that emergence, this second form of the bread of life discourse was added to vv. 35-50 to express a clearer eucharistic meaning. (For the problem of the sacraments in this gospel cf. n. 20.)

The second discourse serves another purpose, however, and that is to stress that humans must take into themselves the whole of the revelation in Christ to gain its benefits. Whether that purpose arose in response to a docetic movement is difficult to say. It is true that the Johannine community was at the time of the writing of 1 John in the throes of an internal conflict which involved separatists who appear to have denied that Christ had come as a flesh-and-blood human (cf. 1 John 4:1-3). It may be that the eucharistic and antidocetic features of the passage fit best the setting of the Johannine epistles. All that notwithstanding, the message of the section is that one must ingest the whole of the revelation, including the scandal of its historicity, in order to know its total benefits.

The Bread of Life Discourse—Conclusion: Belief and Unbelief (6:60-71)

60-61—This long and powerful discourse comes to a dramatic and sobering conclusion. Verse 60 is the third of the four objections and misunderstandings punctuating the whole passage (cf. vv. 41, 52, and 66). This time, however, it is not "the Jews" who are offended (as in vv. 41 and 52) but **many of his disciples.** This section illustrates the fact that John uses the word **disciple** (*mathētēs*) to mean simply "believer" and does not limit the term to the inner circle of the followers of Jesus. His believers are now scandalized by **a hard saying** (*sklēros . . . ho logos*). Whether that expression is to be understood as a reference to the conclusion of the second discourse, vv. 51-59, or the whole of the discourse is not clear. The verb **heard** (*akouō*) is used in the beginning of the verse to mean simply hearing but at the conclusion to mean **listen** in the sense of hearing *and accepting*. **Hard** translates *sklēros* which literally means a "hard thing," used in its figurative sense here as difficult to accept (not necessarily difficult to understand). Verse 61 is another instance of the marvelous knowledge of **Jesus.** The response of the believers is called "murmuring" as the "Jews" murmur in v. 41, bringing to mind once again the desert experience of Israel. **Do you take offense at this?** is the first use of the verb *skandalizō* (cf. 16:1), meaning literally "to scandalize." Again **this** raises the question of what it was specifically which offended the **disciples.** Here it seems to be the identification of the bread of life with **Jesus'** flesh and the command to eat that flesh.

62—If the disciples cannot accept the content of the bread of life discourse, they will be even more offended by the **ascending Son of man.** But the Greek of this verse is confusing, because it is not a complete sentence and states only a condition without the conclusion of the condition (i.e., a protasis without an apodosis). Hence, it may suggest that if the disciples **see the Son of man as-**

cending, they will be either (1) further scandalized or (2) helped to accept that which at first had scandalized them. The context seems to weigh in favor of the former, since the eventual outcome of the conversation is to offend the believers even more (cf. v. 66). The ascension of the **Son of man** is Johannine language for the crucifixion (cf. 3:14; 12:34), and it is by the cross that Jesus returns to the Father, i.e., **where he was before** (cf. 20:17 below). The scandalousness of the language of the bread of life speech is surpassed only by the scandal of the cross. That the unique **Son** of the Father should complete his earthly work by being executed as a common criminal offends the sensitivities of humans (cf. l Cor. 1: 23).

63-65—At first v. 63 seems to disrupt the flow of thought, but it makes sense if it is taken as an effort to overcome or at least partially clarify the disbelief of the disciples. It is **the spirit** which allows one to see truth in Jesus' **words** and to accept them. The contrast of **spirit** (*to pneuma*) and **flesh** (*hē sarx*) is the contrast of the divine and the human, as it is at 3:6 (cf. 8:15). The flesh is not degraded here, nor does this statement contradict the importance of Jesus' flesh in vv. 51-59. Human perspective alone cannot perceive the truth of the bread of life discourse. The risk of faith is required to avail oneself of the spirit. **The words I have spoken** refers not alone to the discourse but to the whole of the revelation in Christ, and it is those words which are the life-giving bread. Verse 64 acknowledges that there are some whose vision is limited to the "flesh," and it is those who **do not believe.** The words of Jesus cause a great division between those who do believe and those who do not. His foreknowledge of those who belong to each side is affirmed. John wishes to say that Jesus is not rendered powerless by unbelief, nor even surprised, but knows beforehand of its reality. The depths of unbelief are represented in the one who betrays him. **From the first** (*ek archēs*) means the first of Jesus' ministry, but may imply preexistence as well (cf. 1:1, *en archē*). The necessity of the insight of the Spirit is linked with the divine activity responsible for faith, and so v. 65 reaffirms that faith in Christ is possible only insofar as **it is granted . . . by the Father.** This expression states the same thought found in vv. 37 and 39 (believers are those "given" by the Father) and v. 44 (believers are those "drawn" by the Father). Here the explanation of the reality of unbelief lies in the election of God (cf. 12:37-40). But still the importance of human decision is not ruled out nor is human responsibility for unbelief dismissed (cf. the freedom implied in v. 67).

66—The words of Jesus do not overcome the offense, nor were they intended to, and **many of his disciples drew back.** This verse constitutes the fourth and final objection in the discourse as a whole (vv. 41, 52, 60, and 66). It is interesting that the four instances form a set of pairs. In the first pair it is the Jews who first murmur against Jesus (v. 41) and then argue among themselves (v. 52). In the second pair it is the **disciples** who first murmur against Jesus (v. 60) and then turn away from him (v. 66). The impact of this progression is to stress the severity and pervasiveness of unbelief. **Drew back** (*apēlthon*) may recall Isa. 1:4-5 and suggest apostasy (cf. the use of the verb at 18:6). **No longer went about with him** translates *ouketi met' autou periepatoun* which means "walked with him no more," a way of describing the end of a relationship between a disciple and master. John expresses the fact of the rejection of Jesus in his earthly ministry by those who at first had followed him. But this verse arises also out of the reality of apostasy within the ranks of the church of the evangelist's day. "The little anecdotes about men who refused the call of Jesus in Mk 10:22 and Lk 9:57-62 were remembered because of the Christians who fell away at a later stage" (Lindars, p. 275).

67-69—In the light of the spreading power of unbelief, Jesus inquires as to the wishes of **the twelve.** This verse and vv. 70, 71, and 20:24 are the only uses of **the twelve** (*dōdeka*) in John. While having references to **the twelve** in traditional materials, John seems to prefer to use the broader expression *disciples*, which encompassed believers of his own day as well as those of Jesus' time. The wording of the question in the Greek anticipates a negative answer (*mē kai hymeis*), but nonetheless it is important that the intimate circle of disciples is asked to make their decision regarding continued faithfulness. The implication is that the believer is never secure from the forces of unbelief and almost daily must choose to believe or not to believe. In the tradition of the Synoptic Gospels,

Peter answered for the group (v. 68). Some have seen in this passage the Johannine version of the confession at Caesarea Philippi (Mark 8:27-30; Matt. 16:13-23; Luke 9:18-22). Peter affirms the claim of Jesus at v. 63b that it is the message of Christ which is the means by which humans may find **eternal life.** Words (hrēmata) is not preceded in the Greek by a definite article ("the"), implying that it is the general message of Jesus' whole ministry which is the source of life. There is no one else who can offer such a gift to humans—another statement of the exclusiveness of the revelation for John (cf. v. 53 and 14:6). Verse 69 indicates one of the ways in which faith and knowledge are related in this gospel. Here it appears that believing leads to knowing, that the confidence of truth results only from the prior step of faith. Knowledge then cannot precede the act of faith. (The same implication is found in 8:31 and 10:38). However, John reverses the order of the two in 17:8 and in 16:30. At 14:7 and 17:3 the two verbs appear to be interchangeable. On the whole, then, John poses a close relationship between faith and knowing without distinguishing any subtle difference between them. (This may be due in part to his concept of knowledge—cf. Kysar, *John*, pp. 78-79.) Peter's confession is that Jesus is the **Holy One of God** (ho hagios tou theou), the only use of such a title in this gospel. Jesus addresses God as the Holy Father in 17:11, and the Spirit is called holy (e.g., 1:33; 14:26; 20:22). (On the meaning of holy and sanctification cf. 17:17f. below.) The title Peter uses is found in the Synoptics (Mark 1:29 and Luke 4:34) spoken by demons. Some see this title as a more universal expression of Jesus' role as compared with the traditional messianic titles of Judaism, especially *Christ.* But John enjoys using a variety of titles for Jesus and implies that each is applicable to some degree (cf. 1:29-51 above). There is nothing in this passage to make us think that there is anything inferior about the title, but it represents genuine, if not yet comprehending faith.

70-71—The chapter closes with the terrible reality of unbelief, namely, the act of betrayal. But first **Jesus** declares that it is his initiative which makes the Twelve his disciples, not their own worth or faith. **Did I not choose** (exelexamēn) **you** is part of the theme of divine initiative in faith which is repeated throughout this chapter

(vv. 37, 39, 44, and 65). The divine election precedes the human act of faith. Once again human freedom and choice are affirmed (v. 67), only to be qualified with the other truth held in tension with the first—divine action is responsible for faith. John tells us nothing of Jesus' actual selection of the Twelve (except 1:29-51). **One of you is a devil** makes the point that unbelief and darkness reside even among the faithful (a reflection on John's experience with his own community of faith?). **Devil** (*diabolos*) appears only two other times, 8:44 and 13:2, where it is used to designate the Prince of Demons, i.e., Satan (mentioned only at 13:27). He is called "the ruler of this world" in 14:30. It is striking that here **Judas** himself is called **devil** (cf. Mark 8:33), when at 13:2 the **devil** uses **Judas**. The suggestion is that Judas' act results from his identification with the forces of evil. "Satan has made Judas his ally, a subordinate devil" (Barrett, p. 307). Jesus' knowledge of Judas and his character is emphasized here so as to assure the reader that the betrayer's deed in no way compromises Jesus' sovereignty and his control over his own destiny. Judas is one of those Jesus has chosen, **one of the twelve.** Only in John do we find Judas called **Simon.** The meaning of **Iscariot** is elusive. Some textual variants in v. 71 propose one of the possible meanings, namely, "man of Kerioth" (a village in southern Judea).

This magnificent and skillfully constructed chapter finds its conclusion in the worst of the expressions of unbelief, Judas' betrayal. While the revelatory words of Jesus reach their penultimate level here (superseded only by the farewell discourses), so too does the reality of rejection and unbelief (superseded only by the actual betrayal and crucifixion). The chapter shows that the revelation of God in Christ divides humanity between those who receive it and those who are offended by and reject it. That division occasioned by the act of God in Christ is an important theme which continues to hold a prominent place in the plot from this point on.

■ In Jerusalem (7:1—10:42)

The unbelief and defection with which chap. 6 concludes establish a tone which persists throughout the remainder of this gospel. It is in the shadow of the formidable force of unbelief that this section begins. John 7:1—10:42 narrates the ministry of Jesus in Jerusalem, at the heart of the forces which will bring him to the cross. This section traces the conflict with the religious establishment and sets the stage for the death plot itself which emerges with finality in chap. 11. The reader has been prepared for the collision of the revealer and the established religion as early as the narrative of the cleansing of the temple (2:13-22), not to mention the announcement of rejection in 1:11. The integrity of 7:1—10:42 is questionable, and it is clear that the evangelist has composed this section from a number of fragments of tradition without much concern for unity and smooth narrative. But it is equally clear that the general purpose of the composite chapters is to show the clash of the revelation of God with human institutions and traditions. (For the order of chaps. 5, 6, and 7 cf. n. 12.)

Introduction: Whether to Go to Jerusalem (7:1-9)

The evangelist heightens the dramatic suspense of the narrative by underlining the dangers of going back to Jerusalem. It would appear that the threat of death in 5:16-18 is the context which John has in mind here, but Jesus' activity in Galilee in chap. 6 is also presupposed. The evangelist wants the reader to be acutely aware of the unbelief Jesus encounters in Galilee but also the greater danger of a resumption of the ministry in Jerusalem.

1—**After this** is John's frequent way of attaching one narrative to another with the least possible suggestion of a temporal sequence (e.g., 2:12; 3:22; 5:1). Jesus is free to travel in Galilee even though he has been rejected by many. **Would** (*ēthelen*) **not go about** may for textual reasons more properly read "was not able" or "could not." The latter (*eichen exousian*) is a textual variant which is difficult to explain, if it is not taken as the original (the same expression is used by John in 10:18 and 19:10). The reading adopted in the RSV would seem to have resulted from the unwillingness of scribes to conceive of the limitation of Jesus' power and freedom. In favor of the RSV reading, however, is stronger external textual evidence and the general tendency of this gospel to stress Jesus' sovereignty (e.g., 7:30). Still, John may have wanted to impress the reader with the dangers of going to Jerusalem and

115

uses the stronger "could not go" to strengthen that impression. **Because the Jews sought to kill him** echoes the same words of 5: 18. **Jews** in this case may mean only "Judeans," but the overtone of opposition found generally in the use of the word is clear. The title (*Ioudaioi*) is most often used in a pejorative way to designate the opposition of unbelief (e.g., 8:22, 59; 19:12), although it appears in a few cases in a purely descriptive sense (e.g., 11:45; 4:22; 5:46). Since the Johannine church itself probably had its roots in Jewish Christianity, it is clearly the case that John did not mean by his use of **the Jews** to judge an entire race of people!

2—This provides a reason for going to Jerusalem and to some degree frames the discourses to follow. **Tabernacles** was a harvest festival rooted in the wilderness life of the Hebrew people after the exodus from Egypt, and the building of shelters recreated the nomadic period of Israel's history. Its meaning for John seems once again to set the words and acts of Jesus within the imagery of the grand salvific event of the exodus.

3-4—**Jesus' brothers** make a sudden and final appearance after their brief mention in 2:12. *Adelphoi* here is usually taken to mean Jesus' blood brothers, sons of his parents, although some interpreters would argue that they are half-brothers, cousins, or "spiritual brothers" (cf. 20:17) and thereby preserve the belief in Mary's perpetual virginity. Their request of Jesus seems a bit confusing, but apparently suggests a new strategy: in the capital city perform a conspicuous mighty work which would convince the disillusioned **disciples** (6:60) of his identity. John puts in the mouths of Jesus' **brothers** the simplistic view that wonders alone produce genuine faith, a view John has disputed several times (e.g., 4:48) and which he here claims constitutes a kind of unbelief (v. 5). Verse 4 further explains the perspective of the brothers, namely, that a mighty display of power will persuade others of Jesus' messiahship. Their words, **no man . . . known openly** are similar to sayings of Jesus recorded in the Synoptics (Mark 4:22; Luke 8:17; 12:22; Matt. 10:26), and it may be argued that the Johannine words are actually a version of a saying elsewhere attributed to Jesus (cf. Lindars, p. 283). The more immediate point is an argument used to question Christian belief in Jesus' messiahship.

John and his community no doubt had been confronted many times with the view that, if Jesus were the Messiah, his acts of power would have been more convincing in his lifetime (cf. v. 30 below). The Johannine response was to say that acts of glory are perceived for what they are only from a perspective of faith.

5—This makes explicit what has been implied, i.e., the suggestion of Jesus' **brothers** comes out of the context of disbelief. John tells us nothing more about the **brothers** that would suggest that they became followers of Jesus, although the view is represented in the tradition that they provided leadership for the church in its nascent period (cf. Acts 1:14; 12:17; 15:13; John 20:17 may mean they received word of their brother's resurrection). John repeats the fact of the unbelief of Jesus' family preserved in Mark 3:21 and the break of Jesus from his family represented in Mark 3:31-35 (cf. Matt. 12:46-50; Luke 8:19-21). For the fourth evangelist their unbelief epitomizes the rejection of the revelation and the saturation of humanity in darkness. Here they offer an alternative which contradicts the Johannine concept of the cross as Jesus' way of glorification.

6-7—Jesus' response contrasts the divine will with the desire and conditions of humanity represented in the unbelief of the brothers. Jesus' **time** (*kairos*) is synonymous with his "hour" (*hōra*), the Johannine designation for the crucifixion-glorification (e.g., 2:4; 12:23). John uses *kairos* only here and in v. 8 and apparently means by it the decisive time of salvation (cf. Mark 13:33). Jesus' life is determined by divine will, and the act by which he will be made known to the world is set by God's plan. That act is a far different one than Jesus' brothers had in mind. In contrast, his brothers' *kairos* **is always here,** which may mean on the simple level that they are free to attend the festival as they wish, or, on a more profoundly theological level, that they are faced in every moment with the crucial decision whether or not to embrace the truth of the revelation. Verse 7 further stresses the distance between Jesus and his brothers. Their request is a desire of the realm of unbelief to have its own view confirmed. The revelation convicts the **world** of its **evil** (cf. 16:8ff.) and upsets its expectations of God. For **hate** of Jesus cf. 15:18, 23-24 below.

8-9—**My time has not yet fully come** repeats the words of v. 6 with the important exception that *peplērōtai* (**fully come**) replaces the more mundane *parestin* ("arrived"). The former suggests the eschatological fulfillment of the divine mission, confirming the notion that Jesus' departure for Jerusalem involves his divinely determined destiny. **Going up** (*anabainō*) is the same word John uses elsewhere for Jesus' ascension (3:13; 6:62; 20:17) and may be a subtle suggestion that Jesus' **going up** to Jerusalem is part of his ascent to the Father. Some manuscripts read **I am not *yet* going up,** which is clearly the scribal effort to make v. 8 agree with v. 10.

Temple Addresses—Division and Opposition (7:10-52)

This section is the first of two discourse episodes which John narrates of Jesus in the temple, the second being 8:12-59. Both are composite collections of sayings materials punctuated with responses from the crowd, and both are intended to stress the distinction between faith and unbelief. Here Jesus meets his opponents on their own grounds—the temple.

10—Jesus does go up to Jerusalem in **private**, in apparent contradiction to v. 8. It appears to be another example of Jesus' refusal to fulfill a human request, only later to do so (cf. 2:1-10; 11:5-15; 4:43-53). The point of this refusal-consent pattern is that Jesus is not susceptible to human influences, that he follows the divine will without compromise. It is another of the evangelist's statements of Jesus' sovereignty. **Not publicly but in private** (literally, "not manifestly but as in secret"—*ou phanerōs alla hōs en kryptō*) suggests that Jesus went up to Jerusalem not in a conspicuous manner to attract attention to himself, but quietly, in contradiction to his brothers' urgings.

11-12—The **Jews** search for Jesus for hostile reasons, we may assume (v. 11), since the use of the term **Jews** later in v. 13 indicates a hostility toward him. Among the **people** ("crowd," *ochlos*), however, there is division—a further bit of evidence that **the Jews** is used by John to mean the Jewish leaders and Jesus' opponents but not the whole **people**. **Muttering** (*goggysmos*) recalls 6:41, 61 and again hints at the motif of the desert wanderings of the exodus. But v. 12 specifies that in this case the people are divided in their view of Jesus. It is such a division which characterizes the reaction of Jesus in the narrative to follow and forms an important theological theme in this gospel. The appearance of the Messiah evokes division in the world, separating those of the light and those of the darkness. **Good man** is intended as a positive but faithless perspective—an openness without trust. **He is leading the people astray,** on the other hand, may echo a serious and legal charge which was raised against Jesus both in his own day and in John's (cf. Matt. 27:63). It is likely that the Johannine Christians confronted the claim that, far from being the Messiah, Jesus was one who had misled the **people** (cf. Martyn, pp. 73-81). One who leads the **people astray** (*planaō*) is part of the early Christian apocalyptic view of the era leading up to the parousia (e.g., Mark 13:6; Rev. 2: 20). Paul speaks of being treated as one who leads the people astray (RSV, "impostor," 2 Cor. 6:8).

13—**Fear of the Jews,** an expression found elsewhere in John (e.g., 19:38; 20:19; cf. 9:22), evidences the condition and state of mind of John's own community in which **the Jews** constituted the major challenge. This phrase also shows that John means the religious leaders when he writes **Jews,** since those said to be afraid are surely themselves **Jews. No one spoke openly of him** may likewise reflect the fact that the Johannine community knew others in the synagogue who were afraid to confess their faith in Christ **openly** (*parrēsia*). In John's day belief in Christ had dangerous consequences, and he is critical of those unwilling to risk those consequences (cf. 12:43; 19:38). (John's treatment of Nicodemus may represent him as one such "crypto-Christian," 3:1-13 and 7:45-52.) That v. 13 comes out of John's own day is clear, since it contradicts the supportive remarks attributed to some of the crowd in v. 12.

14-15—**Jesus** goes into **the temple** to teach, a reference to the outer temple where such could occur. The Mishnah speaks of the activities in the "Court of the Women" during the festival of Tabernacles or Booths (*Sukkah* 5). John intends this context of the temple to enable the reader to understand that the ensuing discourses stand over against all human institutions and are part of the fulfillment of the Hebraic-Jewish tradition. Christ, who is the *new* temple (2:19-21), proclaims the revelation in the old temple. **The middle of the feast** is the third or fourth day of a celebration of either seven or eight days (cf. Deut. 16:13; Lev. 23:36). John, however, is not concerned with exact dating. **The Jews marveled** (*thaumazō*, v. 15) is the expected and proper response to the revelation of God (e.g., 3:7; 9:30). But ironically those who witness Jesus' teaching marvel at his **learning**, rather than respond to his identity (v. 16). Their response is superficial and fails to come to grips with the essential scandal of the revelation of God in human form. **Learning** (*grammata*) means literally "to know letters" or "be literate," but here depicts Jesus' capabilities as an exponent of the Scriptures. John shares the tradition that Jesus spoke as a wise, learned man in spite of his humble origins (cf. Luke 2:41-50; 4:16-22; Mark 6:2-3; Matt. 13:53-58).

16-18—Jesus' reply redirects the discussion to the essential matter, his relationship with the Father. Always in John the primary content of the words of Jesus is the identity of the revealer with the result that one cannot avoid the Christological issue, which for John is *the* question for humans confronted by Christ. That Jesus' **teaching** is not his own, but God's, is affirmed elsewhere (e.g., 12:14). Whatever John claims of the Father-Son relationship, the result is always that in responding to Christ one responds to God (cf. 12:44-45). **Who sent me** articulates one of the central Christological motifs of this gospel, namely, that Christ is the official agent or envoy of the Father (cf. 5:23 above). With the exception of "Father," **who sent me** (*tou pempsantos me*) is the most frequent expression used of God (e.g., 4:34; 5:23, 24, 30, 37; 6:38; 12:44; 15:21). Those whose will is one with God's recognize the origin of Jesus' teaching (v. 17). (More accurately, "If one wills to do his will, he or she will know.") Predisposition determines one's response to Jesus. Whereas this point is sometimes made in such a way as to suggest that human predisposition is predetermined (e.g., 12:36-40), it might be that reference here to **will** (*thelēma*) implies that such a condition is self-determined, but only by faith. For the relationship of **know** and *believe* cf. 6:69 above. In this case, it appears that knowing is a step prior to, but not exclusive of, faith itself in that it is a recognition of the source of Jesus' words (cf. 6:9 above). **My own authority** renders *egō ap' emautou lalō* ("I speak from myself") and asserts (again) that Jesus' revelation is derived from the Father, on whom he is dependent. Jesus is not a "divine man" who in himself possesses supernatural knowledge and powers. This issue is once more pertinent to the evangelist's own time—did Jesus reveal God's will or only his own human views? Verse 18 proceeds from the catch phrase, "speak from oneself," to characterize the true revealer and his followers. It is a question of whose **glory** (*doxa*) is sought. To seek one's **own glory** instead of God's is to betray one's falseness. Only the effort to seek the **glory of the one who sent** Jesus evidences truth. **True** (*alēthēs*) and **falsehood** (*adikia*, "unrighteousness") comprise another expression of the Johannine dualism which frames this whole gospel (cf. light and darkness, 1:5 above). However, only here is the word *adikia* used in John (cf. 1 John 1:9 and 5:17). The word is often used in the LXX to translate "lie" or "falsehood" (cf. 2 Sam. 14:32). The thought of v. 18 is essentially the same as that of 5:23.

19-20—The discussion focuses now on faithfulness to the **law** of **Moses,** which indicates that behind the questions of seeking glory (v. 18) and speaking from oneself (v. 17) lurks a polemic against those who claim to adhere to the Mosaic **law.** The verse is comprised of three loosely related statements, the point of which is that those who **seek to kill** Jesus cannot be faithful to the **law** given by **Moses.** Jesus distances himself from the law—**did not Moses give *you* the law?** (cf. 8:17 and 15:25 and contrast 4:22). Such a separation from the Law (so foreign, for instance, to the Jesus of Matthew, e.g., 5:17-20) is less appropriate to the historical Jesus than the Christ of the Johannine community and bespeaks the separation of that community from its synagogue opponents. **Keeps the law** translates *poiei ton nomon*, literally "do the Law." **The people** (*ochlos*, "crowd") in v. 20 respond by charging that Jesus is **possessed by a demon** (*daimonion*), the equivalent of saying he is insane. John reports such a charge in several other contexts (8: 48, 52; 10:20) and echoes Mark 3:22 (cf. Luke 7:33). In this reaction resides an alternative to faith. Jesus' words and actions inescapably call for response, either acceptance or the conclusion that he is deranged. Faith always stands within the shadow of the possibility that Jesus is not the agent of God but a deluded human. Demons are mentioned in John in only those cases in which Jesus is charged with demon possession and, unlike the Synoptic Gospels, John does not narrate exorcisms. Demons were understood to be a specific expression of the forces of evil.

21—This is only loosely related to the preceding dialog and shifts the subject to signs. The **one deed** (*ergon*, "work") referred to is not clear, but the subsequent remarks suggest the healing in 5:1-15 which sparked a debate over the violation of the Sabbath laws. Still, there is nothing in that narrative of "marveling." Rather, 5:16 reports that his act evoked persecution. Some argue that this discourse is misplaced from the context in 5:1-15, but such efforts at rearrangement are not convincing. Here and elsewhere in this discourse the evangelist has taken bits of sayings material from various traditions to produce a kind of patchwork quilt. John often uses the word *ergon* (**deed**) to designate Jesus' wonders (e.g., 5:20; 7:3; 10:25; 14:11). The thought of vv. 21-25 is that people have been more concerned with the violation of the Sabbath laws than with the act by which Jesus restored health and wholeness. Again, as in v. 15, witnesses marvel at the wrong thing.

22-23—The first two words of v. 22 (*dia touto*) are connected in the RSV with v. 21 and are translated **at it** ("by it," JB). Other translations tie them with v. 22, suggesting that the preceding constitutes some reason for what follows (e.g., "yet, because," NIV). If the latter alternative is taken, the connection between vv. 21 and 22 is that the command to **circumcise** was given to make humans whole. Jesus defends his act of healing on the **sabbath** by reference to the practice of circumcising on the **sabbath.** To obey the law that male infants should be circumcised on the eighth day (Lev. 12:3) **circumcision** was allowed on the Sabbath (Mishnah, *Shab.* 18:3, *Ned.* 3:11). In 5:17 Jesus defends his healing on the Sabbath by reference to his relationship with the Father, but here by reference to tradition concerning the interpretation of the Torah (cf. Mark 3:25-28 and parallels where 1 Sam. 21:1-6 is invoked). Jesus' argument is simply that if circumcision is permitted on the Sabbath then surely healing is to be allowed; thereby he poses one traditional interpretation (circumcision) against another (prohibitions against Sabbath healing). The basis of the argument is a common rabbinic principle "from the lesser to the greater." If it is permissible to treat one part of the human **body** on the Sabbath in circumcision, it is therefore permissible to treat the **whole body** (*holon anthrōpon*, "whole person"). Since the Law was designed for human salvation, Jesus' work of making the **whole body well** fulfills rather than contradicts the Law. The Johannine Jesus is seldom pictured in this way as a rabbi, arguing the interpretation of the Law. The parenthetical comment of v. 22 acknowledges that the command to circumcise is found in the Torah (Lev. 12:3) but its origin lay with Abraham, one of the **fathers** (Gen. 17:10; 21:4).

24—This command is that the people should not superficially conclude that Jesus is a lawbreaker but perceive in faith the real meaning of his work (cf. Isa. 11:3b-4). **Right judgment** means deciding on the basis of more than that which appears.

25-27—The reaction of the people of Jerusalem is described. The Greek word *hIerosolymitōn* is found only here and Mark 1:5. John may intend to distinguish this group from the others of the crowd, but for what reason is not clear. They seem to be unaware of the death plot against Jesus. Verses 25-26 add to the tension and division among the crowd and increase the suspense with regard to the actions of **the authorities** (*archontes*, the same word translated "rulers" elsewhere, e.g., 3:1). The failure of the leaders to act against Jesus raises the question of whether or not he is the Messiah, and this in turn introduces the question of the Messiah's origin. Verse 27 expresses a popular notion that when Messiah came he would remain hidden until the appropriate time and then appear as if it were "out of nowhere." Consequently, no one would know from where he came (1 Enoch 48:6; 62:7 and 4 Ezra 13:51ff.). Ironically, the people conclude that Jesus cannot be the Messiah because they know where he is from (a similar point is made in 6:41-42). The reader, however, knows that Jesus' origins are not earthly at all but heavenly (1:10-11). This ironic misunderstanding further exemplifies v. 24, in that the judgment made of Jesus arises from appearances rather than the deeper truth. Other examples of John's use of irony are found in 4:12; 11:52; 12:12-15, 19; 13:37; 19:19.

28—Jesus responds by challenging what it is the people think they know about him. The RSV translates the first of Jesus' remarks as a rhetorical question, and well it might be (but see NEB). **Proclaimed** is a subdued translation of the verb *krazein*, meaning "to cry out." John uses this verb on several occasions to signal a grave declaration (e.g., 1:15; 7:37; 12:44). In this case, it prefaces the dangers of thinking that we know when we do not. Jesus comes not from himself (*ap' emautou*, **of my own accord**). The Greek expression is the same as v. 17 where the question concerns the source of Jesus' teachings (translated in the RSV as "speaking on my own authority"), and the point is similar, namely, Jesus is God's representative. Opposed to coming **of my own accord** is the fact that Jesus is **sent**. By implication Jesus is made to say that the people's supposed knowledge of his origins is false. But the reason for their mistake is not rooted simply in poor perception but in the fact that they do not know God. The human perspective is determined by a relationship with God, a point John makes frequently. If they are not faithful to the Torah, they fail to perceive who Jesus really is (e.g., 8:39-42). If they do not know God, they cannot truly know Jesus (e.g., 8:55); and here, if they do not know God, they cannot know him **who sent** his agent (cf. 6:45). And yet John can also claim that to know Jesus brings knowledge of God (8:19). Once again (cf. 6:46 above) the view of the evangelist is circular: You cannot know Jesus unless you know God, but you cannot know God except by knowing the one he sent (1:18). But this overlooks a major motif that to know the God of Israel's history is to be able to perceive Jesus' true identity (8:56). That God is **true** (*alēthinos*) may mean that he is "real" as opposed to the false gods (cf. 17:3), and hence Jesus' mission is real. Or it may suggest that God alone is the source of truth and hence, by virtue of having been **sent**, Jesus' words are truth.

29—Jesus **knows** (*oida*) God, since his origins are with God. The word translated **know** in vv. 27-29 is *oida*, except in 27b where *ginōskein* appears. In general John uses these two verbs interchangeably (cf. Brown, vol. 1, p. 514). He can use the former in the sense of ordinary cognitive knowing (e.g., vv. 27, 28a) and in the more profound sense of what arises within an intimate relationship between two parties (which is the frequent sense of the Hebrew *yadah*, e.g., Hos. 4:6). Surely in vv. 28b and 29 the knowledge of God and of Jesus is more than a cognitive knowing and assumes a relationship of faith. For it is only in faith that one can **know** the **Father** and the **Son.**

30-31—Now it is this group (**they** means "some people of Jerusalem," v. 25) who try to arrest him, adding to the forces of opposition already mentoned (v. 1). The mob cannot succeed, however, because of the divine determination of Jesus' **hour** (cf. 2:4 above). Jesus' sovereignty over others is never compromised in John's gospel (but cf. v. 1 above). At that decisive **hour** Jesus *allows* the arrest and crucifixion. In spite of this hostile intent, John tells us in v. 31 **many of the people** (*ochlos*, "crowd") **believed in him,** thereby stressing again the division among humans resulting from the revelation of God. The belief of the crowd is, however, a **signs** faith—they are persuaded that no more wondrous **signs** could be expected of the Messiah than those done by Jesus. The evangelist subtly prepares the reader for the fact that the popular reaction to Jesus in Jerusalem is superficial, even as the reaction of the Galileans in chap. 6. Actually the OT picture of the Messiah does not include the performance of wonders, but by the first century the anticipation of the prophet-like-Moses and the return of Elijah influenced messianic speculation and apparently created a popular notion of a wonder-working Messiah.

32—Verses 32-36 are obviously another independent pericope attached here, for the attempted **arrest** seems unrelated to that in v. 30. It is **the Pharisees** in this case who initiate the arrest. John uses the term **Pharisee** some 20 times, all but one of which (18:3) are found in the first 12 chapters (contrast this with 65 occurrences of "the Jews," 15 of which appear in the passion narrative). It is likely that his tradition employed the title **Pharisees,** while his own inclination was to identify the Jewish leaders as "the Jews." The title **chief priests** appears also to be rooted in the tradition and is used 10 times in John, half of those in connection with **Pharisees. Chief priests** denotes the high ranking of the temple **priests.**

Their combination with Pharisees appears to be John's way of referring to the Sanhedrin (11:47). There is, however, a textual uncertainty concerning the phrase **chief priests and Pharisees,** making it possible that the combination was not John's but that of a later scribe. The **officers** were members of the temple police at the command of the Sanhedrin. **Muttering** (*goggyzō*) is used here as it is attributed to the crowd in v. 12 (cf. 6:41, 61 above). The muttering expresses a discontent of which the leaders want to take advantage.

33-34—These words announce Jesus' departure and return to the Father. At that time it will be impossible either to find or follow **Jesus. A little longer** (*chronon mikron*) appears in different forms elsewhere in this gospel (*mikron chronon* in 12:35 and simply *mikron* in 13:33; 14:19; 16:16, 17, 18, 19). In general this reference to a short time designates the imminent crucifixion-ascension which terminates the earthly ministry of Jesus. The departure motif, so prominent in the farewell discourses (chaps. 14–16), intrudes itself back into this discourse and preshadows the climax of the gospel. **I go to him who sent me** represents the Johannine concept of crucifixion and resurrection as ascension and reminds us that the origin and destiny of the revealer are with God, that Jesus is a stranger in this world and at home with the Father. Verse 34 warns that Jesus will not always be accessible to those who **seek** him. John is claiming that the time available to embrace the revelation is limited, and the time for decision is now. **Seek** (*zēteō*) has been used of opponents seeking to kill Jesus (v. 1) and their search for him at the feast (v. 11), while it is used in the sense of desire in v. 18 and the opponents' efforts in vv. 19, 25, and 30. In v. 34 it is ambiguous—seeking Jesus to arrest him or seeking him to accept him? It includes a note of irony, for while Jesus was present among them they sought him for evil reasons and when he is gone from their midst they will seek him for their salvation. **Where I am** (*eimi egō*) **you cannot come** designates the unique destiny of Jesus, which has to do with both his divine destiny with the Father and the means of his exaltation (the cross); cf. 8:21 and 13:33.

35-36—The audience is suddenly labeled **the Jews,** and they are substituted for the Pharisees of v. 32 (cf. 9:13, 18 below).

Their puzzlement over the meaning of Jesus' remarks is typical Johannine use of the misunderstanding motif (e.g., 3:4 and 4:14-15). Humanity is blind to the truth of the revelation. While Jesus speaks of a transcendent departure, the leaders attempt to comprehend his words in a spatial way (cf. another instance of the misunderstanding of Jesus' departure in 8:21-22). Verse 35 is also an instance of irony. Unknown to the speakers, they express a truth. While they mistakenly assume Jesus is about to journey **to the Dispersion** (*diaspora*), they unknowingly predict that Christ's revelation will be extended to **the Greeks.** The reader has the vantage point from which to see that the words predict the extension of the mission of the church beyond **the Jews** and Palestine. **Dispersion** refers to the scattered Jewish people (e.g., Isa. 49:6). **The Greeks** may mean the people of Greece, the Gentile world united by Hellenistic culture, or proselytes to Judaism from the Gentiles. In this context the meaning is simply Gentiles. Verse 36 underlines the incomprehension of the crowd.

37a—**On the last day of the feast** provides continuity with what has preceded—the beginning of the feast, v. 10, and "the middle of the feast," v. 14. It is not clear whether **the last day** means the seventh or eighth day (cf. v. 14 above), although it seems likely that the seventh day might more appropriately be called **the great day** than the eighth, which was essentially a day of rest. This might also have given the immediate context for the words of Jesus, since the waters of libation were concluded on the seventh day. However, "it is doubtful whether John was deeply concerned about the matter and possible that he was quite unaware of the question raised by his words" (Barrett, p. 326).

37b—More problematic and more important are the questions posed by vv. 37b-38. The issues involved include these: (1) The punctuation of **if any one** through **the scripture has said;** (2) whether it is Jesus or the believer from whom **flow rivers of living water;** and (3) the source of the scripture citation in v. 38. On the first question, it is possible to translate the Greek three different ways. *(a)* "If any one thirst, let him come to me and drink. He who believes in me, as the scripture has said. . ." (the RSV translation). *(b)* "If any one thirst, let him come to me; and let him who be-

127

lieves in me drink. As the scripture has said. . ." (the RSV foot-note). *(c)* "If any one thirst, let him come to me and drink [i.e., he who believes in me]. As the scripture has said. . . ." The argu-ments for each are extensive and too lengthy to repeat here (cf. Brown, vol. 1, pp. 320-323). The translation followed by the RSV is sustained by one chief argument: This punctuation is found in Origen and others, and it renders a construction most typical of John's style (the use of a participle, **he who believes**—*ho pis-teuon*—to form the subject of a new sentence). It must be stated, however, that the arguments for each of the translations are inde-cisive and no final solution is possible. If the answer to the question of punctuation favors the RSV translation, we are left with the fact that it is the believer (and not Jesus) to whom the scripture passage is applied. The third issue, however, is unresolved, namely, what scripture is intended by this citation. Whether one translates the passage to apply the citation to Jesus or the believer, there is no single passage which parallels the Johannine wording. Closest to the citation, if it refers to Jesus, are Isa. 43:19-21 and 44:3 plus Ps. 78:15. The nearest parallels to the quotation, if it describes the be-liever, are Isa. 58:11b; Zech. 14:8; and Prov. 18:4. Of the latter three it is the passage from Zechariah which may be most helpful. There it is said, "On that day living waters shall flow out from Je-rusalem. . . ." It is possible that John means the believer is under-stood to function on the eschatological day as Jerusalem was said to do.

While there is no way to solve the enormous problems of this passage, the meaning is clear if viewed on the assumption of the RSV punctuation and the resulting view that it is to the believer that the scripture citation refers. The saying **If any one thirst, let him come to me and drink** recalls 4:10-14 and invokes the an-cient religious use of water as a symbol. As surely as any thirst for water, so does humanity yearn for the truth of the revelation. Wa-ter is used symbolically in the OT to represent cleansing and sal-vation (e.g., Hos. 6:3; Ezek. 36:35; and Isa. 55:1). Furthermore, the water used in the ceremonies of the feast of Tabernacles may be intended as a context. The Mishnah (*Sukkah*) describes the use of libations in the temple throughout the days of celebration. John poses this claim of Jesus as the source of water over against the ritual waters of the cult. A reference to baptismal water is unlikely.

38-39—One who **believes** and embraces the revelation becomes a source of life for others (i.e., the Spirit, v. 39). John will later claim that the Spirit is given to believers, and they are then "sent" as Jesus is sent by the Father (20:21-22). Those who drink of the revelation become channels for the continued outpouring of the truth. **Living water** (*hydatos zōntos*) may mean "flowing water" but more likely here denotes "life-giving water." **Out of his heart** is in the Greek literally "out of his stomach" (*koilias*), meaning out of the very core of one's being. It appears to be a Semitic expression, since the stomach is the seat of emotional life for the Hebrews. Verse 39 is an aside by the evangelist (cf. 11:51-52; 13:28-29; 18:32) in which he identifies the water with the **Spirit**. Whereas water appears to represent the truth of the revelation elsewhere (e.g., 3:5; 4:10-14), John explicitly ties the symbol here to the Spirit. He assumes that it is necessary to inform the reader in a postresurrection situation of the preresurrection absence of the Spirit. John's view of the bestowal of the Spirit is that the glorification of Jesus must be accomplished before the Spirit is given (16:7). The Christian experience of the Spirit presupposes the revelation in Christ, for the work of the Spirit is for John essentially a continuation of Christ's work (14:15-17). By implication John is saying that the work of the Spirit is evident in the corporate life of his church through which the truth of the revelation is offered to others. It is not necessary to conclude that John denigrates the activity of the Spirit of God in Israel's history. The presence of the Spirit, the Jews believed, had been withdrawn (Ps. 74:9; 1 Macc. 4:46; 9:27; 14:41) and would be restored only in the messianic age. For John that restoration had occurred as a result of Christ's glorification and far exceeded the activity of the Spirit in times past. (Some textual variants occur in this verse, the result of what appears to have been efforts to soften the implication that there was no gift of the Spirit prior to Jesus' glorification.)

40-44—The words of Jesus in vv. 37-38 evoke still another divided response from the crowd. (**Words,** *logōn*, is the preferred reading among an unusually large number of variants, many of

which read "word.") On the one hand, some are impressed by his
words and declare that he is the **prophet,** an apparent allusion to
the prophet-like-Moses who was expected to come in the messianic age (cf. Deut. 18:15-18 and John 1:22 above), or the Messiah
himself (v. 41). On the other hand, some argue that he cannot be
the Messiah, since he is from **Galilee** and the Messiah must be a
descendant of **David** and originate in **Bethlehem.** That the Messiah should be of the line of David roots in 2 Sam. 7:1-17 and 23:5
(cf. Ps. 89:3-4; 132:11-12). The location of the birthplace in Bethlehem has its biblical origin in Mic. 5:2, although this interpretation of Micah is found *only* in Christian documents of the first century. The view that the Messiah should originate in Bethlehem and
not in Galilee (cf. v. 52 below) stands in contradiction to vv. 26-28
where it is said that the origins of the Messiah would be mysterious. John may be showing the weakness of all efforts to specify the
credentials of the Messiah. All such efforts presuppose that the
people know Jesus' origins, when in fact they do not recognize
that his roots are with God. John either does not know or ignores
the traditions that Jesus was of the line of David and born in Bethlehem (Matt. 1:2-16; 2:1 and Luke 2:1-7; 3:23-31). It hardly
seems likely that he would not employ such a tradition in his polemic against his opponents if he knew of it. Here part of the irony
of the situation is that Jesus' Galilean roots are misleading. God's
revelation of himself in Jesus shatters all human efforts to determine the divine plan for salvation and surprises us with the scan-
dalously meager earthly origins of his revealer (cf. 1:46 above). In
v. 43 once again the result of Jesus' words is **division** (*schisma,* cf.
9:16; 10:19; 1 Cor. 1:10; 11:18; 12:25) among the people (vv. 12,
25-27). Verse 44 informs us of still another attempt to **arrest** Jesus
which is also unsuccessful (vv. 23 and 30).

45-51—The closing unit of the chapter describes the spread of
the division over Jesus to the **chief priests and Pharisees** (cf. v. 32
above) themselves. The **officers** (cf. v. 32 above) sent to arrest him
have been impressed by his teaching. The time between the sending of the officers (v. 32) and the present scene (v. 37) is strange
only if we forget that John is constructing his narrative from fragments of tradition. The officers' words, **No man ever spoke like**

this man! are another touch of irony, for this man is unlike any other man. The response of the Pharisees to the report of those sent to arrest Jesus repeats the charge that he leads people astray (cf. v. 12 above). They further argue against Jesus by claiming that none of the leaders (archontōn) or Pharisees believe in him (v. 48). It is they who understand the Torah and alone are qualified to judge the authenticity of Jesus' claims. However, by their own ignorance and failure to obey the law they have made themselves accursed (eparatoi, v. 49), and not the people whom they accuse. The leaders are here made to speak with the contempt in which the "people of the land" were sometimes held by the religious elite, who devote themselves to the keeping of the law (cf. Barrett, p. 332). Ironically, however, in vv. 50-51 one of the leaders points out that they are ignoring their own Law by not trying Jesus fairly (cf. Exod. 23:1; Lev. 19:15; and Deut. 1:16). Who had gone to him before appears to be a gloss better omitted (cf. Gamaliel in Acts 5:34-39). Perhaps John intends a further irony by informing us that one of their own group is a secret believer. Surely ironic is the fact that those who judge are themselves judged by their own injustice and unbelief.

52—This raises certain problems, for there is no OT reference which denies that a prophet might come from Galilee. Indeed, the opposite is the case, as 2 Kings 14:25 demonstrates. Two possibilities emerge as solutions: First, John's knowledge of Jewish thought of the time of Jesus is faulty. Second, a textual variant which reads the prophet is the more authentic text. If the latter is the case, the passage then denies that the prophet of Deut. 18:15-18 ("the prophet-like-Moses") is to come from Galilee and fits better the scope of Johannine thought. Search (eraunēson) means "study the Scriptures." Clearly John is again employing irony as he does in v. 41: Galilee is really not Jesus' origin in the final sense. It would seem safe to conclude that the matter of the origins of Jesus figures prominently in the controversy between the Johannine Christians and the synagogue of John's time.

John 7:1-52 is clearly the result of the welding together of disparate bits by some common themes. John has made little effort to produce a chronological order or a narrative flow to the section, and instead has allowed some common themes to produce that unity. Those themes are at least three: First, division results from Jesus' words, a division which spreads from the crowd through the leaders (vv. 12, 25-27, 40-43, and 48-52). The interchange of the terms "crowd," "the Jews," "the people of Jerusalem," and "the Pharisees" shows that what they all have in common is a schism arising from the words of Jesus. Second is the persistent effort to arrest and kill Jesus (vv. 1, 19, 25, 30, 32, and 44) and the somberness it yields. The third theme is the question of Jesus' earthly origin as a stumbling block to discerning his real origins (vv. 27, 41-42, and 52). The impact of these themes is to drive home the inevitable destiny which awaits Jesus and the inescapable fracturing which results whenever the gospel is proclaimed, whether in the time of Jesus, John, or our own. Whenever humans suppose that they understand and can "package" God's ways for their own certainty, they become blinded to the presence of the divine in their midst and consequently respond without faith. Not only does God continually surprise his children but persistently denies them a security based upon their own reasonings and assumptions.

(The Woman Charged with Adultery [7:53—8:11])

There can be little or no doubt that this pericope was not originally part of the Gospel of John. The evidence of this fact is surveyed adequately in the commentaries found in the bibliography (cf. esp. Brown, vol. 1, pp. 335-336). The narrative is missing in those manuscripts thought to be the earliest (e.g., P[66]) and is present only in later textual witnesses. One group of witnesses includes it after Luke 21:38 (f[13]) and others place it elsewhere in John. While the textual evidence against its place in John is beyond refutation, there are good reasons for regarding it as an early part of tradition. It has the form of a Synoptic conflict- or pronouncement story, with stylistic features resembling Luke. It is, furthermore, an account of Jesus with similarities to those characteristics attributed to him in the Synoptics. It is sometimes suggested that it was a bit of freefloating tradition eventually inserted at this point in the Fourth Gospel as an illustration of 7:24. It seems clear that its function was to help to answer the question of the Christian attitude toward sin, especially adultery. While more Lukan (or at least Synoptic) than Johannine, it will be treated briefly here.

7:53—8:6—Verse 53 seems to be the conclusion of the narrative immediately preceding this pericope preserved here as part of the introduction provided in 8:1. **Mount of Olives** is nowhere else mentioned in John nor are the **scribes** (v. 3). **Adultery** was the act of intercourse between a married **woman** and another man. Jesus is addressed as **teacher,** a form of address common in the Synoptics (e.g., Matt. 22:24, a similar kind of story). **The law of Moses** (v. 5) would be Lev. 20:10 and Deut. 22:21 (cf. Ezek. 16:38f.; Mishnah, *Sanhedrin*). **What do you say** translates an emphasis upon the **you** (*sy oun ti legeis*). Verse 6a specifies what has seemed implied. The Greek is clear that the question is said to tempt (*peirazontes,* **test**) him. In 6:6 **Jesus** uses the same word to **test** Philip. In what sense did the leader suppose to test him? Some would say simply that they wanted him explicitly to deny the Mosaic Law, as his frequent and radical association with tax collectors and sinners seemed to imply (e.g., Matt. 9:10-13). Others find here the suggestion that, if Jesus pardoned the woman, he would be in violation of the Torah; and if he condemned her, he would violate Roman restriction against a sentence of death without the governor's endorsement (cf. 19:31b). Verse 6b has been the subject of a great deal of fruitless speculation. It is probably safer to say simply that Jesus writes while contemplating his response.

7-11—That response avoids the trap which has been set and skirts the issue presented to Jesus. That the hands of the witnesses to an offense are to be the first to execute the punishment is found in Deut. 13:9 and 17:7. With this statement, Jesus resumes his writing; and the crowd slowly disperses, leaving him alone with the **woman** (vv. 7-9). **Jesus** questions the **woman** and asks if there is any one left to condemn her (for **woman** cf. 2:4 above). **Condemned** (*katakrinein*) has more of the sense of an official and legal condemnation than the word John customarily uses (*krinein*). Without witnesses against her, there is no case. The indicative statement that there is no condemnation of her as a result of her sin gives rise, however, to an imperative: **Go, and do not sin again** (cf. 5:14). Forgiveness is followed by the commandment.

It is for good reason that this isolated and homeless pericope has captured the popular imagination, for it is a powerful and poignant tale. In general it warns against too easy judgment of others whose offenses may appear more obvious than one's own. In its setting in early Christianity it was perhaps a warning against the strict imposition of the law and suggests the radicality of forgiveness as it was evidenced in the attitude of the historical Jesus. Furthermore, in concert with the pericope regarding divorce (Mark 10:2-9; Matt. 19:1-9; cf. Matt. 5:31-32 and Luke 16:18) this passage may represent the condemnation on the part of Jesus (and/or the early church) of those laws which discriminated against women. Taken as a whole, it is still another instance of the radical acceptance of sinners on the part of Jesus.

Temple Addresses—Departure and Ancestry (8:12-59)

This section continues the dialog between Jesus and his audience in the temple precincts, as John informs us in vv. 20 and 59. Like 7:10-52, it is comprised of a number of somewhat independent bits of discourse/dialog joined together under the rubric of temple addresses and some common themes. The continuity with what has come before is suggested in v. 12 with the word "again" (*palin*), as well as some of the themes recognized in the preceding unit. Its integrity as a separate unit is found only in a loose time and place structure (vv. 12, 20, 21, 59) and several new themes not found in 7:10-52, e.g., light and the real descendants of Abraham.

Departure, Destiny, and Origin (8:12-30)

12—**Them** is not clear, especially given the shifting audience in 7:10-52, but the chief priests and Pharisees would be the most immediate antecedent. Verse 13 confirms that impression. **I am the light of the world** is the second of the series of powerful "I am" statements with predicates (cf. 6:35, 51 above) and is repeated in 9:5. Another ancient religious symbol, **light,** is here claimed by John to explicate the meaning of Christ. For him **light** stands for the revelation, and the **world** (*kosmos*) represents the realm of darkness set over against God (cf. 1:4-5, 9). **The light of life** resembles 1:4 where the light of the revelation is life-giving. In the **darkness** of alienation from God the revelation illumines human existence, giving meaning and definition to believers. **Light** is both a universal religious symbol and an important metaphor for Judaism itself. It is related to the feast of Tabernacles (cf. Mishnah, *Suk.* 5:2-4) and wisdom thought (cf. Prov. 8:22). (Cf. Barrett, pp. 335-337, for a survey of the religious background of light.) For John Christ gathers up all of the various meanings of light into his person and fulfills all of them. **Follows me** is a reference to discipleship (cf. 1:35-51), and to **walk** designates the specific character of a human life (cf. 11:9-10 and 12:35). The symbols of walking in light or darkness are found in Qumran literature (e.g., 1QS 3:1-9). The way one "walks" expresses a self-understanding, a perspective on reality.

13-15—The **Pharisees** are reinstated in the scene and raise a new issue, namely, that Jesus is **bearing witness** (*martyreis*) to himself. In 5:31ff. the same issue is discussed from another point of view. There Jesus claims other **witnesses** to the truth of his words, and here he claims that the **witness** of his Father verifies his own witness. The self-predication of the "I am" saying in v. 12 is taken to be a witness to oneself. The principle that self-witness is insufficient is found in Num. 35:30 and Deut. 17:6; 19:15. **Jesus'** first response to the charge in v. 14 is to claim that his divine origin and destiny make his **witness true.** Again the origin and destiny of Jesus define his identity (cf. 7:27-28, 35; 9:29-30; 13:36). His origins with God and his eventual return to the Father make him God's official representative and hence entitle him to **witness** to himself, for he cannot but speak the truth. In 5:31 **Jesus** is made to say that his self-witness is not true, while here he asserts the opposite. Still, the thrust of the argument is similar. Jesus' unique identity validates his **testimony** (cf. 5:37). John's discourse and discussion materials obviously bring together disparate and widely differing traditions. If his opponents knew Jesus' identity (his **whence** and his **whither**), there could be no question of the truth of his words. Their **judgment according to the flesh** (i.e., according to appearance; cf. 7:24) blinds them to the truth of his origin and destiny (v. 15). **According to the flesh** (*kata tēn sarka*) does not mean an inherently evil perspective but only one confined to this world with its limitations of time and space. Jesus again seems to contradict himself in v. 15, for in 5:30 he says that he does **judge**. The root of the difference in this case is that judgment is not the primary function of the revelation but only an inescapable consequence. (It may be that v. 15 prompted the insertion of 7:53—8: 11.)

16-18—So, **judgment** is the divine prerogative. Jesus' **judgment is true** because of his relationship with the Father. (The textual difference between *alēthē* and *alēthinē* does not significantly change the meaning of **true**.) This verse clarifies the "functional unity" of the Father and the Son—Jesus' judgment is for and with God. For **he who sent me** cf. 7:16 above. The pattern of vv. 14 and 16 is similar: Jesus picks up an expression from the previous verse (in v. 14 it is "bear witness to myself" and in v. 16 **I judge**) and qualifies the preceding statement. This is a characteristic of Johannine discourse style. Verses 17-18 make explicit what has been implied, namely, that the **Father's** witness is added to Jesus' own to make his **testimony** valid. **Your law** again suggests the distance of Jesus and/or the Johannine community from the Jewish **law** (cf. 7:19 above). The **testimony of two men is true** refers to Deut. 17: 6 and 19:15. The argument is not entirely true to the sense of the OT **law**, however, since the **witness** of the one charged is not allowed. Hence, Jesus has only one **witness**, the **Father**. John cannot escape the fact that Jesus' self-witness is valid because of his divine identity. Verse 18 is the conclusion of the argument concerning witness. The **Father's witness** is joined to that of Jesus. **I bear witness to myself** is literally, "I am the one witness to myself" (*egō eimi ho martyrōn peri emautou*) and concludes the discussion with an "I am" statement as it was begun in v. 12. If the "I am" statement here is taken as a self-predication of the same magnitude as 8:12, it means that Jesus' divine person is witness even as it is light. (Compare Isa. 43:10 which in the LXX is similar to v. 18.) The point of the argument concerning Jesus' witness is that his relationship with the Father gives his witness validity quite apart from the legal requirements for admissible testimony. John's message is simply that the words and the acts of Jesus are a manifestation of God. Furthermore, the evangelist extends the category of witness to encompass the concept of revelation. Witness is not only the means by which humans are brought to the revelation (cf. 1:29-51; 3:22-30; 4:28-30) but also the very nature of the revelation itself (cf. 5:31-40).[15]

19-20—The discussion continues by picking up the word **Father.** (Verse 18 is the first use of the title since 6:65, assuming that the textual variant which adds **Father** in v. 16 is taken to be a scribal clarification.) The Pharisees' question betrays a misunderstanding of **Jesus'** reference to his **Father,** since the question, **Where is your Father?** assumes that Jesus has spoken of an earthly father. Their question reflects their ignorance of the Father and consequently of Jesus as well. Knowledge of Christ's identity both leads to and presupposes knowledge of God (cf. 7:17 above). The error of human blindness is to fail by faith to see the divine glory residing in the human Jesus (1:14). Verse 20 punctuates the discussion with a break. The location of the dialog **in the treasury** is problematic, since the interchange could not have been in the storage rooms used for temple valuables. Offering boxes were located in the court of the women, and hence it is widely thought that the meaning is "near one of the offering boxes" (cf. TEV). But our knowledge of the temple is too limited to judge the accuracy of John's words. Again Jesus cannot be **arrested because his hour had not yet come** (cf. 7:30, 44 above). This verse may be an editorial transition to hold together the discussion in vv. 12-20 with the other parts of the temple address.

21-23—**Again** (*palin*) divides another separable unit (vv. 21-30). This unit is an exemplary passage which reflects many of John's popular themes and his style. **I go away** (*egō hypagō*) is a Johannine expression for the death/resurrection/ascension of Jesus. **Seek me** here means attempt to appropriate the salvific power of Christ. The thought repeats what is found in 7:33. **Die in your sin** is found only here in John and signifies the rejection of the revelation, the essence of sin for John. The phrase may be a legal one, signaling the just consequences of one's actions (cf. Deut. 24:16 and Ezek. 3:18). Here it is sin in the singular, indicating the pri-

137

macy of the rejection of the revelation; the plural appears in v. 24, suggesting that John does not mean a distinction between sin in the plural and in the singular. This is so since both are for him the blindness to Christ's glory. For **where I am going you cannot come** cf. 7:34 above. In v. 22 the opponents are now (and again in v. 31) called **the Jews,** a switch from v. 13 (cf. 7:1, 32 above and 9: 13, 18 below). Again, as in 7:35-36, Jesus' allusion to his going away produces misunderstanding, and it strangely raises the possibility that Jesus will take his own life! As the misunderstanding in 7:35 contains an ironic reference to the Christian Gentile mission, so this one ironically refers to Jesus' death. He will lay down his life for others (10:15) but *they* will kill him, not he himself. Verse 23 is in synonymous parallelism using two pairs exemplifying Johannine dualism—**from below/from above** and **of this world/not of this world.** The first *(ek tōn katō and ek tōn anō)* is a spatial metaphor to describe the realm of God and that of evil or opposition to God, much as the light/darkness dualism does. The second pair designates the same two realities. For **world** cf. 3:16 above. Clearly **world** does not mean simply the material realm, but that realm mistakenly taken to be independent of its Creator. The verse suggests that one is affiliated with one realm or the other and is thereby defined by that association. It is not the case, then, that the distinction intended is between Jesus' unique origin and human origin, but between a proper understanding of self and a false one.

24-25—The words of v. 21 are repeated with the exceptions that sins is plural and the important qualification, **unless you believe that I am he,** is added. The Greek is the simple **I am** *(egō eimi)* without the predicate **he.** (For the meaning of the **I am** without the predicate cf. 6:20 above.) The fate of the opponents can be avoided only by faith. The content of that faith is the assertion that Jesus bears the divine name, i.e., is functionally one with the great **I am.** Whereas John most often speaks of believing *in* Jesus (e.g., *pisteuōn eis eme,* 6:35), he also uses the expression "believe *that*" (e.g., *episteusan hoti sy me apesteilas,* 17:8), as he does here. For him the personal trust in Jesus, which is the heart of the faith relationship, results in belief in statements *about* Jesus; hence John builds a bridge between faith understood as trust and faith understood as creed. In v. 24 one is asked to **believe that** Jesus carries the authority of the divine name. It should be noted that John, however, never uses the noun, "belief" or "faith" (*pistis*), but always the verb, "to believe" (*pisteuein*). Salvation is found only in the correct understanding of and posture toward Jesus. His audience is once again made to misunderstand Jesus (v. 25). They entirely miss the sacred sense of **I am** and ask after his earthly identity, **Who are you?** Ironically, of course, they ask the most vital question, "Who is Jesus?" The response to this question in v. 25b is far from clear. This presents a complicated translation puzzle made worse by the absence of punctuation and spacing between the letters in the ancient manuscripts. The Nestle Greek text and that of the United Bible Societies read *tēn archēn ho ti lalō hymin*. Three proposals are offered for rendering those words: (1) It is taken as a statement, "What I have told you from the beginning" (RSV, JB, NAB, TEV). (2) It may be understood as a question, "Why should I speak to you at all?" (NEB, TEV margin, RSV margin). In this case, *tēn archēn* is rendered "at all" and *ho ti* is taken as *hoti*, "why?" (3) The partial sentence is taken to be an exclamation: "That I should speak to you at all!" Again *ho ti* is read *hoti*, and *tēn archēn* "at all." To complicate the issue, one ancient textual witness (P[66]) reads, in effect, "I told you in the beginning that which also I am telling you." The context gives some strength to the RSV translation of the passage as a statement, and for that reason is to be preferred, even though there can be no conclusive proof. Given the meaning of v. 26, it seems the sense of the statement is something like, "I am what I have told you I am from the very first of my ministry."

26-30—The relationship between the two halves of v. 26 is likewise not clear, but the meaning seems to be that Jesus disciplines himself not to say all that he might to the people in favor of speaking only what he has **heard from** the Father. **To the world** renders *eis ton kosmon* but seems to have the sense of **in** (*en*) **the world.** Verse 27 indicates another lack of understanding which is simply John's way of giving Jesus a further opportunity to speak. **Lifted up** (*hypsōsēte*, v. 28) is one of the Johannine allusions to the cross and its meaning (cf. 3:14 above and 12:32-34 below). On the use of **Son of man** in John cf. 1:51 and 3:14 above. The crucifixion will result in two bits of knowledge: that Jesus is **I am** and that he is a faithful interpreter of the **Father.** The cross is the decisive event which manifests Jesus' true identity. There is an implicit threat in these words to the effect that his opponents will discover too late that Jesus is indeed who he professes to be. Verse 29 is something of a summary of vv. 21-28. The presence of the Father is constant because Jesus is constantly faithful. This theme will become the basis of the imperative to the disciples in 15:1ff., where they are asked to abide in God as Jesus does and to be obedient as Jesus is obedient to the Father. Verse 30 comes as a bit of a surprise, since there has been no indication of a believing response in vv. 21-28. It seems to function as a translation to a new subunit, vv. 31-59. It may be too that John has in mind specifically Jewish believers who nonetheless lack the courage of their convictions (cf. 12:42).

Verses 12-30 explore the identity and function of Jesus interlaced with a number of misunderstandings. Jesus states his gift to humanity in v. 12 but is misunderstood in v. 13. He states his function as a witness to God in vv. 14-18 but must deal with a misconstruing of his words (v. 19). He states the eternal significance of his death in v. 21 but is met again with misunderstanding (v. 22). He states his identity in relationship to the reality of unbelief in vv. 23-26 but without being understood (v. 27). Finally, he states that the cross will reveal his relationship with God (vv. 28-29), and we are given the only hopeful note of a positive response in v. 30. The obstacle to the acceptance of the revelation is the people's difficulty in believing that a single human being could be who he claims to be and to do what he claims he is doing. The revelation is *hidden* in a human person, but paradoxically it is the most obscured of all the acts of that human (his death) which manifests the truth he offers (vv. 28-30).

Ancestry—Jesus' and His Opponents' (8:31-59)

31-33—This unit begins with a reference to **the Jews who had believed in him** and seems hardly appropriate, since those same "believers" quickly become his opponents in the ensuing discussion and even are said to seek to kill him (v. 37). For this reason some claim that the phrase is a later gloss or effort of the final redactor to smooth the transition from v. 30 to v. 32. The Greek is more exactly translated "had believed him" (*tous pepisteukotas autō*), and may suggest that their faith is less than the personal trust John describes as "believe in (*eis*) him." Believing Jesus' words is not enough (cf. v. 24 above). In 7:31 some of the crowd believe, even though disbelief is widespread. It is perhaps best to take the reference to believing **Jews** again (cf. v. 29 above) as John's critique of those Jews of his own synagogue who at first embraced the revelation but then fell aside when the controversy between the Jewish community and the Christians heated up. **Continue in my word** translates what is more exactly "abide" or "remain" (*meinēte*) **in my word** (cf. 15:10 below). The sense here is that one live out of and find one's purpose in the revelation of God in Christ. That is the definition of true discipleship. **Truly my disciples** is opposed to superficially giving credence to Jesus' words. To **know the truth** (v. 32) is to embrace and trust the revelation. **Know** (*gnōsesthe*) has the sense of relationship and not simple cognitive knowledge (cf. 7:28-29 above). **Truth** is John's label for the content and significance of God's revelation and not general knowledge of some kind. The revelation frees the believer from the false self-understanding of the "world" or "darkness." In Jewish thought the Law freed one for the "yoke of the kingdom" (Mishnah, *Aboth* 3:5). This is John's only use of **free** (*eleutheros*), and he means it as a synonym for eternal life or salvation. It is freedom to be what God intends humanity to be; therefore it involves liberation from all oppressive powers. This is so because God's redemptive revelation is opposed to all that prevents a full humanization of his creatures. The response of his audience in v. 33 indicates their bondage to their pride of heritage. Their claim is that being **descendants of Abraham** makes them immune to bondage. Surely John does not intend that they claim freedom from political bondage, for their history proves otherwise. Their real bondage is their assumption that national identity itself assures freedom. **Descendants** is in the Greek "seed" (*sperma*) but seems to be used as a collective singular (cf. Gal. 3:16).

141

34-35—Jesus answers with the claim that **sin enslaves. Every one who commits sin** renders *ho poiōn tēn hamartian*, "the one doing sin," and parallels "doing the truth" (e.g., 3:21). It is the "performance" of sin or the "life-style" of sin that places one in bondage to sin. Barrett finds a twofold meaning: "He who actually commits sin demonstrates thereby that he is already the slave of sin; also, by the very sin he commits he makes himself still further a slave" (p. 345). Life alienated from God has a way of perpetuating itself—a notion expressed in the concept of "original sin." The little parable in v. 35 does not seem entirely fitting at this point in spite of efforts to interpret it otherwise. The point is that the **slave** has no enduring place in the family, while **the son** through inheritance continues (*menei*, "remain") in the family **for ever** (*eis ton aiōna*). The point is that the opponents of Jesus are not children of Abraham, as they claim (vv. 33 and 39), but slaves who have forfeited their inheritance, and it is Jesus, the **Son**, who alone is the true descendant of Abraham. The original meaning of the parable might have spoken of the Christian as the son, but John uses **son** (*huios*) always in reference to Jesus. The parable fits the theme of vv. 32 and 39 but is disruptive after v. 34. It owes its location here to the catchword **slave** in v. 34. Not unexpectedly, John's discourse moves along on the basis of the suggestion of a word or two in the previous verse.

36-38—It is reasserted that true freedom is found only in God's revealer. By God's act one is made truly **free** of the bondage of a sinful life-style. The suggestion of **free indeed** (*ontōs eleutheroi*) is that the freedom the audience claims for themselves is not genuine. Jesus now (v. 37) recognizes that in a sense the opponents are **descendants of Abraham,** at least biologically. But the fact that they **seek to kill** Jesus (contrast with v. 31) indicates that spiritually they have abandoned their ancestry. Biological ancestry is irrelevant (cf. Matt. 3:9; 8:11-12 and Luke 3:8; 13:28-30). What is relevant is whether or not Jesus' **word finds . . . a place in** them (the Greek *chōrei* means "functions in your life"). Verse 38 is unclear, and its lack of clarity has resulted in scribal efforts to improve the sentence. The issues are twofold: (1) Is the **father** mentioned in the second clause God or the "devil" (cf. v. 44)? (2) Is that second clause an imperative or a declaration? Textual witnesses add "your" before the second **father** to yield the meaning that both Jesus and his opponents obey their **father,** but the opponents' **father** is not God but the devil. If those scribal efforts are misleading, then we are left with an alternative. This verse is a statement of Jesus' loyalty to God followed by the command that the opponents **do what you have heard from your father** (God). Since the theme that the devil is the father of the opponents is introduced only later (vv. 41, 44), it seems the latter meaning is the more likely, and Jesus is attempting to call his listeners back to their spiritual heritage. **Seen** implies Jesus' source of knowledge from a preexistent vision or his immediate spiritual knowledge, while **heard** means the opponents have God's will in the written Law.

39-41—Verse 39 suggests a misunderstanding on the part of the listeners (if both the "fathers" of v. 38 refer to God), for they again (cf. v. 33) claim that **Abraham** is their **father.** They persist in their belief that their ancestry secures them! Jesus' answer is marred by difficulties in the tenses of the verbs and textual variants designed to smooth out those difficulties (39b). The best reading would render this translation: "If you were Abraham's children, you would be doing Abraham's works" (cf. TEV). Being a descendant of Abraham in the true sense yields behavior appropriate to such. Their attempt to **kill** one **who has told you the truth** belies their claim. **Abraham** would not reject the **truth** of the revelation in Christ, for it is harmonious with his beliefs and behavior. The reference to Jesus as simply **a man** has disturbed some interpreters, but it reaffirms the genuine humanity of the Johannine Christ. The principle involved in the argument thus far is that one behaves as one's parents behaved. Now on that principle the sarcastic suggestion is made in v. 41 that Jesus' opponents behave as their **father,** the devil, does. (If not in v. 38, now in 41 the point of v. 44 is implied.) The response is to claim that his listeners are not illegitimate children but **have one Father, even God.** They are made to respond to an implicit suggestion that they are bastards, and they make the point that ancestry must finally root in **God.** Is their defense against illegitimate birth an inference concerning *them* in the words of Jesus or a subtle taunt of *Jesus* based on a ru-

mor that his birth was illegitimate? While there is some evidence
of such a rumor later, it does not seem necessary to invoke such a
meaning here. John shows no knowledge of the virgin birth. The
discussion has now moved to the question of true ancestry.

42-44—The argument of v. 42 is similar to what has preceded
it, namely, if **God** is claimed as one's parent, then behavior consistent with that parentage must be in evidence. In this case, that behavior would consist of loving **Jesus,** the very opposite of what his
opponents have attempted, i.e., to kill him (vv. 37 and 40). Such
love is expected, because **Jesus** claims to be functionally one with
God, acting as his representative—a point made repeatedly
through these discourses (e.g., 7:28). Some attempt to find the
subtleties of later trinitarian thought in the words **I proceeded and
came forth from God,** but such attempts are anachronistic and
guilty of reading more *into* than *out of* the text. The challenge in v.
43 is to the effect that their failure to **understand** Jesus belies their
claim to divine ancestry. The Greek is "because you do not know
my speaking *(lalian),* you **cannot hear** my message *(logon)."* The
RSV **cannot bear** is weaker than the Greek "are not able" *(ou dy
nasthe).* Knowing or understanding the speaking of Jesus leads to
the possibility of "hearing" in the sense of appropriating and obeying. Now the implication of v. 41 is made explicit in v. 44. The
parentage of the opponents is with the forces of evil, **the devil** *(diabolos).* **You are of your father the devil** can be translated, "You
are of the father of the devil," but that makes the succeeding difficult. That parentage is evident in the **will** of the opponents. A
succession of statements about the **devil** is made: He is a **murderer
from the beginning** refers to the concept that the devil brought
immortality into humanity (cf. Rom. 5:12) and/or to Cain's murder
of Abel (Gen. 4:8). He is opposed to the **truth,** meaning he is at
odds with the revelation of God. **Has nothing to do with truth**
renders what is more exactly "he did not stand *(estēken)* in the
truth," which may imply the Jewish mythology of the fall of Satan
from his status with God. He is a **liar** in that he is the opposite of
truth. The Greek is less than polished: "He is a liar and the father
of it *(ho patēr autou)."* The Jewish view that the devil in the form
of the serpent deceived Eve may also be implied in this verse (e.g.,
The Life of Adam and Eve 9–11).

144

45-47—Since the opponents do the will of the "father of lies," they **do not believe** Jesus when he speaks the **truth.** This is so in spite of the fact that they cannot prove Jesus guilty of sin (v. 46b). **Convicts** (*elenchein*) is the same word used of the Paraclete's proving the world sinful in 16:8. It is not necessary to argue that this is a reference to the sinlessness of Jesus (cf. Heb. 4:15); it means only that his opponents cannot find fault in his words and behavior. This means that they have no legitimate grounds for rejecting Jesus' words, and it is their parentage in the devil which alone accounts for their stubborn unbelief. Verse 47 states that point with clarity. If their roots were in **God** (*ek tou theou*), they would recognize the truth in Jesus' **words.** They must then not be rooted in God. **Hear** again, as in v. 43, means more than the sensual experience of audition; it is the act of claiming the **words** of Jesus for oneself and living them, i.e., obeying. The theme repeated here is that a person's perspective (or roots) determines his or her perception (cf. 7:28-29).

48-50—Jesus is again accused of being possessed by a demon (cf. 7:20 above and 8:54; 10:20), but here is added the derision that he is **a Samaritan.** A number of interpretations of the latter have been proposed. It may mean he is a heretic or an illegitimate child. It has also been taken to mean the same as being possessed by **a demon** (notice that the response is to the single charge of having a demon, v. 49). Could it also be the case that the Johannine community contained a number of Samaritan Christians, and for that reason suffered ridicule from the synagogue of the city? At the very least we can conclude that the charge of being a Samaritan was as derisive as saying that one was insane. Jesus counters (v. 49) by suggesting that he **honors** the **Father,** and it is that fact which the warped perception of his opponents take to be insanity (cf. 5:23 above). The point of v. 50 is similar to 5:41-44 and 7:18 (cf. above). As God's delegate, Jesus never seeks his **own glory.** In the second line there is no object after **seeks** (i.e., no **it**), but it is common parlance in this gospel that God **seeks** to glorify the Son (e.g., 17:1). It is God who will pass judgment on whose behavior is truthful.

51-56—The argument shifts slightly at this point. **Keeps** (*tērēsē*) **my word** means obedience and hence has the sense of "hearing" in vv. 43, 47. It is to hold Christ's **word** and allow it to control one's life (cf. the use of this expression in 14:15, 21, 23, 24). The promise is that such a person **will never see death,** never experience condemnation to nothingness (cf. 11:25). His audience responds with the argument that **Abraham died,** taking Jesus' words literally. He, of course, referred to spiritual **death** (v. 52). **Never taste death** is synonymous with **never see death** in v. 51. Verse 53 is intended to push Jesus' words to their utterly ridiculous extreme, but ironically speaks the truth. The answer in v. 54 repeats the common theme that Jesus' interests are not in self-aggrandizement but in glorifying **God.** It is God alone who **glorifies** Jesus (cf. v. 50 and 17:1ff.). The claim of v. 55 is that Jesus **knows** God while his opponents do not. Two different words for **know** are used here (*ginōskein* and *eidenai*), but no difference of meaning is detectable (cf. 7:27-29 above). **I keep his word** is to be compared with v. 51 where believers are to keep Jesus' word. As is often the case, the Father-Son relationship is the model for the relationship of believers and Jesus (e.g., 15:9-10; cf. the chart, "Relational Analogies," p. 266). Verse 56 is the claim that Jesus and the Christian movement embrace the Hebraic tradition as their own. What is meant by **Abraham rejoiced that he was to see my day?** It may be that it is a reference to Gen. 17:17 when Abraham saw the beginning of God's fulfillment of his promise. It may also refer to the apocalyptic notion that Abraham was accorded a view of the whole of God's saving history (4 Ezra 3:14). Or it may assume some sort of continued life for Abraham in God's presence which allows him to experience Jesus' ministry (cf. Luke 16:19-31). The last clause, **he saw it and was glad,** seems to be redundant in its effort to emphasize Abraham's rejoicing. **My day** (*tēn hēmeran tēn ēmen*) stands for the whole of the Christ event.

57-59—Still another ridiculous misunderstanding is attributed to Jesus' audience in v. 57. Through this whole discussion they remain trapped in a literalism which blinds them to the meaning of Jesus' words. **Not yet fifty years old** is meant only to stress the years between Jesus and Abraham arising out of the opponents' literalism, and it does not afford any evidence for the age of Jesus during his ministry. The RSV is correct in taking **have you seen**

Abraham? as the preferred reading rather than "has Abraham seen you?" The latter is an attempt to cohere this phrase with the words of v. 56 where it is said Abraham saw Jesus' day. The conversation comes to a climax in Jesus' "I am" saying in v. 58. Abraham was, was "born" or "came to be" (*genesthai*), while Jesus *is*. The statement joins the dramatic theophany of the I am (cf. 6:20) with the implication of Jesus' preexistence. The thrust of the proclamation is to claim the superiority of Jesus over Abraham, a view which characterizes the Christian relationship with the OT tradition, i.e., embracing it while asserting the supersession of Christ over it. The words understandably offend the listeners, and in v. 59 they attempt to stone Jesus for what seems to them is blasphemy (it is not clear, however, in what sense his words are blasphemous). That stoning was the appropriate punishment for blasphemy is stated in Lev. 24:16. Still, this act is a mob reaction and does not give evidence against the view stated in 19:31. Jesus' escape is less mysterious in this case than in 7:30, 44, and 8:20, but delays the inevitable moment of his "hour." With **went out of the temple** John concludes the long series of temple discussions, stretching from 7:14 to this verse.

Ancestry in the unit vv. 31-59 is pressed into service metaphorically to stand for that which gives the human her or his perspective, values, and allegiance. As the parables of the Synoptic tradition so often do, this poetic image breaks open new meaning for the readers and places their "parentage" in question. Moreover, this dialog demonstrates how the revelation shatters human security—in this case, a false security sought in one's "roots." All efforts at securing ourselves falter and collapse over against the manifestation of God. No roots are deep enough until they tap our utter dependence upon our Creator!

In 8:12-59 we detect two cycles of discussion, the one comprised of vv. 12-30 and the other vv. 31-59. The first takes as its focus Jesus' departure and his ancestry in the sense of his origin and destiny. The second develops the ancestry of Jesus contrasted to his opponents. Each is composed of bits and pieces which seem to have some independence on their own. The interconnection of these parts is often no more than a catchword or phrase, suggest-

ing that John or his source is responsible for their union. Verses 30
and 31 seem obviously to be a rather superficial effort to link the
two cycles together. Still, in the composite work of the evangelist
there is a clear intention in this unit taken as a whole. It is designed
once again to raise the inevitable conflict between the revelation
and the established religion and to show the tragic sense in which
humanity is blinded by its own inhibition in this world to the truth
offered in Christ. While John describes the blindness of Judaism, it
is clear that he means the blindness of any human institution which
tries to preserve itself intact in the face of the surprising revelation
of God.

Blindness—Physical and Spiritual (9:1-41)

In chap. 9 we confront one of the best illustrations of John's literary talent. The chapter is a finely polished drama of seven scenes
which shows in an exemplary way how John recites a wonder story
and then proceeds to explore its symbolic meaning. While it is a
physically blind man who is healed, it is his spiritual sight and the
spiritual blindness of the religious leaders that constitute the central message of this section.

1-3—The first scene (vv. 1-7) narrates the healing itself with
masterful economy. **A man blind from his birth** prepares us for
the extent of the wonder of Jesus' act. (The closest Synoptic parallels to the healing are Mark 8:22-26 and 10:46-52.) In v. 2 the
disciples assume that this man's ailment is a result of sin, either his
own or that of **his parents.** The concept that suffering was the consequence of sin and disobedience has a long history in Hebraic and
Jewish thought (e.g., Exod. 20:5), even though such a "retribution
ethic," with its correlative that righteousness always brings blessing and success, was challenged in the books of Job and Eccle-
siastes, among others. It remained one of the resolutions of the
problem of theodicy as late as the first century, i.e., God's justice
understood in the light of human suffering. Jesus' response in v. 3
neither confirms nor denies such a view. Rather, he claims **this
man's** condition was determined for reasons of God's glorification.
The same thought is expressed in 11:4, and it picks up the OT

theme that God sometimes manipulates history in such a way as to heighten the glory of his acts (e.g., Exod. 7:3f.). It is then not sin but God's redemptive purpose which causes the man's condition. **The works** (*erga*) **of God** are those actions by which humans become instruments of God's redemptive will.

4-5—Verse 4 suggests that the opportunity for Jesus and his disciples to do **the works of God** is limited and will eventually be terminated. The pronouns **we** and **me** present a problem. Textual variants at this point appear to be efforts to make the pronouns consistent (i.e., "we. . .we" or "I. . .me"), but the RSV follows the more difficult and hence (in this case, at least) the preferable reading. **Him who sent me** is merely an allusion to God, and the first person plural (**we**) associates, on one level, the disciples with Jesus' mission and, on another level, the Christian community which is called to continue **the works** of God begun in Christ (cf. 14:12). **While it is day . . . work** is possibly a proverb put on the lips of Jesus. **Day** means a life span, but may here denote the time span of the evangelistic work of the church. **Night** in v. 4 seems to trigger the **light** in v. 5. The latter casts a symbolic meaning over the proverb in v. 4. The opportunity for God's work is so long as the light of the revelation is present. Here it is not the solemn **I am** as in 8:12 but the simple, unemphatic *eimi*. Its function, however, is to announce the theme of the chapter: Christ brings **light** to this dark **world** both by giving physical sight and bestowing the truth of the revelation of God. By the association of this verse with the meaning of v. 4 the implication is that Christ is in **the world** both during his earthly ministry and after his resurrection-ascension through the Spirit's presence in the community of believers (cf. 16:12-14 below).

6-7—With the introduction provided in vv. 1-5 the act of healing itself is now told. In the ancient world **spittle** was understood to have magical effects, especially that of a holy person (cf. Barrett, p. 358). Only here and in Mark 7:33 and 8:13 do we find Jesus using spittle in a healing. This feature of the wonder may suggest that the narrative of the healing proper has roots in the earliest Christian tradition, since there seems to have been a tendency to repress such features of magical powers in Jesus' healings (cf. the parallel to Mark 7:33 in Matt. 15:29-31 and the omission of Mark 8:23 from Matthew and both 7:33 and 8:23 from Luke). **Anointed** (*epechrisen*) suggests the OT use of anointing as the empowering of the king (2 Sam. 16:3). (**Anointed is** the most difficult of several textual variants and probably the best.) That the **clay** is used may arise from Gen. 2:7 seems a strained inference. The **man** is given a double command, **go, wash,** and the scene is reminiscent of 2 Kings 5:10-13. **Siloam** would seem to refer to the pool whose Hebrew name is "Shiloah," located south of Jerusalem where the valleys of the Kidron and Tyropoeon converge. John takes some liberties with the etymology of the name and renders it in a passive form, **sent** (*apestalmenos*), one of his favorite words. As Jesus is sent, so also does he send believers (20:21). John (or a later editor) frequently gives his readers the benefit of Greek translations of Hebrew words (e.g., 1:38, 41, 42; 11:16; 19:17). The man obeys the commands of Jesus, and without elaboration it is said he **came back seeing.** It is doubtful that his washing is intended to be a veiled reference to Baptism. The healing is completed, and the man's new sight becomes the basis of his journey through the subsequent verses to spiritual sight.

8-12—The second scene of the drama presents the reaction of the crowd. The crowd is amazed, but some refuse to believe that this sighted man is the same one who once was blind. A frequent element in healing stories in the Synoptics is the public confirmation of the deed (e.g., Mark 2:12; 7:36-37). **The man who used to sit and beg** (v. 8) may have been part of John's source, a detail which he omitted in telling the healing but adds here (cf. Mark 10: 46 and parallels). Verse 9 reports the division of opinion in the crowd and is similar to the division Jesus' words cause his hearers (cf. chaps. 7 and 8). **I am the man** is a purely secular use of the emphatic *I am* (*egō eimi*) construction and has the force of stressing the *I*. That John can use it in such a way as this suggests that not every *egō eimi* on the lips of Jesus is intended to have revelatory meaning. But in another sense, even here it is the revelation of the person of the man who has been healed in a way not unlike Jesus' self-revelation in the formula (e.g., 4:26 above). In v. 10 the man is asked how it is that he can now see (**eyes opened** is an OT expression for the restoration of sight, e.g., Isa. 35:5). Verse 11 is the man's response and the first of a series of witnesses to Jesus he will make in this chapter. Here he affirms only that Jesus was the man responsible for his cure; in later witnesses he gradually uses more significant titles for Jesus. He summarizes the healing with nearly identical words used in v. 7. Such repetition is sometimes evidence of the form a narrative took while being transmitted by word of mouth. **Received my sight** (*aneblepsa*) usually means "to recover eyesight" but is used here and again in v. 18 of the healing, even though the man had never before been able to see (v. 1).

13-17—The third scene comprises the first of the interrogations of the healed **man.** John does not tell us why the man is taken to **the Pharisees,** but presumably it is to investigate the religious implications of the healing. The Pharisees may be a reflection of the council of the elders of the synagogue in John's own city. Verse 14 introduces a new detail into the story of which John has not informed us. The **sabbath** violation is less of an issue in this story than in 5:9, but it leads the discussion to more significant matters. John's narrative style sometimes includes the introduction of a particular detail only when it is immediately necessary to the story (e.g., 4:8). Healing was permitted on the Sabbath only in the cases of emergency (cf. Barrett, p. 359), and the molding of clay may have constituted kneading, also prohibited on the Sabbath (Mishnah, *Shab.* 7:2). To the Pharisees' question the man tells his experience in even more concise terms, v. 15. Again (v. 16), consideration of Jesus' act results in **division** (*schisma,* cf. 7:45-52) as was the case with the crowd (v. 9). Ironically the Pharisees' denial, **this man is not from God,** anticipates the confession of the healed man in v. 33. The precise charge as to how the healing constituted a violation of the Sabbath is not made clear (cf. v. 14 above and Brown, vol. 1, p. 373). Not surprisingly it is the wondrous character of Jesus' act (**such signs**) that causes some to defend him (out of a meager signs faith, it would appear). That **sinners** were not able to perform wonders is not attested, so far as we know (in contrast cf. Deut. 13:2-5). In v. 17 the healed man makes his second witness: **He is a prophet.** The RSV is accurate, since the definite article *the* is missing in the Greek. Hence, it is not the messiah-prophet (as in 1:21; 6:14; and 7:40) the man has in mind but only one who does wonders. Compare the words of the Samaritan woman (4:19). The wonders of Elijah and Elisha may have shaped the notion of a **prophet** as a wonder-worker.

18-21—With the **man's** confession the third scene is ended and the fourth begins (vv. 18-23)—the interrogation of the parents of the healed man. In v. 18 the interrogators suddenly become the **Jews,** a switch similar to the one in 8:13 and 22 and the opposite change found in 7:11 and 32 (cf. above). This may be an indication that John has here begun to think more of the experience of his own day than that of Jesus—an indication borne out by further evidence below. The **parents** are called in, we suppose, to settle the question of the veracity of the man's story and in hopes of escaping the dilemma posed in v. 16 (of one who could do such an act but violate the Sabbath in doing it). The two parents may be the two witnesses needed to verify the man's claims (cf. Deut. 17: 6), although John does not suppose to be describing a legal trial in this questioning. **Until** anticipates the leaders' conclusion that the man had been healed (cf. v. 24). The question they pose in v. 19 seems to assume that the man has been healed. Verses 20-21 contain the answers of the parents and understandably they can witness only to the identity of the man and not the occasion of his receiving sight. They seek to avoid involvement in the religious question by deferring to their **son. He is of age** may mean only that he is responsible for himself or that he is of the age to offer legal testimony, which was probably thirty (cf. Schnackenberg, vol. 2, p. 698, n. 30). With their statement the responsibility for making a decision regarding Jesus is thrust back on the leaders, and they are still left with the dilemma of v. 16.

22-23—We are now given further evidence that John is describing (at one level) the experience of his own community. The **parents** (who in the narrative are clearly themselves **Jews**) are said to be **afraid of the Jews.** Obviously, **Jews** connotes John's own opponents. The claim that believers should **be put out of the synagogue** is anachronistic and imposes a later situation of the church back onto the time of Jesus. **Put out of the synagogue** (*aposynagōgos genētai*) is an expression found only in John (cf. 12:42 and

16:2). The two phases of history between which John moves are indicated in the fact that the *Pharisees* are divided and undecided about what to do with believers (vv. 13-17, a condition in Jesus' own day) and that **the Jews** have already decided to put them out of the **synagogue** (v. 23, a condition of John's time). It has been proposed and is often argued that *aposynagōgos* is an allusion to the formal decision propagated by the Council of Jamnia (ca. 90 C.E.) in the "Twelfth Benediction" (*Birkath ha-Minim*), the benediction against the heretics, to the effect that Christians should not be allowed to remain in the synagogue. Furthermore, the uses of the word *aposynagōgos* reflects the occasion of the writing of the Fourth Gospel, i.e., soon after the Johannine community had suffered expulsion from the synagogue in their own community (cf. Martyn). That this is the case seems clear from this gospel. It is not, however, necessary to assume that it was a formal propagation of the benediction which occasioned the expulsion, and there is some evidence against the existence of such a benediction in the first century. More likely, the expulsion of the Johannine Christians from their home in the synagogue occurred as a result of an informal and local decision of the Jewish community (cf. Introduction above). Verse 22 may then reflect the fear among those Jews who held convictions in favor of Jesus and their concern for the consequences of their convictions should they be discovered. There is pathos in the verse arising out of the agony of both Jews and Jewish Christians divided over their views of Jesus. John was acutely aware in his own experience of the division Jesus causes (e.g., vv. 9 and 16 above).

24-27—Verse 24 introduces the next scene (vv. 24-34) which narrates the second interrogation of the formerly blind **man** by the religious authorities (this time called "the Jews," if we trace the antecedent of **they** back to v. 22). **Give God the praise** means the formal oath required before offering testimony (cf. Josh. 7:19 and 1 Esdr. 9:8) and not the injunction for the **man** to attribute his healing to God and not Jesus (cf. the TEV, "Promise before God that you will tell the truth!") **We know** (*hēmeis oidamen*) is emphatic, and **sinner** seems now to take on the character of a more formal charge (contrast v. 18 above). Verse 25 is the clever and careful response of the interrogated. Regardless of the status of the healer before the law, the fact remains that the healed man has been liberated from his darkness. He begins to emerge here as a contrast to the man healed of his illness in 5:1-18, who turns witness against his benefactor (5:11-16). The witness of the formerly blind man is based upon the experience of redemption, a fact John may want us to see as definitive of all Christian witness. Verse 26 has the markings of the judicial "grilling" of a witness in order to entrap him, but the healed man turns the entrapment against his questioners in v. 27. **Would not listen** translates what is literally "did not hear." The question with which he responds to the leaders is a rhetorical one, implying a negative answer. **Disciples** (*mathētai*) may also suggest the evangelist's own situation. The effect of these words is to make clear what has been gradually emerging: Ironically it is the leaders who are on trial here. Now they must face the decision whether to believe in Jesus or reject him.

28-34—The leaders retreat to their sense of tradition—they are **disciples of Moses** (cf. 8:31-59). With this declaration they have made their decision falsely *between* Moses and Jesus, and in this case against Jesus. The decision posed here is the tragic situation of the Christians and Jews in John's city, where embracing Christ was taken erroneously to be a rejection of Moses. **God has spoken to Moses** (v. 29) is a way of affirming his authority (e.g., Exod. 33:11), and **as for this man, we do not know where he comes from,** a way of denying the authority of Christ. The latter contradicts 7:27 where the physical origin of Jesus is known. The leaders' words, however, are intended to be a denial of Jesus' origins with the Father. The world always leans upon what it assumes it already knows and avoids the risk of faith, for faith is trusting that which may yet be unknown. Verse 30 is the more aggressive answer of the healed man in which he taunts his questioners (who are rapidly becoming the *questioned*). **Marvel** (*thaumaston*) is a high degree of surprise and amazement. The healing should inform one of the origins of Jesus. In v. 31 the healed man adopts the first person plural **we**, suggesting that he is now speaking on behalf of the Christians of the Johannine community, and what he says reflects their response to charges leveled against them by their former colleagues in the synagogue. **God does not listen to sinners** is a common Jewish/OT belief (e.g., Isa. 1:15; Ps. 66:18; Prov. 15: 29). Contrasted to **sinners** is one with two characteristics: (1) a **worshiper of God** (*theosebēs*, used only here in the NT), a characteristic common in Hellenistic literature associated with piety, and (2) one who **does his** (God's) **will,** a typically Jewish characteristic (a "most unusual" combination, says Bultmann, p. 337). In v. 32 **the man** combines the evidence that Jesus must be a good person, since God listens to him, with the marvel of the healing. His words, **never since . . . born blind,** sound like hyperbole, but there are no known claims to the healing of one who had never seen. The conclusion of the short argument comes in v. 33: Jesus must be **from God.** Nicodemus grants the same to Jesus (3:2). This constitutes the healed man's third confession, the previous being "a man" (v. 11) and "a prophet" (v. 17). This earns him the derision of the leaders (v. 34), and he is **cast . . . out.** Their charge that he was **born in utter sin** may reflect their abhorrence of those who failed to study and obey the law, but also their view that his blindness at birth was a result of his and his parents' sinfulness. The leaders are arrogant in their false sense of knowledge. **They cast him out** (*exebalon auton exō*) may be another allusion to the fate of the Johannine Christians at the hands of their alienated companions in the synagogue (cf. 6:37 above).

35-38—The sixth scene of John's drama (vv. 35-38) brings together Jesus and the healed man for the first time since the wonder. Throughout this whole discussion (vv. 8-34) Jesus has been offstage, even though he has been the central figure. In v. 35 Jesus expresses the question which has been slowly emerging in the testimony of the healed man: **Do you believe in the Son of man?** It is again **Jesus** who takes the initiative, as he did in the healing itself (v. 6). He **finds** and comes to the one who has been ejected from among the religious leaders, suggesting that Christ will not allow his followers to be alone in their distress (cf. 14-18). **The Son of man** is the preferred reading of the textual witnesses, the other being "the Son of God." The construction **Do you believe in the Son of man?** (*pisteueis eis ton huion tou anthrōpou*) is unusual for

John and occurs only here. The title is perhaps appropriate, since
in the following scene Jesus is cast in the role of God's judge, and
it is in that role (as well as in association with the passion) that John
most often uses the title **Son of man** (cf. 5:27). The man's question
in v. 36 in response to Jesus occasions the revelation of identity in
the following verse. It is not clear whether the question seeks a
definition of **Son of man** or an identification of him among others.
Sir is the proper translation here of *kyrie*, even though elsewhere
it carries the confessional meaning, "Lord" (cf. 21:15). It need not
be objected that the man should by now know Jesus' identity; that
is not the point of the question. It is rather a transition to Jesus'
declaration. **You have seen him** (v. 37) describes the loftier purpose for which the man has been given the capacity for sight. The
second part of the verse recalls 4:26 but lacks the emphatic *I am*
(*egō eimi*). Nonetheless, the words constitute a self-revelation
made more powerful by the use of the third (rather than the first)
person pronouns (**him, he**). The man's final confession (v. 38) is
simple. **Lord, I believe.** Now the *kyrie* is properly rendered **Lord.**
The man's belief is followed by his act of worship, making him the
model of both Christian faith and worship. **Worshiped** (*proseky-
nēsen*) is the proper response of humans to a theophany (e.g., 17:
3), and John uses it in 4:20-24 and 12:20 as well as here. The
Greek word can also mean to "prostrate oneself before." It is important that the man's faith, while taking its first origins from the
wondrous healing of his eyes, is finally evoked in response to Jesus'
word. In this way he is John's model of the relationship between
"signs faith" and genuine belief or "word faith." Only the revelation of Jesus' identity in word could bring the man to the point of
the real faith decision, however much his experience of the sign
might have prepared him for this moment. The man's progression
of faith is marked by his confession that Jesus is "a man" (v. 11), "a
prophet" (v. 17), "one from God" (v. 33), and finally "Lord" (v.
38) and "Son of man" (v. 35). It is now that the man has been
given sight in the full sense of that word (so far as John is concerned), for at last he is able to see spiritually and not just physically. So, too, is the contrast between him and the blindness of the
religious leaders complete. There is some textual evidence for the

omission of the words **he said** . . . through . . . **Jesus said** (vv. 38-39a). But the weight of the external evidence favors it in spite of its use of some un-Johannine expressions (e.g., *ephē* for **said** in v. 38).

39-40—The final scene of this chapter brings the inevitable confrontation between Jesus and the religious leaders. In v. 39 **Jesus** articulates the impact of the entire story. That he **came** . . . **for judgment** contradicts 3:17 (but not 5:22 and 8:15-16). **Judgment** (*krima*, used only here in John) remains the consequence of the revelation and, insofar as judgment is part of the salvific plan, it brings some to belief and some to unbelief; and thereby it accomplishes God's redemptive task. The language of v. 39, it has been suggested, is fashioned from Isaiah (in particular 29:18 and 6:10), and this presages the use of Isa. 6:9-10 in 12:40. In spite of what may appear to be a suggestion of predestination in these words, the principle at work is expressed in 3:18—rejection of the revelation constitutes its own judgment. The religious leaders have arrogantly maintained that they know the truth and hence **see**, but have in fact fallen deeper and deeper into the darkness of sightlessness. In a sense v. 39b is the Johannine version of the Synoptic saying found in Matt. 19:30 (cf. Luke 13:30). Those who claim to see are the ones blinded by the revelation, while those who are thought to be blind are given sight. The opponents, now called **Pharisees,** appear out of nowhere (v. 40) and overhear the words of Jesus. John's concern is not with the verisimilitude of his narrative but with the theological issue which is the aim of the passage. Their question to Jesus is worded so as to expect a negative answer. But they have in truth of fact understood the condemnation of them in Jesus' words.

41—This final verse underscores the Johannine concept of judgment. It occurs in reaction to the revelation. Insofar as the religious leaders *claim* that they **see** and know, they have piled **guilt** upon themselves. It is not that they are without capabilities to see and know (i.e., believe) but that they are unwilling to do so. **Guilt** is actually "sin" in the Greek (*hamartia*). **Your guilt remains** is more literally "your sin remains" (or "abides"), using *menein*. The Johannine sense is that their fundamental relationship is with that which is opposed to and separated from God. This suggests that they continue to live in the midst of their sin and define their lives out of such a posture. While the condition of their blindness is serious, it is not necessary to assert that this is the equivalent of the unforgivable sin of Mark 3:20 (cf. 1 John 5:16).

In this almost poetic chapter the theme has moved gradually from physical sight and blindness to the more serious matter of the spiritual sight and blindness involved in the human response to the revelation. This is not to say that John regards the healing of such a crippling human ailment as insignificant, only that he views it in the larger context of the overwhelming importance of a human's relationship with God. As the man healed of blindness slowly comes to the light of genuine faith, the religious leaders slowly sink further and further into the blindness of unbelief. All the while what John has been describing speaks directly to his own situation and that of his church. The man healed of blindness represents the genuine believer coming to faith in spite of those who would prevent him from doing so. The religious leaders, on the other hand, represent the members of the synagogue in John's city who fail to see in Christ the continuation of God's redemptive work in Israel. The tragic conclusion of the chapter finds the reality of unbelief even in the presence of genuine faith and discipleship. The reader has once again (cf. chap. 8) been warned of the human tendency to cling to its self-constructed security, a tendency which blinds those who think that they can see to the light of the manifestation of God in their midst.

The Discourse on Sheep and Shepherds (10:1-21)

This section continues the attack upon the blind religious leaders while affirming the special relationship between Jesus and the believers. It fits the mood of the earlier sections describing Jesus' encounters with his opponents in the temple and introduces the first of John's longer "allegories" (cf. 15:1-8). The genre is unique to John within the NT, even though there are traces of allegory in the narrative parables of the Synoptic Gospels (e.g., Mark 4:13-20). Within the larger rubric, parable (meaning simply "analogy"), there are a number of subtypes: the simple metaphor (e.g., 12:24), the narrative parable (e.g., Luke 10:30-36), and the allegory. The latter is a simple analogy which is expanded to compare one reality with another at several points. "Allegory" may not be the best term to describe this genre, but it will suffice for our purposes. John is the master of the allegorical speech. We will find that 10:1-16 is actually the weaving together of as many as four distinct allegories.

The first of the allegorical passages has to do with the access to the sheepfold (vv. 1-5). It is the shepherd of the sheep who has direct access to the sheep. The figurative use of sheep and shepherds is well known in the OT, where both David (2 Sam. 7:8) and God (e.g., Jer. 31:10) are spoken of as shepherds and the people of Israel as sheep. Furthermore, the work of the shepherd over the sheep is used to describe the eschatological work of God in the lives of the people (Isa. 40:11; Ezekiel 34; cf. 1 Enoch 85-90). It is Ezekiel 34 which may best function as a background between false rulers and the good shepherd who is at once David (Ezek. 34:23) and God in his redemptive activity.

1-3a—The allegory is introduced with the solemn pronouncement, **truly, truly,** which telegraphs a revelatory saying. There is little to tie it with the ending of chap. 9, but the reference to the **thief and robber** links the passage to the words spoken to the religious leaders in 9:41. The thought is simply that legitimate access to the sheep is the prerogative only of the shepherd. **Sheepfold** is an enclosed area in which the sheep are contained. The word *aulē* (sheepfold) can also be used of a dwelling (e.g., Mark 15:16) and a courtyard (18:15). **Door** *(thyra)* here means the gate or entryway. **Climbs in by another way** is literally "goes up from another place." Judas is described as a **thief** (12:6) and Barabbas as a **robber** (18:40). It is uncertain who was originally intended by these names, but in the present context it is the religious leaders who are those with no legitimate access to the believers who are in Christ's care. The intruders represent, however, any who would attempt to usurp leadership of the community from Christ. In v. 2 the legitimate owner of the flock is called **the shepherd. The gatekeeper** has authority over those seeking admission (v. 3). The Greek word *(thyrōros)* is used at 18:6 and Mark 13:34.

3b-5—In v. 3b the second of the allegories is taken up. In vv. 1-3a the contrast of those who have legitimate access to the sheep and those who steal their way in is made. Now the point becomes the fact that the shepherd knows his **sheep** and they **him**. It begins with the assumption that shepherds name their sheep, and develops the notion of a close relationship between the sheep and their leader. **His own** (*idia*) recalls 1:11 and implies that there are some who are Jesus' sheep and some who are not, a feature of the Johannine version of election (the "affiliation" theme). **Leads them out** may be a deliberate reference to Num. 27:17-18, the appointment of Joshua. In v. 4 **brought out** is the stronger Greek word "cast out" (*ekbalē*). **The sheep follow** (*akolouthei*) **him** hints at the "following" which is a feature of discipleship (cf. 1:37-42). That the shepherd knows the names of the **sheep** and they **know his voice** are Hebraic features—the importance of the name for identity (cf. 20:16) and the significance of listening to the divine **voice**, the spoken word of God. Verse 5 poses the contrast of the previous verse. **Strangers** are again to be taken as those who attempt to usurp Christ's rightful leadership and in the immediate context is another polemical reference to the Jewish religious leaders.

6—A mention of the listeners' lack of understanding occasions the next allegory (vv. 7-10), a typical Johannine literary feature (e.g., 8:27-28). **They** refers, presumably, to the "Jews" of v. 19 and the Pharisees of v. 40, i.e., opponents—for the most part (although disciples also fail to understand Jesus on other occasions, e.g., 12:16). **Figure** translates the word *paroimia*, a synonym for "parable" (*parabolē*). The suggestion here is that the figurative speech does not facilitate but hinders communication, and that impression is borne out by 16:25-29 where the disciples do not understand the figures (cf. Mark 4:10-12). It is not simply because his audience are not believers that they fail to understand Jesus.

7-8—The third allegory (vv. 7-10) begins again with the solemn **truly, truly,** as did the first (v. 1), and suggests the independence of this figure. The **I am** saying with the predicate **door to the sheep** surprises us, since in vv. 1-3a Jesus is the one who enters by the door. That surprise is witnessed in some textual variants which read "shepherd" instead of door. As with the Synoptic parables, the unexpected is a feature of the Johannine allegories. The meaning is an exclusive claim as the one through whom humans gain affiliation with the sheep of God, the elect community. Hence, this saying affirms what is found in other so-called exclusivistic sayings of the Johannine Jesus, especially 14:6. **All who came before . . . robbers** presents certain problems. The gnostics of the second and third centuries employed this verse as a proof-text of their rejection of the OT. That is clearly a distortion of the Johannine setting of the passage. Others have proposed that it alludes to false messianic claimants of the first century (cf. Acts 5:36-37). Still others are content to take the referent to be the Jewish religious leaders who are obviously the brunt of the attack in vv. 1 and 12f. Textual variants testify to the discomfort caused by this verse in the fact that **before me** (*pro emou*) is in some cases omitted. It may be that it is futile to look for historical figures as the referent of Jesus' words. Bultmann stresses that the language is "completely metaphorical" and that the point is "the exclusiveness and absoluteness of the revelation" (p. 376). Anyone or anything which is taken as a life-giving revelation is hereby dismissed, whether it be OT figures, Jewish messianic claimants, or Hellenistic saviors. For John's first readers no doubt the saying was a direct attack upon those who claimed that Moses and the Law contradicted Jesus' words, and hence for them **all who came before** would be the figures of the OT tradition and contemporary Jewish faith which were taken to be superior to Christ. Such could not sway the community of faith, for they were the elect who listened only to the voice of Christ.

9-10—The **I am** saying of v. 7 is repeated, omitting "of the sheep." Here the allegory with the believer is spelled out, and hence no difference between this saying and that of v. 7 is intended (cf. Barrett, p. 372, for discussion of the background of the concept of **door**). By Christ one enters the eschatological community of faith, and there is **saved. Saved** and **find pasture** are in synonymous parallelism with each other. John does not frequently use **save** (*sōzō*) as a figure for redemption (cf. 3:17; 12:47). Verse 10 poses the opposite of Christ in the figure of the **thief** (cf. v. 1 above). **Kill** translates *thyein*, not John's usual word for **kill** (*apokteinein*), and suggests the slaughtering of animals. **I came** includes the emphatic pronoun (*egō*) to sharpen the contrast with the **thief** (i.e., "*I*, on the other hand, came. . .."). John's rich arsenal of words for the benefits of the revelation is increased by one here as he has Jesus say that the revelation gives **life** (the opposite of what the **thief** brings) and gives it **abundantly** (*perisson*). With the word **abundant** he recalls the concept of the eschatological hope for plenty and abundance with the coming of the Messiah (e.g., Amos 9:13) but speaks of it in terms of a "spiritual" plenty—the full richness of **life** as intended by the creator.

11-13—In v. 11 the fourth allegory begins by picking up the suggestion of v. 2 and expanding it by a contrast with the "hireling" (v. 12). The **I am** construction occurs here for the third time (cf. vv. 7 and 9). **Good** (*kalos*) is variously translated in order to honor the fundamental sense of the word and the context as well, e.g., "ideal," "model," "beautiful," "devoted," etc. But it is intended primarily as the opposite of the hireling in v. 12. The affirmation of v. 11 is startling, however—dying for the **sheep. Lays down his life** (*tēn psychēn autou tithēsin*) is an expression unique to John (cf. 13:37; 15:13; 1 John 3:16) and implies an emphasis upon Jesus' own initiative, i.e., his willingness to die. **For** (*hyper*) is often associated with death in John (e.g., 6:51) and means "for the benefit of" (cf. Mark 14:24). While it may have sacrificial overtones, it does not intimate death in any *cultically* sacrificial sense. Now in v. 12 it is **the hireling** with whom Jesus is compared. **The hireling** (*misthōstos*), we may assume, is responsible for **the sheep,** but they are not his property, as they are the **shepherd's.** The contrast centers in this single matter—the ownership of the flock. While a historical referent is not required, John's first readers would think of the religious leaders as the hireling. It is Jesus' radical commitment to the community of believers that is stressed. **He flees** is added to the Greek by the RSV at v. 13 for clearer meaning. The Greek reads, "because he is a hireling and does not care about the sheep." For Jesus the welfare of his own is a life-and-death matter, unlike the hireling of whom no such commitment is expected.

14-15—The **I am** saying of v. 11 is repeated but moves the thought now in a different direction. Much as v. 9 repeats v. 7 in order to introduce a new but related thought, the construction of this allegory follows a similar pattern. The new focus of this verse and the next is the mutual and reciprocal knowledge between Jesus and believers. For the meaning of **know** cf. 7:27-29 above. Here the intimate relationship of knowing includes commitment and love between the two parties. The relationship between Jesus and the believer is modeled after the relationship between the Father and the Son (v. 15), as is so often the case in John (e.g., 17:11). This relationship between the believer and Jesus should not be construed as a "mystical" one in the sense that the former is absorbed into the latter, for it is a thoroughly *personal* relationship in which the integrity of the persons is preserved. Verse 15b repeats the words of v. 11b with the use of the first person pronoun I. The relationship of knowledge involves a commitment of love which makes possible the surrendering of life.

16—This verse introduces a new and somewhat troublesome thought. Who are the **other sheep** (*alla probata*)? Most commentators agree that it refers to the Gentiles in distinction to the Jewish Christians, and there is sound reason behind such interpretations. It might also be the case, however, that for John and his first readers the other sheep are other Christian congregations beyond the Johannine community. As **the sheep** of the immediate **fold** hear the shepherd's **voice** (v. 3), so too will this **other fold heed** (Greek, "will hear," *akousousin*) the voice of **the shepherd**. A strong textual witness reads "they shall be" instead of **there shall be,** but the difference is of little importance. The theme of unity is an important one in chap. 17 and expresses the Johannine hope for human oneness. It is both the unity of Jewish and Gentile believers and the unity of Johannine and other believers that John has in mind here. The flavor of the passage intimates the ingathering of peoples with the coming of the Messiah (Ezek. 34:11-16).

17-18—With v. 16 the allegories come to their conclusion, and v. 17 begins a new subunit which is a kind of excursus on vv. 11 and 15. The reason for **the Father's** loving the Son is not because the Son goes to the cross, but that the crucifixion expresses the unity of love and obedience between them. The new thought of v. 17 is found in the clause **that I may take it again.** The connective, **that** (*hina*), may suggest that the purpose of Jesus' death is the resurrection. However, in John the crucifixion and resurrection are a single event, inseparably bound together. The latter only expresses in a different way the meaning of the former. Verse 18 states the absolute autonomy of Jesus in his death. A relatively strong textual witness argues for the aorist verb, *ēren* (took), in place of *airei* (**takes**). If the former is preferred, it simply views the cross from the temporal perspective of John and his community. **Power** translates the word *exousia* and means power in the sense of "authority" or "right" (cf. TEV). Whereas the most common expressions for the resurrection in the NT imply that it is God who raised Jesus from death and not Jesus' own power (e.g., Acts 2:24), John's sense of the functional unity of the Father and Son allows him to attribute that power to Jesus. The polemical quality of these words is apparent. John and his community must respond to the charge that Jesus' death demonstrates his powerlessness and proves his messianic claims false. In response John stresses that Jesus died willingly and was not forced. Moreover, the apology would claim that his death was in obedience to God's will. **Charge** renders *entolēn*, more appropriately translated "command."

19-21—This paragraph summarizes the response of the Jews to the allegorical speech and the excursus of vv. 17-18. Now they appear to understand Jesus, unlike their reaction in v. 6. As so often the case, there is **division among the Jews** regarding Jesus' words (e.g., 7:12). The charge that Jesus is possessed by a **demon and . . . is mad** (the two comprise one assertion) is posed over against the marvel of his healing (cf. 7:20; 8:48, 52; and 9:16 above). This little interlude seems clearly to be an editorial transition by the evangelist to move to a new section.

The first half of chap. 10 is a masterful piece of work, even if it is sometimes perplexing. The differing allegories and the author's switching back and forth between the metaphor and his point are at times confusing. Nonetheless, the four allegorical bits bombard the reader relentlessly with imagery that is provocative and moving. John surely here intends to force the reader to consider all that is said of Jesus in such a short space. It is doubtless true that John has knit together a series of metaphors, each of which had an independent life of its own. But he has done so deliberately and effectively. Along with the independence of each allegory we find interlacing among the four. The first (vv. 1-3a) is interlaced with the third (vv. 7-10) by the use of "truly, truly" to introduce each (vv. 1 and 7), "door" (vv. 1 and 7), and "thief and robber" (vv. 1 and 8). The first is linked with the fourth (vv. 11-16) by the use of "shepherd" (vv. 2 and 11). The second is tied with the fourth by the word "voice" (vv. 3b and 16). The third and fourth are interlaced by the use of the **I am** sayings in each (vv. 7, 9, and 11). The composite nature of the section is obvious, but so too is the care with which they have been merged. Collectively they make a number of related points: (1) Jesus' exclusive and intimate relationship with his community; (2) his sole claim to leadership of that group; (3) his person as the singular means of access to the eschatological community in which there is salvation; and (4) his radical commitment to those of that community.

The Encounter at the Feast of Dedication (10:22-42)

This major section (7:1—10:42) is concluded with one final encounter in Jerusalem between Jesus and his opponents. John 10: 22-42 functions to bring the series of allegories to bear directly upon the opponents (e.g., vv. 26-29). Furthermore, it climaxes the temple discourses with the issue of Jesus' identity with the Father (v. 30) and sets the stage for the death plot which arises out of the raising of Lazarus in chap. 11.

22-24—Verse 22 gives us the first indication of time since the beginning of the temple discussion at 7:2 (the feast of Tabernacles, a fall event, approximately October). We are now told it is the **feast of Dedication,** which was the celebration of the rededication of the temple in the midst of the Maccabean revolution, ca. 165 B.C.E. It recalled the restoration of the temple after its desecration by Antiochus Epiphanes IV, and was also called *Hanukkah,* usually observed in December. Its symbolism does not explicitly appear in the discussion which follows, although it may be that this encounter is intended to be the prelude to Jesus' dedication as the new temple. The temple of Herod the Great was surrounded by porticoes, the one on the eastern side dedicated to **Solomon** (v. 23). Jesus' audience is identified in v. 24 only as **the Jews,** which most often but not always denotes opponents (e.g., 9:22 above). Their question poses a translation problem: **Keep us in suspense** is literally "our soul (life breath) take away (or raise)" *(tēn psychēn hēmōn aireis)*. In brief the problem is whether or not the expression implies purely suspense or hostility. That is, does it imply that the questioners are honestly open to the answer or have they already made up their minds? Most commentators and translators favor the former, as does the RSV. While previous discourses have constantly had as their subject Jesus' identity (e.g., 8:12ff.), now for the first time the question is put directly, **If you are the Christ, tell us plainly.** The request implies an honest inquiry. **Plainly** *(parrēsia)* is often used by John in the sense of clarity, as it is here (cf. 11:14; 16:25, 29) and elsewhere to mean "publicly" or "openly" (e.g., 7:13; 18:20). The request is similar to the one found in the trial scenes in the Synoptics (Matt. 26:63; Mark 14:61; Luke 22:67) and gives the discussion the tone of a trial. It also reinforces our impression that John views the whole of Jesus' dialogs with opponents as a trial.

25-28—Jesus' response in v. 25 seems true but evasive. He has in the past affirmed his special relationship with God (e.g., 6:51-52), and the response has been unbelief. But **Jesus,** in this gospel as in the Synoptics (cf. the trial scenes cited above), seems reluctant to embrace the title **Christ** as it is found on the lips of unbelievers. His **works** *(ta erga)* have reinforced his words which informed others of his identity. It is the **works** done **in my Father's name** which show Jesus' functional unity with the Father (cf. 5:43; 17:6). For the witnesses to Jesus cf. 5:31-40 above. Verse 26 brings the allegories of vv. 1-16 to bear upon the audience. They **do not believe because** *(hoti)* they are not part of Jesus' flock. This is another of John's hints that belief and unbelief are determined by one's affiliation (cf. 8:23 above). It is obvious that for John belief and unbelief are ultimately rooted in God's acts and peoples' alliances. Verse 27 repeats the themes of vv. 3, 4, 15, and 16, and introduces vv. 28-30, the subject of which is "the safety of the sheep" (Lindars, p. 369). Verse 28a states the benefits extended to the sheep in a positive and a negative way. **Eternal life** is another way of expressing v. 10 (cf. 3:14-16 above). **Never perish** is the enduring quality of that life. **Perish** *(apollymi)* has the sense of "to

be lost," and hence v. 28b follows logically from 28a. Unlike the
fate of the sheep left in the hands of the hireling (v. 12), the believers cannot be taken from Jesus (a similar thought is found in
17:12). The point is that each believer is infinitely precious to
God, an idea expressed elsewhere in other ways (e.g., Luke 15:1-
10).

29-30—Verse 29 is crippled with textual problems too complicated to review here. In summary, the different readings center on
the gender of **who** (*ho* or *hos*) and **greater** (*meizon* or *meizōn*) and
represent a total of five variations. The final decision comes down
to whether it is **my Father** who is greater or that which is given to
Jesus (i.e., the sheep)—cf. the RSV text and its marginal reading
(Barrett provides a detailed analysis of the problem, pp. 381-382).
Although the problem is beyond resolution, it does seem that the
RSV affords a clear meaning and fits the context. It is the Father's
greatness that insures that the believers cannot be taken away
from Christ. If he holds the believer fast, there is nothing that can
separate them (cf. Rom. 8:35-39). In v. 28 it is Jesus' **hand** that secures the believers, and in v. 29 the **Father's hand.** This implies
the *functional* unity of the Father and the Son which is explicitly
stated in v. 30. It is not to be supposed that John in v. 30 has made
a statement of the metaphysical or ontological unity of the Father
and the Son. **One** (*hen*) is neuter and has sometimes been taken to
mean "in the same category." It is the oneness of will with the Father which is the concern here. In terms of the revelation Christ
brings to the world, he functions in unity with the Father. The unity of essence or nature may be *inferred* from this statement, but it
cannot be defended as John's intended meaning.

31-33—The reaction is again an impulse **to stone** Jesus, as in 8:
59 (cf. above). It is this action which **Jesus answered** in v. 32. The
good works ought to have impressed the audience. This response
suggests that mighty deeds should open the way to faith, even
though they are inadequate in themselves as a basis for faith. **Good**
translates *kala*, the word used to characterize the shepherd in vv.
11 and 14, the wine made from water in 2:10, and now the works
given to Jesus by God (here and v. 33). The sense of "ideal" or
"model" may not be far from John's mind. **From the Father** (*ek*

tou patros) suggests that his mighty deeds are done by virtue of his unique relationship with God. Christ is not a wonder-worker who does his miracles out of his own power. Jesus is for the first time in this gospel formally accused of **blasphemy** in v. 33, although the charge is implied in 8:59. The charges of blasphemy in the Gospels (cf. Matt. 26:65; Mark 14:64) are not clearly in accord with what is known of the Jewish laws regarding the matter. The Mishnah (*Sanh.* 7:5) limits blasphemy to the utterance of the sacred name for God (YHWH). It may be supposed, however, that in the Jewish-Christian dialogs of the first century the claims for the divine authority of Jesus were construed to be blasphemous. Therefore, the setting for v. 33 may be more akin to John's situation than that of Jesus. Christ's hearers take his words to mean he intends to **make** himself **God.** In a strange twist of irony the Jews have taken the words of Jesus in v. 30 literally, and hence misunderstand him but, on the other hand, are correct in their inference insofar as John *does* believe that Jesus is God (1:1 and 20:28). The scene resembles the religious trial of Jesus as it is recorded in the Synoptics (Matt. 26:57-75; Mark 14:53-72; and Luke 22:54, 63-71) and may in fact be in the back of John's mind (although there is little evidence of a dependence on the Synoptics themselves). Such a possibility indicates that for John the whole of Jesus' encounters with the religious leaders is a kind of trial scene.[16]

34—This verse begins the rather strange argument of **Jesus** in response to the charge of blasphemy. It involves two parts: The first in vv. 34-36 is an argument from Scripture, and the second in vv. 37-38 is based on the mighty deeds Jesus has done. In v. 34 **your law** presents two problems. Does Jesus (and/or John) intend by **your** to separate himself from the Torah (cf. 8:17 above)? **Your** is textually weak and most likely is a scribal addition. The second problem is that **Jesus** is about to quote a psalm but is made to refer to it as part of the **law.** It was apparently, however, a common practice to call other sacred writings **law,** as the evidence of the NT itself shows (e.g., 15:25; 1 Cor. 14:21). The psalm cited here is 82:6, in which God speaks to unjust judges, calling them **"gods"** and "sons of the Most High" but assuring them nonetheless that they "shall die like men."

35-36—Jesus' argument is that, if these persons can be called gods without blasphemy, therefore he is not liable to such a charge. Even though such an argument seems fallacious to us and an abuse of Scripture, such reasoning was a common rabbinic practice. Another dimension of Jesus' use of these judges follows the line of reasoning from the smaller to the greater (cf. 7:21-24): If the judges were ones **to whom the word of God came** and could therefore be called gods, then Jesus who is God's word is entitled to speak of himself as God. The parenthetical remark **scripture cannot be broken** (*lythēnai*) means that the instructions of Scripture must not be violated (cf. the use of "break," *lyein*, in 8:23). Verse 36 brings the first argument to a close. Jesus describes himself in two ways: **consecrated** and **sent into the world.** The latter is a familiar expression in John (e.g., 5:36, 38; 11:42), but the former is not. Jesus prays that the disciples will be consecrated (17:17) and consecrates himself (17:19), but only here uses that word (*hagiazō*) to describe himself. Its fundamental meaning is "to set apart for special use" and here signifies the manner in which Jesus has been "set apart" for his divine mission. Numbers 7 speaks of Moses' dedication of the tabernacle and may have been one of the readings for the feast of Dedication. The LXX uses *hagiazō* to speak of that act. It is possible that for reasons of its association with the feast John uses **consecrated** in this context. The title **Son of God** (*huios tou theou*) surprises us here, since it is not used in v. 30. It is, of course, implied by that verse and suggested by the psalm quoted in v. 34 which speaks of the judges as "sons of the Most High" (on **Son of God** cf. 1:34 above). Jesus' unique relationship with God claims for him status as God and Son of God.

37-38—The second argument begins at v. 37, reasoning that Jesus' wonders demonstrate he has a unique relationship with God. Verse 37 appeals to the theme of vv. 32-33 and invites the listeners to disregard his wonders, if they can, and refuse to **believe** (an imperative, *pistuete*). Verse 38 explores the opposite. If Jesus' **works** are God's, then let that be a basis for a believing response. **Know and understand** translates *gnōte kai ginōskēte.* The connection of an aorist subjunctive and a present subjunctive here means "know and keep on knowing" (over a period of time).

Scribes must have thought the two to be redundant, and therefore substituted "believe" for **understand**. The knowledge which is a part of faith is an ongoing growth, just as believing itself is a process. There is a note of desperate appeal in these words, which may arise from the efforts of the Johannine community to evangelize among the Jews. **That the Father is in me and I am in the Father** constitutes the third of the self-affirmations in our passage. The first is "I and the Father are one" (v. 30) and the second "the Son of God" (v. 36). This third affirmation makes clear that for John the meaning of the first two is found in the personal relationship of mutual indwelling of **the Father and the Son**. Here John uses his alternative expression **in** instead of "abide" (*menein*, cf. 14:10; 17:21). The affirmation is stated in such a way as to imply that belief in a creed is in mind, i.e., **know and understand** *that* (*hoti*, cf. 14:10). Such a view is not unknown in this gospel (cf. 11: 27, 42), and it is clear that John saw a close relationship between the personal trust in Jesus (**believe** "in") and statements about Jesus (**believe** "that"). Here, however, the "belief that" serves as the foundation upon which a more personal faith might arise (cf. 4:50 above). Just as signs faith is but a preliminary stage of believing, so too here (at least) what is sought is merely an openness to Jesus which creates opportunity for faith.

39—The discussion is now ended and the whole of the encounters in the temple brought to a conclusion. This verse restates the attempt to arrest Jesus found in 7:30, 32, and 40 and ends the episode on the somber note of unbelief and opposition. The whole of the temple discourses, then, seems to produce no faith.

40-42—This paragraph is an editorial transition to the next scene. Jesus moves out of the especially dangerous region of Jerusalem **across the Jordan** east into Perea, part of the area ruled by Herod Antipas, the tetrarch. John 1:28 speaks of the area in which the baptizer worked as "Bethany beyond the Jordan." Verse 39 does not encourage us to think of a popular following for Jesus, but vv. 41 and 42 clearly do, at least in the region east of the Jordan. The **many** may be those attracted by the ministry of the baptizer. Again the focus is the signs. The baptizer is reduced once again to only a witness (cf. 1:19ff. above), one who was not empowered to do wonders to confirm his words. But the **many** (*polloi*) understand that the baptizer's words are borne out by the ministry of Jesus, even though the baptizer's promises that Jesus would take away the sin of the world and baptize with the Spirit (1:29, 33) are not yet realized. The openness to faith on the part of the residents of this locale is to be contrasted with the failure to believe on the part of the Jews of Jerusalem. However, we are not told precisely who the **many** of v. 42 are and why they **believed.** But John ends this section on an upbeat, in order to clear the way for the remarkable sign of the raising of Lazarus.

John 10:22-42 is an appropriate conclusion to the long midsection of the gospel which finds Jesus in dialog with the opponents on their own ground, the temple. This is the case because it so well articulates the question of the identity of Jesus and relates it to the matter of Jesus' wonders. It is these two matters and their close association which will be addressed vividly by the narrative in chap. 11.

■ Casting the Die (11:1—12:50)

In chaps. 11 and 12 we reach the climax of the first half of the gospel and are skillfully directed into the concluding half. While these chapters are a transition from the focus on the revelation of glory in Jesus' ministry to that of the glorification of the Son, they are at the same time one of the richest sections of this gospel. It is here that we find the climactic sign of the resurrection of Lazarus, the anointing at Bethany, and the scene which signals the coming of the long-awaited "hour." Taken as a whole, however, they function to bring to its crescendo the efforts of the religious leaders to take Jesus' life. Here the twin forces which result in the crucifixion—the death plot against Jesus and his own willingness to lay down his life—converge to bring to reality that which has lurked within the plot line from the very first of the gospel, even the prolog. The revelation meets with opposition and hostility of such a kind that the revealer's life is to be taken. But the taking of that life is the apex of the revelation itself.

The Sign of the Resurrection of Lazarus (11:1-44)

The subject of the signs and the faith they evoke has been a constant theme in the previous chapters. Now John narrates for us the grandest of the signs, but paradoxically will tell us in the next subunit that that sign elicits the death plot against Jesus. The story in vv. 1-44 is filled with dramatic action and rich symbolism. As we saw in chap. 9, John exploits the wondrous acts for their symbolic value, and the resurrection of Lazarus is no exception. Lazarus is brought from death to life, and that is surely important. But this tale is also the enactment of the fact that Christ brings life to humanity in its fullest sense, life understood as a symbol for the benefits of the revelation.

1-4—The first paragraph is the dramatic and suspenseful setting for the narrative. Verse 1 introduces the cast of the drama and its locale. The name **Lazarus** is mentioned outside of chap. 11 and 12:1 only in Luke (16:19-31). The name in Hebrew means "God helps," but there seems to be no effort on the part of the evangelist to use that etymology. **Bethany** is a reference to Bethany of Judea, not (apparently) to the village in Perea mentioned in 1:28. **Martha** and **Mary** are mentioned only in Luke 10:38-42 outside of this gospel. While these connections with Luke are interesting, it is very difficult to prove by them a knowledge of the third gospel on the part of John. Verse 2 is a parenthetical comment to link Mary with the anointing to be related in 12:1-8 and uses the language of that narrative (e.g., **anointed, ointment**). **Lord** in this case appears to be a title for Jesus (not a simple "sir" as it is in v. 3) and is unusual for John. It may be that v. 2 is a later gloss added to clarify for the reader the identity of Mary. In v. 3 Jesus is informed of Lazarus' illness, and a link of affection between him and Lazarus is established. **He whom you love** is the basis for the suggestion that it is Lazarus who is the "beloved disciple" mentioned later (e.g., 13:23 and 19:26). While this is the best internal evidence of the identity of the mysterious disciple, such a conclusion is purely speculation. **Love** here and in v. 36 is *phileō* but *agapaō* in v. 5. This shows the likelihood that John used the two words for love interchangeably. Verse 4 assures the readers that Lazarus' **death** is not final. Instead, the presence of **God** in his redeeming activity will be demonstrated by these circumstances. John tells his readers what to expect. **Jesus** will by this mighty deed reveal **the glory of God** but will also **be glorified.** In the resurrection of Lazarus we have a bridge between the two parts of the gospel: Jesus reveals glory but, in anticipation of the crucifixion-resurrection, also receives glory. This sign foreshadows the glorification of Jesus himself. **Son of God** is unusual as a self-designation on the lips of Jesus (but cf. 5:25; 10:36). On the title itself cf. 1:49 above. There is some evidence that **Son** was the original reading.

5-7—The necessity of v. 5 is doubtful, unless it is to reassure the reader of **Jesus'** love in spite of the delay in going to the scene mentioned in v. 6. But that delay is all the more puzzling because of Jesus' affection for **Lazarus.** It would seem to find its place in the story for two reasons: (1) It has sheer dramatic power, lifting the suspense of the narrative. (2) But it is still another of those incidences in which John depicts Jesus' acting solely out of his own determination and not that of humans (cf. 2:4; 4:48; and 7:2-10 above). It may therefore fit that scheme of request/refusal/compliance evidenced in those passages. (The suggestion that his delay represents the delay of the parousia is ingenious but hardly Johannine.) Verse 7 concludes that delay and makes clear that Jesus' decision to go to Bethany is his own, unforced by human pressures. The **two days** does not appear to have a symbolic role.

8-10—We are reminded of the dangers inherent in going to Judea. If the delay of two days heightened the suspense of the story with regard to the welfare of Lazarus, this conversation increases the suspense with regard to **Jesus'** welfare. These verses are comparable in structure to 4:35-38 and betray one of John's narrative techniques. In both 4:35-38 and here the evangelist interrupts the flow of the story with a brief discussion between Jesus and **the disciples** which in both cases includes a short parable. **Seeking to stone you** channels into the episode the dangers explicated in 10: 31. Jesus acts in full knowledge of the consequences of his decision, and the subsequent events in Judea are not unexpected. The little metaphor of walking in **the day** and in **the night** (vv. 9-10) is both very simple and very complex. It is comprised of an introductory question (v. 9a, the common division of daylight into **twelve hours**) and two balanced lines (vv. 9b and 10) which form an antithetical parallelism. The metaphor is founded on the obvious fact that travel is possible during the daylight and nearly impossible at night. On one level, its meaning is simply that the time for Jesus' ministry is limited, and he must act while there is still time to do so. On another level, however, it is more complicated Johannine theology. **Jesus** is the **light of this world** (8:12) by which humans may live (**walk**, *peripateō*); and without the light (cf. 1:15) of the revelation humans will **stumble** (cf. Isa. 8:14) and lack an inner light which leads them through life. John could hardly have used these words without implying their deeper symbolism. **The light is not in him** apparently alludes to the concept that sight is possible by means of light coming from within the person, possibly that exterior light is absorbed and then emitted. Its symbolic meaning is that one who does not embrace the light of the revelation has no light in him or her.

11-13—Following the little excursus on light, v. 11 reintroduces the concern for **Lazarus. Our friend** (*philos*) indicates Lazarus' place within the "family" of Jesus and the disciples. *Philos* may mean Christian (cf. 15:13-15). **Sleep** is a common metaphor for death in the NT (e.g., 1 Cor. 15:6) and in classical Greek literature (e.g., *Iliad* 11). The metaphor is transparent—Lazarus is dead, but for Jesus Lazarus' resurrection is but an awakening from **sleep** because Jesus holds power over life and death. As clear as the passage is to the reader, it is equally unclear to **the disciples!** Verse 12 is another use of the technique of misunderstanding. As is the case elsewhere (e.g., 3:4 and 4:31-33), the disciples interpret Jesus' words in a literal fashion, and their response is foolish and even humorous. They suggest that Lazarus should be allowed to sleep so that **he will recover. Recover** translates the verb *sōzesthai* (literally, "he will be saved"), which is often used in the NT to mean recovery of healing (e.g., Mark 5:15). But it also conveys its other meaning of redemption. There may then be a kind of subtle irony in the disciples' misunderstanding. They entirely miss Jesus' meaning but in their words they unconsciously articulate his thought—Lazarus will be "saved." It should be noted, however, that "save" is used in John in its redemptive sense only four times—3:17; 5:34; 10:9; and 12:47. Verse 13 is John's clarification of Jesus' meaning in case the reader is unsure as the disciples are.

14-16—Jesus corrects his followers, telling them explicitly that **Lazarus is dead.** For **plainly** cf. 10:24 above. He continues in v. 15 to state that what is about to happen is for their benefit. The Greek construction is a bit clumsy. **That you may believe** is a parenthetical comment. The implication is that, if Jesus had been **there,** he could have prevented Lazarus' death, a point made in faith by Martha and Mary below in vv. 21 and 32. The notion that faith should arise from the experience of witnessing Lazarus' resurrection is consistent with some of the views of signs throughout this gospel (e.g., 2:11) and with the thought of v. 4. **Thomas'** courageous words in v. 16 conclude the dialog. The Aramaic name rendered **Thomas** means "twin," and hence John gives us the

Greek translation, *didymos*, **twin.** It is possible that **twin** is only the meaning of his name and not an indication that Thomas was a twin. (All speculation that he was Jesus' or Judas' twin has no foundation in this gospel.) He is mentioned three times elsewhere in John (14: 5; 20:24f.; and 21:2) but is found only in lists of the disciples in the Synoptics (Matt. 10:3; Mark 3:18; and Luke 6:15). His words reflect a still further use of irony. He does not understand the nature of Jesus' death and yet speaks the truth that discipleship does mean, for many of this little band of followers, martyrdom.

17-19—The fact that **Lazarus** has been **in the tomb four days** is made to assure the reader that **Jesus'** friend is truly dead and to prepare her or him for the exceeding marvel of Jesus' deed (cf. the way John does the same thing in 9:1 above). Jewish thought of the time held that there might be opportunity for resuscitation before the fourth day, since the spirit of the deceased hovered around the grave for three days before departing for its abode in Sheol (Bultmann, p. 400, n. 8). Hence, Lazarus, beyond question, is dead, and the process of decay has begun (v. 30). This is another example of the way John heightens the marvelous quality of Jesus' signs. Let there be no doubt that this is a genuine resurrection and not a resuscitation (contrast Matt. 9:18-25)! It could be that in the dialog with their opponents the Johannine Christians were confronted with the accusation that Jesus' wonders were not extraordinary and that John is attempting to respond to that view. Verse 18 places **Bethany** near **Jerusalem** for two likely reasons: (1) It accounts for the presence of "Jews" from Jerusalem (vv. 19 and 45) coming to console Mary and Martha, and (2) it makes explicit the intense danger for Jesus. **Two miles** is literally 15 stadia. A stadium is the Greek measurement of approximately 200 yards. In v. 19 **the Jews** means simply residents of Jerusalem and not necessarily hostile opponents of Jesus. **Many** suggests that there was a large crowd to witness Jesus' wonder. Mourning followed the actual burial in Palestine, since the burial occurred soon after death. **Console** translates the word *paramythēsōntai*, which is not common in Christian literature but occurs in 1 Thess. 2:11; 5:14; and 4:18. This sets the stage for the large group of mourners mentioned in v. 33.

20-22—Martha is the first to meet Jesus. **Mary sat in the house**—sitting was the common posture for mourning (Job 2:13). John has two separate conversations with the sisters in order to increase the opportunity for Jesus' speaking and to lengthen the narrative and hence strengthen the suspense. Martha's greeting in v. 21 is a statement of faith and shows that she is a believer, even though her belief will grow in the course of this story. While her words recall Jesus' own in v. 15, they nonetheless express a hint of resentment that Jesus did not act in time to save her brother. Still, v. 22 reaffirms her confidence in Jesus. Our faith is not without feelings of anger in times of crisis. Martha's vague confidence (cf. 14:13-14) will be confirmed and transformed by the subsequent events.

23-24—Jesus' remark in v. 23 directs the conversation to a more specific hope for resurrection. His words express a general and vague hope for life beyond death. They may refer to resurrection on the last day, as Martha understands them in the next verse, or the wonder about to occur as Lazarus is called out of the tomb. The latter is the meaning John implied in the words. **Martha affirms her faith in the resurrection at the last day** (v. 24; cf. 5:28-29), but there is an implied tone which suggests that such hope in a far-off event is of little comfort for now. The inadequacy of that hope for a final resurrection is precisely what will be corrected in the present reality of Jesus' act of raising Lazarus. The resurrection at the final time was a common Jewish belief held by the Pharisees and others influenced by Jewish apocalypticism and was taken over by the early Christians. **At the last day** (*en tē eschatē hēmera*) is a Johannine expression found elsewhere (6:39, 40 44, 54; 12:48) but not beyond John, although the plural "last days" is frequent in other NT literature (e.g., Acts 2:17). Why John prefers the singular (day) is not clear. Might it intend to echo the prophetic concept of the "day of the Lord" (*yom YHWH*, e.g., Amos 5:18; 9:11)?

25-26a—Another **I am** saying with the predicate (cf. 6:35, 51; 8:12; 10:7, 9, 11, 14 above) occurs. **Resurrection** translates *anastasis*, the root word used in these verses as well as vv. 23, 24 and 5:29 and 6:39-45. It is also used once of Jesus' own resurrection

(20:9). *Egeirein* in the passive is the more common NT word for **Je-sus'** resurrection (e.g., 2:22 and Acts 3:15; 4:10). **And the life** (*zōē*) is missing in some important textual witnesses. Its addition is easier to explain than its omission, even though external evidence favors its presence. While it is most likely that it was an addition by scribes to produce a balance with the next lines, its absence does not alter the essential meaning of the statement. As opposed to the belief that resurrection occurs in that distant "last day," Jesus' very presence means resurrection. Where Jesus is, there death has already been overcome, and life (in its rich symbolic Johannine meaning) is present. **He who believes in me** (*ho pisteuon eis eme*) is the Johannine construction meaning a personal, trusting relationship with Jesus. **Though he die** insists that the believer is not immune to death but must face it as do all humans. But it is not the final word for the believer. In spite of death, **yet shall he live.** Verse 26 adds in parallelism the same thought worded differently. **Lives and believes** are near synonyms, since embracing the revelation of God in Christ (believing) yields the result of life in the sense of the quality of existence intended by God and not threatened by death. **Shall never die,** however, seems to contradict "though he die" in the previous verse. It appears that a subtle change in the meaning of **die** has occurred between the two verses. In v. 25 it seems to mean the experience of *physical* death, while in this verse it carries the sense of *spiritual* death or death which lies in the failure to believe. The believer experiences the physical reality of death but has been saved from the spiritual death which is part of the realm of darkness and unbelief (cf. 6:49-50 for the same double use of **die**).

26b-27—In addition to Martha's belief in the resurrection of the last day, she is now asked to **believe this.** What she is about to witness is the truth of Jesus' pronouncement, but Martha must understand that Lazarus' resurrection is an expression of the new reality of which Jesus speaks. She is asked *first* to trust Jesus' words and *then* to see them documented in the sign. This is still another of John's subtle means of elevating "word faith" above "signs faith" (cf. 4:50-53 above). In v. 27 Martha makes her grand confession. Although she does not yet fully understand the implications of Jesus' words for her brother's condition (cf. v. 39), she confesses her faith in his identity. The expression, **I believe that** (the perfect with *hoti*) indicates that she trusts Jesus (the sense of "believes" in vv. 25 and 26) and goes beyond that to embrace a statement of his identity. Again, we have an instance where creedal faith arises in close association with faith as a personal relationship with Jesus (cf. 10:38 above). Martha's words sound very much like a formal creed and might possibly reflect such a creed used in John's church. Her words are comparable to 20:31, where the evangelist states the purpose of his writing, and are similar to Peter's confession (6:69). It is important that John puts this high Christological confession on the lips of a female disciple. This reflects his high regard for the role of women in the church (cf. 20: 11-18 below). She uses three titles, which in effect all affirm the same thing: **Christ, the Son of God, he who is coming into the world.** They reflect the titles traditionally associated with messianic belief (cf. 1:41, 49 and 10:24f. and 36). The last of the three has roots in the primitive Christian confession (e.g., Mark 11:9) and may be associated with the Mosaic-prophet concept of Messiah (cf. 6:14). Hence, the three taken together gather up the range of expressions used to affirm Jesus' identity as the Messiah and the fulfillment of God's promise. Clearly John presents Martha to his readers as a paradigm of Christian faith in the face of that which they do not entirely understand. So, too, for us she demonstrates the manner in which creeds enable us to hold fast to faith even when we do not yet fully comprehend what God is about to do.

28-32—Verse 28 concludes the conversation with Martha and sets up the discussion with Mary. It is not clear why Martha speaks **quietly** to **her sister.** The word *lathra* means "secretly" or "in private." Is it that Jesus wants to speak to Mary alone? **Teacher** is a subdued title given Martha's confession in the previous verse, but it is a noble title in John's view, as 20:16 witnesses. **Calling for you** is not a part of the conversation between Jesus and Martha to which the reader has been privy. In v. 29 Mary acts as a model disciple and comes at her Lord's beckoning. **Went to him** (*ērcheto pros auton*) may have symbolic meaning for coming to faith, but such is not clear. Verse 30 is not entirely understandable in terms of the narrative either, but it again prolongs the delay in rescuing Lazarus. If John intends for us to understand that Jesus wanted to speak with **Mary** privately, v. 31 shows that it was not possible. By **the Jews** coming with Mary, however, the scene is set for the wondrous act. **Weep** (*klausē*) means to wail and is used too of Mary Magdalene in 20:11,15. John is constructing a scene which is filled with the realism of mourning. In v. 32 Mary assumes a posture of respect and pleading, a token of her faith in Jesus. She repeats the exact words of her sister in v. 21, perhaps an indication that John would have us understand that the entirety of Jesus' conversation with Martha is repeated with Mary.

33—This verse poses a classical problem of both translation and theology. At the sight of Mary's **weeping** and that of **the Jews**, Jesus is (first) **deeply moved in spirit** and (second) **troubled.** The first of those expressions, **deeply moved,** translates *enebrimēsato,* which is customarily used of anger (Mark 1:43; 14:5; and Matt. 9:30, cf. Dan. 11:30, LXX), A variety of translations may be found, each of which shies away from the obvious sense of anger (e.g., "his heart was touched," TEV; "he sighed heavily," NEB; and "said in great distress," JB). A textual variant exists which also attempts to lessen the evidence of anger in the expression: "was troubled *as if* angry." The difficulty is the matter of at what or whom Jesus is angry. A range of suggestions has been made by modern commentaries, but the simplest solution seems to be that Jesus is made angry by the destructive force of death among humans. That is, he is angry at the reality of death that produces such suffering and pain as he witnesses in the sisters and their guests. The Creator is repulsed and horrified at the way in which death and suffering distort the goodness of creation and mangle the lives of humans.

The second term, **troubled,** is literally "troubled himself" (*etarazen heauton*). The same verb is found in 12:27 and 13:21 where it expresses respectively Jesus' feelings with regard to his impending suffering and his betrayal by Judas. However, it is linked here so closely with the setting and with the previous verb that we must conclude that sorrow and pain at the sight of the mourners is intended. These two expressions, along with the recurrence of **deeply moved** (in anger) v. 38 and the tears shed in v. 35, demonstrate the realism of Jesus' humanity for John and/or the passionate nature of his divinity. While there is much in this gospel to stress Jesus' divine distinction from humans, there are passages such as these which witness to the thoroughgoing incarnation (cf. 2:15-16; 4:7; 12:27; 19:28). These then are *human* feelings of the one who is the Word made real flesh and blood. But they are more. They are expressions of the agony stirred within God by human suffering. Jesus' tortured emotions are those of the Father moved by the ravaging of humanity by pain and death. The passionate God of the Christian faith suffers when his creation suffers.

34-37—In v. 34 Jesus asks to be taken to the grave and is led there. The powerful emotions of the moment are articulated in the simple words **Jesus wept** (v. 35). The verb is *dakryō*, meaning "to shed tears," and not *klaiō*, the word used of the wailing of the mourners (v. 31). We may assume that these are tears arising from the deeply felt anger and sorrow, a combination not unusual in situations of mourning. John is forcefully suggesting that the God who holds power to lift humans from the clutches of death nonetheless shares the pain of bereavement and loss. Verses 36 and 37 present two reactions of the crowd to Jesus' emotions. The first is to conclude rightly that Jesus **loved** Lazarus. But the observers state more than they mean, for Jesus' love for Lazarus and all humans far exceeds the tears of the moment. Indeed, he loves so deeply that he will lay down his life for humanity (cf. 15:13). The second reaction restates the words of Mary and Martha (vv. 21 and 32), and poses the question of why Jesus did not try to save his friend. There is an element of misunderstanding in this reaction, for the speakers do not realize what Jesus is about to do. Their words once again have the effect of tightening the suspense of the narrative.

38-41a—Verse 38 reiterates the anger of **Jesus** as he approached the grave; he is **deeply moved** (cf. v. 33 above). The Greek adds "in himself" which is synonymous with "in spirit" of v. 33. Natural caves were often used for graves; they were then covered with a **stone.** The command of Jesus in v. 39a comes unexpectedly. One of the results of the emphasis upon the feelings of Jesus in vv. 33-35 is to conceal his intentions so that now the first step of the wonder catches the reader off guard. **Martha** is reintroduced at this point as **the sister of the dead man** which seems redundant in the light of the earlier part of the narrative and may suggest that John has at this point returned to his source which did not include the earlier conversations of Jesus with the sisters. A primitive form of embalming was used, as is evident from v. 44, but it was insufficient to preserve the body for as long as **four days.** That Lazarus **has been dead four days** (cf. v. 17 above) stresses the magnitude of the wonder about to be done—Lazarus is truly dead. Martha's reaction need not be taken as a failure of the faith she expressed in v. 27, for she had no idea what Jesus' immediate act would be. It is not necessary to suppose she thinks Jesus wants to view the deceased. Jesus' response in v. 40 pulls together vv. 4 and 25-26; Martha is about to see **the glory of God** as Jesus enacts his statement of v. 26. There is a qualification, however—**if you would believe.** This statement hints that **the glory of God** is seen in Jesus' actions only through the eyes of faith. That is the evangelist's view of signs. That the signs *evoke* faith is more likely the view of his source (e.g., 2:11), but John allows both views to stand side by side because both are in a sense true. The wonder does cause a kind of faith, but faith is required to see the wonder in its fullest sense as an expression of **the glory of God** (cf. 1:14).

41b-44—The wondrous act is now described. The prayer of Jesus in vv. 41b-42 is typical of the prayers in this gospel (cf. 12:27; 17:1-26), for they suggest that the relationship between the **Father** and the Son is one continuous prayer. **Lifted up his eyes** suggests that the common posture for prayer among the Jewish people was to stand and look up (e.g., Luke 18:13), and that is also the common posture for Jesus' own praying on a number of occasions (cf. 17:1 and Mark 6:41). The words **thou hast heard me** reflect Jesus' confidence that his desire to bring Lazarus to life has already been heard long before it is articulated. The relationship between Jesus and the Father includes a continuous "hearing" (v. 42a). The prayer is itself done for the sake of the crowd, not that they might be impressed by Jesus' piety, but that they might be prepared for what is about to happen and understand that it is God who is being revealed here and not just the power of a wonder-worker. **That thou didst send me** reminds us that it is the identity of Jesus as God's special agent that is found in the glory of God revealed in the wonder. In v. 43 Jesus commands **Lazarus** to **come out.** (Is the **loud voice** meant to awaken the sleeping friend?) The scene is a performance of Jesus' words in 5:25 and 28 and signals the fact that "the last day," the day of resurrection (v. 24), is already here in the person of Jesus. In v. 44 Lazarus obeys the words of his Lord and appears with the garments of the grave still clinging to his body. **Bandages** (*keiriais*) would seem to mean the strips of linen used to wrap the body. In Prov. 7:16 (LXX) it is used to mean "bed clothing." For **cloth** cf. 20:7 below. The narrative ends abruptly with the command of Jesus, **Unbind him and let him go.** John places at the apex of the narrative the declaration that in Christ God is at work liberating humans from all those forces which imprison and oppress, not least of which is death.

In the last of the signs John has explicated the way in which the Word in flesh brings *life.* Whereas in chap. 9 he plays with the physical and spiritual meanings of eyesight, now he uses a resurrection from death to physical life to illustrate the gift of life. In that previous chapter the sign is narrated first and then its spiritual meaning explained in the subsequent discussions. Here the meaning of the act is stated to Martha in vv. 25-26 and then acted out in the resurrection. This is not to minimize the fact that John believes actual life beyond physical death is offered as a benefit of the revelation (just as he believes physical eyesight is vitally important), but to help us see that for him life has a far more important spiritual dimension as well.

The other dimension to this narrative is the manner in which it foreshadows Jesus' own resurrection. It is clear that the evangelist wants his readers to sense in this bestowal of life to a deceased friend the way in which Jesus himself will rise beyond the confines of death. As God is glorified in Jesus' wondrous act, so he will be glorified by his Father in his own resurrection. The resurrection of Lazarus is to the first half of this gospel (in which Jesus reveals glory) what Christ's resurrection is to the second half (in which Jesus receives glory). In this most marvelous of signs John has informed us of how God will exalt his Son. But this mighty deed is not without its negative consequences—which John now relates.

The Death Plot against Jesus (11:45-57)

It is not without reason that John attaches to the resurrection of Lazarus the plot on Jesus' life. Painfully the evangelist tells us that the greatest of gifts to humanity (life itself) evokes from the darkness of unbelief the effort to smash the giver of that gift. The contrast of the beneficence of God in his revelation and the malevolence of the human religious institution brings us face to face again with John's sobering estimate of human nature. The revelation is met not just with rejection but with hostile resistance. While the plot to kill Jesus comes as nothing new (e.g., 7:1), its finality here indicates that Jesus' "hour" is imminent.

45-48—This sign, like the others and like the words of Jesus, produces a division among the witnesses. Some believe as a result of the wonder; others seek ways of expressing their unbelief. The Greek of v. 45 may be rendered as the RSV has it or with the sense that all of **the Jews** present **believed.** The second sense would mean that the "some" of v. 46 are others not present for the wonder. The former seems more likely, given John's insistence that the signs never produced unanimous belief. **Seen . . . and believed** states John's understanding of the close relationship between the sensual experience of seeing and hearing Jesus with faith. To see the manifestation of God in Christ is often a prerequisite of faith and leads to faith (cf. 11:40 and 20:8 as well as 1:39 and 46, but contrast 20:29). That only **Mary** is mentioned here is strange and may hint at the greater importance of Mary due to her act of anointing Jesus (12:1-8). **Some** tell **the Pharisees** what has taken place (v. 46), supposedly for the purpose of their reaching a decision regarding Jesus. That the Pharisees are spoken of as a single, unified group gathered in one place informs us more of the Judaism of John's time than that of Jesus. On **chief priests and the Pharisees** (v. 47) cf. 7:32 above. **The council** is the Sanhedrin (*synedrion*), John's only use of the word. It was composed of **chief priests,** elders, and scribes. Many of the scribes were Pharisees.

The words of the Pharisees can be translated, "What are we doing now?" with the implication that nothing is being done. **Many signs** is actually not accurate, for Jesus does few signs in this gospel; but the impact of his popularity makes the exaggeration understandable (cf. the "many Jews" who believe in v. 45). Verse 48 includes the same exaggeration —**every one will believe in him.** The fear expressed in the words of the members of the Sanhedrin contains a note of irony. Even though they take action against Jesus, **the Romans** nonetheless do exactly as the Pharisees fear—in the later war which climaxed in the destruction of the temple in 70 C.E. **Holy place** is simply "our place" in Greek (*hēmōn . . . ton topon*) and means the temple. The perspective of a post-70 view is evident in the verse, and it may reflect a Jewish apologetic for the death of Jesus, one which the Johannine community had encountered firsthand. That a messianic movement would evoke Roman response is reasonable.

49-50—Caiaphas was **high priest** 18-36 C.E. (cf. 18:13, 14, 24, 28). **Who was high priest** *that year* seems to imply that John understood the tenure of the office to be a single year, while in fact it was a lifetime position (cf. Num. 25:11-13; 35:25, 28). It is true that the Romans deposed high priests at their pleasure, but still it seems unlikely that John would not know the custom of the Jewish Law. The problem is made worse by his emphatic mention of **that year** again in v. 51 (missing in some manuscripts) and 18:14. It seems best to assume that John means by **that year** "the notorious year," i.e., the year of the passion. Caiaphas' insult, **you know nothing at all,** is intended ironically by the evangelist, for Caiaphas himself is bogged down in the pit of ignorance so far as Jesus is concerned. In v. 50, however, he is made to speak prophetically. The principle he cites appears to have been widespread in Judaism and is illustrated by 2 Sam. 20:14-22 and Jonah 1:8-16 (cf. Schnackenburg, vol. 2, p. 519, n. 97). This is the epitome of Johannine irony. Jesus will **die for the people** and will save the **whole nation,** but not in the way Caiaphas supposes. Textual witnesses suggest the absence of **for you** and **for the people,** but no essential meaning is lost if those are taken to be scribal additions.

51-53—Verse 51 gives John's reason for Caiaphas' words. His statement is an unconscious and unwilling declaration of the truth.

There is a possibility that the **high priest** was thought to have prophetic powers by virtue of his office, but for John the point is that God expresses his truth through the opponents of Jesus as well as the believers. The preposition **for** (*hyper*) here and in the previous verse might hint at a sacrificial death, but such an idea is not strongly represented in this gospel (cf. however 1:29). It is better taken to mean simply "for the benefit of." Verse 52 would appear to be the evangelist's assurance that in Christ people of belief will be brought not only out of the Jews but from every part of the world. **Children of God** (*ta tekna tou theou*) at once speaks of those who are made part of the divine family in faith (1:12) and those who are elected to become part of that family; for there is a sense in which those who believe are chosen by the Father (6:44). The thought of this verse reminds the reader of 10:16 and the "sheep" of another flock. **Who are scattered abroad** picks up the OT theme of the ingathering of both Israel and the Gentiles (e.g., Isa. 43:5 and 56:6-8). For John that eschatological event finds its fulfillment in the Gentile mission of the church, as well as in the Jewish converts. Realized or present eschatology is evident in the mission of the church, thinks John. Verse 53 is the solemn declaration that the **death** plot will be carried out this time. This conclusion prepares us for the advent of the final "hour."

54—This verse reflects the seriousness of the situation and signals a near conclusion to the public ministry of **Jesus. Openly** is the same word (*parrēsia*) used of "speaking plainly (clearly)" (e.g., 10:24). The location of **Ephraim** is debated, but the two main candidates are just northeast of Jerusalem (cf. Brown, vol. 1, p. 441 for a discussion of the sites). Textual witnesses divide equally between **stayed** and "spent some time." In Ephraim Jesus awaits the Passover and his final visit to Jerusalem.

55-57—This transition belongs as much to 12:1ff. as it does to 11:45-54. In v. 55 John mentions the third **Passover** of Jesus' ministry (the fourth, if the unnamed feast of 5:1 is taken to be Passover). It is a pilgrim feast, and **went up** (*anebēsan*) is used of the journey to **Jerusalem** (cf. 2:13; 5:1; 7:8). Certain acts of purification were required for the pilgrims (cf. Num. 9:6ff. and Mishnah, *Pes.* 9). Verse 56 repeats the thought of 7:11 and intends to stress the danger of Jesus' appearing in Jerusalem in the light of the plot against his life. The death plot has now taken the form of ordering that Jesus' presence should be reported (v. 57). Verse 57 integrates vv. 55-57 into the subsection 45-57.

John 11:45-57 has the singular impact of anticipating the inevitable arrest of Jesus toward which the plot of this gospel develops with unmistakable certainty. The evangelist wants to increase the apprehension of the reader with this section, while still planning to delay the actual arrest even more.

Anointing—A Preparation for Death—and the Plot against Lazarus (12:1-11)

The narrative of the anointing is parallel to those found in the Synoptics at Matt. 26:6-13; Mark 14:3-9; and Luke 7:36-50, although it has been thoroughly remolded into the flow of the plot of John. It is a sequel to the resurrection of Lazarus insofar as it is set in Bethany and Mary is featured. It is connected with 11:1-44 also by the fact that it foreshadows the death and burial of Jesus, even as the Lazarus story presages the resurrection of Jesus. Still further, the Johannine story seems to anticipate Jesus' act of washing the feet of the disciples (13:1-20), for here it is the feet of Jesus which are anointed (for a comparison of this story with the Synoptic accounts cf. Brown, vol. 1, pp. 449-454). This passage is one of only a few places in the Fourth Gospel where a dependence on one or more of the Synoptics seems plausible.[17] John again sobers the reader by attaching to this narrative, which depicts a beautiful act of love and devotion, one which characterizes the worst side of human nature— the plot against the life of Lazarus (vv. 9-11).

1-2—The story begins with a designation of time and place. **Six days before the Passover** would be the day of Saturday evening and Sunday, since the Passover itself is dated on Friday evening and Saturday (13:1 and 18:28). No symbolic meaning is evident in the number of days mentioned here. In light of 11:54 we are to assume that Jesus travels back to **Bethany** from Ephraim. The identification of the village as the home of **Lazarus** and the description of him seem quite unnecessary given the proximity of this narrative to 11:1-44. John may be using a source or working with an edition of the gospel which did not have these two stories in close proximity. Verse 2 continues to set the scene. It is apparently an evening meal, perhaps hosted by Lazarus and his sisters. The suggestion that the meal was accompanied by the ceremony of *Habdalah*, which celebrated the end of the Sabbath, is not borne out by the text.

3—Pound is literally *litran*, the Greek and Roman measurement which equals about 12 ounces. **Ointment** was probably a perfume used for a number of purposes, including the preparation of a body for burial. **Nard** is a plant from which the oil was extracted. **Pure** translates a word whose meaning is not clear, *pistikos*. Its literal meaning is "faithful" and hence the rendering **pure** or "genuine." **Mary's** act is puzzling at two points: (1) Why is it **the feet of Jesus** which are anointed? Anointing the head would, of course, have messianic symbolism, but not so the anointing of feet. John had mixed features of the anointing of Jesus' head in Mark 14:3 (and Matt. 26:6) with the penitent woman's wetting the feet of Jesus in Luke 7:38. Perhaps John means to suggest that in Mary's act Jesus is prepared for his burial. Her anointing implies that her master's entire body would be embalmed. (2) Why does **Mary** wipe **his feet with her hair?** If the anointing is in some sense an anticipation of Jesus' act of washing the feet of his disciples, the wiping would betoken that feature of Jesus' later act (13:5). In fact the Greek verb here translated **wiped** (*ekmassein*) is used only in connection with these two stories in John (11:2; 12:3; 13:5) and the anointing in Luke (7:38, 44). The last clause of the verse emphasizes the abundance of the **ointment—the house was filled.** . . .

4-6—The introduction of **Judas** in the tale is a distinctively Johannine feature and probably reflects the evangelist's own creative work. Judas is described here as he is in 6:71 in nearly identical words as **one of his disciples (he who was to betray him).** Textual variants of this verse attempt to harmonize the passage with 6:71 by adding "Simon" or "son of Simon" and "from Kerioth" for **Iscariot** (cf. 6:71 above). Judas' words (v. 5) are close to those of the unidentified speaker(s) in Mark 14:5. (This similarity is one of the bits of evidence used to argue for John's dependence on Mark.) The denarius was the average day's wage for the time, and so the ointment was indeed extravagant! In v. 6 John comments on the character of Judas. He is called a **thief** (*kleptēs*), the same word used in 10:1ff. for those who threaten the welfare of the flock. That he was the treasurer of the small band is nowhere stated outside of this gospel (cf. 13:29). **Money box** renders *glōssokomon*, another word used only here and 13:29. It was originally a box designated to carry reeds and tongues of musical instruments. John alone attributes to Judas the character flaw of greed, although it may be implied in Matt. 26:14-16. This shows the way in which tradition tended to increase the villainy of the betrayer, but it may also imply that for John it is such flaws of character which allow opportunity for evil of a far worse kind (cf. 13:2).

7—**Jesus'** words present a translation difficulty. The Greek sentence is elliptical and confused by the evasive sense of "that" (*hina*) after **let her alone** and the meaning of **keep** (*tērēsē*). Among the possibilities are these: (1) "Allow her to keep the remainder" of the ointment for Jesus' burial (an unlikely meaning since we hear nothing more of the ointment, and Jesus' body is generously embalmed according to 19:39). (2) "Should she keep it until the day of my burial?" (a possible but not persuasive proposal). (3) "She has kept the ointment until now" to embalm Jesus (suggested by a textual variant which attempts to improve the sentence). (4) Let her "remember" this act on the day of Jesus' burial (a proposal which stretches the meaning of *tērēsē* to include "remember"). None of the alternatives is satisfactory, but the general impression of the obscure Greek is that Mary should be allowed to do what she has with the ointment, for unknowingly she has prepared Jesus for **his burial.**

8—This saying is troublesome for other reasons. It is identical to Matt. 26:11, and since some manuscripts exclude it entirely, its presence in John may be due to scribal accretion from a knowledge of Matthew. This may be, but the verse is not without purpose in the story. It drives home the point that Jesus' burial, alluded to in the previous verse, is imminent. It does not denigrate concern for **the poor** but exhorts attention to Jesus, since he is soon to be killed. It may be an intentional allusion to Deut. 15:11 with the addition that appropriating the revelation in Christ takes precedence over the command to care for **the poor.**

The anointing at Bethany has several meanings which should now be summarized. First, it is an act by which Mary has (unknowingly) performed ahead of time the preparation for the burial of Jesus. Second, it is an act which anticipated the servant deed of Jesus in washing the feet of his disciples. But, third, it is also Mary's gift of love and gratitude to Jesus. If Martha is honored by means of her confession (11:27), Mary is now honored as one who expresses a love which is exemplary for the believer.

But as John followed the mighty deed of the resurrection of Lazarus with the account of the death plot against Jesus, he appends to this story of exemplary love another death plot.

9-11—The large **crowd** is presumably the crowd of pilgrims mentioned in 11:55 which now comes to Bethany. **Lazarus** has become a public curiosity— one who has returned from death. But it is Lazarus' walking testimony to Jesus that worries the officials in v. 10. The words recall 11:53 except now it is **the chief priests** alone who plot the **death.** Verse 11 is another of those statements which supposes a popular movement among the people in support of Jesus (cf. 7:31; 8:30; 10:42; 11:45). John more consistently gives the impression of such a movement than do the Synoptics. **Going away** (*hypēgon*) is meant metaphorically of a movement of faith from Judaism to Christianity. The latter would reflect a situation in the church of a later time, and may be reminiscent of Jewish converts to the Johannine community.

The place of these verses in the chapter is only to show once again the dastardly reactions of humans to the revelation. We are never told if the death plot is actually executed. Even he who represents the evidence of God's liberating love must be crushed in order to protect the religious status quo.

The Entry into Jerusalem (12:12-19)

Again we are confronted with a Johannine narrative which has Synoptic parallels (Matt. 21:1-11; Mark 11:1-11; and Luke 19:28-40), and again it is Brown (vol. 1, pp. 459-463) who provides the most helpful comparison of the accounts. It is obvious that John (or the tradition before him) has abbreviated the narrative and given it a new theological meaning, as compared with the Synoptics. One might say that this scene is an interpretation of the title "King of the Jews," given to Jesus in the crucifixion (18:33 and 19:19). It stands at its present place in the gospel plot in order to anticipate the derisive bestowal of that title and the insights the disciples will gain only after the resurrection. It is also a comment on the popular mass movement in support of Jesus (cf. 12:11 above).

12-14—The next day would be Sunday or Monday, if our interpretation of 12:1 above is correct. John, however, is interested only in the most general kind of chronological order. The **crowd** would seem to be those mentioned in 11:55 as well as 12:9. In v. 13 that crowd welcomes Jesus as they might welcome a king. **Branches of palm trees** were regularly used in certain festivals and in welcoming a victorious monarch (for the latter cf. 1 Macc. 13:51). Whether or not palm trees were available in Jerusalem at the time of Passover is not known, but they were clearly a celebrative implement. **Hosanna!** is a Greek transliteration of the Hebrew which means "Save us now, please." By the time John wrote, the word had probably lost its intercessory meaning to become only a shout of praise. The quotation is from Ps. 118:26, and there has reference to the pilgrims coming into Jerusalem. But the additional words, **the King of Israel,** interpret the **he who comes** in messianic terms. The use of the palms and the citation of Psalm 118 were common in the feast of Dedication, but that does not mean that they could not be used appropriately on Passover. Clearly the scene is one of nationalistic and religious fervor. **Young ass** (*onarion*) is the diminutive form of the "ass's colt" (*pōlon onou*) mentioned in the quotation in v. 15. Of some significance is the fact that John has the selection of the animal *after* the crowd's acclamation (the reverse order found in the Synoptics, e.g., Mark 11: 2-10), suggesting that the act of riding on the ass is a *correction* of the crowd's notion.

15—This quotation is formed out of Zech. 9:9, but John's version follows closely neither the Hebrew nor the Greek text. Either John (or his tradition) has carelessly quoted from memory or else he has consciously merged Zech. 9:9 with another passage. **Fear not** does not appear in the Zechariah passage; rather it has "Rejoice greatly, **O daughter of Zion!**" The remainder of the quotation is an abbreviation of Zech. 9:9 which describes the king as "triumphant and victorious" and "humble." It blends the tone of royalty with a sense of humility. The mighty king rides not a war horse but an ass! The phrase **fear not** could have come into the writer's mind from a number of passages (e.g., Isa. 40:9), but some believe that Zeph. 3:16 (the Masoretic text) is intentionally in mind as an interpretation of Zech. 9:9. While the Zechariah passage is clearly nationalistic in tone, the setting for Zeph. 3:16 is universalistic (cf. Zeph. 3:9-10). It is possible that John means by this subtle allusion to Zephaniah to qualify the nationalistic quality of the quotation of Zech. 9:9. But if this is so, the allusion is subtle indeed. However, if John does want to correct the crowd's nationalistic fervor, Zech. 9:9 itself subdues that enthusiasm with the image of the king on a lowly beast of burden.

16—We are told that the **disciples did not understand** (literally, "did not know," *egnōsan*). Only after the crucifixion/resurrection did the event make sense to them (cf. 2:21-22). However, it is not entirely clear what it was the disciples came to understand. Surely it is not the messianic quality of the procession itself, for even the crowd understands that. Perhaps, then, it is the subtle way in which Jesus had been presented, not as a nationalistic Messiah mounted on a war horse, but the peaceful (and universal?) Messiah riding on a donkey (cf. 20:9 below).

17-19—These verses seem to be an addition to the story which is intended to fit the narrative into the context. Verse 17 suggests that those who witnessed the resurrection of **Lazarus** had shared their experience with others, and v. 18 gives that as the reason for the **crowd's** enthusiastic welcome of Jesus. **The Pharisees** in v. 19 are understandably threatened by Jesus' popularity. On one level, their statement **the world has gone after him** is simple hyperbole. On another level, given the context of the statement, **world** prepares us for the coming of the Greeks in v. 20. While **world** means "everyone" in the sentence, it is also John's word for the realm of unbelief for whose salvation Christ has come (3:16). There is a note of irony here both in the way the Pharisees are correct and in the way in which they are wrong. The whole world will eventually follow him; but everyone is running to Jesus for the wrong reasons, and this popularity will be turned on its head in a short time.

The narrative of Jesus' royal procession is clearly written to describe the misunderstanding of his messiahship. The crowd has in mind a warrior-king Messiah who will liberate them from Roman oppression. Jesus' reservations about being cast in that role are evident in 6:15 as well as here. Furthermore, John has again suggested that the reason for the crowd's enthusiasm is Jesus' wonder-working power (v. 18), and John has consistently shown that such faith is superficial (e.g., chap. 6). Just how John intends us to understand the riding of a donkey as a proper reinterpretation of messiahship is less than clear. But surely the substance of it is found in 18:36—"My kingdom is not of this world." John will maintain that Jesus ironically is king, even as Pilate (19:14) and the placard on the cross (19:19) proclaim. Riding on a donkey is symbolic of the crucifixion, as the resurrection is symbolic of Jesus' kingship—it is only by means of a humble death that Jesus is enthroned.

The Greeks and the Arrival of the "Hour" (12:20-26)

This is the first part of a collage of narrative and discourse which together with vv. 27-50 function to bring an end to the public ministry of Jesus and ready the transition into the private time with the disciples before his arrest. This first segment is comprised of two parts. In the first the Greeks come seeking Jesus (vv. 20-21), and in the second Jesus announces the arrival of his "hour" and the meaning of his death (vv. 22-26). This section, along with its subsequent unit, communicate a solemnity which ushers in the passion story.

20-22—The Greeks are doubtless Gentiles. *Hellēn* is most often used of non-Jewish persons of the Hellenistic world (e.g., Mark 7:26). Their presence in Jerusalem for the feast might presuppose that they are converts to Judaism or even Greek-speaking Jews. But their function in the narrative is clearly symbolic, for they are immediately dropped after their introduction. For John they represent the Gentile mission of the church wherein the peoples of the Hellenistic world come seeking the revealer, and the evangelist has no interest in making their presence in Jerusalem believable. Their reason for speaking to **Philip** in particular in v. 21 is not clear, although Philip is represented as a missionary in 1:43-45. **Bethsaida,** if we have the correct site in mind, is actually in Gaulanitis (but only by a short distance) and not in **Galilee.** Bethsaida might have been associated in popular mentality with Gentiles. **See Jesus** may be shorthand for "have an interview with Jesus." **See** (*idein*) is sometimes joined with faith (e.g., 20:8) and hence may indicate an openness to believe. It is also the word used in the phrase, "come and see," in 1:39 and 46 as an invitation to discipleship. John intends to attribute symbolic significance to the request of the **Greeks. Andrew** is introduced in v. 22. He is also mentioned in 1:40-42 in a missionary role, as well as appearing in 6:8. The two of them take the request of the Greeks to Jesus. Should we understand this rather strange way of bringing the Greeks to Jesus in a symbolic way? The Gentiles were to be introduced to the Christian church only through the Jewish Christians, their intermediaries to Christ. Perhaps that fact lies behind the manner by which the Greeks come to Jesus; however, it is difficult to say with any certainty that that is John's meaning.

23-24—Jesus' answer is not really an answer at all. It does not seem that his words are intended directly for the Greeks, and they are immediately withdrawn from the story. It is, however, the presence of the Greeks which occasions Jesus' declaration that his **hour** (*hōra*) has come, for their presence means the readiness of the world for the glorification of the Son. On three occasions it has been said that Jesus' hour had *not* yet come (2:4; 7:30; 8:20) and on another three occasions Jesus will speak of his *impending* hour (12:27; 13:1; 17:1). His hour means that process by which God will glorify him, and his earthly ministry will be completed (cf. 2:4 above). For **Son of man** cf. 1:51 above. It is often used both in this gospel and the Synoptics in association with the crucifixion. **Glorified** is the Johannine understanding of the crucifixion-resurrection whereby God's presence is climatically expressed in Christ. Verse 24 presents a metaphor which sheds light on the way in which Christ will be glorified. As is so often the case, John draws from a rich and almost universal religious symbol, namely, that of dying and rising in seeding and growing. It is found in the ancient fertility religions and the Hellenistic mystery cults, as well as in the Christian tradition itself (cf. Mark 4:3-8, 26-29; and 1 Cor. 15:35-41). Here its application is as a simple parabolic understanding of the way in which Christ is glorified in his death and resurrection. The Greek reads, *the* **grain of wheat,** perhaps suggesting the symbolic identification of Jesus as the seed. **Much fruit** stands for the rich benefits of Christ's death, including the offering of the revelation to the Greeks represented in v. 20 (cf. 15:1-16 below). **Remains alone** (*monos menei*) stands in parallelism as the opposite of **bears much fruit,** and means that it has no consequences beyond itself. It is not impossible that this simple saying has roots back to the historical Jesus himself. The death of Jesus is then a necessary completion of the revelation which allows it to influence the existence of all humanity.

25—The way in which dying yields **life** is now applied to discipleship in vv. 25-26. The saying in v. 25 has Synoptic parallels, and together with them this passage constitutes the fourth wording of the same thought. We find it expressed in terms of "save-lose-save" (Mark 8:35 and Luke 9:24), "save-lose-find" (Matt. 16:25), "gain-lose-preserve" (Luke 17:33), and "love-hate-keep" (this passage). It is clear that this saying was preserved in several different forms, possibly originating in the teachings of Jesus himself. It is perhaps the most widely attested saying attributed to Jesus in the NT, since it has representation in the Markan, Q, and Johannine traditions. The Johannine admonition that one must not **love** but **hate** her or his life is the most radical of the four forms. The love-hate (*phileō-miseō*) pattern may be an instance of Semitic hyperbole like those found elsewhere in the Gospels (e.g., Matt. 5:29 and 19:24). These harsh words are a drastic way of expressing the matter of preference, that is, to love one's life is to value it above all else, while to hate one's life is to prefer a higher value than one's own existence. It is unthinkable that the saying should be taken literally, any more than Matt. 5:30. If the saying has genuine roots far back in the Christian tradition, and possibly in Jesus himself, the phrases **in this world** (*kosmos*) and **eternal life** are Johannine interpretations. The former carries the meaning of the realm of darkness and unbelief (cf. 1:10 above) and connotes that one must throw away trust in oneself even in the midst of an environment which counsels the opposite. **Eternal life** stands in antithetical parallelism to world and represents the whole range of the benefits that stream from embracing the revelation, but most particularly the reality of life which stands apart from unbelief and endures beyond the grave (cf. 3:16 above). **Life** translates *psychē*, sometimes rendered "soul" (e.g., 1 Thess. 5:23), but here it has the more Semitic sense of that living quality (*nephesh*) which is a part of the whole person. **Lose** (*apollynai*) means "destroy" and so perhaps here "lose it entirely." The saying counsels that one must embrace a loyalty beyond one's self or lose the highly valued self.[18] As Jesus surrenders his life for his followers, so must the disciples be willing to lose their lives for the benefit of the revelation.

26—This verse focuses the meaning of discipleship even more precisely. It contains three statements. In the first (**if any . . . me**) discipleship and service (*diakonia*) are equated. To serve (*diakoneō*) means to **follow** (*akoloutheō*; cf. 1:35-51 above). The nature of the service will be explicated in 13:4-17. The second statement (**and where . . . be also**) implies the consequences of discipleship. On the one hand, this means that the disciple will **follow** Jesus to the cross—**where I am** means suffering; but, on the other hand, the statement suggests the rewards of discipleship. Discipleship means, alongside of suffering, the reward of being with Christ, as 14:3 promises. The third statement (**if any one . . . honor him**) makes more explicit the reward of discipleship. **Honor** (*timaō*) is to value highly. As Jesus **honors the Father** (8:49) and humans are invited to **honor** the Son and thereby the **Father** (5:23), so now it is said that God reciprocates that gift. The three statements taken together trace the nature of discipleship from following and serving to its ultimate benefit—being prized by God.

This short section stands by itself because of its pivotal importance in this last chapter of the first half of the gospel. It announces the meaning of the "hour" and its consequences for believers.

The Last Public Discourse and Its Results (12:27-50)

Like the two loosely related parts of vv. 20-26, this discourse has drawn together several disparate bits. They are blended skillfully, however, into a powerful conclusion to the first half of the gospel. John has placed the agony of Jesus' decision to face his course and his loneliness in that decision (vv. 27-36) alongside a pronouncement on unbelief (vv. 37-43) and a discussion of the identity and mission of the revealer (vv. 44-50). With these verses, supported by 20-26, John readies the reader for Jesus' private ministry and his passion.

27-28a—These verses compress the agony of Jesus' decision to face the cross into a few words. Behind v. 27 lies the tradition of the Galilean's wrestling with his fate in the garden of Gethsemane (Matt. 26:36-46; Mark 14:32-42; Luke 22:39-46), but it is evidence of how an independent Johannine tradition has been shaped in a manner very different from that of the Synoptics. It may have been the evangelist's own decision to make this agony a public matter, leaving the prayer of chap. 17 one of triumphant, confident faith. The language of v. 27 has been influenced by the psalms, e.g., 42:6; 6:3. **Now** (*nyn*) suggests the moment of the arrival of the hour (v. 23). **Soul** translates *psychē*, the same word rendered "life" in v. 25. The thought is that the total person of Jesus is involved in his agony. **Troubled** (*tarassein*) is the same word used in 11:33 (cf. above) and 13:21. It conveys the sense of radical emotion. The prayer for rescue is presented as a passing thought, for Jesus is sure of what he must do. **Father** is John's most frequent name for God on the lips of Jesus, but here it may represent the "Abba, Father" of the Synoptic tradition (e.g., Mark 14:36; cf. 5: 18 above and n. 11). **Save me from this hour** may be punctuated as a question (as the RSV has it) or as a statement, a petition (as the NEB). While Jesus' hour has been sometimes represented as a time of glorification (cf. v. 23 above), it is here spoken of with the full force of its suffering and tragedy. For that reason, it is likely John represents Jesus briefly asking that he be spared the ordeal. The very **purpose** of the hour, however, dismisses any thought of avoidance, for it is the redemptive meaning of Christ's life. **Purpose** is not found in the Greek: *dia touto ēlthon*, "for this I came."

The prayer ends in v. 28a with the affirmation, much as the Gethsemane prayer ends, "not my will, but thine, be done" (Luke 22:
42).

28b-30—The agony of Jesus is short-lived, and immediately his
resolution receives divine confirmation by a heavenly **voice**
(*phōnē*). Such a voice is referred to in the Synoptic accounts of the
baptism and transfiguration (e.g., Matt. 3:17 and 17:5) but only
here in John's gospel. The voice is unlike the *Bath qol* of the rabbinic tradition, for there the **voice from heaven** is an inferior echo
of the Torah. John leaves no doubt that it is the voice of God himself speaking to affirm Jesus. The Father has **glorified** Jesus
throughout his ministry (e.g., the signs which express glory, 2:11)
and will **glorify** him still further in the cross and resurrection.
Verse 29 once again asserts the division which revelation causes
amid humanity. Some think that they have heard **thunder** and others the voices of **angels**. (Does this mean that 5:37 is a reflection of
the absence of a willingness to hear God's words rather than the
fact that he does not speak directly?) Thunder is linked with the
voice of God in a number of places in the OT (1 Sam. 7:10 and 19:
16) and the NT as well (Rev. 14:2). But John clearly means that
some of the crowd heard no voice at all but only thunder. Jesus'
words in v. 30 claim that the voice was for the sake of the people,
not his. Typical of the Johannine Jesus, he needs no such external
confirmation, for his relationship with the Father is a continuous
confirmation. We see in the relationship of this verse to Jesus'
prayer in v. 27 the tension between the humanity of Jesus and his
special divine status. For John, Jesus' questioning of his fate can
only be a passing matter. That the crowd does not discern evidence of the divine confirmation in the voice only further stresses
the fact that humans cannot comprehend even the most blatant act
of God for their benefit.

31—Jesus' words continue, beginning again with **now** (*nyn*).
Perhaps we are to think of Jesus' agony (vv. 27ff.) as the first consequences of the arrival of the "hour" of his glorification and
God's triumph over the forces of evil as the second. Two an-
nouncements are made side by side, each signaled with **now: Judgment** has come, and Satan is dethroned. John's rather complicated

and not always consistent view of judgment is found in 3:19 and 5:
22-30 (cf. above). Clearly the cross and resurrection have a secondary result of judgment, while their main purpose is salvation,
not judgment (cf. v. 47 below). As some are deaf to the voice from
heaven, so some will be unresponsive to the cross. Judgment
means, in the second announcement, that the forces of evil are
subdued and their grip on this world broken. **Ruler of this world**
(*ho archōn tou kosmou*) is a peculiarly Johannine expression for the
devil or Satan (cf. 14:30 and 16:11). Even so, the thought of the
passage is harmonious with the concept of the two eras, one of the
rule of Satan and one of God's rule, and the confidence that Jesus
brings the dethroning of Satan (e.g., Luke 11:20; 10:18; and Col.
2:5). While John's dualism has a cosmic and existential quality,
there remains in his tradition the notion of a temporal dualism.
The ruler of this world will soon be replaced by God's kingship in
Christ.

32-33—If v. 31 expresses the meaning of the "hour" in terms of
judgment and the overthrow of Satan, v. 32 expresses its powerfully redemptive effects in other ways. **Lifted up** (*hypsoō*) means
the enthronement of Christ, replacing the disempowered force of
evil, but it also means crucifixion. John intentionally uses this ambiguous word to speak of the dual reality of the cross (cf. 3:14
above). **From the earth** employs a further spatial metaphor to indicate that the "lifting up" is into the divine realm. Jesus **will draw**
humans into the realm of the rule of God. **Draw** translates *helkō*,
the same word used in 6:44 (cf. above), and in both cases it refers
to the divine power which attracts human faith. **All men** reads "all
things" in some manuscripts, implying that the redemption
wrought in the cross is cosmic in dimension, but in all probability
the variant is a scribal interpretation of the crucifixion. All humans
will be lured by the power of the cross. This is the best evidence
for the proposal that John was, finally, a universalist who believed
all humanity would be brought to faith. That is an attractive view,
but the strong emphasis on the reality of unbelief (cf. vv. 37-41 below) makes it hard to accept as an accurate view of John's thought.
Clearly, however, the cross affects all human life. We have here
one part of John's essentially nonsacrificial view of the atonement:

The cross unleashes the magnetic power of divine love which pulls persons to faith. John's concept of the divine responsibility for faith (e.g., 6:44) is here tempered with the thought that all are elected. Verse 33 is his care to make certain the reader understands the otherwise ambiguous words of the revealer.

34—The crowd objects. They correctly understand Jesus' words to mean that he must die, but fail to grasp the other meaning of the expression **lifted up,** namely, the exaltation as king. Hence, their confusion comes from their assumption that the **Christ** will be a glorious figure. **From the law** means from Jewish Scripture, but we know of no passage which states that the Messiah should never die (unless the promise of the eternal Davidic dynasty was taken to mean that the Messiah would rule forever; cf. 2 Sam. 5; Ps. 89:36; Isa. 9:7; Ezek. 37:25). Actually Jewish messianic thought included contradictory notions both of the temporally limited reign of the Messiah (i.e., he is to die, 4 Ezra 7:28-30, or to be taken into heaven, 2 Bar. 30:1) and his eternal reign (T. Reub. 6:12 and Sib. Or. 3:48). It would appear that the crowd equates **Christ** and **Son of man,** and the concept of the death of the latter is not consistent with their expectations (e.g., Dan. 7:14). But their last question suggests that they recognize the possibility that the equation of **Christ** and **Son of man** is mistaken (for **Son of man** cf. 1:51 above). All of this notwithstanding, John represents the crowd as finding it absolutely incredible that the Messiah (Son of man) should be crucified. Still, they are made to ask the right question—**Who is this Son of man?**

35-36—The subject of these verses seems to have little to do with the query of the crowd. The composite character of the section is betrayed by this abrupt transition. The relationship between vv. 34 and 35-36a nonetheless makes some editorial sense. The inability of the crowd to conceive of a Messiah who would be crucified as a means of being exalted cannot be removed by any answer Jesus might make. It stands for the immovable blindness of unbelief, and to that blindness there is nothing more to say except a warning that their time of decision is short. That is the point of the little metaphor in vv. 35-36a—act now, for **the darkness** will soon **overtake you.** While the metaphor is based on the notion that the traveler must journey during the daylight (cf. 11:9-10 for the same metaphor), **walk** (*peripatein*) is a Johannine figure for discipleship, as 8:12 shows. **A little longer** (*mikron chronon*) stands for the time until the crucifixion as it does in 16:16. **Overcome** is the same word that is used at 1:5 (*katalambanō*), where it means that the darkness of the world cannot subdue the **light** which is Christ. While the darkness cannot overcome the light, it can and does overcome humans. Verse 35b suggests the Johannine meaning of redemption, i.e., to **know where** you are going and who you are. Verse 36a states the crisis of the moment—**believe** (imperative, *pisteuete*) **in** (*eis*) **the light** (cf. 1:12 above). **Sons of the light** is synonymous with "children of God" in 1:12-13. It implies a dualistic division of humanity, much as the distinction between those who are Jesus' "sheep" and those who are not (10:26). The expression (**sons of the light**) is found in the Qumran literature where it is the opposite of the "sons of darkness" (1QS 3:13—4:26) and where the two are opponents in the final eschatological battle. The end of the conversation comes abruptly in v. 36b and really is the end of the public discourse. He **hid himself** (as in 8:59) to avoid being stoned. The opportunity to accept the revelation is ended (for now), as Jesus warned that it would be.

37-39—Unbelief dominates this conclusion to the public ministry of Jesus (as it often has the whole of his ministry, e.g., 6:66), and so it is appropriate that John should at this point insert a statement designed to help his readers understand why it is that people reject the revelation. Verse 37 contrasts unbelief and the **signs** of the preceding chapters. While "signs faith" is not mature faith, signs invite consideration. The statement may have in mind Moses' invitation for the people of Israel to believe on the basis of God's mighty acts of the exodus (Deut. 29:2-9). Verse 38 states that the reality of unbelief comes as no surprise, but fulfills **Isaiah 53:1**. John uses a formula here to introduce Scripture fulfillment, **the prophet Isaiah might be fulfilled** (compare Matt. 1:22). While the figure of the suffering servant of Deutero-Isaiah is often used of Christ in the NT (e.g., Luke 24:26), this is the only use of Isaiah 53 to demonstrate the reality of unbelief. John follows the LXX of the passage closely. The sense of the words is the tragic failure of persons to accept the announcement of God's actions. Although not interpreted messianically by the Jews, the rejection of the suffering servant provided the early Christians with a way of understanding the enigmatic death of their Messiah (e.g., Acts 8:32-35). The force of the verse is to demonstrate that Israel could do none other than reject Jesus. Verse 39 makes that explicit. It is the introduction to v. 40 and refers ahead to it more than back to v. 38. (**Therefore** is a somewhat misleading translation of *dia*.)

40-41—Verse 40 is the classical NT explanation of unbelief. John's quotation of Isa. 6:10 is a mixture of the Hebrew and Greek texts, although nearer to the former. It appears in several places in the NT—Acts 28:26-27; Rom. 11:8; and Matt. 13:15 (cf. Mark 4: 12 and 8:17). In its original setting it represents the difficulties facing Isaiah of Jerusalem as a spokesperson for God. John's use of the passage is not so much to declare that unbelief is predestined by God as it is to offer an explanation for the disturbing reality of the refusal to believe. He regularly states both sides of the issue of the responsibility for faith—divine election and human decision (cf. 6: 35-67 above). His position would seem to be that faith is more than human will, although it includes the act of the individual, and at the same time humans are responsible for their unbelief.[19] In v. 40 the evangelist intends to claim that unbelief is a part of the divine economy of salvation and does not surprise nor frustrate God's redemptive efforts. Behind this lurks the disappointment over the evangelistic efforts of John's church among the Jews. Verse 41 proposes that **Isaiah's** words are a result of the prophet's vision of the coming of Christ and his **glory**. A similar thing is said of Abraham in 8:56. A textual variant makes it unclear whether one should read **because** (*hoti*) or "when" (*hote*), but the meaning is changed little by this difference. Isaiah's vision of the divine throne room (6:1-13) included, according to John, a view of Christ, for in seeing God he saw the Father's Son and the redemptive plan centered in the sending of the revealer.

42-43—These verses are a still further expression of the Johannine community at the time of the writing of this gospel. There were some Jews in the synagogue who refused openly to **confess** their Christian faith for **fear** of its consequences. John clearly condemns them and not without some personal hostility. **Authorities** (*archontes*) is a general term and illustrates the author's none-too-careful distinctions among the groups in Judaism at the time of Jesus. **Fear of the Pharisees** suggests that they were the dominant force in the synagogue of John's city (cf. "fear of the Jews" in 9:22; 20:19). **Put out of the synagogue** (*aposynagōgoi*) is another reflection of the setting of the writing of this gospel (cf. 9:22 above and Introduction §1). John condemns that belief that cannot let go the security of social position on behalf of Christ. He knew firsthand that faith often involves an almost reckless willingness to grasp the truth at whatever price (cf. 5:44 above).

44-45—The themes of belief and unbelief, as well as judgment, lead to a final discourse, vv. 44-50. It seems quite clear that the evangelist has formulated (or placed here from his tradition) a discourse which typifies Jesus' public ministry, and therefore provided an appropriate climax to the first 12 chapters. The subsection begins with a declaration of Jesus' relationship with God. **Cried out** is used in 7:28 and 37 to introduce proclamations (cf. above). Verses 44b and 45 comprise two parallel statements of Jesus' authority. **Believes in me** in v. 44 is parallel to **sees me** in v. 45 and **him who sent me** is repeated in both. These lines stress the functional oneness of Jesus and God and show the manner in which faith and sight are nearly equated in this gospel (cf. 14:9 below). **Him who sent me,** along with *Father,* are the two most frequent ways of referring to God in John.

46-48—As vv. 44-45 are good summaries of the view of Christ in this gospel, so v. 46 is an often-stated view of his mission (cf. 8:12 and chap. 9). **May not remain** employs the favorite Johannine expression *menein,* which means to abide in a relationship and to take one's orientation from that relationship. Humans need not live forever in the darkness of misunderstanding. In v. 47 the description is of those who have failed to believe, even though they have heard Jesus' words—a reference to those who are the subject of vv. 37-43. **Does not keep** (*phylaxē*) **them** does not mean for John failure to obey certain commandments but rather the unwillingness to take the revelation as the basis of one's life (cf. 15:9-17). Again we find, as we did in 3:17-18, the assertion that judgment is not the purpose of the revelation (v. 47). Judgment is the second-ary result of God's redemptive work, and for that reason John could have Jesus say in some situations (as this) that the revealer does not **judge,** and in others that he does (e.g., 5:22, 27; 8:16, 26). A gift extended to another unintentionally demonstrates that person's willingness to accept a gift. The way judgment does arise from the revelatory work of Christ is stated in v. 48. One judges oneself by the decision to accept or reject the gift of God in Christ. **The word** (*ho logos*) one **rejects** will be the **judge on the last day** (cf. 6:39ff. and 11:24 above). Here we have a rare indication of the way John relates the present and realized eschatologies of his gos-pel (cf. 5:24-29 above). In the present one believes or does not, and the latter has eternal consequences of a negative kind. Unbe-lief may in some sense be predetermined by God (vv. 39-40), but the unbeliever is held accountable on the last day for his or her failure to accept the revelation.

49-50—This little monolog begins with the authority of Jesus (vv. 44-45) and now returns to that theme in its conclusion. The reason the word of Jesus has eternal consequences is because it is God's word. Jesus does not speak on his **own authority,** literally, "not out of myself" (cf. 7:16 above), but only in obedience to the Father. Again the thrust of this verse is the functional unity of Christ and God—what Christ speaks is God's word—or the single will of the two. The image of the prophet-like-Moses may have shaped this view of Christ, for of that prophet it is said in Deut. 18:18 that God will speak through him and he will transmit God's **commandments.** In a very concise statement v. 50 makes clear that the commandment of the **Father** is itself **eternal life.** That is to say, the invitation to believe is the invitation to live the fullness of life. The final sentence of this summary passage reiterates that Jesus does not speak for himself but only obeys what the Father asks him to say. Chaps. 1–12 end, then, much as they started—with the claim that Jesus is the Word of God, and he has been the Word of God by constantly obeying the Father's will.

This section shows certain signs of having been drawn together by the evangelist without great concern for coherence. Still, as a transitional piece, it works perfectly, summarizing some of the themes of earlier chapters and anticipating the passion story. Taken as a whole the impact is to stress once again the awful reality of unbelief. John will paint more vividly the benefits of the life of faith in the chapters to follow, but here must show that, while there are many who believe, the force of unbelief weighs more heavily. Only with such powerful unbelief can John make credible the offense of the execution of Jesus.

Jesus Receives Glory (13:1—20:29)

■ Love and Rejection (13:1-38)

Chapters 2–12 have narrated the public ministry of Jesus and centered in the dialog between Jesus and the crowds, both believers and opponents. In words and actions Jesus has for believers revealed the glory of the Father. With the conclusion of chap. 12 we find ourselves in the second major division of the gospel, called "the book of glory" because it focuses on the glorification of Jesus in the passion story. Here the "horizontal" revelation of the first chapters is replaced by the "vertical" outpouring of God's presence on to Jesus. Jesus' ministry in this second half is limited to the body of believers and his public execution. It includes three sections: First, Jesus' ministry with the disciples in the setting of a supper (13:1-38), followed by his final instructions to his disciples (14: 1—17:26), and concluded with the exaltation of Jesus in the crucifixion and resurrection (18:1—20:29). John now builds his story to its grand climax.

Chapter 13, the first unit of the final half of the gospel, is a carefully designed and balanced literary piece which is comprised of a pair of events, each of which includes an expression of love followed by the prediction of rejection. The first is the act of Jesus' washing the feet of his disciples followed by the prediction of Judas' betrayal. The second is the discourse which includes the commandment to love succeeded by the prediction of Peter's denial. John here treats his readers to the paradox of the revelation of God and the human reaction to it, as he has so very often done.[20]

The Foot Washing and the Prediction of Judas' Betrayal (13:1-30)

1—The first indication in this gospel of a date for the last supper and the crucifixion different from that in the Synoptics is given abruptly: **before the feast of the Passover.** In effect, John's dating of these events is one day earlier than that which we find in the Synoptics (e.g., Mark 14:12; cf. 19:14 below). A reference to Jesus'

hour is followed by a brief statement of its meaning, to depart out
of this world to the Father. For hour cf. 2:4 above as well as 7:30
and 8:20. Departure (*metabainō*) is a metaphorical allusion to the
crucifixion-resurrection whereby Jesus returns to the Father. In 5:
24 and 1 John 3:14 the same word is used to speak of "passing
from death to life" (but it is used at 7:30, as well as several places
in the Synoptics, e.g., Luke 10:7, for simple geographical movement). World (*kosmos*) presages the importance of the disciples'
relationship with the reality of unbelief, to be discussed in the farewell speeches. The narrative about to be related is focused on
love, and that focus is introduced here. His own (*idios*) recalls 1:11
and the designation of Jesus' own sheep (10:3, 4). This is another
of John's ways of speaking of the affiliation of believers with Jesus.
To the end translates *telos*, which means both "completely" and
"conclusion." It is possible John meant to emphasize both of those
denotations, as he sometimes plays with words of multiple meanings (e.g., 3:8 above). The preface to this chapter, in which love is
so central, stresses that Jesus throughout his ministry has loved
(*agapēsas*) and will now express that love in the single act (*ēgapē-
sen*) of his death.

2-3—Verse 2 gives further features of the setting of the foot
washing. It must be understood in the context of the betrayal to be
predicted in vv. 21-30. The contrast between Jesus' love in v. 1
and Judas' intent to betray Jesus is vivid and pathetic, as John
wants it to be. It is important that Judas is included in the foot
washing, for it demonstrates Jesus' inclusive love. There is a textual variant which might be considered the more difficult reading,
"put into the heart *that* Judas," rather than put it into the heart *of*
Judas. The former would make little sense unless it is "the devil's
heart" that is meant, and the latter is to be preferred. For the devil
cf. 6:70 and 8:44 above and 12:31; 13:27; and 14:30 below. Notice the comparison with Luke 22:3. For Judas cf. 6:71 and 12:4
above. While John shares the view that Judas' betrayal was effected by the power of evil, he nonetheless maintains Judas' responsibility for the act. Verse 3 is still further qualification of the
circumstances of the foot washing. In v. 1 we are told "Jesus knew
his hour had come," and now we are informed of two additional

things that Jesus knows: (1) **The Father** . . . **hands,** meaning by the **all things** (*panta*) authority over all in general and/or all that would accomplish God's redemptive plan. In either case, his sovereignty is stressed as a contrast to the humble servant deed he is about to perform (cf. 3:35 above). (2) **That he had come** . . . **to God** communicates both the identity of Jesus as God's envoy and the importance of the "hour" in v. 1 as the completion of Jesus' mission. **Was going to God** means the "departure" mentioned in v. 1 and suggests that by his lowly death he will be exalted. In this sense then the footwashing is representative of his willingness to submit to his lowly death.

4-5—The shedding of **his garments** and putting on of the **towel** may be symbolic of Jesus' laying aside his life (since the same verb used here, *tithēmi*, is used of his life in 10:11, 15, 17, and 18) and taking it up again in resurrection (since the same verb used here in the translation, **girded himself,** *lambanein*, is employed of his receiving his life again in 10:17-18). While the foot washing is a foreshadowing of the crucifixion (vv. 6-8), it may be too much to find such symbolism in the act of robing for the act. Verse 5 states the act with extreme simplicity. **Basin** (*niptēr*) is a word not found in koine Greek outside of this passage. It is fashioned from the verb "to wash" (*niptein*), and hence would be an implement used in washing. Jesus' act is a radical departure from custom, since not even servants were required to **wash** the **feet** of their master. It reverses the relationship of the disciple and teacher (cf. 2 Kings 3:11). Peter's surprise and resistance in v. 6 are entirely understandable. **Disciples** raises the question of who is present on this occasion. *Mathētēs* is used in this gospel for any faithful follower (e.g., 6:66), and John describes those present not as the "Twelve" (for its use cf. only 6:66, 70, 71 and 20:24), implying that a wider range of believers may have participated. It appears John deliberately plays down the role of the Twelve in order that his readers and all believers might identify with the disciples. (John does not use "apostle" in its technical sense, but cf. v. 16 below.) The broader audience is assumed throughout the farewell discourses as well as here.

6-11—When **Peter's** turn comes, he protests Jesus' actions. Peter is represented elsewhere as typical of the lack of understanding of the passion on the part of the disciples (e.g., v. 36). In the Greek the pronouns **you** and **my** are side by side, indicating a contrast. Peter's question expresses a bewilderment. **Jesus** promises that the meaning of his act will become clear **afterward** (v. 7), literally, "after these things" (*tauta*). Are the "things" the explanation of the foot washing in vv. 12-17 or Jesus' death and resurrection? It seems more likely that it is the second option which is intended, as it is in the cleansing of the temple (2:22) and the entry into Jerusalem (12:16, where *tauta* is also used). The disciples, as well as the opponents of Jesus, do not understand Jesus' ministry until after the crucifixion-resurrection. Verse 7 shows the essentially synonymous meaning of the two words John uses for **know** (*oida* and *ginōskein*). Peter's reply in v. 8 has the force of an oath, for the negative is emphatic (*ou mē*, "no, never"). The point is not to denigrate Peter but to emphasize again the drastic nature of the servant deed performed by Jesus. Peter understandably does not want his master acting in such an unthinkable way. Jesus' reply expresses the symbolic importance of the foot washing. Being washed by Jesus is to be granted the benefits of his redeeming work. So, it would seem that the foot washing is representative of the cross and its saving effects as well as those of the entire revelation. Peter in v. 9 swings to the opposite stance—"since you put it that way, give me a bath!" It is possible that the author wanted Peter's words to denote his misunderstanding of his master. Jesus' meaning is the symbolic importance of the act, while Peter, like so many who misunderstand Jesus, is thinking of the physical washing. In spite of this dialog, Peter never really understands what Jesus is doing. The verb **bathed** (*louein*) is introduced in v. 10 but is used only in synonymous parallelism with **wash** (*niptein*). Behind Jesus' words may lie a proverb which has been adapted. The point is that those who embrace the revelation are "cleansed" by it, so that other "washings" are not necessary. The crucifixion makes the believer **clean** of the unbelief of the world. It is not the case that these words give a sacrificial interpretation of atonement, for the sacrificial cleansing is not implied. Although Judas has received the gift of washing, the act alone is not sufficient to make him clean, for he has already rejected Jesus' spiritual gift. While it is possible that the symbolism of the act is a veiled allusion to Baptism, it is difficult to argue thus. John's references to Baptism are all so uncertain that it is difficult to say that washing in this case was intended to suggest Baptism. In v. 11 **who was to betray** is literally, "who was giving him over." The second half of the verse, **that was . . . clean**, is likely a scribal addition for emphasis.

12-15—These verses comprise an explanation of the foot washing, which is not the same as the meaning suggested by the dialog between Peter and Jesus concerning cleansing, although it does not exclude that meaning. The emphasis of this explanation is on the exemplary quality of Jesus' act. **Resumed his place** is literally "reclined again," since the meal was eaten in a reclining position. **Do you know** may be the understanding mentioned in v. 7. The two titles in v. 13, **Teacher and Lord** (*ho didaskalos kai ho kyrios*), establish Jesus' identity with regard to his disciples, important in the discussion of the humble act of service. Both titles are common in John, and both were used in addressing one's rabbi. But the fuller Christian meaning of **Lord** is doubtless implied as well. In v. 14 the simple logic of the event is articulated: If the Teacher, then the student. Just how the expression, "washed the feet of the saints," in the description of the requirements for the office of widow in 1 Tim. 5:10, should be related to Jesus' point, if at all, is not clear. It is doubtful that the expression should be taken as evidence of a use of foot washing as a religious practice in the church. In v. 15 the word **example** (*hypodeigma*) is also found in Heb. 4: 11; 8:5; 9:23; James 5:10; 2 Peter 2:6.

John has told the story of the foot washing and conveyed two significantly different (although not incompatible) meanings. In the dialog with Peter (vv. 6-11) the deed is interpreted in terms of the atoning value of Christ's death with the metaphor of cleansing. In vv. 12-15, however, a simpler interpretation is given. Jesus' act is a humble service of love which is offered as a model for the relationship among the disciples (i.e., within the church). It is difficult to say just how the narrative of the deed was given the two distinctive meanings. The tradition possibly contained only the deed with its simple lesson of humble love, and John has inserted within that narrative the dialog with Peter to articulate what had been implied in the traditional form, namely, the significance of Jesus' death. Since the foot washing was a deed which in quality anticipated Jesus' death, the addition of the cleansing motif only heightened the allusion to the cross. Jesus' death was a humble servant deed done in love which has the effect of cleansing humans of their alienation from God. If the foot washing was practiced liturgically by the Johannine community, which is likely, it may have taken on overtones of a preparation for martyrdom, especially after the community became enmeshed in the controversy with the synagogue. As the foot washing was a deed which expressed Jesus' willingness to lay down his life for his disciples, believers washed the feet of their colleagues as a sign of their readiness to die for the faith.[21]

16—Verse 15 concludes the interpretation of the foot washing itself, but John has appended here a saying related to service. It is possibly an independent saying found within his tradition. The point is simply that the **servant** (or slave, *doulos*) cannot expect better treatment than his **master** (*kyrios*). The saying has some similarities with several Synoptic passages, Matt. 10:24-25 and Luke 6:40, the closest being the Matthean saying. John's version adds the second line (synonymous parallelism) in which the **servant/master** pair is followed by **he who is sent/he who sent him,** the latter reflecting typical Johannine language. **He who is sent** translates *apostolos* (apostle), but it is not used here in its technical sense of one of the followers of Christ (as in, e.g., Luke 6:13). Here two different words are used for **sent,** and they occur without significant difference (i.e., *apostellō* and *pempō*). Verse 16a speaks with Johannine ambiguity of both Christ as the one sent and of believers (cf. 20:21b). But in the shadow of the cross this saying means that discipleship involves a commitment which includes a willingness to suffer martyrdom. Disciples can expect any honor afforded them to arise only out of suffering, as it did for their master. John's first readers may have known some persecution and hence found these words reassuring.

17-18—It is not clear what **things** (*tauta*) are referred to, and it is equally unclear as to how one might "do" what is described in v. 16. Perhaps the antecedent is back to the foot washing, and v. 16

is parenthetical. More likely, this is another independent saying John has linked loosely to this context. John 12:47 counsels the same point, namely, obey what is heard (cf. Luke 11:28). **Blessed** (*makarioi*) describes a state which reflects the reign of God, that is, a condition like that which God desires for his creatures. Such a condition reflects both the gift of God and the willing response of the humans. Verse 18 once again casts the shadow of betrayal over the discussion. As John punctuates the narrative at v. 10b with an allusion to Judas, now he does so again. Judas has disqualified himself from the state of blessedness just mentioned. But this verse is also concerned to show that Judas' betrayal did not come as a surprise to Jesus. In his sovereignty Jesus knew what Judas would do, and yet still Jesus agonizes over the fact of the betrayal (cf. v. 21 below). It is not clear whether it is Judas who has been **chosen,** and hence is predetermined to betray Jesus, or whether the others have been chosen, but not Judas. John 6:70 seems to suggest that the options are not exclusive. All the disciples are chosen, and one is chosen in full knowledge of his future act. The betrayal (certainly embarrassing to the earliest Christians) is done to **fulfill scripture.** The fulfillment of Scripture is used to explain Judas' deed elsewhere in the NT (e.g., Acts 1:16). In this case, the passage is Ps. 41:9, which was sometimes interpreted in the light of Absalom's betrayal of David (2 Samuel 13). John's quotation does not carefully follow either the Hebrew or the Greek text here, but seems closer to the former. The meaning is that one who has shared a meal with the psalmist has now turned against him. **Lifted his heel against me** is apparently a loose translation of a Hebrew idiom for scorn. Just how the lifting of the heel is scornful is obscure. Some suggest it means "kicking me from behind" and others that showing one's heel to another was an insulting gesture among Arabs. It is not necessary to see an allusion to the Eucharist in the mention of **bread.** The point is the bitter experience of having one with whom you have shared the intimacy of a meal turn against you.

19—This verse attempts to turn what might be a scandal for faith into a cause for belief. It is again stressed that Judas' betrayal is not unexpected, and Jesus is here actually foretelling what will transpire. When the disciples experience what will happen, they will remember how Jesus predicted it and **believe that I am he.** Prophecy fulfillment is a common occasion for faith, as 8:28 shows. **I am he** translates *egō eimi.* The predicate (**he**) may be implied or it may be another instance of the absolute **I am** (cf. 6:20; 8:24, 28, 58 above). Isaiah 43:10 is evoked by these words. The message is that even the dastardly deed of betrayal is turned on its head to become an experience that nurtures faith. Even the actions of the unfaithful may be used by God to call forth faith. Such is his sovereignty.

20—This saying returns once again, after the intrusion of the discussion of the betrayer, to the subject of discipleship. It is another loosely related saying placed here by the evangelist because of the catchword "sent"—**send** (cf. v. 16). It has a theme similar to 5:23 but is best explained by 20:21. In the view of John, the mission of the church and of the disciples takes its model from the relationship between the Father and the Son and the mission of the revealer. Hence, mission arises from a Christological base and is inferred from the act of God's sending his Son (cf. Matt. 10:40; Luke 10:16; and Mark 9:37). The logion traces the lines of authority from God to Christ to the disciples and may have served the early church as an authorization of the community's mission.

21-23—The betrayal has been referred to twice already in this section (vv. 10b and 18-19) but now becomes the main subject in vv. 21-30. Verse 21 speaks of the agony of the thought of betrayal. **Troubled in spirit** (*etarachthē tō pneumati*) employs the same verb found in 11:23 and 12:27 (cf. above). **Testified** (literally, "testified and said") sounds almost as if the words are a formal charge, althought the charge is not named (cf. 1:32 and 4:44, where *martyreō* is used to introduce a declaration). The disciples do not understand this (v. 22), and so they attempt to get help (v. 23). At this point in John the mysterious "beloved disciple" is introduced. Here his intimacy is emphasized by **lying close to the breast of Jesus** (cf. Introduction §2).

24-27—The exact position of the beloved disciple need not concern us (i.e., how in a reclining position the disciple would have been close to Jesus' breast), for John only wishes to stress the closeness of the relationship with Jesus. In v. 24 **Peter** tries to gain some insight into Jesus' words by asking the beloved disciple to intervene. Peter assumes here the role of spokesperson for the disciples, as he is often pictured doing (cf. 6:68; Mark 8:29). **Beckoned** translates *neuei*, which describes a gesture rather than a word, i.e., "nodded" or "motioned" (cf. TEV). Textual witnesses are divided from that point on in this verse. There are two major readings, that of the RSV and "to ask who it was about whom he was speaking." The first assumes that the beloved disciple knows the identity of the betrayer while the second asks the beloved disciple to learn who it is. The second appears to be a scribal effort to harmonize the verse with what is said of that disciple in the next sentence. Verse 25 literally describes the beloved disciple "falling back" (*anapesōn*) on **the breast of Jesus.** He then asks Jesus the question which in the Synoptics appears on the lips of the disciples as a whole, "It is I, Lord" (e.g., Matt. 26:22). Here the word is **breast,** *stēthos,* while in v. 23 it is *kolpos,* "bosom" (cf. 1:18 above). In v. 26 **Jesus** takes the initiative and gives **Judas the morsel.** John again intends that we see that Jesus has full knowledge of what is to happen, but here extends a gesture of love and acceptance to the betrayer. It may be bread that is dipped or, if the narrative still contains remnants of a Passover meal setting, it might be bitter herbs that are dipped in a sauce. Efforts to see here eucharistic features are farfetched (compare Mark 14:20 and Matt. 26:23). For Judas cf. 6:71; 12:4; and 13:2 above. Ironically the moment in which Jesus expresses his act of love is the occasion of the betrayer's resolution to fulfill his plans (expressed in the mythological symbol of **Satan** invading Judas' will, v. 27). This is the only time John uses the term **Satan.** "Devil" is more common (cf. 6:70; 8:44; and 13:2). With his next words Jesus actually starts the process of the betrayal itself, another hint of John's insistence on Jesus' sovereignty in the situation. **What you are going to do, do quickly** means either "do what you are about to do" or "do what it is you are determined to do" (compare Luke 22:3).

28-30—Verse 28 is hardly believable in terms of verisimilitude, for surely the beloved disciple could have discerned what was taking place, if not also the other disciples present. But John is not primarily interested here in convincing narrative. His intent is more theological than literary. Even among Jesus' most intimate followers there is still not the faintest notion of what is about to transpire. John's motif of misunderstanding increases the sense of incomprehension of the will of the Father, for such is the disciples' immersion in darkness. The misunderstanding is stated in v. 29. It presupposes what has been stated in 12:4-8 (cf. above). That Judas would go to **buy what we need for the feast** (Passover) suffers from the doubt that purchasing for the Passover meal would take place after sundown. But **that he should give something to the poor** might have been encouraged on the eve of the feast. On the other hand, **night** (*nyx*) in v. 30 is less a designation of time than a theological statement: Judas belongs to the darkness by virtue of his willful act of treason, the same darkness into which Christ came to bring light (1:5). The night that was to end Jesus' ministry (9:4; 11:10; and 12:35) has arrived.

The pairing of the foot washing and the prediction of betrayal is deliberate on the part of the author, for he wants to underscore the tragic irony of divine love and evil will. Out of the most intimate of situations and the context of love the betrayer is set on his course. John will now illustrate the same point in another pair of narratives.

The Love Commandment and the Prediction of Peter's Denial (13:31-38)

The terrible paradox of divine love and human betrayal is emphasized once again, this time with the revelation of the will of God in the command to love and the anticipation of Peter's unfaithfulness. In the first, the meaning of the foot washing is articulated in another injunction (cf. vv. 14-15 above). While the prediction of Peter's denial parallels Judas' betrayal, its tragic dimension is visible only in the context of the request that the disciples love as Jesus loves. This short unit provides an important introduction and transition to the discourses of the three following chapters.

31-32—This discussion is prefaced with the announcement that Judas is no longer privy to the matters of the family of faith, specifically this discourse and the ones that follow in chaps. 14–16. For **Son of man** cf. 1:51 above. The glorification of Jesus takes place supremely in his death, the nature of which is indicated in the foot washing. **In him God is glorified** means that God's powerful and loving presence is manifested in Jesus' death. Glorification in the cross is found in the divine love which is expressed there. Glorification is spoken of here in the past tense, betraying the perspective of John and his community. But in v. 32 the perspective switches back to Jesus' time, and the verb is future—**will . . . glorify.** It is difficult to decide whether **if God is glorified in him** should be preserved in the reading, for the phrase is missing in some significant witnesses (e.g., P^{66}); but its loss is more easily imagined than its addition. The phrase repeats the sense of v. 31c and makes the glorification reciprocal. That is, since God is made known in Jesus, Jesus will be honored and his identity broadcast in God (**in himself**). The close relationship of the Father and the Son means that as one's nature is manifested so is the identity of the other. Christ's love reveals God's love, and God's love confirms Christ's. **At once** (*euthys*) signals the imminence of the crucifixion-resurrection (cf. v. 33 below) and implies perhaps that, as distinct from some future eschatologies, the glorification of Christ need not be postponed until the parousia but occurs in Good Friday and Easter.

33-35—**Little children** (*teknia*) is an address of endearment found only here in this gospel but seven times in 1 John (2:1, 12, 28; 3:7, 18; 4:4; 5:21). Its occurrence here might reflect the fact that the final discourse of John's gospel underwent some revision at the hand of the author of 1 John.[22] Its use suggests the author has in mind his own readers. Gradually there emerges in the relationship of Jesus and his followers (including the readers) a sense of a family grouping (cf. 1:12 above). For **a little while** cf. 7:33 and 12:35 as well as 14:19 and 16:16-17 below. The "now" and "at once" of v. 31 stand in tension with a **little while** here. That tension is characteristic of the transcendence of temporal distinctions in John's version of Jesus' passion (e.g., 20:17 below). For **seek me** cf. 7:34, 36, and 8:21 above. The reference **as I said . . .** is to 8:21. **I am going** (*hypagō*, cf. 7:33 above) captures the whole process of

Jesus' departure, the crucifixion-resurrection-ascension by which Jesus moves into the divine realm. The disciples cannot go with Jesus, but he promises eventually to come and take them with him (14:3). They share the human limitations of time and space with Jesus' opponents. **Jews** appears here on the lips of Jesus, but clearly reflects the situation of the evangelist.

34—The disciples are not now able to follow Jesus into the divine realm, but they can realize in this world a feature of that realm—they can **love one another.** The bond of mutual love (here *agapē*) in the community is a feature of John's realized eschatology. As believers may be glorified and made one in some future experience (cf. 17:1ff. below), they can now love one another in a way that anticipates that future life. **Commandment** (*entolē*) appears eight times in this gospel, all in chaps. 12–15, and will be a featured theme of the final discourses (e.g., 14:15, 21; 15:10, 12). What is **new** about this commandment is not found in the injunction itself (cf. Lev. 19:18) but in the source and function of the love. It arises from Jesus' own caring for the community—**as I have loved you.** The model and source of love is Jesus' death, the supreme expression of love (15:13). The disciples are not left on their own to conjure up concern for one another out of a determination of will, but are empowered to love by themselves being loved (cf. 1 John 4:7-12). Another vital dimension of this love will be stated later, namely, that it is modeled after the love relationship between the Father and the Son (cf. 14:21 and 15:9 below). **New** (*kainos*) is used only here and 19:41 in this gospel and three times in the Johannine Epistles (1 John 2:7, 8 and 2 John 5). The implications of the motif of the new covenant are not found in the passage nor its setting; covenantal theology is not one of John's interests. While the Greek word *agapaō* is used here for love, John can as easily use *phileō* without a change of meaning (e.g., 16:27). The other new thing about the commandment is its function, expressed in v. 35. It serves as a revelation of one's relationship with Christ. It is striking that Jesus' death "will draw all (*pantas*) persons" to him (12:32), and mutual love among Christians will inform all persons (*pantes*; note that **men** is not in the Greek) of the disciple's commitment. It is only that quality of concern which dis-

tinguishes the believer from the world. The emphasis of this commandment is on a love *within* the community (cf. 15:12) and nothing is said of loving those outside the community (contrast Matt. 5:
43-45). Given the situation of the Johannine church (cf. Introduction), it is not surprising that what is nurtured here is a kind of sec-
tarian love. It should not be forgotten, however, that the believers
are "sent" into the world for others—a world God loves (3:16; cf.
20:21).

36-38—In v. 36 the attention shifts to **Peter** and his forthcom-
ing denial. He yearns for a continued relationship with **Jesus** and
has not understood the words spoken in v. 33, even as Jesus' audience misunderstood the same remark in 7:35. (Again, the disciples possess no special knowledge that separates them from Jesus'
opponents, but only a faith that hangs on in the midst of ignorance.) Peter thinks of a physical, geographical "going." John 16:5
demonstrates the likelihood that v. 36 came from a different
source and/or was introduced into this gospel at a different stage of
editing than the third form of the farewell discourses (cf. below).
In Jesus' answer, **follow** (*akolouthēsai*) means discipleship (cf. 1:
37ff. above) but with the implication here of martyrdom! To be a
disciple has just been described as a following which may lead to
death (12:25-26). **Afterward** (*hysteron*) denotes the occasion of
Peter's martyrdom, spoken of again in 21:18-19. At the time of his
martyrdom Peter too will follow Jesus into the presence of God.
Peter's inflated confidence is expressed in v. 37. He uses the very
words of Jesus in 10:11 (*psychēn tithenai*) which makes his boast ridiculous, since he cannot **lay down** his **life** in the same sense as
Christ does his. There is both irony and pathos in Jesus' answer in
v. 38. The irony is that Peter *will* die for his Lord but not as or
when Peter thinks. The pathos is in the tragedy of human frailty
even in the midst of noble intentions. It is only the results of the
cross and resurrection that will empower Peter at a later time to
lay down his life for Jesus. For now, his weakness must be expressed in denial (18:15-18, 25-27; compare Matt. 26:30-35;
Mark 14:26-31; and Luke 22:31-34).

In two pairs of narratives John has affirmed divine love and human failings. But what emerges as the leitmotiv is the centrality of

love, both as it is expressed by Christ and made the badge of Christian discipleship. That theme is carried over into the following chapters, with the result that as the tragedy of human blindness is worked out so is the eminence of divine love.

■ Parting Words: The Farewell Discourses and Prayer (14:1—17:26)

These chapters are among the most difficult and the most important of this gospel. Their importance is found in the suggestion that they are the concluding private instructions of the disciples by Jesus, not to mention the giant theological themes which make up their content (e.g., the Paraclete). However, they are also among the most puzzling of the sections of John, due to their apparent composite character. There is, first, a high degree of repetition among the chapters (e.g., the power of asking in prayer, 14:13-14; 15:7, 16b; 16:23-24, 26). Second, there are a number of sudden disjunctures in the flow of the discourse (e.g., 14:31 and 16:4b; cf. below). Finally, there are topics scattered in a disorganized fashion throughout the chapters (e.g., the Paraclete, 14:15-17, 26; 15:26-27; 16:7-14).

It is widely held that in these chapters we find several forms of one essential discourse. John 14:31 is generally taken to be the break between a first and second form of the discourse. Whether or not chaps. 15–16 comprise a single unit, forming the second version of the discourse, is debatable. Some find in 16:4 a division between what might be the second and third versions. Within that single verse there seems to be a change of thought ("I have said these things. . .I did not say these things. . . "). From this arises the proposal that there are three forms of one discourse— 14:1-31; 15:1—16:4a; and 16:4b-33. The relationship of 13:31-38 to these seems to be that of a transition to one or all of the discourses.

It appears that a single discourse has undergone revision and expansion not once but twice, with the result that all three versions found their way into this gospel. Why this should occur we can at best merely speculate, but they have the appearance of statements of counsel and encouragement to a community suffering abandonment and uncertainty soon after what might have been the division of the community from its Jewish home in the synagogue. The evangelist or members of the church have interpreted and reinterpreted some traditional words of Jesus in an effort to address them to the critical situation of the community. There is some evidence that the order of the three discourses in this gospel reflects a chronological order of composition, for instance, the ever-increasing sense of a dualistic relationship with the "world" in each of the three. It is on the basis of this hypothesis that I will proceed with the commentary. The chart, "Themes in the Farewell Discourses" (p. 235), will serve as an overview of the major motifs of the discourses and a comparison of the contents of the three sections.[23]

Discourse I—Loss and Restoration (14:1-31)

1—The setting for the beginning of the first discourse would seem to be the departure of Jesus mentioned in 13:33. But that explicit setting is broadened by an implicit one—the sense of the absence of Jesus from the community and the delay of the parousia. In the original setting the departure of Jesus might have been the crucifixion, but in the church's interpretation it has become the more general sense of abandonment which the Johannine Christians acutely felt in the schism with the synagogue. Verse 1, then, appropriately begins with words of comfort. **Hearts** is singular in Greek (*hē kardia*), perhaps an instance of the "distributive singular" (cf. Luke 1:66). **Troubled** has been used of Jesus' emotions (11:33 and 13:21, *tarassō*). **Believe in God . . . me** can be translated a number of ways, depending on whether the verbs are to be taken as indicatives or imperatives (i.e., "You do believe" or the command to believe). Since **troubled** is an imperative (*tarassesthō*), **believe** should also be understood as such. The close relationship of the Father and the Son implies that belief in one includes belief in the other. Here Jesus seeks to encourage the believers' confidence in him.

2—This verse introduces the concept of **rooms**. Heaven was widely understood as the dwelling place of God, hence his **house** (e.g., Ps. 2:4; 103:19; 123:1). The concept of heavenly apartments for the righteous is also attested in Jewish thought (e.g., 1 Enoch 39:4f.). The Greek word rendered **rooms** (*monai*) meant temporary shelters used by travelers. But it is the noun formed from the important Johannine verb *menein*, "to abide, remain." Since the latter in John has reference to a close and reciprocal relationship (e.g., vv. 10, 17), the noun **rooms** would mean the condition or state of living in that relationship. The thought is then that there is a condition of intimacy with the Father awaiting the believer. It has to do more with a *relationship* than with a *place.* While this promise has to do with the heavenly existence of the believers, there is also a sense that this relationship is realized in the association of Christ with his church (cf. v. 3 below). The remainder of the verse, **if it. . .for you,** is difficult to translate due to the lack of punctuation in early texts. First is the question whether **if it were. . .told you** constitutes a complete sentence and whether that sentence is a question ("If it were not so, would I have told you?") or a statement ("If it were not so, I would have told you"). The second issue is the relationship of **that I go to . . .** with the previous sentence. (**That,** *hoti,* is omitted by some manuscripts, an apparent effort to clarify the meaning.) If the clause continues the **if it were . . . told you,** it may then be a statement or a question. Furthermore, *hoti* may have the force of either "that" or "because." The best possibility seems to be the following: "If it were not so, I would have told you. I am going to prepare a place for you." **That** is thereby taken as an introduction to the last clause (cf. TEV). The meaning of this is the assurance (1) that Jesus would not mislead his followers with such a promise and (2) that he goes ahead of his followers, forging a place for them. **I go** (*poreuomai*) means the same as "I am going" in 13:33—Jesus' death, which is his ascension to the Father. His passion is the means by which he makes available the opportunity to dwell in relationship with the Father.

3—**When** may be translated "if" (*ean*), but the reassuring quality of these words indicates that the RSV is preferable. **Come again** is ambiguous in this setting. Is the author thinking of the parousia, the resurrection appearances, or the coming of the Spirit-Paraclete? It is likely that the original meaning had reference to the parousia, but John intends it to apply *equally* to the presence of the resurrected Christ in the Spirit which makes his presence an immediate reality for the readers. Similarly, that place to which Jesus **will take you** has both a future-heavenly referent and a present reality in the church. Such an ambiguous meaning is necessitated by John's consistent effort to see the future eschatological hope realized (at least in part) in the present life of the believer (e.g., 5:24-29 above). This means that while John holds out a hope for a future and heavenly relationship, he affirms that that relationship exists already for the life of faith. The heart of the promise is expressed in the last phrase of the verse—it is the presence of Christ that makes the difference for the believer (cf. 17:26). Where the believers are in the presence of Christ, there they are safe.

4-6a—"Where I am" in v. 3 occasions the theme of **the way**, turning "attention from the destination to the *route*" (Lindars, p. 417). The Greek of v. 4 is obscure, and a clearer reading is found in some textual witnesses: "Where I am going you know and you know the way." But the shorter reading translated in the RSV is to be preferred, if only because it is the more difficult. The verse is clearly designed to introduce Thomas' question in v. 5 and should be translated in the light of that. **The way** (*hodos*) would seem to mean, on the first impression, the way of the cross, a suffering route to exaltation. **Thomas'** question in v. 5 serves only to occasion Jesus' further pronouncement in v. 6. Thomas is mentioned here, 11:16; 20:24ff.; and 21:2. Verse 6 is another of the "I am" sayings with the predicate (cf. 6:35, 51; 8:12; 9:5; 10:7, 9, 11, 14; 11:25; 15:1, 5). The meaning of **the way** seems to shift here, since in the previous verse it refers to Jesus' way which is the cross. Now it is the Christians' way which is under consideration. The two meanings are connected in that Jesus' death and resurrection (his way) makes him the way by which humanity comes to the Father. Way is used only in this discussion in John (except for 1:23 where it is employed in a different sense). That may possibly mean that the word hints at a traditional saying John has embodied in the discourse. The word is found in the OT (*derek*) to speak of the moral path of obedience (e.g., Josh. 22:5) and the direction led by wisdom (e.g., Prov. 3:17). It became a self-designation for the Qum-

ran Essenes (e.g., 1QS 9:21) much as it did for Christians (Acts 9:
2). In Hellenistic religions it was used to speak of the process by
which the initiate became divine (Bultmann, pp. 603-604). John
means that Jesus is the medium by which one is given the revealing love of God which brings with it proper self-understanding and
a peaceful relationship with God. The next two nouns, **truth and
life,** are intended to qualify and explain **way.** It might, however,
be the case that **way** is intended to identify the means to the goal
and **truth** and **life** the goal itself. The first of the alternatives is
more in keeping with Johannine thought. The path to truth and
life is none other than the one who is that truth and life (cf. 1:4 and
4:24 above). In effect, then, the three nouns designate three synonymous functions effected by Christ. The revelation is itself truth
which yields life in its truest sense, and the revelation is the way by
which those benefits are extended to humanity. In sum, it is Christ
who is all that humans need in order to find release from the realm
of darkness and misunderstanding.

6b-7—The second half of v. 6 draws the obvious conclusion of
the first half: Jesus is the only means by which the revelation is bestowed. These words are best seen not as a universal declaration
for all time and place but as a confession of the Johannine community in the midst of their own situation. The exclusiveness of
this statement had its source in the difficult and threatening dialog
with the synagogue and affirms over against Judaism the effectiveness of Christian faith. Neither Jesus nor John had in mind a judgment of world religions unknown to them. The thought of the
clause emerges, moreover, out of the relationship of Christ and
God and declares the functional reality of that relationship for humans. Jesus serves as the passage to **the Father** (cf. 10:7). Verse 7
brings the conclusion of the line of thought pursued in vv. 1-7, and
its promise is that the disciples do **know** (*ginōskein*) and **see** the **Father.** However, the first half (**if you had . . . Father also**) depends
upon a difficult textual decision. The sentence is found in two
forms with nearly equal textual support. In the one case, the condition is contrary to the fact. This is the reading followed by the
RSV. The other reads as a promise rather than a reproach ("If you
have come to know me as you have . . ."). This reading is adopted

by the Greek texts of Nestle (26th edition) and the United Bible Societies and is followed by the TEV. The second is harmonious with the latter half of the verse (and hence constitutes the easier reading). The first reflects the influence of 8:19. Commentators are divided, and the decision is tenuous at best. In either case, however, whether the first half of the verse is a reproach or a promise, the second half is an assuring statement. It expresses an accomplished fact—the disciples **know** and **have seen the Father. Henceforth** (*ap' arti*) is the pivotal expression, and it means that as a result of Jesus' exaltation the disciples are assured of grasping the revelation.

8-9—Philip's question indicates, however, that the revelation of the exaltation is not yet complete. Philip has played a role several places in this gospel (cf. 1:43ff. and 12:21f. above), and on the occasion of the feeding of the multitude is also given a question which reflects lack of understanding (6:5ff. above). His question here is little more than a foil by which Jesus is allowed to continue the discussion. His query does, however, reflect the existential longing for the vision of the ultimate reality for which there is a universal search. Perhaps his words reflect Exod. 33:18. **Show** (*deixō*) is an imperative which, if fulfilled, will suffice to fill human need. Verse 9 is now clearly a reproach, even if v. 7a is not. The whole life and ministry of Jesus have been windows through which God is seen. To know **Jesus** is to be brought to the **Father.** The last sentence is the simplest summary of John's view of the revelation in Christ. It involves a "seeing" which perceives the historical Jesus but which also senses more than the physical human. It is to see in a more profound way, a faith seeing (cf. Kysar, *John*, pp. 73-77). John's words here address the reality of doubt among the Christians of his community, doubt stirred by the challenges of the conflict with the synagogue (cf. 20:24-29). In this sense, the whole of the gospel is a commentary on 1:18.

10-11—Philip's question shows a failure of faith, as v. 10 suggests. The perception of **the Father** in Jesus depends upon a perspective of belief and cannot be documented in such a way as to preclude faith. **I am in the Father and the Father in me** expresses one dimension of the relationship among God, Christ, and the believer. John states that relationship alternatively with the preposition in (*en*) and the verb "dwell in" (*menein*). The formulation found here is taken up in 14:20 and 17:21. While the sense of being in has been sometimes taken to refer to a unity of being (ontological) or a mystical union, Johannine Christology in general shows that it is a functional oneness that is meant (but cf. 1:1f. for its ontological implications). Philip's question misses the point Jesus has repeatedly made, namely, that his words and acts are not his own but those of the Father (e.g., 12:44ff. above). Verse 10 moves from Jesus' words (**speak**) to **works** (*erga*). God's word and his acts are ultimately the same. (*Dabar* can mean both "word" and "deed" in Hebrew.) Hence, the revelatory words of Jesus and his acts are finally one and the same; each supplements the other. However, while this gospel favors faith in Jesus' words (e.g., 4:50b above), his mighty **works** are the more easily believed revelation (cf. 10:38). God's presence in Christ expresses itself in both the spoken word and the enacted word. Verse 11 restates the thrust of the discussion. As in v. 1, Jesus commands belief (the imperative of *pisteuein*), possibly signaling a closure of sorts for the unit vv. 1-11. Here, however, the faith requested is faith in Jesus' statement **that** (*hoti*) **I am in the Father.** . . . Faith is by implication giving credence to a proposition (cf. 11:27 above). If it is not possible to embrace the statement of the relationship of the Father and Christ, the disciples are urged to **believe** on the basis of the **works** mentioned in v. 10. Such faith in Jesus' deeds is an introductory level of believing which is positive only insofar as it leads the believer to a higher level of faith (cf. 20:29).

12-14—These verses state the results of the life of faith, if the condition of believing spoken of in the previous verses is filled. But the belief on which the results are founded is the personal, trusting relationship with Jesus—**believes in me** (*ho pisteuōn eis eme*)—in contrast to the creedal faith mentioned in v. 11. The results of this faith are twofold: In v. 12 it is the privilege of doing **greater** (*meizona*) **works.** Works (*erga*) should be understood as inclusive of wonders, but it means more widely all acts which express God's redemptive concern for humans. The **greater works** are the evangelical spread of the kerygma through the mission of the church—

a spread which far exceeds that of Jesus' ministry. This is possible
for the church only because, first, the revelation of Christ will have
been accomplished and, second,the Spirit which empowers the
church will have been given (20:21-22). Both of these are **because**
(*hoti*) Jesus goes **to the Father.** It is not then that Jesus is de-
meaned by this prediction, rather the opposite. It is he who makes
the **greater works** possible. The second result of faith is expressed
in v. 13. This is a statement made in several different ways
throughout all three of the forms of the discourse (cf. 15:7, 16; 16:
23, 24, 26), as well as in 1 John (3:21-22; 5:14-15; cf. Brown, vol.
2, pp. 634-636 for a comparison of the verses). The disciples are
promised that their prayers will be heard. **Whatever** (*ho ti an*) emphasizes the inclusiveness of the power of their asking, but **in my
name** (*en tō onomati mou*) closely qualifies it. While invoking the
name of a divine person was in the ancient world a way of performing magic through that one's power, the name of Jesus brings
power but also responsibility. To **ask in my name** means to ask
what is harmonious with the will of Christ and consistent with the
Father's love. **I will do it** comes as a shock, for we expect Jesus to
say that *God* will do it (compare 15:16 and 16:23). But in the context of the functional unity of the Father and the Son what God
does Jesus does as well. The implication is that Christ continues to
work, even after his return to the Father; and that work continues
in the future to glorify Christ even as God has **glorified** him in his
earthly ministry. Verse 14 may be a scribal repetition (it is omitted
in some manuscripts) or a repetition of the thought of v. 13 for emphasis. This promise of answered prayer needs to be seen in the
light of the evangelical mission of the church alluded to in the previous verse. Those "greater works" of the expression of God's redemptive love come through the believers who ask for them. The
asking is part of the ongoing work of God.

15—A new thought comes with abruptness, and its relationship
with the previous discussion is a bit uncertain. **Love** means obedience in John's view and binds the believer to God/Christ. **You will
keep** is one of three manuscript readings. In some it is future (*tēr-
ēsete*) followed by the RSV, **you will keep.** In others it is imperative (*tērēsate*). And in still others we find the subjunctive (*tērēsēte*,

"love me [and] keep my commandments, then . . . "). The first best suits what is said in the conditional clause, **if you love me. Commandments** in the plural is strange, for we know of only one commandment, namely, to love one another, 13:34. The singular is also found in 15:12, although the plural is used as well in 14:21 and 15:10. But vv. 23 and 24 show that it is not the single commandment to love which is meant here but Jesus' message as a whole (his *logos*, singular in v. 23 and *logoi*, plural in v. 24). So the injunction to **keep my commandments** is the same as "hearing" Jesus' word(s) (8:47; 12:47; 5:24) or "abiding" in them (15:7) or "continuing" in them (8:31). Those "words" in John mean to believe and live a life-style of faith, at the heart of which is love. It is not the moral content of the life of faith which interests John as much as it is the posture of faith; for he seems to have thought that morality followed naturally from such a posture. (It is this very matter which is one of the problems facing the author of 1 John, e.g., 2:9.)

16—The first of the Paraclete passages is vv. 16-17. It is related to the context in that the giving of the Spirit is implied in vv. 12-14, but it is far from an integral part of the chapter. Each of the passages dealing with the Paraclete is only loosely related to its context, which suggests that they may have been insertions in the process of the evolution of the farewell discourses.[24] In this case, v. 16, it is Jesus' prayer which evokes the giving of the Paraclete by the **Father** (contrast 15:26; 16:7). **Counselor** translates *paraklētos*, but it is difficult to find an adequate translation. Within the judicial realm the word could mean "intercessor" or "advocate" (the NEB translation; cf. 1 John 2:1 RSV), and in the sphere of religious thought it was used to mean "proclaimer" (cf. Rom. 12:8) and "comforter" (the KJV translation, e.g., Acts 9:31). Its immediate background, so far as John was concerned, might have been the role attributed to angels in some Jewish thought of the first century (cf. Kysar, *Fourth Evangelist*, pp. 234-240). John or his tradition enlisted this word and pressed it into service to become a means by which a new and richer view of the Spirit might be conceived and communicated. In this case, the Paraclete is called **another** (*allon*) **Counselor**, which suggests that Jesus was the first.

Hence, there is a continuity of function between the Spirit and the historical Jesus. (The Paraclete is Jesus' alter ego!) Unlike Jesus, the Paraclete remains with the believers **for ever**. It appears, then, that one of the functions John assigns to the Spirit-Paraclete is to provide a permanent presence of God with the community of believers. That figure fills the void left by the absence of Jesus due to the delay of the parousia. John does not terminate the presence of the resurrected Christ with the ascension followed by the bestowal of the Spirit, as does Luke (Acts 1:9-11), but has the one presence flow into the other without temporal distinction (20:22). Nonetheless, it is clear that this fourth evangelist thought of the Paraclete as the continuing presence of the resurrected Christ in the church. On the other functions of the Paraclete cf. below 14: 26; 15:26-27; and 16:7-14.

17—Here the Paraclete is called the **Spirit of truth** (*to pneuma tēs alētheias*), as is also the case in 14:26 and 16:13 (however, in 14:26 the Paraclete is called "the Holy Spirit"). **Truth** in this gospel means the revelation of God in Christ (1:17) which is synonymous with Christ himself (cf. v. 6 above). The Paraclete is **the Spirit of truth** in that she/he brings the revelation to the community in *any* age and leads it to "all the truth" (16:13), which is to say all of the ramifications of the revelation (cf. 1 John 4:6 and 5: 6). Such a Spirit of truth appears in the Qumran literature as one who purifies the faithful (e.g., 1QS 4:12). Verse 17 in effect states two things about the Counselor: First, it is not known or accepted by **the world** and, second, it *is* with the believers and known by them. World (*kosmos*) designates in the farewell discourses the realm of unbelief between which and the church there is hostile opposition (cf. 1:10f. and 3:16 above). **The world** is blinded to the reality of the Paraclete by its inability to perceive the revelation. **Know** (*ginōskei*) means not just creedal acceptance but a trusting relationship as well. The verbs **sees** and **knows** are in the present tense, betraying the perspective of the evangelist and his community. **Dwells** is the familiar Johannine word *menein* which suggests a mutual relationship of intimacy. John will use this verb to construct the pattern of relationships among God, Christ, the believer, and the Spirit (cf. below). In this first of the Paraclete passages the function of the Counselor is limited to the inner life of the church. The Spirit is accessible only to those who dare to perceive the present in faith.

18-19—The promise with which the chapter begins is resumed, and it flows from the promise of the giving of the Paraclete. **Desolate** (*orphanous*) is literally "orphaned." Commentators point out that the concept was used for disciples being deprived of their masters both in Judaism and Hellenism. Doubtless it is a state of affairs experienced by the Johannine community cast out of its home with its "parents" in the synagogue. **I will come to you** repeats the promise of v. 3 and raises again the problem of which *"coming"* is meant (cf. v. 3 above). It is, however, the coming of the Paraclete which is most relevant here. **Yet a little while** (v. 19, *mikron*) refers to the impending crucifixion (cf. 13:33 above as well as the related expression "a little longer" at 8:33 and 12:35 above). It is because of his death that **the world will see me no more**, and because of his resurrection that **you will see me**. There is a play on the word **see** (*theōreō*) here, for in the first instance it means no more than physical sight, while in the second it is a perception which is the result of faith (i.e., the resurrection appearances are experiences of faith). The semicolon after **see me** is one way of relating the previous sentence with the clause **that I live . . . live also**. It is better, however, to run the sentence on through that clause. **You will see me; because I live . . . I live** is then an affirmation of Jesus' resurrected life. The Greek literally reads, "**because I live** *and* **you will live**." As a result of Christ's having life after resurrection, the believers too are given life. These two verses describe the promise of the resurrection to believers; for it means they are not left alone (deprived of the divine presence), and they are given life.

20—The monolog goes on to state still another promise fulfilled in Christ's death and resurrection. **In that day** has the ring of eschatological language, for the expression summarizes the OT concept of the "Day of the Lord" (e.g., Amos 5:18) and is used in Christian apocalyptic thought (e.g., Mark 13:32). The reference here, however, is to the resurrection of Christ, and hence it speaks of the promise of the eschatological time already fulfilled in the community of faith (cf. the same expression in 16:23, 26 and "the last day" in 6:39, 40, 44, 54; 11:24; and 12:48). In that realized eschatological day the believers will know what they have been invited to believe in v. 11. What is spoken of here is the relationship which exists between God and Christ and the way in which the believers' relationship with Christ will become like that divine relationship. This is the first clear indication of the Johannine scheme by which the believer's relationships are modeled after the Christological relationships (cf. the chart on p. 266). In this case, the believers are incorporated into the Christological relationship, making them part of the network of divine love.

21—The association of the believer and Christ is exegeted in v. 21 in terms of love. First, there is a restatement of the contents of v. 15, so that the discourse has spiraled back to that theme even as it has forged forward. To love (*agapaō* in this case) is once again to obey; one without the other is unthinkable. Having the commandments does not differ from keeping them. On commandments cf. v. 15 above. The second half of the verse, however, seems to imply that obedience (and hence love) is a precondition for receiving the Father's love as well as Christ's. There is ample evidence in this gospel for God's unmerited and prevenient love (e.g., 3:16; 13:34 and 15:9, 12). But the thought here has to do with being included in the mutual relationship of love which exists between Christ and God. Participation in that relationship requires faith (the essential meaning of keeping the commandments) and love. Without these interrelated themes there can be no meaningful integration into the divine family. It might be that John implies two equal kinds of divine love. The one is the "natural" love which God has for his creation, and the other is the love he has for those who have become his children as a result of the revelation (1:12). Jesus' love includes his manifestation. "To manifest" (*emphanizein*) is employed in John only here and in the next verse, so it is somewhat unclear what we are to make of it. The same word is used, however, in Matt. 27:53 to describe the resurrected persons resulting from Christ's crucifixion, and Acts 10:40 utilizes a related word (*emphanēs*) to speak of Christ's resurrection. It is fair, then, to say that the manifestation to the believers here has a first reference to the resurrection appearances. As a consequence of love and faith comes the firsthand experience of the risen Lord. The resurrection then is not to be understood as the grand sign which evokes faith from unbelievers but as a confirmation of faith and caring. But the resurrection appearances in John represent more—they stand for the continuing presence of Christ in his community through the Spirit-Paraclete. Hence, the manifestation referred to is not different from the experience of the Spirit in the church.

22-25—**Judas'** question, like the other queries posed by disciples (vv. 5 and 8), serves as a reason for the advancement of the discussion. **Judas (not Iscariot)** may be linked to the "Judas, son of James" mentioned in Luke 6:16 and Acts 1:13, but the relationship should not be pressed. John has not restricted the participants in the dinner scene to the Twelve, and it is clear that his list of the Twelve (if he had one) differed from those found in the Synoptics (Matt. 10:2-4; Mark 3:16-19; and Luke 6:14-16, as well as the list of the eleven in Acts 1:13-14). **Not Iscariot** may be a gloss to make clear a distinction between this figure and the betrayer. (Some manuscripts read *kai* after **Lord**, which adds continuity with what comes before.) The question poses the distinction between the believers and the **world** and may assume a grandiose picture of the parousia in which Christ is to be made known to the whole of creation. **Jesus'** answer in vv. 23-24 repeats the difference between those of his family and those who eliminate themselves from that circle by their failure to believe and love. If **Judas'** question presupposes the manifestation at the parousia, Jesus' answer once again seems to have to do with the resurrection appearances and their continuation in the work of the Spirit-Paraclete within the church. Only faith and love can "see" the resurrected Christ and the Spirit. Verse 23 repeats the sense of v. 21 with the difference of **we will come . . . with him,** which is in effect a clarification of "manifest myself to him" in v. 21. **My word** is synonymous with "commandments" above (cf. v. 15 above). **Home** is *monēn*, the same word utilized in v. 2 for "rooms." Now the dwelling place of the divine is with the human, and the heavenly dimension of the "rooms" in v. 2 is described as a reality in the present experience of the believers. John's so-called "heavenly eschatology" is realized in the church. John has Jesus saying in different ways throughout this discourse that the divine is present in the believers' lives (cf. vv. 3, 16-17, 18, and 21). Verse 24 repeats the meaning of v. 23 in the negative. **Word** refers to the message of the revelation as a whole. It is not Jesus' message but God's, by whom he has been **sent**.

25-26—Verse 25 introduces the second of the Paraclete sayings which occurs here as a further explanation of how Christ and the Father make their "home" with the believers. **These things . . . spoken to you** appears six other times in the parting words of Jesus (15:11; 16:1, 4a, 6, 25, 33). It serves as a refrain to underscore the seriousness of the contents of these last remarks. **Still with you** (*par' hymin menōn*) employs the theme word "abide." It is a bit confusing here, for Jesus has just said that he and the Father will remain permanently with the believers (v. 23), but now speaks of his death as a conclusion of his remaining with the disciples. This is done to introduce the manner in which the Paraclete will resume Jesus' place. The Paraclete is identified with **the Holy Spirit**. John uses this title only three times—here, 1:33, and 20:22. Only here does it appear in the full sense of a title, i.e., "*the* Spirit *the* Holy." The title seems to have been part of his tradition and not necessarily his preference. The Paraclete is sent by **the Father** in Jesus' **name**, not unlike 14:15 but quite different from 16:7b. A function of the Paraclete is to **teach all things** and keep the believers mindful of all Jesus communicated. **All things** (*panta*) may contrast with "these things" in v. 25; but its meaning is "the entire ramification of Christ's revelation." This meaning is clear by the way in which all things is in synonymous parallelism with **all that I have said to you.** The Paraclete does not bring a new revelation but communicates the historical revelation in Christ to other times and places and steers the church in the interpretation of that revelation. The two functions named here, teaching and reminding, are two aspects of the same work. **All things** anticipates "all the truth" mentioned in 16:13.

27—In his final words with his disciples Jesus says his "adieu," employing the Jewish custom of using *shalom* (**peace**) as both a greeting and a farewell. **Peace** occurs in John's gospel only in the farewell discourses (here and 16:33) and in the resurrection appearances (20:19, 21, 26). Assuming its Hebraic connections, **Peace** (*eirēnēn*) denotes a wholeness of person, including both "spiritual" well-being and material prosperity. On the lips of the Johannine Jesus it becomes a synonym for salvation or eternal life. But it is a benefit of the revelation which puts humans in harmony with themselves, their God, and one another. **Leave you** (*aphiēmi hymin*) has nearly the sense of a passing on of one's inheritance. The **peace** differs from that which the world promises, hence it is not the contentment we often assume is meant by peace. It is rather a wholeness known only by those harmoniously related to their Creator. In the light of this gift of peace, the words of v. 1 with which this discourse began can be repeated, this time in antithetical parallel construction with **neither let them be afraid**.

28-29—Verses 2-4 are recalled. But here the disciples are chastised for not loving Jesus and correctly understanding the meaning of his departure. The unfulfilled condition (**if you loved me**) is softened in some manuscripts, but clearly the RSV reading is preferable. From proper love flows an appreciation of the benefits of Jesus' death which in turn is a cause for rejoicing. Rejoicing is the result of the resurrection, as 16:22 indicates. **The Father is greater than I** is not to be taken as a metaphysical statement having to do with relationships within the Godhead. Such is far from John's mind. The agency concept of Jesus, which we find in this gospel, implies that the envoy is subordinate to the one he or she represents. Moreover, the description of the Father-Son relationship also implies a subservience of Christ to God (e.g., the Son obeys the Father, 8:25; 10:15; 15:10, 15). But the context of these words shows that what is meant is that the Father is able to bring glory out of the tragedy of the cross. In going to the Father God's love transforms the apparent failure of the cross into a victorious exaltation. Verse 29 repeats the point of 13:19 (cf. above). The disciples cannot now understand the meaning of Jesus' departure, but on the other side of the resurrection these instructions will allow them to understand and believe.

30-31—Verse 30 signals the conclusion of the first form of the discourse. (That **much** is left to be said shows the original version of this discourse did not precede two more chapters of discussion.) For **ruler of this world** cf. 12:31 above. **Is coming** is less of a reference to Judas than to the whole evil action about to be thrust upon Jesus. But he is not powerless in the face of these events. **He has no power over me** is literally "he has nothing in me" (*en emoi ouk echei ouden*). It is idiomatic for "has no claim on me" and may carry the forensic meaning of having no legal charge against another. The point is that the **ruler of this world** can lay no claim of power against one who is of another "world." The relationship of vv. 30-31 is not clear, but the RSV punctuation is probably correct in suggesting the continuation of the flow of thought from v. 30 to v. 31. Jesus is elsewhere said to be obedient to the Father (e.g., 8: 25). Such obedience shows love. The **world** can **know** of Jesus' **love** by the cross. It is **love** which will finally vindicate Jesus.

Efforts to understand **Rise, let us go hence** as a spiritual rather than physical movement are straining to avoid the problem it raises. That John intended for us to think that the next three chapters take place as Jesus and the disciples are walking to the garden is likewise dishonest. The first form of the discourse concludes here, and originally it led into the journey to the garden (18:1).

This first version of the "parting words" may be said to address the ever-present danger of a sense of the absence of God within this world. There is a legitimate feeling of loss and fear which accompanies those times when God seems to have abandoned the people, and it was a feeling known to the members of John's community. But the word of hope in this section is that every such experience can find its cure in the presence of God through the Spirit-Paraclete, a continuation of the risen Christ. Transformed by that presence, the community which sometimes feels "orphaned" can find comfort and empowerment.

Themes in the Farewell Discourses

14:1-31	15:1—16:4a	16:4b-31
Promise of Jesus' Return (1-3, 15-17, 18, 27-28)		Promise of Jesus' Return (as Paraclete, 1-7)
"The Way" as a Way of Knowing (4-7)		Parables and Knowing (25, 29-30)
Faith as Seeing (8-10, 19) ("little while," *mikros*)		Faith as Seeing (16-20) ("little while," *mikros*)
Works as Revelation and Faith Living (10-11)		
Power of Asking (13-14)	Power of Asking (15: 7, 16b)	Power of Asking (23-24, 26)
Indwelling (15-17, 18-21, 23-24)	Indwelling of Believers in Christ (15:1-10)	
Love and Obedience (21-24)	Bearing Fruit, Loving, Obeying (15:1-10, 16a)	
Peace (27)		Peace (37)
Son as Agent of Father and Functions for Father (24, 28)	Son Obeys Father and Is Identified with Him (15:9, 10, 15, 23-24)	Son Sent by Father and Possesses What Is the Father's (5, 15, 32b)
Ruler of the World Overcome (30)	The World and Believers (15:18-25)	Christ, Paraclete, Believers, and World (8-10, 28, 33)
Rejoice in Son's Departure (28)	Eschatological Joy (15:11)	Eschatological Joy (20-22, 24)
	Faithfulness in Persecution (16:1-4a)	Prediction of Desertion (32)
	Servants Become Friends (15:15)	
	Love One Another (15:12-14, 17)	
Father Loves Believers Because of Obedience (23)		Father Loves Believers Because of Obedience (27)

Discourse II—Intimacy with Christ and Hostility with the World (15:1—16:4a)

1—Many of the same themes occur again in the second form of the discourse, although fresh emphases and thoughts do emerge (cf. chart, "Themes in the Farewell Discourses," above). This section begins with what is the second of the grand allegories of this gospel, 10:1-16 being the other. Like the first it is a more developed metaphor than the simpler "I am" sayings with the predicate (e.g., 9:5). It begins this chapter with abruptness. **I am the true vine** calls to mind the frequent use of the **vine** and the vineyard as symbols for Israel in the OT (e.g., Ezekiel 17 and Jer. 2:21). But John employs the vine as a symbol for Christ. The polemical tone is therefore inescapable—Christ is God's servant who stands in the place of Israel. This was possibly the original setting for the metaphor in the life of the Johannine community, although it may have served earlier in tradition in a less polemical way. **True** means the **vine** is related to the revelation in Christ in contrast to other understandings of God. **The vinedresser** (*ho georgos*) is the one who prepares the soil for the **vine**, and it is unwise to press the allegory further as a description of the relationship between Christ and God.

2-3—The Father functions as the judge of the relationship between the believers and Christ. That the **branch** stands for the believer is not mentioned until v. 5, but it is already implicit here. It is the function of pruning to prevent unfruitful branches from interfering with the fruit-bearing of others. **Fruit** (*karpos*) is the life of faith and love demanded of those allied with Christ, as v. 10 indicates. Unfruitful Christians are those whose faith has died and consequently their love has lost its basis. John's message is that the Christian community is better off without those apostate Christians whose discipleship has withered. The unfruitful branches first represented those believers who had fallen away under the pressure of the division from the synagogue and later came to symbolize those who had divided themselves from the community and demonstrated a lovelessness. There is in the Greek a play on the verbs **takes away** (*airei*) and **prunes** (*kathairei*). The two are not often found with the meaning implied by this context. This shows that their use is in part due to their respective sounds (an indication that the passage was originally in Greek and not Aramaic but also, possibly, that its origin was in oral speech, not writing). The verb **prunes** in the Greek is the key to the association of v. 3 and v. 2, since in the former the word **made clean** is the adjectival form, *katharoi.* The wordplays on the double meaning of *kathairei* as "cut" (in v. 2) and "cleanse" (in v. 3). In 13:10 it is Jesus' act of surrendering his life which cleanses the disciples; here it is his **word** (*logos*). **Word** means the whole of Jesus' message, including his life and death as well as his spoken proclamation.

4—The idea of "abiding" (*menein*) plays an important role in the whole of the allegory (vv. 5, 6, 7, 9, and 10). It stands for the faithful relationship between Christ and the believer in which the two are bound together. It is first expressed in an imperative form, suggesting that the disciples by virtue of their decision of faith can effect the alliance. The proper connection between **abide in me** and **and I in you** is not precisely clear. It may have the sense of a comparison (**abide in me** *as* I abide in you) or a condition (If you **abide in me,** *then* I will abide in you) or a declaration (Let there be a mutual abiding). In any case, the importance of the believer's intent for the relationship is clear. Without the faith and trust of the person, the life of discipleship is doomed. Here John stresses the responsibility of the human for faith, in spite of the fact that one cannot claim faith as an accomplishment of one's own (e.g., 6:65).

5-8—Verse 5 repeats the thought of v. 4 while introducing an emphasis on the helplessness of the believer without Christ, a qualification of the importance of the believer's act of faith stated in v. 4. For the first time believers are explicitly identified with the **branches** (for **much fruit** cf. v. 8 below). Verse 6 develops the metaphor of the pruning used in vv. 1 and 2, and its meaning is clear: "An unfaithful Christian suffers the fate of an unfruitful branch" (Barrett, p. 475). **Fire** suggests eternal punishment, but such a view is generally missing in John. It is better to understand the verse to describe more generally the meaninglessness of a human life separated from Christ/God. Verse 5 states the positive features of the relationship with Christ, and v. 6 the negative results of breaking the association. Now in v. 7 attention returns to the positive features of "abiding." For **ask whatever** . . . cf. 14:13-14 above. In v. 3 "the word" is singular, *logos*. Here **words** is the plural, *hrēma*. The latter may refer to specific sayings as opposed to the general message in the former; but no sharp distinction should be imposed. Jesus' words are his message, and he himself is the message. To **abide in me** is not essentially different from abiding in Jesus' **words.** Whether **by this** in v. 8 refers back to v. 7 or forward to the bearing of **much fruit** and the demonstration of discipleship of v. 8, the meaning is clear: The life of the believer glorifies God. God glorifies Jesus (e.g., 8:54) and Jesus the Father (e.g., 12:28) and now the believers glorify the Father. With the departure of Jesus the community of faith becomes the concrete expression of the divine presence (cf. 17:10), and the relationship between the Father and the Son is paradigmatic of that between the believer and God (cf. chart, "Relational Analogies," p. 266). Through the life of faith God reveals himself to the world. The incarnation of God's presence moves from Jesus of Nazareth (1:14) to the community of faith. A textual variant makes it difficult to know whether glorifying the Father is synonymous with proving **to be my disciples** or whether the latter should be taken as the *result* of the disciples' glorification of God (in the first case, the subjunctive, *genēsthe*, is taken to be the preferred reading and in the second the future indicative, *genēsesthe*). Since the two are so closely related, the difference is minor. In either case, **prove** is literally "you will become" (or "you are becoming"). In 13:35 mutual love is the evidence of discipleship which shows that to **bear much fruit** (*karpon polyn pherēte*) in vv. 5 and 8 means to love.

With v. 8 the extended metaphor of the vine is completed. Its point is the life-giving connection of the believer with Christ. The essence of Christian life and faith has no other source than the association of the human with the revealer. As water (chap. 4) and bread (chap. 6) have been pressed into service to symbolize the life-giving quality of the revelation, so here the vine/branch symbol restates that fact. While a eucharistic meaning was soon read into the metaphor, it is doubtful that John consciously intended such a meaning.

9-11—The implicit allusion to 13:35 in v. 8 makes logical the movement in vv. 9-10 to the subject of love. At this point the connection described in the vine metaphor as a mutual abiding is explicated in terms of **love.** The Father-Son relationship is used as a model to express the character and extremity of Jesus' love for the disciples (cf. chart, p. 266). The aorist verbs (**Father has loved . . . have I loved you**) suggest the historicity of the singular act of divine love in the revelation. But they do not preclude the continuous love of God (e.g., 3:35). The imperative **abide** (*meinate*) suggests again the believer's responsibility for the relationship (cf. v. 4 above). Humans must accept the gift of love extended to them in Christ if they are to benefit from a life in harmony with God. In v. 10 what is meant by accepting that gift is spoken of in different words—**keep my commandments.** On the meaning of this expression cf. 14:15 above. In this and the following verses John gives the closest to what might be called the ethical dimension of the Christian life. It comprises two simple and interrelated points: (1) The disciples' model of faithfulness and obedience is found in the relationship between Christ and God; ethics is founded on Christology. (2) It is defined in terms of love, so that the obedience of faith finds its expression in love (cf. Gal. 5:6; Phil. 2:5-12). In v. 11 **these things I have spoken to you** is the clause employed in 14: 25 of the first discourse, here and 16:1 in the second, and 16:25 and 33 in the third. It functions as a transitional bridge and a logical binding of the previous statements with those yet to come. In v. 11 **these things** (*tauta*) refers to the whole description of the alliance between Christ and the believer. That alliance yields a **joy** (*chara*) which is characteristic of conditions at the end-time. It is eschatological, but it is also Christological in that it is derived from the relationship between the Father and the Son. **Be full** (*plērōthē*) can only look ahead to the **joy** of the Easter faith.

12-14—In v. 12 the "new commandment" of 13:34 (cf. above) is repeated in nearly identical terms. The complex relationship is now complete: The Father loves the Son (vv. 9 and 17:26); the Son loves the believers (v. 9); and now the believers should **love one another.** The model of Christian love is found in Christ's obedient act, stated here in the aorist (**I have loved,** *ēgapēsa*). Out of that one historic act of love emerges the continuous **love** (*agapate,* present subjunctive) on the part of believers for one another.

Verse 13 goes on to characterize that love on the basis of Christ's loving act. On the human level the most extreme form of friendship is found in the life-giving sacrificial deed. That truism expresses the greatest of human gifts. It is the metaphor of that human relationship of radical friendship which John uses to characterize God's relationship with humans in Christ. **Lay down his life** echoes 10:17 where the same verb (*tithēmi*) is utilized (cf. 13:37). **His friends** is literally "the ones he loves" (*philōn*) and shows the way John uses *phileō* and *agapaō* interchangeably. It is from the metaphor of that human love that the declaration of v. 14 is drawn. **Friends** (*philoi*) must be taken, then, as those whom Jesus loves so dearly that he will sacrifice himself in death, a meaning which bursts the normal boundaries of our everyday use of the word **friends**. Jesus' friends are those who benefit from his love, stated in vv. 9 and 12. **If you do** . . . should not be construed to mean that Jesus' friendship is conditional on the basis of the obedience of the believers. "The phrase . . . specifies the condition whereby what they already are can be fully realised in them" (Bultmann, p. 543; cf. 1 John 4:19). While this is true, it must also be stated that a friendship depends on reciprocal love, and the disciples can forfeit their alliance with Christ by willful unbelief (cf. 6: 66 above).

15—But this declaration that the disciples are **friends** involves a transformation of the usual **servant**/master pattern. *Doulos* can mean both servant and slave, and it is perhaps the latter which is in view here. Friendship implies a relationship of reciprocality and intimacy, as opposed to the singular quality of the obedience demanded of the slave. While servanthood is typical of the Christian (13:12-17), the relationship described as "abiding" or "remaining" is one which makes the Christian more of a friend than a servant (cf. Wis. 7:27). What marks the difference is a kind of knowledge. The servant is not privy to the intent and plan of the master but only blindly obeys what is asked of him or her. The Christians, by virtue of the revelation of God in Christ, know the plan and intent of the Father. Such knowledge is typical of the confidence and sharing of a friendship, and like that relationship is not simply cognitive consciousness but an acquaintance resulting from mutual love. The surprise and radicality of this thought can hardly be overstated. So efficacious is the expression of the love of God that it radically transforms the relationship of the creature to the Creator, so that it approaches that of partners!

16-17—This radical transformation, however, depends entirely upon the initiative of God, as v. 16 states. Lest it should be thought that humans by nature are "friends" of God, Jesus is made to say that it all depends on his choosing. In the Greek the "I" is emphatic. A tone of predeterminism is not infrequent (cf., e.g., 6:65, 70). The verb "to choose" (*eklegomai*) is used only four times in John—here, 6:70; 13:18; and 15:19. The verb **appointed** (*ethēka*) stands in parallelism with **chose** but is somewhat clumsy. It is the same verb translated "lay down" in v. 13 above (*tithēmi*). Commentators tend to think that its use here reflects a translation from Hebrew which would mean "to give or ordain" (cf. Num. 8:10, LXX). The verb is followed by two *hina* clauses (**that** or "in order that"). In the first the enduring **fruit** of the disciples' lives is connected with their mission (**go**). This connotes that the life of faith and love is directed outward to the world, even as the Father's love is so directed (3:16). It is not an inward oriented life, but one designed to glorify the Father for the benefit of the world. It is in such a mission posture that the **fruit should abide** (*mene*), i.e., it should endure within the relationship with Christ. The second clause (**so that whatever. . .**) restates the promise of 14:13-14 and 15:7 (cf. the former above), but here is qualified by the mission to which the believers are **appointed.** The promise is qualified not only by the expression **in my name** but also now by the outward directed nature of the life of faith. Requests arising from the mission are granted. Some would understand that the second clause is conditioned by the first (i.e., the promise depends upon the believers' bearing **fruit**). But it is more likely that they are separate coordinates. Verse 17 both summarizes what has been said and points ahead to the following verses. Love characterizes the relationship just described, and to love one another is essential to the mission of the believers.

18-19—The opposite of love is the essence of the attitude of **the world** toward the disciples. The relationship of the Father and the

Son has been used as a model for the association of the believers with Jesus (e.g., v. 10). Now the relationship of the Son with the world (*kosmos*) is paradigmatic of the relationship between believers and unbelievers. There is in the sequence of the three discourses a mounting sense of alienation from the world (cf. 16:8-11, 33b). It is only to be expected that the disciples experience the hostility of the world, since Jesus did (7:7; cf. Matt. 10:17ff.).

Know (*ginōskete*) may be either indicative or imperative, but the latter is more likely. **World** is used here and in the following discussion in a pejorative way, meaning the whole realm of unbelief. Its meaning for John arose from the hostility and persecution (cf. v. 20 and 16:2) experienced by the Johannine community. The condition stated in v. 18a is real, while the condition introducing v. 19 is contrary to fact—the disciples **are not of the world. Of the world** is literally "out of" or "belonging to the membership **of the world**" (*ek tou kosmou*). **Its own** is neuter (*to idion*) but refers to a group of humans. The **love/hate** contrast is typical Semitic hyperbole (cf. 12:25 above). The disciples' relationship with the **world** is a result of Christ's election. It terminates their affiliation with the world and reverses their status with regard to those alienated from God. This is characteristic of John's radical motif of affiliation by which persons are members of one or the other group, depending on their perspective on Christ (e.g., 10:26-27; 3:20-21). There is no intermediate position; it is either one or the other. His view differs from that of the later gnostics insofar as one is not affiliated by nature but by virtue of his or her response to the revelation in Christ.

20—The saying in 13:16 is recalled. While it is used in the previous chapter to encourage imitation of Jesus' servant life, it is employed here to suggest that the consequences of that life are the same for the disciples as for their master. Believers can expect to fair no better in relationship with the darkness of the world than did Jesus. Hence, they may expect persecution. This surely reflects the fact that the Johannine community knew persecution and that John attempted to make that experience meaningful for his readers by showing how it flows naturally out of the fate of Jesus. The last clause of the verse seems to suggest the opposite fact:

as some accepted Christ, some will accept the gospel preached by the church. Set amid the statements stressing the rejection of the message, this positive possibility surprises the reader. But the point is that the efforts of the church will not be entirely futile. For "keeping" Jesus' word cf. 8:51-52 and 14:23-24 above. That the title **servant** reappears here after v. 15 may suggest the independent composition of the two sections, vv. 12-17 and vv. 18-25.

21—**All this** refers back to the negative reaction of the world. **On my account** is literally "on account of my name" (*dia to onoma mou*), an expression found nowhere else in John. His more common expression is "in my name" (14:13, 14). It means simply "because of me." It may, however, reflect a traditional saying attributed to Jesus here taken on by John (cf. Mark 13:13 and Matt. 10:22 where the same construction is found). The disciples suffer for the same reasons Jesus did, namely, a failure to recognize the divine source of the revelation (cf. 7:28-29 above).

22-23—These verses establish the guilt of those who have rejected Jesus. They are rightly understood as an apology for the Johannine community over against its opponents. **Sin** for John is simple unbelief. Without the revelation there would be no occasion for rejection and unbelief, but with it there is an inescapable judgment as well as an offer of acceptance (cf. 3:18-21 above and Rom. 5:12-14). The revelation has both a negative and a positive result. While intended to save, it also puts humans in question and results in judgment if the revelation is rejected. Here the **word** of the revelation is mentioned, and in v. 24 the "works" of the revealer are used to say the same thing, which implies the unity of the work and word of Jesus. **Excuse** (*prophasis*) is used nowhere else in John and nowhere in the NT with precisely this sense (cf. Phil. 1:18 where it means "false reason"). But its intent is clearly to affirm the responsibility of those humans who have rejected the revelation. Verse 23 restates the principle that one's reaction to Christ comprises his or her reaction to God (e.g., 13:20b). Hence, to **hate** Jesus is to **hate** God.

24-25—The sense of vv. 22-23 is restated here. Again the responsibility for rejection is affirmed this time by reference to **the works** of Christ as opposed to his "word" in v. 22. The works and message of Christ are one, but the former are understood to be more easily comprehended as expressing divine authority (10:38). His deeds are unique (**no one else did**), since they express the divine presence, i.e., glory. **Seen** hints at the powerful visual force of the signs, yet still the world has seen and rejected them. In John's situation v. 25 had the force of pointing out that the opponents of the community by their rejection of the gospel were fulfilling their very own Scripture (cf. 10:34 above where Jesus speaks of "your **law**" and cites a psalm while referring to it as law). The exact psalm quoted is not certain, for 35:19 and 69:4 both speak of the innocent and righteous person being **hated. . .without cause.** Those who reject the revelation do so without any defense (cf. 9: 39-41). If sometimes John speaks as if the human cannot take credit for believing (e.g., 6:37), he nonetheless holds with equal conviction the fact that humans are responsible for their unbelief.

26—The third of the Paraclete sayings is attached loosely to the preceding and closing verses of the second discourse. Nonetheless, in the face of the hostility and persecution the disciples are promised the divine presence to sustain them (cf. Matt. 10:19-20). Now the Paraclete is said to be sent by Jesus **from the Father** (contrast 14:16, 26). Again the Paraclete is identified as **the Spirit of truth** (cf. 14:16 above). **Proceeds from the Father** (*ho para tou patros ekporeuetai*) means nothing more than **sent to you from the Father.** The presence of the Paraclete arises from or grows out of the will of the Father for the community. John should not be read here as a theologian attempting to penetrate the inner being of the Godhead! The function of the Paraclete is to testify to Christ. The **witness** of the Paraclete is none other than his teachings (14:26) or her speaking and glorifying Christ (16:13-14). To **witness** (*martyreō*) is to sustain the truth of a matter, and the disciples are promised that amid their difficulties in the world the Paraclete will continually reaffirm the truthfulness of the revelation in Christ. The Christocentricity of the concept of the Paraclete is clear in each of the passages. The Paraclete provides the witness on which the proclamation of the gospel is based. This passage means that the Paraclete was understood as the source of the prophetic inspiration known to the community.

27—The witness of the disciples is related to the witness of the Paraclete. Their message is an expression of the message given them by the Paraclete. **Also** *(kai)* should not be taken to mean in addition to the Paraclete but as a result of the divine presence. **From the beginning** *(ap' archēs)* denotes the commencement of Jesus' ministry (cf. 16:4b below; 1 John 2:24; and 8:25 above). (Contrast the use of **beginning** to mean "before creation," 1:1, 2.)

16:1-2—The paragraph vv. 1-4a resumes the discussion of the relationship between the disciples and the world. Verse 1 is spoken out of the experience of apostasy known in John's church. For **I have said all this** cf. 15:11 above. **Falling away** is literally "being scandalized" *(skandalisthēte)*, which is also found in 6:61, where Jesus asks if his difficult words have "scandalized" the disciples (cf. Mark 14:27-31). The experience of opposition and persecution tempts the Christian to turn away from the gospel. Verse 2 includes one of the three references to expulsion **from the synagogue** *(aposynagōgous,* cf. 9:22 and 12:42 above). **The hour is coming** means that Jesus predicted the circumstances being experienced by John's first readers. **Hour** *(hōra)* is utilized of Jesus' time of suffering (e.g., 2:4 and 12:23), and its use here implies the relationship between Jesus' pain and that of the church. John's readers are encouraged to view their own predicament as a continuation of the redemptive work of God in the cross. **Service** *(latreia),* found only here in John, elsewhere in the NT is associated with temple worship (e.g., Rom. 9:4). Hence, it may suggest the offenders consider their work against the Christians an act of worship. In its present context this surely refers to the Jewish persecution of the Johannine Christians in John's own village. There is little evidence of that persecution having reached the extremes of Christian martyrdom and was surely a localized incident.

3-4a—In v. 3 the reason for unbelief and persecution is again stated to be a lack of the recognition of God in Christ (cf. 15:21 above). The whole tragedy, John has Jesus say, roots in a grand misunderstanding. What is being done as a service to God actually arises from ignorance. The irony in John's words speaks of a deep and tragic rupture of the two bodies, Jews and Christians. Verse 4a repeats the sense of v. 1 and restates the words **I have said these**

things (cf. 15:11 above). The disciples will be strengthened in their time of trial by the fact that their master had predicted it. John 14:26 attributes to the Paraclete the function of helping the disciples **remember** what Jesus had said. It is by the leading of the Spirit that the disciples will recall Jesus' foretelling of the persecution. **Their hour** (*hē hōra autōn*) would seem to mean the persecutors' time (for the Paraclete cf. 14:15-17, 26; 15:26-27 above; and 16:7-14 below).

Clearly, there are two motifs that emerge in the second form of the discourse. The first is the alliance of the believers with Christ and all that that entails. The second is the relationship of the believers with the world and the consequences of that relationship. Taken as a whole the passage reflects the nature of the Christian life viewed negatively (the hostility of the world) and positively (the intimacy of the association with Christ and God). It is the power of the latter which enables the believer to deal with the pain of the former. This bespeaks the conditions of the Johannine community and the good news John shares with them. The worst can be endured if the divine presence is known.

Discourse III—Tribulations and Assurance (16:4b-33)

The third form of the discourse shares some common themes with both the first and the second. More of its content can be found in one of the other forms than is the case with either the first or second forms. Nonetheless, this third version of the "parting words" forges some new ground not least of all in a further delineation of the believers' relationship with the world and the Paraclete.

4b-6—Verse 4b builds a bond with the previous discourse by means of some common terms (**the beginning,** 15:27, and **these things,** 16:1). **These things** refers to the threat of persecution which arises for the disciples only after Jesus is no longer **with** them. For **from the beginning** cf. 15:27 above. Verse 5 reintroduces the theme of departure as the meaning of Jesus' death and resurrection (cf. 13:33ff. above). **Him who sent me** is John's common title for God (e.g., 4:34; 5:23; 7:33). **None of you asks . . .** shows the independence of at least 15:1—16:33, for Jesus has been asked **where** he is **going** (cf. 13:36 and 14:5). The point is that the sorrow of the disciples is due to their failure to understand the meaning of Jesus' death and his eventual destiny. Verse 6 begins the emphasis of this discourse on **sorrow** (cf. vv. 20-22). For **these things** cf. again 15:11. The referent of **these things** in this case would seem to be the departure of Jesus and the subsequent persecution.

7—To combat the sorrow of the disciples, the fourth of the Paraclete sayings occurs in vv. 7-14. This passage is clearly an attempt to compensate for the absence of Christ by reference to the Spirit. **I tell you the truth** may mean only "what I am about to say is not a lie" (cf. 8:45-46). But **truth** may also mean the content of the revelation itself and anticipate the naming of the Paraclete "the Spirit of truth" in v. 13. **Advantage** (*sympherei*) has the sense of expediency and is used only three times in John (here, 11:50, and 18:14), in each case with reference to the death of Jesus and its benefits. The disciples will profit from Jesus' death, even though it is a painful experience. Part of that profit is the coming of the Spirit. Jesus' death ushers in the eschatological era which is marked by the giving of the Spirit. That the Spirit and Christ cannot have concurrent ministries suggests that the presence of the Paraclete only can result from the exaltation of Christ. Now the Paraclete is sent by Christ in contrast to the assertion that he or she is sent by the Father (14:16, 26).

8-11—These verses describe the work of the Paraclete with regard to the **world,** but they are hardly clear. Commentators differ on their meaning. The arguments center on the meaning of **convince** (*elengchein*), the preposition translated **concerning** (*peri*), and the three *hoti* (**because**) clauses. It is difficult to determine a meaning which makes sense of the three words **sin, righteousness,** and **judgment.** But the best understanding of them is derived if they are taken to mean that the Paraclete convicts the world of being wrong at three points: (1) at the point of its failure to believe in Christ (**sin**); (2) in its sense of justice in that **the world** persecuted Jesus but the Father exalted him; (3) in its sense of **judgment,** which is controlled by evil, and evil is overthrown by the crucifixion of Christ. How the Paraclete accomplishes this "con-

victing" or "exposing" is not stated, but would seem to be related
to the message of the church proclaimed to the world under the
guidance of the Spirit (cf. 15:26 above). So it is by means of the
church's proclamation that the Paraclete does its work, and
thereby assures the believers of the truthfulness of the revelation.
In v. 10 **righteousness** translates *dikaiosynē* which can also be rendered "justice." Unbelief is the essence of sin for John (cf. 15:22-
24 above). **I go to the Father** is the crucifixion-exaltation of Jesus
in which God confirms his Son. **You will see me no more** can only
allude to the change of the nature of the divine presence among
the believers from the visible incarnation of the word (Jesus) to the
invisible reality of the Spirit. This clause is inserted almost as an af-
terthought and does not function significantly in the immediate argument, although it underlines the transition spoken of in v. 7b. In
v. 11 **judgment** (*krisis*) means condemnation, as it often does in
John (e.g., 3:18). For **ruler of this world** cf. 12:31 above. In these
verses the Paraclete functions as did Christ to judge the world
(e.g., 5:30). This is the only role assigned to the Paraclete beyond
the community of faith itself, and even this role has to do with the
proclamation of that community to the world. The divine presence always results negatively in convicting the darkness of the
world, even though its goal is redemption.

12-13—Verse 12 bridges the Paraclete saying of vv. 7-11 with
that of vv. 13-14. It introduces the role of the Paraclete as a guide
to truth (v. 13). The reason for the reference to **many things** to be
said may be John's defense of his interpretation of the tradition in
which, under the guidance of the Spirit, he attributes new words
to the Jesus represented in the tradition. **Bear** (*bastazein*) means
"to endure," which here may stand for no more than "understand." The Paraclete saying itself, vv. 13-14, is prefaced with the
naming of the Paraclete, **the Spirit of truth** (cf. 14:16 above). As
the Spirit of truth, she or he is said to lead the believers to **all the
truth** (*tē alētheia pasē*). The phrase means the whole of the revelation in all its implications and does not necessarily contradict the
statement that the Paraclete brings only the revelation of Christ
(14:26). Obviously John has in mind the unfolding of the tradition
and the working out of its consequences. (The slight difference be-

tween the manuscripts which read *en* before **all the truth** and those which support *eis* does not seem significant, for the context dictates the meaning just described.) **Guide** (*hodēgein*) is related to the word *hodos*, "way" (cf. 14:6), and suggests direction along a path to truth. As Jesus spoke only what was given to him by the Father, so the Spirit speaks by divine command. Manuscripts vary as to the tense of the verb **hears** (*akouō*), with the main alternatives being the present and future tenses, for either of which a case can be made. The future tense is perhaps more likely, hence "he will hear." **Declare** (*anangelei*) is used in reference to the divine message in numerous places in the NT, and at 4:25 of this gospel it has similar meaning. **The things that are to come** (*ta erchomena*) probably refers to eschatological events, but specifically here means developments in the life of the Johannine community. The Christian need not be worried about the future. Again, as in 15:26-27, there is the implication that the Spirit lies behind the experience of prophetic speech in the Johannine community. John is confirming the charismatic character of his church (cf. Käsemann).

14-15—It is said that the Spirit **will glorify** Christ. That is, the Paraclete brings to the consciousness of the community the divine presence which is found in Christ. He will do this by making the revelation accessible to believers of later times. Persons can embrace the revelation because the Spirit offers it to them. Again **declare** (*anangellō*) is employed of the saving message which has its source in Christ—**what is mine** (*ek tou emou*). Verse 15 reasserts that the Father's saving will is found in Christ. The community is promised that they will share all that which came to expression in the Christ event, and hence they are at no disadvantage simply because they live in another time (cf. on the Paraclete, Kysar, *John*, pp. 93-98, and the excellent summary in Brown, vol. 2, pp. 1135-1144).

16—Now a sudden resumption of the discourse on a new theme. For **a little while** (*mikros*) cf. 14:19 above. There the expression seems to refer to the crucifixion and burial, and here it has the same meaning. The second **little while** until the disciples will again **see** Jesus is perhaps the period between the crucifixion and resurrection—another form of the expression "after three days" (e.g., Matt. 27:63). It is likely that this was the meaning of the saying in the tradition, but John adds an ambiguity in order to address his readers with the hope of "seeing" Christ again in the Paraclete. For this reason, the promise is placed after the sayings of vv. 7-11 and 13-15. Therefore, he meant by the second **little while** the time between resurrection and the gift of the Spirit. In any case, the good news is that the sorrow of the disciples will be overcome by a return of the divine presence.

17-19—Here the discussion is furthered by means of a question. The **disciples,** not surprisingly, do not understand what has been said in v. 16 and what is stated about Jesus' departure in v. 10. This introduces the lack of understanding which will be the topic of conversation in vv. 25ff. This failure to understand Jesus is a subtle suggestion to John's readers that the eyewitness **disciples** were even less privy to comprehension than are later generations gifted with the Paraclete. Verse 19 is another of several instances in which Jesus is portrayed as having omniscience at least with reference to what others are thinking (cf. 2:14-15 above). The repetitiousness of this passage may suggest that its origin was in the spoken homily of the church, where repetition was helpful for understanding.

20-22—Jesus' long-awaited answer is by no means clear, since it is comprised of a metaphor. Verse 20 interprets in advance the metaphor of childbirth. The disciples will experience loss as with the death of a loved one. **Weep** (*klaiein*) is used in connection with the mourning of Lazarus' death (11:31, 33). In contrast, those of unbelief will **rejoice. Sorrow** (*lypē*, cf. v. 6 above) is an anguish not always associated with death (e.g., 2 Cor. 2:2, 4, 5). The reference to the transformation of **sorrow into joy** surely has the resurrection in mind. It is the short-lived nature of that sorrow and its abrupt reversal which is the point of the figure of childbirth in v. 21. The pains which accompany labor are real but soon are forgotten in the joyous excitement of a human birth. There is no need to allegorize the comparison, but it may be significant that the "birth pangs of the Messiah" was standard apocalyptic thought, comparing the suffering of the last time before the appearance of the Messiah with a woman's labor pains. **Child** translates *anthrōpos*, "human being." In v. 22 the **sorrow** of the moment (*nyn*, **now**) is contrasted with **I will see you again** in place of "you will see me" in v. 16. There may be an allusion to Isa. 66:14 (**LXX**), but there too the passage reads, "you shall see." The change to the promise that Christ **will see** the believer emphasizes perhaps the more important truth that God sees and cares for the believer. Thus, even if believers do not **see** (20:29), they can trust that God *sees them*. It does not contradict v. 16 as much as it views the experience from a different perspective. **No one will take your joy from you** underlines the inviolable relationship between Christ and Christians described in 15:1-8. The word of hope to a persecuted community is the assurance that God sees and holds the divine family close to him.

23-24—In v. 23 two different verbs are used for the two occurrences of **ask**. The meaning of the second (*aitein*) has clearly to do with prayer (e.g., 11:22), and in some cases the first (*erōtaō*) is also employed in connection with prayer (e.g., v. 26). But *erōtaō* can further be utilized for asking questions (e.g., 1:19), and this is doubtless its meaning here. Jesus is looking toward **that day** when the disciples will not have to ask questions. **That day** (*ekeinē tē hēmerā*) carries the implications of the eschatological time which for John is fulfilled in the cross and the giving of the Spirit (cf. 8:56). The second sentence of v. 23 repeats the essential thought of the promise found in 14:13-14; 15:7; and 16b (cf. above) but with the surprise twist that the giving and not the asking are **in my name.** This is the preferable textual witness to others which have the phrase connected with **ask,** since the latter appears to be scribal efforts to harmonize the saying with the next verse and with 15:16b. For God to answer prayer in Jesus' name is to act by virtue of Christ's love (and not on the basis of the believer's faith; cf. 14:26). But now in v. 24 the disciples are commanded to **ask** (*aiteite*, an imperative), and they **will receive.** Note the similarity with the Synoptic saying in Matt. 7:7 and Luke 11:9. Asking is once again related to **in my name,** with the result that both the asking and the giving are done in the light of Christ's life and death. With such a relationship between God and the believer in Christ, **joy** reaches its fulfillment (*plēroō*; cf. 15:11 and 17:13).

25-26—Jesus' words return to the theme of the disciples' lack of understanding introduced in vv. 17ff. For **I have said this,** cf. 15:11 above. **Figures** translates *paroimia* (cf. 10:6 above). It is contrasted in this verse with *parrēsia* (**plainly**) and carries more of a sense of "obscure." The point is that the whole of Jesus' life and teachings remains unclear until after his exaltation and the arrival of the Paraclete. In much the same way as Mark holds back the high Christological confession of a human until the centurion at the cross (15:39), so John suggests that the historical Jesus is understood only from a post-Easter vantage point (cf. 20:28). **The hour** (*hōra*) in this case means the simultaneous exaltation and bestowal of the Spirit. In the light of Christ's death and resurrection and under the guidance of the Spirit, the Christ figure is clearly illumined. (Again, John is encouraging second-generation Christians to realize that the eyewitnesses held no advantage over them.) **Tell . . . of the Father** means the revelation is proclaimed by the church under the influence of the Paraclete. Verse 26 summarizes v. 23 and makes clear that on the eschatological day believers will experience the power of their asking. Jesus is here made to remove himself as an intermediary between Christians and God for, as v. 27 makes clear, no intercessor is needed (cf. 14:13).

27-28—Verse 27 affirms God's love, but it appears that human love and belief are conditions of that divine gift. The point is, however, similar to that found in 14:21, 23, and 15:14. What is in view here is not the conditions of the **Father's love,** for 3:16 demonstrates that God's love bursts out of all conditions. What is the point is once again that the human bears some responsibility for the relationship with the Father. Textual variations leave us unsure (1) whether the last clause of v. 27 (**that I came from the Father**) is properly related to v. 28 and (2) whether the last word of the final clause of v. 27 should read **Father** or "God." The longer reading as found in the RSV is the more likely, with "God" and not **Father** (as in TEV). John repeats himself, as he often does, with just a few changes (i.e., "God" to **Father**). Verse 28 serves as a summary of Johannine thought expressed in four balanced lines. The first two lines state Jesus' origin and the incarnation; the second two the passion and exaltation. With the latter we are brought full circle back to the first thought of the discourse in 16:4b.

29-30—The closing paragraph (vv. 29-33) is filled with painful irony. The **disciples** are made to think that the time of complete knowledge predicted in v. 23 has arrived. Without the experience of the exaltation and the guidance of the Paraclete, they claim in v. 29 that they fully understand Jesus. For the contrast of **figure** and **speaking plainly,** cf. v. 25 above. In v. 30 (with some unclear logic) they conclude from Jesus' marvelous knowledge that he **came from God.** Some have proposed that behind the logic of this statement stands the theory of the divine man (*theios anēr*) whose superknowledge betrays his identity. Be that as it may, John with considerable pathos points out the fragility of the faith the disciples profess; for they still lack the proper comprehension, as their imminent desertion of Jesus will show.

31-32—Jesus' response corrects his overly enthusiastic followers. Verse 31 may be read as a question or a statement, but in either case it casts doubt upon the confidence of the disciples. **Now** (*arti*) is emphatic, even as the disciples' statements stressed the "now" (*nyn*, in both vv. 29 and 30). In v. 32 the **hour** (*hōra*) is in this case the passion. It stands in contrast to the hour mentioned in v. 25, which from the disciples' perspective is yet to come. **Scattered** (*skorpizein*, cf. Mark 14:27) may be an allusion to Zech. 13: 7, which was used in the early church to understand the failure of the disciples in the face of the crucifixion (e.g., Mark 14:27). **To his home** is literally "to his own." (Is this the source of the setting of the resurrection appearance in Galilee, according to 21:1?) John may be offering an apologetic for the fact of the desertion of Jesus by the disciples, an embarrassment at best. Jesus is left to face his ordeal **alone.** But Johannine Christology cannot allow that Jesus is ever separated from the Father (e.g., 8:16, 29; contrast Mark 15:34).

33—This is an appropriate conclusion not only for this discourse but the whole series. **This** (cf. 15:11 above) doubtless refers to the whole of the discourse but especially to the promises (e.g., vv. 13ff.). For **peace** cf. 14:27 above. **Tribulation** (*thlipsis*) is the same word rendered "anguish" in v. 21. It connotes the eschatological difficulties (e.g., Mark 13:7-9), which may have been identified in the Johannine community with its own persecution. **Be of good cheer** is the imperative of *tharseō* and might be translated "take courage." Both it and *nikaō* (**have overcome**) are found only here in John; the latter is a military word suggesting victory in warfare (cf. 1 John 2:13, 14; 4:4; 5:4, 5). It is important to note that the reference to **tribulation** is described in the present tense (**have,** *echete*), while **overcome** is in the perfect tense (*nenikēka*). The perspective is that of John and his church, for whom the victory of Christ over the forces of evil is an event of the past with continuing effect, and the suffering of the Christians for their faith is still a present reality. **World** (*kosmos*) occurs here in its negative sense as the entire realm of existence opposed to Christ and the church. The meaning is the same as the declaration of victory over "the ruler of this world" (12:31). The Christians, John says, are immersed in a vicious struggle for their own existence but can be confident of the outcome of that struggle. God's act in Christ seals the fate of the forces of evil.

Clearly this last discourse stresses more than do the others the plight of the church in the world. The sense of opposition with the world is the keenest in this passage, but so too is the assurance of victory. The disciples are promised the power of prayer, the certainty of knowledge, and the assurance of the Paraclete. John's ordering of the three forms of the discourse, like the progress of his thought so often, is spiraling. The final discourse brings us back to the themes of the first but now at a higher level of intensity and assurance. With it he powerfully concludes the final teachings of Jesus for both the original disciples and the church of any time.

A Final Prayer (17:1-26)

The grand climax of the "Parting Words" is a prayer. It is the longest of the prayers attributed to Jesus in the Gospels. The structure of the passage resists analysis. It is almost a stream-of-consciousness prayer which seems void of order. There are, however, two themes which stand out: first, the relationship of the Father and Son; second, the nature of discipleship. Those themes appear in something of an order. Verses 1-5 is Jesus' prayer for his own glorification. In vv. 6-23 the disciples are featured—their protection, unity, joy, mission, and their belonging to Christ. In vv. 24-26 the themes of the relationship of the Father and Son are combined with the disciples and their place in the world. The progression of thought, however, is more like a chain reaction in which one thought gives rise to another, and then it in turn sparks still another, etc. Perhaps what is most striking about the prayer is the love in which Jesus holds the disciples, a love which is concerned only for his mission to humanity and the well-being of his followers (for a brilliant treatment of this chapter, cf. Käsemann).

1-2—**These words** harks back to the whole of the farewell discourses in chaps. 14-16. The prayer is the capstone of the whole section. **Lifted up his eyes to heaven** is a natural posture for prayer for the Jews (cf. 11:41 above). **Father** suggests the intimacy of the relationship between God and Christ. For **hour** (*hōra*) cf. 2:4 and 12:23 above. It is the period of time in which **Jesus** completes his mission and climaxes in the crucifixion-resurrection. The cross is the means by which the divine presence is poured out on Jesus, and for this Jesus prays **glorify thy Son** (*doxason sou ton huion*). Whereas Jesus has revealed the divine presence in his words and actions, now the Father is about to make himself evident in Christ in the revealer's exaltation. But the glorification of the Son has but one purpose— to make God known. The relationship of the Father and the Son is such that Christ's death points to the presence of God in the power of his love. The sentence begun in v. 1 continues in v. 2. **Power** (*exousia*) **over all flesh** implies the authority of judgment and of life (cf. 5:21f. above). **All flesh** means in this context "all humanity." **To give** . . . is actually a second *hina* ("that") clause of the sentence, with the first occurring in "that the Son may glorify thee" of v. 1. The structure suggests that the glorification of the Son will result in two things: (1) the glorification of God and (2) the giving of **eternal life** to believers (**since** . . . **flesh** is a parenthetical comment). For **eternal life** cf. 1:4 and 3:16 above. The cross completes the work of Christ whereby a new quality of **life** is offered to humans. Those who believe are **all thou hast given** Christ (cf. vv. 6 and 24 below). The suggestion that the believers are brought to Christ only as the Father hands them over to the Son is part of the Johannine understanding of the act of faith (cf. 10:25-26 above).

3—The mention of **eternal life** in v. 2 triggers the statement of v. 3 which describes that **life**. But this verse has all the characteristics of a gloss. **The only** (*monos*) **true God** occurs only here in John, and **Jesus Christ** only here and at 1:17 (which is also often claimed to be a gloss). It is strange to have **Jesus** refer to himself with this title, **Jesus Christ.** If it is a gloss, it is Johannine gloss, for the thought of the statement is consistent with the theology of the gospel. That **eternal life** is comprised of knowing does not shock us, for John uses **know** and *believe* in nearly synonymous ways (cf. 8:31; 10:38; 17:8; and 6:69 above). Knowledge was identified with salvation in Hellenistic thought (cf. Barrett, p. 503) and Hebraic religion (e.g., Hos. 4:6). It became the basis of the gnostic Christianity of the second and third centuries. For John knowledge meant (much as it did in the OT) a relationship and not a cognitive consciousness. **Eternal life** then is described as the result of an affiliation of love with the Father and Son, **Whom thou has sent** indicates that the knowledge which yields eternal life is a relationship resulting from the revelation of God in Christ.

4-5—In v. 4 it is unclear if the perspective is the time of Jesus or that of John. In v. 1 the subjunctive form of *doxazō* ("to glorify") is used and looks forward to the cross. Here the aorist is employed (*edoxasa*), meaning an accomplished fact. It is possible that it points to the life and ministry of Jesus, but it is more likely a demonstration of the perspective of the evangelist, for whom the cross was a fact of history. **Accomplished** (*teleiōsas*) uses the same root as the word translated "It is finished" (*tetelestai*) at 19:30 (the last word of Jesus on the cross). **The work** here means the whole of the mission of the Son. As a result of the completion of his mission Jesus prays that he might be restored to that status which was his before the incarnation. **In thy own presence** and **with thee** mean the same thing and refer to the heavenly relationship of the Son (Word) with the Father. Unlike the view of the hymn found in Phil. 2:6-11, Christ's status after the resurrection and ascension pictured here is not a higher one than that which he held before his earthly mission. So, the exaltation restores Christ to his rightful, heavenly place. **Before the world was made** recalls Prov. 8:23 and speaks of that "time before time" alluded to in 1:1.

6-7—The prayer for the disciples begins here and remains the subject through at least v. 23. But the disciples are not exclusively the original Twelve, for it is clear that John wants his readers to recognize that Jesus prays for them in the following words (cf. 6: 66-67 above). **Manifested thy name** is the equivalent of "I glorified thee" in v. 4. It suggests that Jesus has revealed the character of God. **Name** (*onoma*) stands for the identity of God and represents a way of speaking of the essential being of God. But such a revelation is only for the elect. These are the ones who belong to God and are now given to Christ (cf. v. 2 above and 6:65-67 above). **Out of the world** implies that faith separates humans from the realm of darkness and unbelief. **They have kept thy word** makes clear that the disciples have been faithful, since **word** (*logos*) means the divine message expressed in the revelation and not any single commandment. John here may be affirming the faithfulness of his own community. At v. 7 a textual variant is found which would be translated "I know" (*egnōka*) instead of **they know** (*egnōkan*), but most agree the latter is preferred. The **now** (*nyn*) must again be the perspective of John, i.e., after the cross and resurrection. The time of full understanding anticipated in 16: 23 and 25 comes after the exaltation. The content of that understanding is nothing else than the certainty that the revelation is truly of God. If v. 7b sounds clumsy, it may result from the effort of John to demonstrate Jesus' dependence on the Father.

8-9—The description of the disciples begun in the previous verse continues. Jesus has given **them the words** which come to him from God. **Words** (*hrēmata*) probably means the same as "word" (*logos*) in v. 6 and represents a variation in style sometimes typical of John. **Received them** implies an act of willful acceptance which stands in tension with the predeterministic emphasis above (v. 6). **Know** and **believe** are used in synonymous parallelism and show how closely John related these two. Likewise, **I came from thee** and **thou didst send me** are synonymous. The content of belief/knowledge here is Christological, i.e., Jesus' origin with the Father. In v. 9 **praying** is literally "asking" (*erōtō*). His refusal to pray for **the world** should not be taken as a disregard, for 3:16 must be kept in mind. John's church felt isolated from and was at odds with its society, and so it is to be expected that it is Jesus' concern for the disciples and not the world that is in the forefront. The remainder of the verse repeats the statements made in v. 6.

10—This verse begins with a parenthetical comment concerning the previous statement that the disciples belong to God. **All mine are thine, and thine are mine** describes the common ownership of the Father and Son which arises from their relationship. The pronouns in the Greek are neuter (*ema panta . . . sa ema*, i.e., "all things") which seems to mean a broadening of the ownership to all creation as well as persons (cf. 16:15 above). Hence, the thought goes beyond the claim that the Father owns the disciples to the statement that ultimately all things belong to the Father and hence to the Son as well. The last clause of v. 10 (**I am glorified in them**) returns directly to the last thought of v. 9, and **them** (*autois*) identifies the disciples. The perspective is still the time of John and his church, and what is said is that in the ministry of the church Christ continues to be shown to be God's historical act for human salvation (cf. v. 22 below).

11—This verse speaks of the new situation of the believers following Jesus' departure. They are left in the world, meaning that they must cope with the hostility and oppression of life amid unbelief. Jesus has spoken frequently of his departure (i.e., his death and exaltation; cf. 14:2 and 16:5 above), and now that fact is stated to God in terms of Jesus' **coming** to the **Father.** The disciples must deal with the oppression of **the world** without Jesus' presence, at least in bodily form. **Holy Father** (*pater hagie*) is found only here in John, although it is understandable in the light of the OT (e.g., Isa. 6:3; 57:15) as well as occasional early Christian usage (e.g., Luke 1:49; Rev. 4:8; 6:10; and Did. 10:2). The title may be suggested by the attention to the *sanctification* of the disciples and the *consecration* of Jesus (both words stem from the same root as **holy,** *hagios*) in vv. 17-19. **Thy name** stands for the nature of God revealed in Christ (cf. v. 6 above). **Keep them in thy name** asks for the protection of the faith of the disciples, i.e., their trust in the revelation and their effort to cling to it through persecution. The remainder of the verse is marred by textual problems. Some manuscripts omit the entire clause, **which thou. . .are one,** and others the words **that they may. . .are one.** Retaining the whole clause seems the harder and therefore in this case the preferred of the readings. But then we find a difference concerning the pronoun **which.** Is it a reference to **name** or to disciples? Most commentators contend that the better sense is the former. The revelation of God identified as **thy name** comes from God to Christ and from him to the disciples. The unity of the disciples is the subject of the prayer in vv. 20-23 below. Here the essential element of that unity is found: It is derived from the oneness of the Father and the Son. The unity of the community of faith has no source except the Christological one (cf. "Relational Analogies," p. 266).

12-13—Verse 12 states the protection of the believers Jesus has provided. Jesus has **kept** the disciples in their faith, as he prays God will now keep them. The same problem plagues the pronoun **which** here as in the previous verse. Again it is better to take it as a reference to **name** rather than **them. Guarded** (*ephylaza*) is a synonym for **kept** (*etēroun*), although it has a military connotation which suggests protection against an enemy. **None is lost** echoes 10:38. One wonders how John understands v. 12 in relation to 6:66, where it appears that some of his believers (but not the Twelve) did turn away from Jesus. The exception to the faithfulness of the disciples is Judas. **Son of perdition** is used in 2 Thess. 2:3 (cf. Rev. 17:8, 11). Such a concept has its antecedent in the destructiveness associated with the efforts of the forces of evil in the eschatological time. In 2 Thess. 2:3 the emphasis is on the fact that the parousia cannot occur until the **son of perdition** has had his time. By identifying that figure with Judas, John implies that the eschatological insurgence of evil has already occurred in Jesus' own time. This would seem part of John's insistence on a realized eschatology. Again, Judas' deed is understood as a fulfillment of **scripture** (cf. 13:18 above). **Joy** (*chara*) in v. 13 is another eschatological characteristic. In the fullness of the Easter joy the anticipation of the gladness of the last day is realized. For **coming to thee** cf. v. 11a above. **These things** may refer to the discourses of chaps. 14-16 as well as the prayer, or to the prayer only. But in either case Jesus' concern is that the believers experience the positive side of his crucifixion and exaltation. **In the world** stresses the tension between the two settings of the prayer, i.e., Jesus' own last days and the time of the evangelist. Here the former is in view. For **joy** cf. 15:11 and 16:24 above.

14-16—The time perspective is once again that of the evangelist, for the hatred of **the world** is regarded as an established fact. The giving of God's word to the disciples repeats vv. 6-8, and is an allusion to the content of the revelation, above all, God's redemptive love. Opposition from the world is natural, since the world stands for the opposite of belief, and Christian faith involves a rebirth "from above" (3:3), which means that believers take their orientation from another realm than this world. **Even as I . . .world** is most likely a scribal addition. It is not appropriate to ask that the believers be taken **out of the world** (v. 15). Their mission is there (cf. v. 18). Neither an ascetic withdrawal from the world nor an apocalyptic anticipation of being taken out of the world (1 Thess. 4:17, "the rapture"!) is God's will. What is God's will is that in their proper place in the realm of unbelief they should be protected against the dangers of apostasy, a real danger for the Johannine community as for all the people of God. **Evil one** (*tou ponērou*) may be translated as a personal embodiment of evil (as the RSV implies) or an impersonal force of evil (as the RSV marginal note suggests). In either case, this petition is similar to that of the Lord's Prayer (cf. Matt. 6:13) and is one of the bits of evidence advanced by some to claim that the Lord's Prayer has been embellished in this Johannine prayer. Verse 16 repeats the theme sounded in vv. 6, 11, and 14. The believers must suffer the same consequences as their master (cf. 13:16 above), and hence are related to the world as Christ is (cf. "Relational Analogies" p. 266). The repetition of v. 14 in this verse has caused some scribes to omit v. 16 entirely.

17-18—The relation of the disciples to the world is now further described. While remaining in the world the believers are "set apart" (sanctified, *hagiazō*). **Sanctify** means to be commissioned for a special task and hence made "holy" (cf. Jer. 1:5; Exod. 28:14;

and 10:36 above). The disciples are to be made holy as Jesus also is in v. 19. The same word, *hagiazō*, is translated **sanctify** in this verse and "consecrated" in v. 19. Hence, **sanctify** here is synonymous with "send" in the next verse. **The truth** means the whole of the revelation and is the equivalent of **word** (cf. v. 6 above). It is the content of the revelation (i.e., God's character as redemptive love) which is both the sanctifying power and the purpose for the consecration (commissioning) of the believers. Verse 18 restates the meaning of v. 17 with the language of agency—**send. . .sent.** The mission of the disciples in relationship to **the world** is modeled on that of Christ's relationship with humanity (3:16). The mission of the church arises from God's mission executed in Christ. Again, the emphasis is upon the disciples' life in and for the world rather than upon a separation, and it is mission which is the substance of their sanctification/consecration. The latter is not a state of purity so much as it is a task.

19—This verse restates the meaning again with words related to "making holy." The self-consecration of Jesus surely means his willingness to take up his special mission in the world, namely, his death on the cross. The sense of cultic purity (e.g., Exod. 19:22) is left behind in these words. As with the disciples' sanctification, it is Jesus' being set apart for his mission that is in view here. **For their sake** (*hyper autōn*) does not necessarily imply a sacrificial notion of atonement but only that Jesus' willing death benefits humans. As a result of Jesus' act, the believers are **consecrated**, i.e., set apart in the world for a mission to the world. **In truth** (*en alētheia*), although it lacks the definite article before **truth**, means the same as sanctified "in the truth" in v. 17 (cf. 10:36 and v. 17 above).

20-21—The attention of vv. 20-23 is focused on the unity of disciples, especially those beyond the circle of the original disciples. In v. 20 it is the believers who will in later times come to faith as a consequence of the mission of the original disciples that are the subject of the petition. These later believers are the fruits of the mission for which the disciples are sanctified in vv. 17 and 19. **Those who believe** . . . are the same as the "other sheep" of 10:16, and the "one flock" mentioned there corresponds to the one-

ness of believers about to be the subject of Jesus' prayer here.
Verse 21 states a number of things about the unity of the believers
that Jesus seeks: (1) Their unity is based on and derived from the
unity of the Father and Son and hence is Christological in nature
and not the result of human effort. (2) The oneness occurs in the
relationship the disciples share in Christ and in God. (3) The oneness has the purpose of proclaiming to the world the origin of Jesus. This last point is a reaffirmation of 13:35, where it is the disciples' love for one another which is the proclamation. This motif
of unity betrays the concern of John for the integrity of the church
of his time, which had doubtless been fractured as a result of the
controversy with the synagogue. This concern may also reflect the
Sitz-im-Leben of the Johannine Epistles, although there is no evidence of redactional addition here from the time of the Epistles.
The unity of the Father and Son is a unity of love, as we have seen
(e.g., 15:9 and 14:31). Hence, the unity of believers is one of love
(not organizational structure or doctrine, for instance). In this way
the close tie with 13:34-35 is clearer. (On the remarkable struc-
tural parallelism of vv. 21-23, cf. Brown, vol. 2, p. 769.)

22-23—In v. 10b Jesus says that he is glorified in the disciples;
now in v. 22 we find the more radical statement that the **glory**
(*doxa*) Jesus has from the Father is transferred to the believers.
(The tense of the verbs is perfect, connoting an event in the past
which continues into the present.) **Glory** means the presence of
God in power. Now that divine presence is found in the community of faith by virtue of Christ's exaltation. Hence, the glory perceived in the incarnate word (1:14) is now perceptible in the
church! Because of that divine presence, the church can communicate the revelation to the world. Giving the divine presence to the
community assures their oneness and consequently their proclamation. It should be said that the glory given the community is,
like God's glorification of Christ, found in the midst of the suffering in mission. The flow of thought rushes on relentlessly into v.
23. The first thought is that of 14:20—the mutual indwelling of
the Father, the Son, and the believers. Again it is the unity of the
Father and Son which produces the unity of the believers. **Become perfectly one** is literally "be completed (*teteleiōmenoi*) into

one" (cf. v. 4 above). Again the unity of believers makes a proclamation, this time concerning the origin of the Son and God's **love**
of the believers. It is interesting that this oneness arising from the
relationship with God/Christ is completed in this world, for it
would seem more appropriately an eschatological fulfillment. The
impression is that John has conceived of the realization of the eschaton in the community of faith—they are already **one**. A textual
variant reads that it is Christ, rather than the Father, who **hast
loved them**. But the RSV is doubtless correct, since it is the more
radical of the two statements and is still consistent with Johannine
thought. With the same unsurpassable love with which God loves
the Son he loves the believers (cf. 14:21, 23)!

24—Verses 24-26 represent a near summary of the themes articulated in the prayer. They bring together the complex of relationships involving the Father, the Son, the world, and the believers. Verse 24 expresses the ultimate state of the relationship of
Father, Son, and believers at the eschaton. That relationship is not
yet complete in the life of the church in the world. **Desire** (*thelō*)
seems little more than a stylistic variation from "pray." **They . . .
whom thou hast given** is once again an instance of the neuter (*ho
dedōkas*) to mean a wide range of persons (cf. v. 10 above). A heavenly reunion of the believers with Christ is promised in 14:3.
There is an eschatological fulfillment of the believers' perception
of Christ's **glory,** which comes with the reunion with the revealer
in his exalted status. That glory resides in the **love** God has for
Christ **before the foundation of the world** (cf. 1:1). The ultimate
fulfillment of the believers' faith is found in witnessing the Father's
love for the Son. **Foundation** (*katabolē*) is found only here in John
and 10 other places in the NT (e.g., Eph. 1:14). Its meaning here
is the same as "before the world was made" in v. 4 (cf. above). For
John the **love** of God for Christ is the root of Christ's **glory** and of
his mission.

25—**Righteous** is the second adjective used in naming God (cf.
"holy" in v. 11 above). Since the remainder of v. 25 deals with
judgment, it is appropriate that the righteousness (or justice) of
God should set the context (cf. the use of *dikaiosynē* in 16:8-10

above). The construction of the sentence in this verse is a bit clumsy, but it seems to be based on a "but/and" polarity (*kai . . . kai*) with the words **but I have known thee** inserted as a parenthetical comment. The structure intends to contrast the fact that **the world** is ignorant of God, on the one hand, and that the disciples **know that thou hast sent me,** on the other hand. In his righteousness God is asked to judge between the two. The ignorance of the world is in harmony with the way that realm has been characterized in the prayer (e.g., v. 16) and this gospel as a whole (e.g., 1:10). In contrast to the world, the disciples know that Jesus is from God and hence by implication know God (cf. v. 8 above). That knowledge, however, has been mediated to them through the revelation in Christ; hence the insertion, **but I have known thee.** The thought recalls v. 16.

26—The prayer is concluded with an emphasis on the mediation of God to the believers. **Made known . . . thy name** is synonymous with "I have manifested thy name" in v. 6 (cf. 15:15). The first use of the verb "to know" is aorist (**made known,** *egnōrisa*), which refers to the past ministry of Jesus. The second is future (**will make it known,** *gnōrisō*), which speaks of the continuation of the ministry of Jesus through the Spirit-Paraclete and the community. The revelation has but one purpose, namely, that (*hina*, "in order that") the divine love may be present among humans. **In them** (*en autois*) occurs twice in v. 26b, and in each case can mean either "within them (individually)" or "among them." The meaning may transcend such a distinction; but the emphasis of the context is on the community. So it is better that we understand the phrase to mean "within the corporate body." The presence of the divine **love** is identified here with the presence of Christ, **I in them.** The longing for the dwelling of God among humans (e.g., Isa. 7:14) is accomplished in the Christ event, even as Matthew declares with the name Emmanuel (1:23).

One is safe in asserting that in vv. 22-26 the whole of the gospel and not just the prayer is summarized. For therein is found a digest of Johannine theology. Indeed, chap. 17 pulls together nearly all of the prominent themes of John's thought and restates them in condensed form in a collage of petitions. The Christology of the

gospel (as well as its soteriology) is recapitulated and its consequences for the life of faith unfolded. Within this maze of affirmations one pattern emerges among others. It is the pattern of defining Christian life along the lines of divine relationships. The chart,
"Relational Analogies," on p. 266 attempts to capture some of that
modeling within the complex of interrelationships. The conclusions one might draw from those analogies and from the whole of
the "Parting Words" is that authentic human relationships are derived from divine relationships and, more specifically, Christian
existence is defined by Christology.

■ The Exaltation (18:1—20:29)

John now begins the narrative of Jesus' reception of God's glory
itself, following the extensive teaching section that frames the passion story with special meaning. Not surprisingly, his account of
the passion parallels that of the Synoptic Gospels rather closely, at
least when compared with many of his other narratives. It is clear
that the Johannine community preserved what must have been a
form of the early Christian tradition concerning the death and resurrection of Jesus. That some kind of tradition has restricted John's
narrative is illustrated by the fact that his normal propensity for
discourse is entirely subdued. In some form John received and
employed a source which contained the passion narrative.
Whether or not that source was part of a larger source, e.g., the
signs source, we cannot be certain. That he worked with his own
source rather than with one or more of the Synoptics seems more
likely, but again that cannot be proved. This much we can say with
some confidence: John's passion narrative is derived from a source
already influenced by earlier traditions concerning the climax of
Jesus' ministry.

But we can with confidence say, too, that John or the Johannine
community before him radically shaped that earlier tradition. We
see evidence of that in what might be called the special characteristics of the passion narrative in John: First, it betrays a high Chris-

Relational Analogies in Chapters 14–17

1. Relationship of Father(F) and Son(S) as a Model for the Relationship of Son(S) and Believer(B)

F remains (*menō*) in S (14:10)	Bs remain (*menō*) in S (15:4)
F is in S (17:23); S in F (14:10, 12) (*en*)	S is in B (17:23); B in S (14:20; 15: 4; 16:33) (*en*)
F gives S glory (*doxa*) (17:22)	S gives Bs glory (*doxa*) (17:22)
S obeys F (14:31)	Bs obey S (14:15)
S obeys F and remains (*menō*) in his love (15:10)	B obeys S and remains (*menō*) in his love (15:10)
F loves S (17:26; 15:9)	S loves the Bs (15:9, 12)
S loves the F and obeys him (14: 31)	Bs who love S obey him (14:15, 21)
F sends (*apostellō*) S into world (17:18)	S sends (*apostellō*) Bs into world (17:18)

2. Relationship of Father(F) and Son(S) as a Model for the Relationship of Father(F) and Believer(B)

F's glory is shown in S (14:31)	F's glory is shown in Bs' bearing much fruit (15:8)
F loves S (17:23)	F loves Bs (17:23)

3. Relationship of Father(F) and Son(S) as a Model for the Relationship of Believer(B) and Believer(B)

F and S are one (*hen*) (17:11, 21, 22b)	Bs are one (*hen*) (17:11, 21, 22b)

4. Relationship of Son(S) and Believer(B) as a Model for the Relationship of Believer(B) and Believer(B)

S loves the Bs (15:12)	Bs love Bs (15:12)

5. Relationship of Son(S) and World(W) as a Model for the Relationship of Believers(B) and World(W)

W hates (*miseō*) S (15:18)	W hates (*miseō*) Bs (15:18)
W persecutes or obeys S (15:20b)	W persecutes or obeys Bs (15:20b)
S does not belong to W (17:14, 16)	Bs do not belong to W (17:14, 16)
S is consecrated (*hagiazō*) (17:19)	Bs are consecrated/sanctified (*hagiazō*) (17:17, 19)

tology common to the whole gospel, with the result that Jesus is pictured less as a humiliated servant of God than as God's unique Son going to his enthronement. He is always in control of the situation and regal in his posture. Second, arising from the first point, the cross is the exaltation of God's love expressed in Christ and is not viewed primarily as a sacrifice for sin. It is shaped by the suggestion that Jesus is the Passover lamb, liberating humanity, but that lamb is not conceived of with sacrificial notions.[25] Third, there is in John's concept of this grand climax no temporal distinction among resurrection, ascension, and the giving of the Spirit. Moreover, even the crucifixion and resurrection are hardly distinguished, so closely bound are they. With the cross John moves into a transtemporal mode, and hence collapses together what others (especially Luke) had seen as separable events into one event. Finally, John's passion narrative is distinctive in literary form by dramatically conceived staccato scenes. The narrative flows through short episodes fashioned with artistic care. (Cf. Brown, vol. 2, pp. 787ff. and Schnackenburg, vol. 3, pp. 218ff. for more extensive analyses of the passion narrative.)

Betrayal and Arrest (18:1-12)

1-3—The first scene of the narrative is told with economy. The agony of Jesus' struggle narrated in the Synoptics (e.g., Mark 14:32ff.) is entirely missing and 12:27-28 is the closest John comes to a depiction of Jesus' emotional disturbance as he faces his death. In v. 1 **these words** is literally "these things" (*tauta*), and gives us no clue as to precisely what is intended—the prayer of chap. 17, the first form of the discourse, or all three. The link between this narrative and what precedes it is vague. **Kidron valley** (*tou cheimarrou tou Kedrōn*) refers to a spring east of Jerusalem which carried water only in the winter (cf. 2 Sam. 15:23; 1 Kings 15:13). **Garden** (*kēpos*) may designate a plot used to grow food or flowers. **Disciples** does not mean exclusively only the Twelve (cf. 6:66-67 above), so we are at a loss to speculate who exactly were with Jesus at this time, according to John. Verse 2 introduces **Judas** (cf. 6:71; 12:4; 13:2, 26, 29 above) and the reason the betrayer knew he would find Jesus there. (The Synoptics lack this detail, except

Luke 22:39.) John, however, has neglected to mention the spot in earlier narratives. No symbolic meaning should be attached to **garden** (e.g., garden of Eden). Verse 3 describes the arresting **officers**. **Procuring** is a misleading translation of *labōn*, which here means only "taking" in the sense of "guiding." The arresting **officers** include two groups, Roman **soldiers** and temple police. John alone introduces the Romans at this early state of the passion narrative, and perhaps wants to indicate already that both secular and religious forces opposed Jesus. **Band** renders *speira*, which more exactly refers to a cohort of soldiers. But a group of that size (either 600 or 200) is ridiculous; we must assume that the evangelist means a smaller contingent. Some military forces may have been at the disposal of the religious authorities to guard against insurrection. **Some officers from the chief priests. . .**means the temple guards (cf. 7:32 above). For **chief priests and Pharisees** cf. 7:32 and 11:47 above. **Lanterns and torches** may be only a narrative detail, but John may also intend that they are the futile attempts of those in the darkness of unbelief to find their way.

4-7—With the stage now set the narrative itself begins with typical Johannine drama. **Jesus, knowing all that** sets a tone for the whole passion narrative. With his supernatural knowledge he is not victimized by the events. For Jesus' wondrous knowledge cf. 13:1, 3; 2:25; and 16:19 above. Here, as throughout the passion, **Jesus** is the one in control of events. **All that was to befall him** is more exactly "**all that** which was coming to him" (*panta ta erchomena*). **Whom do you seek?** is a dramatic means by which **Jesus** takes the initiative in the scene. Does the verb **seek** (*zēteō*) suggest the spiritual seeking it sometimes connotes (e.g., 7:34, 36; 8:21; 13:33)? The group's answer in v. 5 is an infrequent name for **Jesus** in John (only here, v. 7, and 19:19 with the adjective *Nazōraios*, and 1:45, "from **Nazareth**," *apo Nazaret*). **I am he** is in the Greek the naked **I am** (*egō eimi*). That this is the divine utterance known elsewhere in this gospel (cf. 8:24, 28, 58; 13:19 above) is clear from the effects of the words described in v. 6. Again, John shows that Jesus has absolute power over the circumstances and allows them to occur. **Judas who . . .** is a clumsy insertion which plays no clear function. However, it may be intended to heighten the drama by delaying the results of the **I am** and necessitating the repetition in v. 6. It may also be a statement of the dramatic encounter of the betrayer with **Jesus.** Verse 6 narrates the overpowering effect of the divine utterance, indeed the effect of a theophany! Verse 7 repeats the question and the answer of vv. 4b-5a made necessary by the awful experience of Jesus' self-identification.

8-9—**Jesus** again uses the sacred "I am" in v. 8, but this time without the awesome results and, properly, with the implied predicate **he.** He protects his own sheep in acquiring their release (cf. 10:28 and 17:12 above), but not necessarily by means of his own sacrifice. There could be implicit in these words an apology for the fleeing of the disciples described in the Synoptics (e.g., Mark 14:50 but omitted by Luke). Jesus sanctions their escape. But there is little evidence elsewhere of an effort to preserve the reputation of the disciples (e.g., 16:29-32). Verse 9 is rightly suspected as an editorial gloss from a later hand. It supposes a rather materialistic interpretation of 17:12, for **lost** there has to do with falling away from faith and here with physical well-being. Be that as it may, the verse ascribes to Jesus' words the status of Scripture. Only here and in v. 32 is the word **fulfil** used of Jesus' words. But the verb (*plēroō*) is often found in connection with Scripture (e.g., 12:3; 13:18).

10—The incident recorded in vv. 10-11 is found in the Synoptics (Mark 14:47ff. and parallels) but without naming the actor or the victim and with a different saying as a conclusion to the incident. The addition of details such as names may indicate a longer development in the tradition. But such elaborations may just as easily be explained as an earlier form of the tradition from which details were later dropped. The image of **Simon Peter** as an impulsive person is sustained by John (e.g., 13:8). **Sword** translates *machaira* which more accurately designates a dagger. **Right ear** is another instance of detail in the scene. **Ear** is *ōtarion*, taken as a diminutive by some; hence, Brown's translation, "earlobe" (vol. 2, p. 812). The name **Malchus** is not usual, as far as we know; it means "king." That leads some to seek symbolic meaning in the detail—Jesus' kingship is at stake. But such is unlikely. **Peter's** act is foolish insofar as it represents a puny effort to detour events which have cosmic proportions and divine design.

11-12—That is the meaning of **Jesus'** words in v. 11. **Cup** (*potērion*) is used only here in John and without its associations with the suffering of Jesus common in the Synoptics (e.g., Mark 14:24). It appears to be drawn from John's source in which it may originally have had those Synoptic connotations; but it has been drastically revised by the Johannine tradition or the evangelist himself. Here it symbolizes the divine destiny of the Father accepted without reserve as part of the glory Jesus is to receive, i.e., a gift from the Father. It is only natural that Jesus should will the events of his passion, since they are his Father's will. And he shares the Father's will (cf. 10:30 above). Verse 12 closes the scene abruptly with the securing of Jesus. The **captain** is more exactly a "tribune," a commander of a force of 1000. The first occurrence of **the Jews** in the passion narrative is typical of the whole section. It consistently names the opponents of Jesus.

Thus John has shown his hand by the manner in which he tells this first scene. Jesus' supremacy and control of the situation and the casting of "the Jews" as the protagonists are set in place for the subsequent episodes.

Jesus' Trial and Peter's (18:13-27)

The religious trial or hearing is punctuated with the segments of Peter's denial. What is evident in this section is that the real trial is Peter's, not Jesus'. The narrative alternates between Jesus before the religious leaders and Peter before his accusers. But John's account of the religious trial bristles with problems of both a literary and historical kind. The story, vv. 13-14 and 19-24, is unclear at best, if not garbled. We are told that Jesus is taken to Annas, who is first called the father-in-law of the high priest (v. 13) but then by implication the high priest himself (v. 19). We are finally informed that Jesus is taken to Caiaphas, "the high priest" (v. 24), but then abruptly find him before Pilate (v. 28). Manuscript evidence shows that scribes have tried by numerous ways to rearrange the passages so as to force them into some sense. But no such rearrangement is entirely successful. We are faced with a fragmented narrative and, perhaps, a disarranged narrative as well, for which there is no explanation. The only recourse is to assume that John has left out crucial parts of the story, or that they have been excised from his work. The historical problems are no less difficult. John never informs us of a formal religious charge brought against Jesus, although such are implied in 18:33 and 19:7. There is no account of a meeting of the Sanhedrin. Caiaphas, the high priest, would surely have been involved in such proceedings. No witnesses are presented in the course of the hearing. Finally, Annas, who may have had informal influence as the deposed high priest, had no formal powers; yet he is the only one said to interrogate Jesus. We can only conclude that John was not interested in the religious trial, perhaps because he felt that trial had already taken place (cf. 11:47-50). Given his tendency toward anti-Jewish polemic, we would expect the religious trial to have played a more important role in John's passion narrative. Why the lengthy trial before Pilate (18:28—19:16) and none before the Sanhedrin? Is John presupposing some acquaintance with the matter on the part of his readers? Is his point that the religious trial was a total farce? Has his preoccupation with Peter's denials caused him to be careless to such a degree with the antiphonal scenes with Jesus?

13-14—These verses comprise the first hearing. **First** indicates that John thought the religious trial involved two hearings, as do Mark (14:35 and 15:1) and Matthew (26:57; 27:1) but not Luke. **Annas** is mentioned only by John (here and v. 24) and Luke (3:2 and Acts 4:6), and it is John alone who identifies him as **the father-in-law of Caiaphas.** Annas was high priest from 6 to 15 C.E., when he was deposed by Roman authorities. The deposition was probably not recognized by the Jewish people. For them, such an action represented foreign intervention in a religious matter, and Annas doubtless remained a powerful figure. John is alone in claiming that Annas interrogated Jesus. Although here it is said that it is his son-in-law who was **high priest,** vv. 19ff. seem to refer to him as the holder of that office. It is possible that he was regarded with such respect and his deposition so totally ignored that he was called the high priest (much as Americans continue to address a former president, even one defeated in election, "Mr. President";

cf. 7:32 above). Caiaphas is identified as the high priest at this time only by John and Matthew (26:57). On **high priest that year** cf. 11:49 above. Verse 14 reminds the reader of 11:50.

15-18—The first of **Peter's** denials punctuates the story of the trial. The **another disciple** of v. 15 is often identified with the beloved disciple, although there is little basis for such (cf. Introduction §2). That he was **known to the high priest** argues against the identification of the mysterious disciple with the beloved disciple and in turn the beloved disciple with John, son of Zebedee. It is unlikely that a Galilean fisherman would be an acquaintance of the high priest. **Known** (*gnōstos*) is not clear in its implications, but may have the force here of "friend" or even "kinsman." **Court** (*aulē*) may refer to the central part of a Roman home or to the area inside the temple. More specific identification is hindered because of the ambiguous nature of the hearing as John records it. We are not sure whether it is likely to have been in Annas's home or in the temple area. Verse 16 seems to imply that the setting was a home. **Maid** is more precisely "portress" (*thyrōrōs*), i.e., a female doorkeeper. Her question in v. 17 is not entirely free of difficulties. The question is a cautious statement which anticipates a negative answer (*mē*). But **you also** (*kai sy*) implies the opposite. Presumably, she is suggesting that Peter must also be one of Jesus' disciples, as is the "other disciple." If this is true, there is nothing hostile or threatening about the question, and it is a casual matter of curiosity. Is **I am not** (*ouk eimi*) intended as a contrast with Jesus' "I am he" in v. 8? As boldly as Jesus defends his disciples, Peter boldly denies association with the prisoner. Verse 18 adds narrative color to the tale, producing verisimilitude. John may be touching up his source.

19—Over against Peter's first denial, John sets the hostile interrogation of **Jesus.** We are left without assurance as to whether the **high priest** who conducts the hearing in v. 19 is Annas or Caiaphas. Verse 13 would suggest the latter, but v. 24 the former. We can only guess that John is here calling Annas high priest on the basis of what was mentioned above on v. 13. All three of the essential elements of the Synoptic account of the religious trial are missing in John: the witnesses against Jesus, the question of his messianic claims, and the charge of blasphemy (e.g., Mark 14:56, 61, 64). Instead, the interrogation centers on Jesus' **disciples and his teaching.** The first may imply fear of the gathering of a group of insurrectionists. The second may reflect the questions put to John's church by members of the synagogue. There could be an ironic tone to the references to disciples, given Peter's failure just narrated.

20-21—Jesus' response in v. 20 claims that his **teaching** has been public (**openly,** *parrēsia,* cf. 7:13, 26; 10:24; 11:14; and 16: 29 above), in contrast to **secretly** (*kryptos*; cf. Isa. 45:19). This surely does not deny Jesus' private teachings to his disciples, but instead implies that Jesus has not propagated subversive teachings. This would be a further indication that concern for the disciples was that they had rebellion in mind. While John does represent Jesus' teaching publicly, it is not the case that he regards those teachings "open" in the sense of "clear" (e.g., 10:24); so the point here would seem to be that his teaching is innocuous so far as social stability or esoteric doctrines are concerned. His teaching in the **synagogues** in John is limited to 6:59 but is frequent **in the temple** (e.g., 7:14; 8:20). The mention of **Jews** makes the statement incredible as a record of Jesus' own response, for all concerned were Jews. This is a clue to the fact that Jesus' trial is recounted in the light of the trials of the Johannine Christians of John's time. The whole content of this answer to the high priest makes more sense as a typical response of the Christians to interrogation in John's own city. Verse 21 is a demand for trial by witness, in other words, a proper legal inquiry. That none are present indicates that John conceived of this situation as only an informal hearing. The truth of Jesus' claims for himself are to be sought in those who are witnesses to him (i.e., Christians).

22-24—Verse 22 is the Johannine version of the mistreatment of Jesus at the religious trial in the Synoptics (cf. Mark 14:65 and Matt. 26:67). Exod. 22:28 sanctions punishment in cases in which a leader is improperly addressed. Verse 23 repeats the demand for witnesses and asserts that Jesus has not acted **wrongly** (*kakōs*). Again it appears that John is trying to underline the inappropriate hostility directed at Christians by members of the synagogue. Barrett observes, "The truth is always objectionable to those who are concerned to establish a case at all costs" (p. 529). Verse 24 is part of the larger problem of this account of the religious trial (cf. above). **Then** (*oun*) may suggest that on the basis of Jesus' appeal for a formal trial with witnesses he is **sent** to the Sanhedrin, presided over by **Caiaphas.** Such a transition need not have been among different buildings. Caiaphas might have been present for the hearing. But all such conjectures do little to ease the confusion of the narrative.

25-27—It is clear, however, that Peter's denials are juxtaposed to Jesus' situation. While Jesus is faced with the real danger of death and yet does not compromise the truth, poor Peter cannot even admit to having been a **disciple** of the prisoner. Verse 25 reaches back to pick up Peter's story from v. 18. **They** are presumably the "servants and officials" of v. 18. Their question is worded in a nearly identical way with that of the maid in v. 17 (*mē kai su*). **Denied it . . . I am not** is redundant, perhaps for emphasis. **One of the servants** becomes the questioner in v. 26. For dramatic reasons this servant is said to be **kinsman** (*syngenēs*) of Malchus in v. 10. John suggests the increasing futility of Peter's efforts at concealing his identity, a feature of the Matthean account as well, except that there it is his Galilean accent which betrays Peter (26:69-75). That John's details are evidence of an eyewitness account is an attractive suggestion, but not a necessary one. Verse 27 records Peter's last denial and brings the narrative to an abrupt end (cf. 13:38).

In spite of the enormous difficulties of John's version of the religious trial, this section is an effective story. By Jesus' regal posture, the evangelist vividly contrasts the failure of human allegiance with Jesus' loyalty to his divine destiny. The trial, John insists, has humanity and not Jesus on the docket!

Jesus and Pilate (18:28—19:16)

The literary problems of the religious hearing stand in sharp contrast with the skillful and dramatic telling of the political trial. This narrative is carefully constructed in eight scenes which alternate between glimpses of Pilate with Jesus, on the one hand, and

Pilate with the religious leaders, on the other. Throughout we sense the significance of the engagement of the revelation with the political powers of this world, and we see Pilate become gradually transformed from a disinterested cynic into a frightened official of state, trying to preserve his power and dignity. In the midst of the portrayal of Pilate stands the persistently kingly figure of Jesus. Historical problems, however, plague this narrative, as well as 18:12-27. Not least among them is the vagueness of the actual charge brought against Jesus and the understanding of Roman and Jewish law reflected herein. The historicity of the account is difficult to assess, but it is obvious that historical concerns have been subjected to theological motives (compare Mark 15:1-5 and parallels).

28—From the house of Caiaphas is literally, "from Caiaphas" (*apo tou Kaiapha*) and gives us no help in solving the problems of the previous story. **Praetorium** (*praitōrion*) was the term used for the residence of the Roman governor. Pilate normally resided in Caesarea (cf. Acts 23:35) but might well have kept a residence in Jerusalem for such "dangerous" occasions in the city as Passover. The Jerusalem location may have been Herod's palace near the Jaffa gate, or it may have been the Antonia fortress in the northwest temple area. **Early** (*prōi*) is a reference to the last period of the night by Roman calculations, hence 3:00 A.M. to 6:00 A.M. (cf. 19:16a below). The defilement mentioned is a bit difficult, for it is impossible to know exactly what John (or his source) had in mind. Defilement could result from contact with Gentiles in general (and with their homes), according to later rabbinic law. Whether or not such an understanding was operative in the first century is impossible to say for certain. Other possible dangers of defilement in this setting include contact with menstruating women and their husbands, unleavened bread, and graves. More important is the note of irony implicit here. While plotting to destroy the revelation of God in their midst, the religious leaders are meticulous in the observance of their law! **Might eat the Passover** may have reference to Num. 9:7-10, which provides for a delayed observance of Passover by one defiled by contact with a corpse.

29-30—The first scene of the drama (vv. 29-32) begins with **Pilate** confronting the religious leaders. Pilate was the Roman gov-

ernor (most likely a "prefect" and not a "procurator") 26–36 C.E.
John assumes that his readers are acquainted with the figure and
gives no introduction. Pilate's question to the leaders assumes that
the Sanhedrin had tried Jesus and were bringing him to Pilate for
confirmation. But it also suggests that he intends to conduct his
own trial. The answer in v. 30 shows that John will try to demonstrate the relative innocence of the Romans and the culpability of
the religious leaders for Jesus' death. **Evildoer** (*kakon poiōn*) is vague but points away from a charge of political rebellion. One wonders if this expression reflects the charge leveled against Christians
by the synagogue in John's own time. **Handed him over** is the
verb which has been used of Judas' betrayal (*paradidōmi*, e.g., 12:
14 and 13:2). It may intimate that the religious leaders are as
guilty as Judas.

31-32—Verse 31 raises thorny issues regarding legal rights and
procedures. First, do the words of **Pilate** mean that the Sanhedrin
was actually allowed to handle such cases without appeal to the
Roman authority? In all probability John has little interest here in
such legal technicalities and intends only to make it clear that the
forces resulting in the crucifixion were Jewish rather than Roman.
Such an apologetic stance toward Roman government is evident to
some degree in all the NT treatments of the trial of Jesus. Second,
is the response of **the Jews** a reflection of an actual historical situation? This is the first we have heard of a formal death penalty
against Jesus. The debate wages on in scholarly circles regarding
the meaning of these words and their accuracy. Some argue that
Roman law prohibited the Jewish authorities from carrying out
formal executions; others dispute that historical judgment. Others
argue that it is the rabbinic law which prevented the leaders from
acting on their own; others deny that such law was in force at the
time. The resolution may finally lie beyond the reach of historical
research. John's motive is, however, clear. He intends by this
statement on the part of the religious leaders to explain why it is
that the Jewish establishment is responsible for Jesus' death even
though the execution was carried out by Roman officials. The
apologetic theme may have been rooted in Johannine tradition or
may reflect the evangelist's own view. John's theological interest

in the matter is expressed in v. 32. The reference is to Jesus' calling his death "a lifting up" (3:14; 8:28; and especially 12:32-33). Again, the evangelist uses **fulfill** (*plēroō*) to refer to Jesus' words (cf. v. 9 above). Stoning would seem to have been the normal means by which Jewish law would apply the death penalty (cf. Deut. 22:21 and Ezek. 16:38-40).

33-36—The second scene (vv. 33-38a) finds **Pilate** face to face with **Jesus**. Pilate's question is a clue to the whole narrative. It is ironically true that **Jesus** is **King**, even though in a much different way than Pilate imagines, and it is Jesus' kingship which sets Pilate over against him. This is a charge for which John has not prepared us, but which seems to be clear later in the story (19:14-15). This question begins the political trial of Jesus in all of the Gospels (Matt. 27:11; Mark 15:2; and Luke 18:33). **King of the Jews** carried political connotations, of course, and may have been a Roman perception of the Jewish concept of Messiah. Jesus' response in v. 34 attempts to elicit a commitment from Pilate. The governor's posture throughout the trial is that of neutrality, but John will show that such neutrality is impossible—one is either of the light or of the darkness. Pilate's attempt at neutrality is clear in v. 35. He pleads ignorance and claims the charge is brought by **your own nation**. He will try to disentangle himself from the whole matter, but without success. Verse 36 focuses the issue on the nature of Jesus' **kingship**. **Of this world** employs the preposition *ek* (of) meaning "arising from" and "belonging to." **World** (*kosmos*) carries its Johannine sense of the realm of unbelief. Jesus is not referring, therefore, to a spiritual kingdom over against an earthly one, but a kingship which is set apart from the evil of unbelief. But such a kingship is distinctly different from the nature of rule in the world of darkness, and it does not involve the use of violence but suffering love. **Servants** (*hypēretēs*) is the same word used in v. 3, translated there "officers." The disclaimer of Jesus has to do both with the violence used by such persons and implicitly the exclusion of such "servants" from among his subjects. **If . . . were** is a condition stating a situation contrary to reality—servants of this kind are no more a part of his kingdom than its being **of this world**. The contrast is intended to show the disparity of God's means of accomplishing his will and human means.

37-38a—The reader, of course, knows the nature of Jesus' kingship, but not Pilate. And so in v. 37 he speaks without understanding Jesus' words. With typical Johannine misunderstanding, Pilate interprets Jesus' words in a literal fashion—Jesus claims to be a **king** but not of the Jews (cf. 3:4 above). Jesus' answer is neither a denial nor an affirmation. In a sense, yes, he is **a king**, but then he must define the nature of his kingship. That definition involves a proper understanding of Jesus' mission. **Born** and **come into the world** are parallel and mean the same thing, Jesus' earthly ministry. **Truth** (*alētheia*) on the lips of Jesus betokens the content of the revelation of God (inseparable from Jesus himself—14:6). **Every one who is of the truth** (*ek tēs alētheias*, cf. v. 36 above) is one of John's "affiliation" designations, which means those who are "drawn" by the Father (6:44) and responsive in faith (6:40). **Hears my voice** recalls 10:16. By implication Jesus' words set Pilate over against those responsive to God's call in Christ. Pilate's rhetorical question demonstrates this (v. 38a). For all of his efforts to remain neutral, he has no comprehension of the revelation and is therefore part of the world. Although challenged by the revelation in Jesus' words, he remains unmoved.

38b-39—The third scene (vv. 38b-40) has **Pilate** with the religious leaders. Pilate declares Jesus' innocence for the first of three times (cf. 19:4 and 6; compare Luke 23:4ff.). John continues his insistence that Roman authority was not responsible for convicting Jesus, although at the same time he asserts Pilate's culpability on other grounds. Verse 39 represents the first of the efforts of Pilate to win the crowd's approval while still avoiding his involvement in a miscarriage of justice. The **custom** (*synētheia*) to which he refers is not documented elsewhere beyond the NT, but is entirely possible (cf. the Synoptic accounts, which do not attribute the offer of the release of one prisoner to custom as such, e.g., Mark 15:9-10). Why John has Pilate refer to Jesus as **the King of the Jews** in this situation is not entirely clear. It may be an effort to impute a sarcasm to the ruler or to have him appeal to popular opinion (as he understands it) against the will of the religious leaders. At any rate, for John it keeps the central issue before us—Jesus' true kingship over against that ascribed to him.

40—This verse seems to be a digest of a more elaborate narrative, since it is said the people **cried out** *again* (*palin*). There is no indication of their having done so earlier. Moreover, **Barabbas** is abruptly interjected into the story without any preparation (contrast Mark 15:7). John may be editing his source for his own purposes. Barabbas is probably not a personal name but a family name and means "son of the father." Speculation that his name too was Jesus, based on a textual variant of Matt. 27:16-17, is intriguing but pointless. More promising, if we are to do something symbolic with the etymology of the name, is the contrast of Barabbas and the true "Son of the Father." But John usually signals his reader when etymology is important (e.g., possibly 9:7). Barabbas is called only a **robber** (*lēstēs*; Mark 15:7 identifies him as a revolutionary). The word may mean one engaged in insurrection. The fact that **robber** is used in 10:1, 8 to describe the illegitimate authority of the religious leaders may indicate a further intention of irony. One who represents the distortion of an understanding of God and the Torah is preferred over the revealer of God.

19:1-3—In this fourth scene **Pilate** is again in the presence of Jesus. Verse 1 relates the scourging. There is some confusion in the order of the events, for the flogging of the victim would normally follow the sentencing and serve as a preparation for crucifixion. John does not make it clear at what precise point the sentence of Jesus has been determined (cf. v. 16 below). The flogging seems in John's scheme to represent a minor punishment by which Pilate hoped to appease the crowd (compare Luke 23:22 and Mark 15:15). The RSV is accurate in representing the Greek, which has it sound as if Pilate himself **scourged** the victim, even though v. 2 makes it clear that was not the case. Verse 2 describes the mockery of Jesus and indicates that the understanding of the charge against Jesus is that of claiming to be a **king. Plaited** renders the verb *plekō*, "to weave" or "twist." The exact nature of the thorny branches is not known. **Robe** is *himation*, "a garment," and especially an outer piece of clothing. Verse 3 depicts the soldiers as approaching Jesus as if to pay homage, only to strike out instead.

4-6—The fifth scene (vv. 4-7) finds **Pilate** once again before the leaders, this time with Jesus. John is emphasizing the pathetic irony of the situation—the true King being mocked by a pretender to royalty. Verse 4 is the second declaration from Pilate that Jesus is innocent (cf. 18:38 and v. 6). It is not easy to read this account as history and to learn what Pilate intended to accomplish. But it appears John would have us think that Pilate is mocking the people, as well as Jesus, and perhaps seeking an "out" for himself. Verse 5 brings a penultimate climax of the section with the words **behold the man** (*ho anthrōpos*). The meaning of this pregnant expression has been sought in numerous proposal (e.g., "this poor fellow," the Son of man, etc.), including a possible scripture fulfillment (cf. Zech. 6:11-12). It is entirely possible that John intends a theological meaning. "**Man**" may have been a messianic title in some circles, related to the title "Son of man." Or it may be that in this lowest of moments the incarnation is fulfilled (1:14). Certainly, John finds in the governor's words an unconscious statement—this is indeed the man through whom God has worked. Verse 6 reminds us that the "Jews" referred to in the narrative (e.g., 18:38) are not a "crowd" in the sense of ordinary people, but **the chief priests and officers** of the temple guard. Now the specific nature of Jesus' death is expressed for the first time in this gospel: **crucify** (*stauroō*). The dramatic tension is increasing as John advances his tale. Pilate's words in v. 6 seem impossible, if we are to suppose this to be a description of the historical event. Would a Roman authority abdicate his responsibility to such a degree as to allow the people to do as they wished with an accused? Or does the author want us to take these words as Pilate's taunting of the gathering? His offer, if serious, would seem to contradict 18:31. Two observations are in order: (1) John wants to convey the increasing frustration and futility of the Roman which find their result in v. 8 ("he was the more afraid"). (2) The evangelist and his tradition again transfers (unhistorically?) responsibility for Jesus' death entirely to the religious leaders. Pilate is given still a third pronouncement of Jesus' innocence (cf. 18:38 and v. 4).

7—This verse brings a revelation. The accusers now claim that Jesus is guilty of blasphemy, assuming Lev. 24:26 is the **law** to which reference is made. Furthermore, the blasphemy finds its locus in Jesus' claim that he is **Son of God** (the Greek title is anarthrous, without articles). Perhaps John has prepared his readers for this with 10:33, but his defective account of the religious trial makes the surfacing of this charge unexpected. Did John suppose his readers would think there were two charges brought against Jesus—he claimed to be "King of the Jews" and he blasphemed? Or are we to understand that the second is the more strictly religious view of the former charge which had the more political significance? At any rate, Brown is correct when he writes, "the evangelist reflects the common tradition that Jesus' claim of relationship to God was a decisive factor in the hostility of the authorities toward him" (vol. 2, p. 877). **Son of God** here may stand in contrast with "man" in v. 5 and together with it express the basic Christian paradox: the man who is the Son of God.

8-10—The sixth scene (vv. 8-11) begins with a description of Pilate's predicament: He is **more afraid**. The source of Pilate's fear (a fear which heretofore has been implied but not articulated) is the fact that he is caught between some semblance of justice and the pressures of the religious leaders, whose powers to have him censured by Rome are very real. It may be that the claim that this Jesus is some sort of divine man aroused superstition in him. If the latter is the case, his question to Jesus in v. 9 is more understandable: By asking Jesus **Where are you from?** he is trying to assess the victim's alleged claims. Again John has Pilate uttering more than the governor intends (cf. v. 5), for it is Jesus' origin which is the key to his identity and authority (cf., e.g., 3:31 above). If all the parties involved knew the correct answer to Pilate's question, none of this would be happening! John implies that secular humanity unconsciously asks the right questions at times. Jesus remains silent—as he does more consistently in Mark's and Matthew's accounts (e.g., Mark 15:5; Matt. 27:14). **Pilate** then threatens the victim in hopes of eliciting information (v. 10). He claims **power** (*exousia*) or authority in the presence of one whose authority is absolute.

11—Verse 11a typifies John's portrayal of the passion—all is allowed to occur as part of the divine plan. It is in this sense that Pilate's **power** is from **above**. **Above** (*anōthen*) should be read here in terms of its theological meaning for John—the realm of the divine (cf. 3:3ff. above)— and not as a simple reference to Rome. Verse 11b is vague because of the uncertainty as to whom **he who delivered me** refers. The verb *paradidōmi* has been used of Judas (e.g., 12:4) and the religious leaders (e.g., 18:30) and might also be taken to refer to Caiaphas (18:28). The thought is that Pilate has acted unwillingly, although not without **sin**, as opposed to the one(s) whose acts have been deliberate. It is best to read the verse as a reference to Judas, although in John's own milieu the intent might arise from the anti-Jewish feelings of the time and refer to the Jewish leaders. **Greater sin** (*meizona hamartian*) is unique to this passage in the Johannine literature. John does speak of "greater works" (14:12) and "greater love" (15:13). He also claims the religious leaders are more responsible for their rejection of Christ (9:41). Having had an intimate relationship with Jesus as one of the disciples and having shared table fellowship with him, Judas' act of betrayal is greater than Pilate's cowardice.

12—Scene seven is a short summary of Pilate's final effort to have Jesus released. **Upon this** is an apparent reference to Jesus' words in v. 11. **Pilate** seeks to **release** Jesus because he is even more convinced of the victim's innocence; but he does not have the courage to oppose the will of the religious leaders. Their threat is not veiled; they will find Pilate guilty of betraying the trust of **Caesar** if he frees Jesus. **Caesar's friend** (*philos*) recalls the declaration of Jesus that his disciples are his friends (14:15). Now the choice is squarely before Pilate—to be Caesar's friend or Christ's. By Pilate's time "friend of Caesar" may have been used as a technical and honorific title for representatives of the empire. If such is the case, the ironic contrast John poses is all the more poignant.

13—In the final scene of this dramatic portrayal (vv. 13-16) all the actors are brought together (as in v. 4) for the climax. In v. 13 **heard these words** seems to say that the reply of the leaders forces **Pilate** reluctantly to pass sentence. **Judgment seat** (*bēma*) means the chair or bench on which the governor sat when issuing decisions, although its literal meaning is "platform." It is used of God's judgment seat elsewhere in the NT (e.g., Rom. 14:10). **Sat down** (*ekathisen*) can be taken either as a transitive ("sat") or as an intransitive ("caused to sit") verb. Is it Pilate who sat down so as to offer sentence, or Jesus who is forced to sit there as a continuation of his mockery? Arguments can be offered for each of these, but the matter comes down finally to a decision regarding the nature of John's narrative. If John is seriously representing history, it is impossible to suppose that he would have Jesus placed on the **judgment seat**. If, on the other hand, history has entirely given way to theology, then it is conceivable that the evangelist would suggest that Jesus is really in the position of judgment, even as sentence is passed on him. Of course, the distinction between history and theology is itself false, since both are part of John's total purpose. History is put at the service of theology. So the solution is a difficult one. Perhaps it is the case that John has consciously intended an ambiguity at this point. It is feasible that he plays with the double meaning of the verb, even as he has played on the ambiguity of other words (e.g., *anōthen*, "again/above," 3:3; *pneuma*, "wind/ spirit," 3:8). He would, if this is the case, want us to picture Pilate taking his place on the bench, when in fact it is Christ who is passing judgment on his accusers.

This verse has still more puzzles. **The pavement** (*Lithostrōtos*) means a street or court paved with stones and (possibly) a mosaic. **Gabbatha** would appear to be the Aramaic name for the Greek *Lithostrōtos* (as e.g., 5:2), but such is not the case. The meaning of the Aramaic is not clear. Most often it is thought to mean "high" or "ridge." This could describe (1) either of the proposed locations for the praetorium, for both the palace of Herod and the fortress of Antonia (cf. 18:28 above) were at high points, or (2) the height of the judgment seat or the platform on which it stood. The discovery of a paved area within the site of the Antonia has stirred proposals that it is the pavement cited by John. This has excited opinions regarding the historical accuracy of the Johannine narrative. While the discovery might indeed be the area of the sentencing of Jesus, even a degree of probability is not possible.

14a—This sentence seems clearly to be included here for symbolic reasons. **Day of Preparation** renders *paraskeuē* which is a Semitic reference to the "eve" or "day before." It is used of the day preceding the Sabbath (e.g., v. 42) when preparation was made for the day free of work. It was also used of the day before a feast, even as John intends it here. For the author's dating of the events of the last week of Jesus' life cf. n. 20. **The sixth hour** stands for noon, on the assumption that John's hours count from daybreak (and not midnight). This contradicts Mark's dating of the crucifixion on "the third hour," 9 A.M. (15:25; cf. 18:18 above). Textual witnesses show that there have been efforts to harmonize John with Mark, and others have speculated about the possibility of a misreading of the letters that supply the numerical value. The result of John's chronological note is that Jesus is crucified at the very hour the Passover lambs are being slain in **preparation** for the meal that evening. The intent is clearly to suggest that the events transpiring here are those of the "new Passover" and the means by which God will liberate humanity even as Israel was liberated in the exodus. The exaltation of God's love on the cross leads his people into a new "land" of eternal life. John has thus framed the sentencing and the crucifixion in such a way as to orient his reader's attention to the meaning of the cross.

14b-16—Again truth is put on the lips of an unaware Pilate. John supposes that those in his narrative understand Pilate's words as a ridicule of the leaders—"this is the closest you will ever come to having a King." But John knows too that his readers will recognize the truth of Pilate's words—Jesus is truly King; compare v. 5. The response of the leaders in v. 15 is inspired by Pilate's ridicule. **Away with him** translates *airō*, which can mean "take away" but also "lift up, take up." Associated as it is here with **crucify**, the possibility emerges that John wanted once again to suggest his enigmatic view of the cross as an exaltation even while it is an execution (cf. the use of *hypsoō*, "lifted up," at 3:14; 8:28; and 12:32-34). Pilate further ridicules the leaders with his response in v. 15, once again referring to Jesus as **your King**. In the Greek **your King** stands first in the sentence for emphasis: "your King— shall I crucify him?" The rage of **the chief priests** impels them headlong into their own blasphemy: **We have no king but Caesar**. Yahweh alone is King, their tradition dictates; yet they have abandoned their tradition. "So with splendid irony John makes the Jews utter the ultimate blasphemy in the same breath as their final rejection of Jesus" (Lindars, p. 572). Now it is they who choose Caesar as their "friend" and not Christ, even as Pilate does (v. 12). **Handed him over** . . . is the closest John comes to having Pilate issue a formal sentence (v. 16). With another use of the verb *paradidōmi* John completes a series of "handing-overs" beginning with Judas' betrayal, followed by the religious leaders' sending Christ to Pilate, and now the governor's dispatching troops to accomplish the execution—a string of human agents conspiring in their rejection of the revelation. **Them** would seem to refer to the chief priests, but that would mean that the religious leaders were allowed to crucify Jesus, which is clearly not the case. The antecedent is surely the soldiers. Has John simply been careless with his pronouns, or is he taking to extremes the effort to paint the Jewish authorities as entirely responsible for the death of Christ? It could mean, too, that Pilate has bowed to the wishes of the leaders, and it is in that sense that **he handed him over to them.**

John's so carefully constructed narrative of the political trial of Jesus has skillfully honed both sides of one blade. On the one hand, he continues and intensifies the tendency of the early Christian tradition to exonerate the Romans and convict the Jewish leaders of responsibility for the death of Jesus. The unfortunate tendency to do so blackens the history of Jewish-Christian relationships. But for John's church it was of uppermost importance that the Jewish leaders bear that responsibility, since it was they who posed the greatest threat to the Johannine community. On the other hand, the evangelist has shown by means of Pilate the impossibility of a semicommitment to Jesus. Pilate is condemned by John's story for trying to preserve his own security while dealing with Christ. Pilate is humanity, in the sense that there can be no believing response to Christ that does not surrender the securities of this world. Pilate could not act both justly and prudently, and neither can any of us, John wants to say. In the alternation between his confrontations with the religious leaders and with Jesus Pilate is forced to choose between truth and expediency. With typical Johannine irony, however, his rejection of the truth is turned on its head by God's plan for the exaltation of his Son.

The Crucifixion and Burial (19:17-42)

John has prepared us for his understanding of the cross, and so this section contains few surprises. This is the portrayal of the enthronement of the King, and that view is carried through with consistency. Most noticeable by their absence are some of the horrifying features of the execution known to us from the Synoptics (e.g., the cry of dereliction, Mark 15:34), and yet the death is genuine. John balances his narrative with the assurance that the cross is an enthronement and with the inescapable fact that Jesus does indeed die. It is that death which is the essential fact of the coronation (cf. Mark 15:21-47; Matt. 27:31-61; and Luke 23:26-56).

17-18—**Went out** indicates that the site of the crucifixion was outside the walls of the city (cf. Mark 15:20b and v. 20 below). In the Greek phrase translated **bearing his own cross**, the emphasis is upon **his own** *(heautō)*. John omits the feature of the use of Simon of Cyrene to carry the cross (cf. Luke 23:26), if he knew about it, in order to stress the sovereignty of Christ (another royal feature) and the sufficiency of his single act for salvation. **Cross** is in this case probably the crossbar which was attached to an upright pole permanently fixed in the ground. **The place of a skull** correctly translates the Greek which does not use a definite article before **skull**. **Golgothâ** renders the Aramaic *gulgoltâ*. Several theories are proposed to explain the name of the site. The two most prominent are (1) that a rocky knoll had the appearance of a human skull and (2) that human skulls remained around the place where public executions had taken place. In v. 18 Jesus' arms are nailed (or bound) to the crossbar, he is hoisted up on the vertical stake, and his feet nailed (or bound) to it. John repeats the tradition that Jesus was **crucified** with two others but does not inform us of their crime (compare Mark 15:27 and Luke 23:32).

19-22—The **title** affixed to **the cross** is the subject of these verses. It is at once the charge for which Jesus is being executed and the proclamation of John's view of the event; for Jesus is truly **King**. For **Jesus of Nazareth** cf. 18:5 above. Verse 20 tells the fact that John alone has the title written in three languages, which for him stands for the universal significance of the revelation. Such polyglot signs were doubtless common in the empire. The reaction of the Jewish leaders to the title (v. 21) underlines the irony of the situation. This one whose kingship they have rejected is truly their King, although the words had been written to mock both them and the claimant. The effort to have Pilate change the proclamation is particularly important in the light of the declaration of the leaders in v. 15 that their only king is Caesar. John is driving home the point that the crucifixion is at once an indictment of the leaders, as well as a salvific event. The *judgment* of the cross is the inevitable consequence of God's revelatory act, even though its purpose is not judgment but salvation (cf. 3:17-21 above). Verse 22 is intended to bring a penultimate climax to the scene. Pilate doubtless refuses to change the title, for hostile reasons. He is seeking vengeance for being forced to this deed by the religious leaders. But the meaning of his declaration, **What I have written** . . . is that the deed has been accomplished once and for all. John has the unwilling Pilate proclaim the fulfillment of the redemptive act of God, which can never be changed now that it is done.

23—Attention shifts to **the soldiers** and Jesus' **garments**. This feature of the narrative is occasioned and controlled by the use of Psalm 22. This psalm was utilized by the early Christians as a way of understanding the crucifixion, and it shaped the details of the narratives of the event. Verse 23 mentions **four parts** of the clothing, divided among the soldiers, but it would be dangerous to assume from this that John is informing us of a historical detail (i.e., that it was four soldiers who were responsible for the crucifixions). **Garments** (*ta himatia*, cf. 13:2, 12 above) could refer to the outer robe alone or more generally to clothing. **The tunic** was the undergarment. That the tunic was **without seam** is a tantalizing detail. Is John mentioning it simply as narrative coloring, or does he want the reader to detect some symbolism in this detail? Symbolic meaning has generally been sought along two lines. (1) The fact that the high priest's tunic was seamless tempts one to understand this as John's way of indicating that Jesus is priest as well as king. If that is the intent of the evangelist (or his source), there is no other evidence for such a view of Christ in this gospel. (2) The single unity of the community is symbolized in the seamless quality of the tunic. Such unity is clearly a Johannine theme, as 17:11 and 20-23

287

evidence. So, if there is symbolic meaning in the seamless tunic, it is found in the second theory, but clear signals that John would have us so interpret this detail are missing.

24—This verse shows that John's only concern is to demonstrate the fulfillment of Ps. 22:18. It could be that he has made the tunic seamless in order to explain why the soldiers have to cast lots for it and hence fulfill the **scripture**. The quotation of the psalm follows the LXX exactly. John alone among the evangelists quotes the passage explicitly. He has taken the two words for the clothing found in the psalm and apparently distinguished between them, although in the psalm they are synonymous ("garments" and "raiment" in the RSV of Ps. 22:18). Whether he misunderstands the parallelism of the psalm or consciously manipulates the passage for his own purposes is not known.

25-27—**So the soldiers did this** in v. 25a may be meant as a contrast between their perception of the event taking place and that of the believers who are featured in vv. 25b-27. Verse 25b raises the question of whether it is likely the women would be allowed to stand near **the cross**. But it is clear from vv. 26-27 that John's interest is theological and not historical. Hopelessly problematic is the question of the number of women named by John. The RSV assumes three of them, but the Greek can as well be translated to mean two or four persons. **Mary, the wife of Clopas** may be a single description of Jesus' **mother** (if so, this would be the only place in John where Jesus' mother is called Mary). Or the four listed may be Jesus' **mother**, her **sister**, **the wife of Clopas**, and **Mary Magdalene** (cf. Brown, vol. 2, pp. 904-906 for a comparison of the women named here and those found near the cross in the Synoptics). **Mary Magdalene** is mentioned here for the first time, even though she will be given the honored position as the first to whom the resurrected Christ appears (cf. 20:1-18). The purpose of describing these witnesses is found in vv. 26-27. For **the disciple whom he loved** cf. Introduction § 2; he is mentioned here for the first time since 13:23 (unless the unnamed disciple of 18:15 should be identified with the beloved disciple). This is the only time he appears in this gospel without Peter also present. For **woman** cf. 2:4 above. The words of Jesus to his mother and the beloved disciple have been understood by some as a use of the adoption formula, but that is not certain. In v. 27 **his own home** is *idia* (some have linked Acts 12:12 to this passage as the basis of identifying John Mark as the beloved disciple). The meaning of the incident is debated. On one level, it is Jesus' simple expression of concern for the welfare of his mother, which testifies as well to the importance of the beloved disciple. Commentators, however, are inclined to find some symbolic meaning in the new association of Jesus' mother and the beloved disciple. Some of these proposals are farfetched and examples of "eisegesis" (e.g., Jesus' mother is Jewish Christianity and the beloved disciple Gentile Christianity—Bultmann, p. 673). More likely is the suggestion that together "they form the nucleus of the new family of faith. The other disciples are 'brothers' and members of his family; all believers are the children of God" (Culpepper, p. 122; see John 1:12). The cross marks the formation of a new people of God, at the center of which is the symbol of faithful discipleship, the beloved disciple.

28-29—The death of Jesus is told briefly. The narrative begins (v. 28) and ends (v. 30) with the use of **finished** (*tetelestai*; cf. 17:4 above), suggesting that in this short scene the plan of God's expression of his love for humanity reaches its goal (cf. the use of *telos* at 13:1). Jesus is in control of all that is happening, and hence it is his word, **I thirst**, that initiates the offer of vinegar in the next verse (contrast Mark 15:39). John's more frequent word to signal the fulfillment of **scripture** is *plēroō* ("fulfil," v. 24), but here it is *teleioō* (**fulfil**). This may be due to nothing more than a desire to vary style, or it may be occasioned by the proximity of the verb **finished** (*teleioō*), just used. If the latter is the case, the evangelist is suggesting that **scripture** finds its completion in the accomplishment of Christ on the cross. The scripture mentioned is surely Ps. 69:21. The reference to scripture is explicit here whereas it is only implied in the Synoptics (e.g., Mark 15:36). **I thirst** is a statement from the cross unparalleled in the Synoptics and fashioned for the sake of the Johannine interpretation of the crucifixion. To show the reality of Jesus' suffering is important for a narrative which emphasizes his royal composure through the whole experience.

Verse 29 appears to represent a compassionate gesture on the part of the soldiers (**they**; in Ps. 69:21 the act is meant to be cruel). **Hyssop** (*hyssōpos*) is used in a strange way here. It was a common plant (weed) whose branches were far too weak to support the **sponge**. Efforts to solve this problem include the suggestion that the word for "javelin" (*hyssos*) originally stood in the text and was accidently changed to **hyssop** (*hyssōpos*). Could it be, however, coincidental that hyssop was used in the Passover celebration (Exod. 12:22)? That may be pressing John's narrative too hard for symbolism, however. Still, he was not terribly concerned to make the details of his account historically plausible, as we have seen.

30—The death is calm and confident. The dreadful "loud cry" (Mark 15:37) becomes for John a declaration of victory: **It is finished** (cf. v. 28). The expression carries two meanings, both of which John probably intended. It signals the end of Jesus' earthly ministry and the completion of his mission. Characteristic of John's portrayal of Jesus, the next two verbs depict his own acts—**bowed his head and gave up his spirit**. The point is that Jesus has not had his life taken from him but has of his own will surrendered it (cf. 10:18). The second of the verbs, **gave up** (*paradidōmi*), is the same as that used for the "handing over" of Jesus by Judas to the authorities (e.g., 18:2), by the high priest to Pilate (18:35), and by Pilate to the soldiers (19:16). Now Jesus by his own will completes the process designed by his Father, a process he has controlled from the very beginning. **Spirit** (*pneuma*) means Jesus' life and should not be construed as the issuing of the divine Spirit as a result of the revealer's death. That act is narrated in 20:22. With calm dignity John's Jesus dies on the cross, a manner quite different from Mark's account, and necessarily so, since this is above all an enthronement we have been witnessing in John's gospel.

31-32—The treatment of the body is the concern of the next verses through the end of the chapter. Those verses are dedicated to the assurance of the reality of Jesus death (vv. 31-37) and his dignified burial (vv. 38-42). Verse 31 represents the religious leaders' attempt to have **the bodies** removed before **the Sabbath**. **Day of Preparation** here means the day before **the Sabbath**, while at v. 14 it is used to designate the day before the Passover. It appears to have been the case that on this occasion Passover fell on a Sabbath, and thus the same **day** is referred to here and in v. 14. **High day** describes the Sabbath on which the feast began. John seems to think that the motive for removing the bodies is to avoid its being done on the Sabbath, whereby the regulation against work would be violated. Deut. 21:22-23 forbids allowing a body to hang overnight. The Romans, perhaps, would have left the bodies as a warning to others tempted by thought of insurrection. The breaking of **the legs** of victims of crucifixion was a normal way of hastening death (through shock, bleeding, and perhaps asphyxiation, since breaking the legs left all of the weight of the body on the extended arms), and Brown cites the discovery of skeletons of crucifixion victims whose **legs** are **broken** (vol. 2, p. 934). In many cases, it mercifully shortened the suffering of lingering for days on the cross. In v. 32 the wish of the leaders is carried out on the other two crucified with Jesus.

33-34—Verse 33 agrees with the witness of Mark 15:44 that Jesus' death was relatively fast. As to the reason for such, it is pointless to speculate. John uses this fact drawn from his tradition for his own purposes pursued in the **spear**-thrust of v. 34. He may want us to suppose that the stab of the spear was to discern whether Jesus was indeed dead. But he obviously attaches importance of a theological kind to the emergence of **blood and water.** On a purely physiological basis such a **flow** would be possible, if the water was the fluids collected in the lungs. The search for the symbolic meaning of the two liquids has not been as easy. The primary question is whether or not the two are symbolic of the sacraments, and that seems clearly not to be the case. **Water** functions elsewhere in this gospel to symbolize the Spirit (e.g., 7:39) and the revelation of God (e.g., 4:10ff.). While that might be the sense of **water** here, this verse is not intended as a fulfillment of 7:39 (cf. above). The **blood** might stand for the benefits of Jesus' death flowing out from the cross, chief among them the gift of the Spirit. 1 John 5:6-8 seems to be an interpretation of this passage, but that does not mean that the sense of the verse in the epistle is necessarily the sense the evangelist had in mind. All in all two observations are called for: (1) The primary point to be established by this verse is the reality of Jesus' death. This need not presuppose an anti-docetic polemic, but instead a simple effort to balance the emphasis upon Jesus' kingly deportment with the reality of his death. John wants to stress both. That is the most evident meaning to be derived, and the importance of the reality of Jesus' death occasions the content of v. 35. (2) John may also have wanted to hint at the outpouring of the benefits of the crucifixion for the believer. Such an interpretation is not as clear as the first, but it is nonetheless within the range of Johannine thought. In this case, the water may indeed symbolize in part the Spirit.

35—The author further attempts to document the reality of Jesus' death, but v. 35 raises more questions than it answers. Some take it to be an interpolation by the redactor responsible for chap. 21 and see 21:24 as an expansion of the present verse. It is clear that in its present positon it intends to say that the piercing of Jesus' side was witnessed firsthand, probably by the beloved disciple. The second **he** (literally, "that one," *ekeinos*) is unclear, but seems to refer to the eyewitness of the first part of the sentence. **That you also may believe** means Christian faith in general and not simply credence to the flow from Jesus' side (cf. 20:31). It seems best to see this verse as an effort on the part of the evangelist (or the redactor) to confirm the basis of the tradition on which this gospel is based. It is, moreover, the beloved disciple who is most probably thought of as having been the source of the Johannine tradition. Verse 35 does not contribute significantly to the whole question of whether the evangelist himself was indeed the witness referred to here. The repetition of **true** may suggest that this verse is answering some charge that the tradition is false. Its position after the piercing of Jesus' side tempts one to say that among the contentions against the Johannine community was that Jesus had not actually died.

36-37—Verse 36 returns to the content of v. 34 and further evidences the possibility that v. 35 is an interpolation or at least a parenthesis. Unlike the **scripture** cited at v. 24 the reference of v. 36 is uncertain. There are two candidates: (1) The righteous person who is divinely protected against **broken bones** in Ps. 34:20; (2) the Passover lamb whose bones are not to be broken in preparing it for the feast (cf. Exod. 12:46 and Num. 9:12). In the light of John's interest in paralleling the death of the Passover lambs and Jesus, the latter presents itself as more persuasive. The quotation in v. 37 is more easily isolated. It is Zech. 12:10 in which the **him** refers to God (cf. Rev. 1:7). John's quotation seems to have more in common with the Hebrew text than the LXX and raises an unanswerable question as to whether he is responsible for the translation or is using a collection of texts employed by Christians in elucidating the kerygma with OT passages.

38-39—The burial is simply told. **Joseph of Arimathea** is mentioned in each of the Gospels as the benefactor who provided a grave for Jesus (Mark 15:43; Matt. 27:57; Luke 23:50). He is not mentioned elsewhere. The location of Arimathea is unknown, although it is often proposed to be Ramathaim-zophim (cf. 1 Sam. 1:1), northwest of Jerusalem. The bodies of the crucified were sometimes left to the vultures. Secret **disciples** are mentioned in 12:42. The implication of v. 39 is that **Nicodemus** (cf. 3:1ff. and 7:50 above) too is a secret believer. The author may be implying that the crucifixion brought these "closet believers" to public confession. Thereby he is perhaps taunting those Jews of his own time who had not had the courage to express their Christian faith when faced with expulsion from the synagogue. **Mixture** (*migma*) would indicate a blending of a number of liquid drugs. An alternate and more difficult reading has *heligma*, denoting a "package" of dry drugs. **Myrrh** was commonly used with embalming, while **aloes** were not. The latter provided a perfume mentioned in other connections (cf. Prov. 7:17). The quantity of the fragrances is excessive for such an occasion. **Pounds** (*litra*) is a Roman measurement; the equivalent in U.S. pounds would be about 75. The abundance reminds one of 2:6 and 12:3, offering another reference to the "royal" character of Jesus' burial.

40-42—Verse 40 describes the preparation for burial. **Bound it in linen clothes with the spices** probably means that **the body** was wrapped in strips of **linen** with **the spices** placed between the layers of the cloths. Does John mean to recall 12:1-8 (cf. above) and the fulfillment of Mary's act of love there? **Custom of the Jews** intends to assure the reader that the burial afforded Jesus was proper in every way—another element of the "royal" treatment of the body. A further such element is found in v. 41, specifically in the **new tomb** used for the burial. Only John specifies the location of a **garden** in Golgotha. Presumably it was an orchard or vegetable plot (cf. 18:1). It would not be surprising that **tombs** were located near the site of the crucifixion, especially if that site was often used for executions. The evangelist's tradition concerning the burial seems to have contained elements from both the sources of Matthew (Joseph's "new tomb," 27:60) and Luke ("where no one had ever yet been laid," 23:53). For John the **tomb** was suitable for one of unique stature, i.e., a king. In v. 42 for **day of Preparation** cf. vv. 14 and 31. The burial was accomplished with dispatch, due to the approaching of the Sabbath-Passover. Burials were apparently not permitted on the Sabbath, although some preparation of the body was allowed (cf. Mishnah, *Shab.* 23:4-5).

John narrates the account of the crucifixion and burial in short episodes, each of which briefly explores a single feature (e.g., the title on the cross, vv. 19-22, the death of Jesus, vv. 28-30). The impact is a gradually ascending crescendo up to the words, "It is finished," in v. 30 followed by a descent to the completion of the burial (v. 42). The story is characterized by an enigmatic tension between John's view of the cross as the coronation of the new king and the reality of the horrid death itself. Humiliation is noticeably absent, even as sovereign control is present. Sacrificial notions of atonement are not expressed, but in their place perhaps is the clear suggestion of a "new Passover." Taken together, all of this defines the cross in John as an exaltation of Jesus as king (even as he is "lifted up" on the cross) and thereby of divine love. The exaltation enthrones divine love as monarch of humanity. It is that divine love which has the power to effect a "new exodus" from amid the darkness of this world. But the exaltation is not yet complete, for John draws only the slimmest of lines between the crucifixion and the resurrection. The former is completed only in the latter.

The Empty Tomb Discovered (20:1-10)

The discovery of the empty tomb is an integral part of John's whole theme of exaltation, for, as we shall see, it is an occasion for faith (v. 8). Like the Synoptics, he includes the empty tomb as a prelude to the appearances of the risen Christ (cf. Mark 16:1-8; Matt. 28:1-8; Luke 20:1-13), but for the fourth evangelist the empty grave plays an additional role. As in all four of the Gospels, the discovery by the women announces the resurrection and, as in Matt. 28:9-10, it is accompanied by a resurrection appearance. But John and/or his tradition made of the tomb an opportunity for faith on the part of the community's founder and ideal of disciple-ship, the beloved disciple. The empty tomb includes an angelo-phany which John has linked closely to the appearance of the risen Christ to Mary (cf. vv. 11-18). More basically, it functions as a kind of "sign" for those who have the eyes of faith to behold it. It is likely that John's community knew the empty tomb narrative to be an angelic proclamation of the resurrection, suggesting that the story is an adaptation of the earliest creedal proclamation of Christ's resurrection (e.g., 1 Cor. 15:5-8). John's unique contri-bution to the formation of the empty tomb narratives is to treat it as a "sign" for the faithful.

1-2—John agrees with the Synoptics that it was **Mary Magda-lene** who was the first to find the empty tomb, although John elim-inates the other women (cf. Mark 16:1; Matt. 28:1; Luke 24:10). Her name suggests that her home was Magdala on the sea of Gal-ilee, southwest of Capernaum. While she is mentioned by John only here, v. 11, and 19:25, she is given a pivotal role in the res-urrection narratives. The author does not indicate a reason for her trip to the tomb, unlike the Synoptics, but says it was **on the first day of the week** (i.e., between 6 P.M. on Saturday and 6 P.M. on Sunday). **Early, while it was still dark** is usually taken to mean early Sunday morning before sunrise (contrast Mark 16:2). **Dark** (*skotias*) may have symbolic meaning, since the discovery for Mary at least leads her to think only that those of unbelief have done violence to the body (cf. v. 13 below). John has not mentioned the sealing of **the tomb** with a stone and expects his readers to take it for granted. Neither does he bother with the question of how the stone was removed (contrast Matt. 28:2). In v. 2 Mary reports the news to **Peter** and the beloved **disciple**. The earliest of the tradi-tions refers to Peter as the one who first learned of the resurrec-tion (cf. 1 Cor. 15:5 and Mark 16:7). **The *other* disciple** may link the beloved disciple with "another disciple" of 18:15 (cf. above, and v. 8; also 13:23 and Introduction §2). This is the first time John has used *phileō* (**loved**) in the expression **whom Jesus loved**. In previous references it has been *agapaō*. This simply shows that the fourth evangelist uses these words interchangeably. Mary's announcement is surprising, since it has not been stated as yet that she had examined the tomb (cf. v. 11). But her conclusion that the body has been stolen appears here as a contrast to that of the beloved disciple in v. 8. Tomb robbery was a common problem of the time. The use of the plural in the expression **we do not know** may be an indication that John's source contained an account of a number of women finding the empty tomb (compare Mark 16:1). Mary interprets her experience in the most negative of ways, for she has not yet encountered the risen Christ.

3-6—**Peter** is mentioned first, in deference to the early tradition, but in the footrace to **the tomb** in v. 4 the beloved **disciple** is the first to reach the goal. The Johannine special regard for the nameless disciple is hinted at in his arrival first, even given Peter's honored place in the previous verse. The beloved disciple is the first to witness the empty tomb (v. 5) and the first to believe in the resurrected Christ (v. 8). But he is not the first to enter the tomb, that honor being accorded Peter. We are either to suppose that there is now sufficient light for the beloved disciple to see into the grave or to interpret the darkness of v. 1 in a purely symbolic manner. For **linen cloths** cf. 19:40. Verse 6 has Peter entering the tomb and seeing what the beloved disciple is just reported to have seen. **Following him** employs John's word for discipleship (*akoloutheō*; cf. 1:37ff. above) and may be one of several indications in the narrative of John's subordinating Peter to the beloved disciple. A different verb for seeing is used here of Peter (*theōreō*) than of the beloved disciple in v. 5 (*blepō*), but no difference of meaning can be detected (cf. *eiden* in v. 8 and *heōraka* in v. 18).

7—**The napkin** (*soudarion;* cf. 11:44, "cloth") was a small towel used over the face of the body. The description of its position vis-à-vis **the linen cloths** is ambiguous in the Greek, so that it is difficult to conclude exactly what was meant. In particular the verb employed to describe the **napkin** (*entylissein*) can mean either "neatly rolled up" or "wrapped up" (in the linen cloths). **With** (*meta*) may mean "with," "like," or "among." Details aside, two things are intended by John's description: (1) The appearance of the burial garments means that the body had not been hastily taken from the tomb by robbers. (2) Whatever the form of the resurrected body of Christ, it has passed through the burial wrappings, which means that John thinks of the risen body as a transformation which "consumes" the physical body (compare Luke 24:12, margin).

8—The experience of the beloved **disciple** is in contrast to Mary's fear of the worst and Peter's apparent lack of a conclusion. The beloved **disciple saw and believed** (*eiden kai episteusen*), but we are not told exactly what it was he believed. Some commentators understand that v. 9 qualifies the meaning of **believe** in v. 8 so as to make clear that it is not resurrection faith that John attributes to the **other disciple** (cf. v. 2 above). But if that is the case, what else is it that the beloved disciple believed? The only other option is that he is said to have accepted Mary's report that the body is indeed gone. Such a proposal makes of his belief a petty matter, and it is clear that John attaches more importance than that to the conclusion of this central figure of his gospel. He is presented here as a model of Easter faith for the readers, who like him must believe without the benefit of a resurrection appearance. In this sense, then, the faith of the beloved disciple is an example of "belief without seeing" praised in 20:29, even though he does "see" the evidence of the empty tomb. His belief too is an example of "seeing" a sign at the deepest level, discerning it as an act of God in the midst of human life. Hence, John has put before the reader three options for viewing the experience of the empty tomb: For Mary it is tragedy, for Peter it is uncertainty, and for the beloved disciple it is faith.

9-10—Verse 9 is not necessarily a delimiting of the beloved disciple's faith as much as it is an indicaton that the disciples did not fully understand the resurrection of Christ until they had reflected on it in the light of the OT. The **they**, therefore, refers to the whole body of the disciples, including the beloved disciple. This assertion is expressed in 2:22 and 12:16 as well and presents the point of view that the Christ event is understood only against the background of God's work in Israel. But what is **the scripture** that suggests the resurrection of Christ? There is no answer to that, even as the reference in 1 Cor. 15:4 is uncertain. It may mean in both cases a general context of the whole of the OT. Proposals for a specific passage include Ps. 16:10; Hos. 6:2; and Jonah 1:17; 2:1. A more general reference seems the more likely. **That he must** (*dei*) betrays the view that the death and resurrection were predetermined aspects of God's plan of salvation (cf. 3:14 and 12:34). Verse 10 contains an unusual construction for John (*pros autous* instead of *pros ta idia*). It may evidence his use of a source at this point. The function of the verse is simply to close the scene and leave Mary alone at the tomb, setting the stage for her experience in vv. 11-17.

The primary role of vv. 1-10 is to demonstrate the exemplary faith of the beloved disciple in contrast to Mary and Peter. It is clear, however, that John does not intend to depreciate the discipleship of Mary, for he will honor her with the first resurrection appearance. Neither does he intend to degrade Peter but only to picture him as one who could not venture faith as does the beloved disciple. The relationship between Peter and the beloved disciple here is not to be taken symbolically or polemically. John is not attacking the legitimacy of Peter's centrality, but he is again lifting up the beloved disciple as the ideal. In a certain sense it is the beloved disciple who is the model of Easter faith, even though he is not individually the beneficiary of a resurrection appearance. John's story in vv. 1-10 may be an effort to compensate for the fact that tradition had not included an account of an appearance of the risen Christ to the community's founder and hero. It is, nonetheless, his faith the readers of John can duplicate, for they too have not had the benefit of a vision of the risen Christ. The ideal disciple's perception of God's work in the empty tomb invites us to find signs of God's continued work in our world.

The Appearances of the Risen Jesus (20:11-29)

Aside from the epilog in chap. 21, John presents three appearances of the risen Christ. In one sense he follows the pattern of appearances found in other traditions. The central narrative features appearances comparable to 1 Cor. 15:5; Luke 24:36-43; and Matt. 28:16-20. But he, like Matthew, knows of an appearance to the women also (i.e., Mary, cf. Matt. 28:9-10). It seems that his sources place the appearances in Jerusalem, as Luke has it (24:13-53) and not in Galilee (Matt. 28:16-20), even though chap. 21 is set in Galilee. While John's accounts appear to have roots in traditions related to those behind the Synoptics, it is clear too that John has stylized the appearance stories for effect. In each of the following we will discover a pattern with the following features: (1) The beneficiaries of the appearance are engulfed in a human emotion (Mary, grief; the disciples, fear; and Thomas, doubt). (2) The risen Christ appears to them in the midst of their condition. (3) As a result, their condition is transformed (Mary, mission; the disciples, gladness; Thomas, faith). Thereby John depicts the appearances as experiences of liberation, much as Christ liberated Lazarus from the grip of death (cf. 11:44 above) and as his own death is a "new Passover."

The Appearance to Mary (20:11-18)

11—John has really joined together two independent pieces, vv. 1-10 and 11-18. The latter picks up the situation described in v. 1 with **Mary** standing **outside the tomb**. Perhaps vv. 1 and 11-18 were part of John's source, and he has inserted vv. 2-9. At any rate, we have not been told that Mary has returned to the tomb after delivering her message to Peter and the beloved disciple (vv. 2-3). Her **weeping** would seem to be her distress over the supposed fact of the stolen body. **Stooped to look** is the same verb found in v. 5 with regard to the beloved disciple (*parakyptō*).

12-13—The angelophany is told with amazing brevity, which suggests that it has lost some of its importance now that it has been combined with the appearance to Mary (contrast Mark 16:1-8 and Luke 24:1-12).[26] For **saw** cf. v. 6 above. **Two** (*duo*) is omitted by some manuscripts. The number and description of the heavenly messengers in the various accounts of the empty tomb differ. John alone describes them as seated **one at the head and one at the feet** (cf. the Gospel of Peter 39ff., 55ff.). But the function of the heavenly creatures is to announce the resurrection. For **woman** in v.

13 cf. 2:4. Mary's reponse to the question is a simple repetition of her words in v. 2. In the author's abridged version of the role of the angels he omits any mention of Mary's awe or fear. The incident is overshadowed by the far more significant event about to take place.

14-15—The risen Christ continues the announcement of the angels, further suggesting that the angelophany of vv. 12-13 has been nearly completely transformed into a Christophany. The failure of Mary to recognize Jesus need not be explained in terms of narrative features (e.g., it is still too dark) or symbolism. It is a classical literary device, namely, the recognition motif. It plays a role in many of the resurrection appearances (e.g., Luke 24:16-30 and John 21:4-7 below). Theologically this suggests the dominance of the initiative of Christ in the appearance scenes. Jesus' words in v. 15 sound similar to those of the angels in v. 13. That Mary mistook Jesus for **the gardener** is a reflection of the location of the tomb in a garden (19:41). This is the third time Mary has expressed her dreaded thought that someone had stolen the body (cf. vv. 2 and 13 above). This repetition plus her weeping in v. 11 is John's way of stressing the plight of Mary's totally consuming fear. Her mistaking Jesus for the gardener is a narrative form of Johannine misunderstanding, usually expressed in discourse materials (e.g., 3:4). Mary misunderstands the presence as a purely human phenomenon when it is actually divinity.

16—The recognition scene pivots on Jesus' personal address to **Mary**. One cannot but yield to the temptation of thinking here of 10:3. For John the resurrection appearance is a personal experience based on Mary's relationship with Jesus. At the sound of her name, **Mary** again **turned** toward Jesus (cf. v. 14). Her attention is focused exclusively on Jesus. **Rabboni** is a more personal address to a teacher, one which reflects warmth and affection. John's translation (**Teacher**) is consistent with 1:38, although "my master" might be a more exact rendering of the Aramaic. (John calls it **Hebrew**, as he is prone to do with Aramaic words, e.g., 19:13.) Mary's surprised encounter with the risen Christ evokes her faith commitment in a way similar to that of Thomas in v. 28.

17—This verse presents a number of problems. The first is the command to Mary, **Do not hold me** (*mē mou haptou*; cf. Matt. 28:

9), a present imperative which assumes Mary has taken hold of him or is about to do so. It can be translated "Do not *touch* me" or "Do not *cling* to me." A problem arises when this is compared to v. 27, in which Thomas is invited to touch the risen Christ (although it is not said that Thomas actually does so). A number of explanations have been offered, of which two are worthy of attention. The first would argue that John has employed two different traditions, one here and one involving Thomas (vv. 26-29). Two different understandings of the resurrected body were presumed in each. In the one behind vv. 11-18 the body is spiritual and not "touchable" and in the one utilized in vv. 26-29 it is materialized. The first adheres more closely with the Christian concept of the resurrected body as a "transformed" entity in the manner Paul conceives it (1 Cor. 15:44-57). The second image of the body may reflect an older Jewish notion of the restoration of the physical body in the resurrection. It is conceivable that different traditions of the resurrection appearances employed the two different ideas of the risen Christ. The second explanation stresses the present tense of the verb and proposes the command is that Mary not **hold** on to Jesus. He cannot be detained, but more importantly Mary cannot relate to the risen Christ in the same physical way she did to the historical Jesus. The resurrection calls for a new and spiritual relationship.

The reason Jesus gives for the command is that he has **not yet ascended.** The Greek is more ambiguous than the translation and may not necessarily mean that the incomplete ascension is the reason for the command. As the next occurrrence of the verb **ascend** (*anabainō*) shows, the ascension is under way (**I am ascending**). The ascension is in John a process which involves the crucifixion and resurrection as a whole and not a separable historical event (as Luke has it—24:51 and Acts 1:9). The ascension is a transtemporal event which is the return of the Son to the Father in a nonspatial way (cf. 3:13 and 6:62 above). It is, in other words, a restoration of the preexistent status of Christ. As such it means the beginning of a new relationship between the disciples and their master, one that is not physical in the sense of the historical Jesus, but spiritual in the sense that it is a relationship in the Spirit-Paraclete. **My brethren** (*adelphous*) may mean either Jesus' blood brothers (as in 7:5) or the disciples (as in 21:23). The second is surely intended here, for the crucifixion-resurrection means the creation of a new family of faith (cf. 19:26-27 above). The believers have become "children of God" (1:12). **My Father . . . your God** indicates the commonality of loyalty in that new family. Jesus' Father and God are now the disciples' as well, by virtue of the revelation. Mary's personal encounter with the risen Christ is not a private experience alone, for out of it issues a command to share the encounter with others. Mission arises from the appearance as an indispensable part of the Easter faith.

18—**Mary** is obedient to the command to share her experience. The RSV represents the strange combination of direct and indirect discourse which is in the Greek. This has caused some scribal efforts to improve the grammar of the verse and has led some commentators to see here a combination of the conclusion of what might have been a separate angelophany and a Christophany. Mary's joyful sharing of her experience, **I have seen the Lord**, implies the whole of the Easter faith and stands in sharp contrast to her sorrow and fear earlier in the narrative (vv. 1, 2, 11-15).

In this first resurrection appearance John has done honor to the probable historical fact that women played a key role in the beginnings of Christianity, and he demonstrates that there were women among those whom he calls disciples. While Mary in some sense is contrasted with the beloved disciple in vv. 1-10, here she is the model of discipleship. Immersed in her sorrow over what she supposed to have been the violation of Jesus' grave, the risen Christ appears to her and transforms her condition. She becomes a joyful and obedient witness to the resurrection.[27]

The Appearance to the Disciples without Thomas (20:19-23)

19—With great economy this both sets the stage for and narrates the appearance of Jesus. **That day, the first day of the week** corresponds to v. 1. All three of the appearances in chap. 20 occur on Sunday, suggesting the practice of Christian gatherings on that day. Whether or not **that day** is intended to connote the eschatological **day** of the OT (e.g., Jer. 30:4-9) is difficult to say. It may also allude to the day mentioned in 14:20; 16:23, 26—the time of the glorification in which the revelation is completed. The precise reason for **the fear** (*ton phobon*) is not clear and probably not important. John is suggesting that the early **disciples** shared the **fear of the Jews** with his contemporary readers. The point is that the disciples are paralyzed with fright, much as Mary is overwhelmed by sorrow in the previous narrative. **Disciples** (*mathētai*) in John means believers as such, and does not tell us it was the inner circle of followers alone who are involved. The resurrected Christ of vv. 19-23 and 24-29 appears in a mysterious and transformed body. The point is less that he can pass through locked doors than that he comes to believers in the midst of their human condition. **Came and stood among them** connotes the transcendent nature of his appearance. **Peace** (*eirēnē*) was a common Jewish greeting (*shalom*), meaning something like, "May all be well with you." Here, as well as in vv. 21 and 26, it denotes the eschatological condition made real by Christ's presence (cf. 14:27 above). The wholeness and fulfillment of Christian life is summarized in this word, and it is presented as a gift from the risen Christ.

20—The risen Christ proceeds to demonstrate that he is to be identified with the crucified Jesus. This demonstration tells us that John's concept of the risen body is mysterious, to be sure, but has the appearance of a physical body. That the **hands and his side** are references to the wounds acquired in the crucifixion is made clear only by v. 27 below. The accounts of the crucifixion do not testify to the fact that Jesus was *nailed* to the cross (cf. 19:18 above), but Brown cites evidence that victims were at least in some cases nailed to the crossbar (vol. 2, p. 1022). His side refers to 19:34. The result of the appearance of the risen Christ is that the **disciples were glad** (*chairō*), in marked contrast to the fear which controlled them in v. 19. Again, the risen Christ has transformed a human predicament. The gladness of the disciples fulfills Jesus' promise in 14:28 and 16:22 ("rejoice," the same verb here rendered **glad**). Like **peace**, this is the gladness of the eschatological time, when the whole of human desires is fulfilled. **Lord** is unusual in John outside of direct address to or of Jesus (e.g., v. 18 above) and may reflect the use of a source in this verse.

21—The greeting, **Peace**, is repeated for the sake of emphasis on that eschatological factor in the scene (cf. v. 19 above), but it may also indicate the linking of two different traditions. There follows the commissioning of the disciples, i.e., for John, believers in general. (John knows nothing of an elite group within the church bearing a special mission, in contrast to Luke 24:36ff. and Acts 1: 2-8). The commissioning is to be understood on a Christological model: **As the Father sent me, even so I send you** (cf. "Relational Analogies," p. 266 and 17:18 above). The two verbs translated **sent** and **send** are different in the Greek. The first is *apostellō* and the second *pempō*. The two are used in synonymous parallelism here, and there is no basis in this gospel for distinguishing between their meanings (cf. Barrett, pp. 569-570). The remarkable feature of this commissioning is that the believers bear the same divine authorization as did Christ. The nature of the mission of the church can only be understood in the light of the mission of Christ. The same self-giving love is asked of the believers in their mission as is evidenced in Jesus' fulfillment of his.

22—For the mission of the church there is given the gift of the **Spirit**. **Breathed on them** (*enephysēsen*) recalls the ancient association of spirit with breath and surely invokes Gen. 2:7 (and perhaps Ezek. 37:5). John suggests that in the giving of the Spirit God has created a new humanity. The new family of faith (cf. v. 17 above) is a new creation. This act is the fulfillment of the promise of the Spirit scattered throughout this gospel (1:33; 7:39; and 16: 7). Here the Lukan distinction between the resurrection appearances and Pentecost is absent, and the risen Christ gives the Spirit even as he said he would. The exaltation of the crucifixion-resurrection results in a new form of the divine presence. The definite article in **receive the Holy Spirit** is missing in the Greek, as it sometimes is in other NT passages (e.g., Acts 2:4). The tradition employed by John may have thought of the Spirit in a nearly materialistic way, but John's equation of the Spirit with the Paraclete (e.g., 14:26) shows that he understood it in a far more personalized way. John 1:33 and 14:26 are the only other occurrences in this gospel of the title **Holy Spirit** (*pneuma hagion*). The gift of the Spirit is for John continuous with the Christ figure (cf., e.g., 14:16 above) and signifies God's prolonged presence with humanity.

23—The power to **forgive** and **retain sins** is directly related to the gift of the Spirit, even as 16:8-15 suggests. This is a variant of

Matt. 16:19, and it may have been developed along the lines of Isa. 22:22. If (*an*) may also be rendered "when." **Forgive** (*aphienai*) means literally "to release" or "let go." **Retain** translates *kratein* which means "to hold on to" and is nowhere else used in this sense of "holding sins." It seems to occur as a result of seeking a parallel to **forgive**. The tenses of the two verbs are different. This leads some to think that forgiving (an aorist subjunctive) is a single action confined to one point in time, while retaining (a present subjunctive) implies an ongoing state of affairs. It is clear that the church is commissioned to continue the work of Christ with regard to forgiveness (cf. 9:41) under the power of the Holy Spirit. What it originally meant probably had to do with the proclamation of the church. Forgiveness is granted with the acceptance of the proclamation and retention when it is rejected. It is the gospel which offers forgiveness and hence causes humans to judge themselves by their response (cf. 3:18ff. above). For the Johannine community that probably had particular relevance to their struggle with the Jewish synagogue. It is worth noting again that John does not picture this power being given to a select group within the church (as Matt. 16:19) but to believers as a whole.

This passage depicts the appearance of the risen Jesus as having a number of results: (1) The eschatological *peace* is given as a sign of the believers' life in the newly formed creation of God. (2) A *mission* which grows out of a proper understanding of Christ is bestowed. (3) A gift of authority and power for that mission, the *Holy Spirit*, is given. (4) With the mission and authority comes *responsibility* to execute the divine will among humans in the form of forgiveness. With these the risen Christ transforms fear into joy.

The Appearance to the Disciples with Thomas (20:24-29)

24-25—John has not told us of the absence of **Thomas** from the experience of the disciples, so now he must do so to set the stage for the third appearance of the risen Christ. **Thomas** appears in this gospel four times—here, 11:16; 14:5 (cf. above); and 21:2. Here, as in 11:16, he is designated as **the Twin**. He is called **one of the twelve** which suggests that John conceives of the Twelve (actually the eleven) as among the disciples in vv. 19-23. This is the last of only four references in this gospel to the Twelve (cf. 6:67, 70, 71 above). The witness of the disciples in v. 25 is identical to the words of Mary in v. 18, except that a plural instead of a singular verb is used. Thomas demands evidence of their claim. In particular he needs evidence that the one seen by the disciples is indeed the crucified Jesus; moreover, a spiritual body will not suffice. The motif of doubt is present elsewhere in the resurrection tradition (e.g., Matt. 28:17 and Luke 24:37-38). This is due in part, at least, to an apologetic necessity for the early church's proclamation, and Thomas' concern might be a response to the claim that it was only a "ghost" the disciples witnessed (cf. esp. Luke 24:37-38). John has graphically described another human plight, that of doubt. He will now show us again how the risen Christ transforms the human condition.

26-27—Jesus appears once again on the next Sunday (cf. v. 19). John seems unconcerned about the location of the appearances, although we may assume he means that they took place in Jerusalem. He does not share a concept of the theological meaning of the locale of the appearances as do Mark (Galilee) and Luke (Jerusalem). **For peace** cf. vv. 19 and 21 above. The second sentence of v. 26, **the doors were shut . . .** , duplicates v. 19 with only a few variations. In v. 27 Thomas is invited to experience for himself that which he claimed he needed (v. 24) in order to believe. Jesus' invitation is patterned after v. 24 (compare Luke 24:39). **Do not be faithless but believing** (*mē ginou apistos alla pistos*) means literally "Do not become unbelieving but believing." The suggestion is that Thomas has started down the road to unbelief but can now reverse his direction. **Be** may be translated "show yourself to be." The adjectives, *apistos* and *pistos*, are used only here in John. The former designates the non-Christian in other passages of the NT (e.g., 1 Cor. 7:12). Thomas is given the option of unbelief or faith. The risen Christ does not force faith on those to whom he appears. As strong as John's view of the role of God in producing faith is (e.g., 6:44), here the human must make his or her own decision to believe or not to believe.

28—This is the denouement of the gospel! Appropriately, Thomas' confession is the final statement of a disciple in the body of this gospel. His words envelop the entire Christology of the Fourth Gospel, subsuming all other motifs under this one expression. The combination **Lord** and **God** (*kyrios* and *theos*) was familiar to the reader of the LXX, since it is used regularly to translate the Hebrew *Yahweh Elohim* (e.g., Gen. 2:15). But it was also common in Hellenistic religions in general, so that Barrett can conclude: "John's language is carefully chosen so as to be both biblical and Hellenistic" (p. 573). That Jesus is **Lord** is a frequent early Christian confession, probably of creedal origin (e.g., Phil. 2:11 and Rom. 10:9), and hence it is not surprising. But the use of **God** in reference to Jesus is unusual. John may be the only NT writer to use this title of Christ unequivocally (but cf. Titus 2:13 and Heb. 1:8). With this confession the evangelist has bracketed the entire gospel between two affirmations that Jesus is God (cf. 1:1 above). John's Christology, for all of its explorations of various motifs, stands finally on the radical claim that Jesus is none other than the divine ultimate reality. His deliberate and delicate argument against the charges of bitheism from among the Jews of his city does not deter him from what for his church was the inescapable conclusion that Jesus is to be fully identified with God. Thomas' words are what the Christian is finally driven to say of Christ in the light of her or his faith.

29—John follows the climactic words of Thomas with a final blessing from Jesus intended especially for readers of this gospel. As significant as Thomas' words are for Johannine Christology, so this beatitude is for the Johannine view of faith. With these words John puts into proper perspective the view of the historical eyewitness of Jesus and most especially the experiences of the risen Christ. **Have you believed . . . ?** is taken as a question by the RSV, and properly so, although it could as well be rendered as a statement. Jesus' question is not to diminish the authenticity of Thomas' faith, or that of the beloved disciple in v. 8 and Mary in v. 16. But believing without having seen, John suggests, is **blessed** (*makarios*) in a special way. He speaks to the second and third generation Christians of his own time and assures them that they are not second-class citizens of the family of God just because they were not fortunate enough to have been eyewitnesses to the his-

torical Jesus or the risen Christ. John has carefully explored the relationship between seeing and believing throughout the gospel (cf.
Kysar, *John*, pp. 73-77). While he shows his suspicion of a faith
that is based solely on the experience of witnessing wonders (e.g.,
4:48), he affirms the basic relationship between sensual perception and faith (e.g., 14:9) and sometimes even implies that a certain kind of seeing is synonymous with faith (e.g., 12:40). But now
he qualifies all of that with the assurance that a faith founded solely
on a positive response to the proclaimed word (the witness of the
church) is equal to any faith blessed enough to have as its base a
firsthand experience of the incarnate word of God in Jesus. For to-
day's Christian the beatitude affirms that a faith that has no marvelous experiences to which to appeal is especially valued by
God.[28]

Appropriately, with Thomas' confession and Jesus' blessing,
John has brought his work to its conclusion. With this confession
and blessing he has stated the goal of human faith and the divine
regard for a faith of even the most meager kind.

Conclusion: Endings (20:30—21:25)

■ Conclusion I (20:30-31)

The present gospel has two conclusions, 20:30-31 and chap. 21. While the appending of the last chapter appears in some ways to flaw the literary quality of the conclusion in 20:30-31, to someone the double ending seemed appropriate. The author responsible for chap. 21 thought that his or her work enhanced and did not diminish the effectiveness of the gospel's conclusion, in spite of the powerful climax found in 20:28-29. For that reason we treat the two endings as part of the larger conclusion of the gospel.

30—The first conclusion of the gospel, vv. 30-31, was the original ending of the document (cf. below). In it the evangelist makes two statements, one having to do with the limitations of his work (v. 30) and the other with its purpose (v. 31). John may have adapted these verses from his signs source (cf. Introduction §1), and the appearance of *enōpion*, **in the presence of,** in v. 30 confirms that possibility. It is a word not found elsewhere in this gospel. The word **signs** (*sēmeia*) is ambiguous. Does it refer to resurrection appearances or to marvelous works? Probably John intended the word to cover all of the various narratives he has used, although the word in the source must have meant strictly "wonders." The author demurs here in the face of the task of saying all that there is to say about the historical Jesus and the Christ of faith. Perhaps he is apologizing that this or that favorite story or saying has been excluded.

31—This states the purpose of the signs source and so also of John's gospel. **May believe** is the focus of a hotly debated textual problem. In some manuscripts the verb is *pisteusēte*, an aorist subjunctive, meaning "may come to believe." In others it is *pisteuēte*, a present subjunctive, properly rendered "may go on believing." The former is better attested in the manuscripts than the latter, and the latter may have arisen to harmonize the verb with the present subjunctive, **you may have** (*echēte*). Still, the present subjunctive is favored by many commentators. The distinction is important for what it may tell us about the destination of John's gospel (or the signs source). If the author means "may come to believe," it implies that he addresses his gospel to those who are not believers with the hope of winning them to faith. If his meaning is "continue to believe," the gospel is directed to the community of believers to strengthen their faith. However, no decision regarding the destination of the whole gospel can be based on this verb—for several reasons: (1) The verb may tell us more about the destination of the signs source than John's gospel. (2) John's use of verb tenses is free enough to allow for either of the options. We have seen that for the most part the gospel is directed toward Christians to strengthen them in the midst of their difficulties, and that impression stands, regardless of how this textual decision may be concluded. The expressed purpose to evoke and/or strengthen faith **that Jesus is the Christ, the Son of God** betrays the presumption of a Jewish background on the part of the reader of the gospel (and/or the source). The question of who is the Messiah was the central issue in the Christian-Jewish dialogs which were the backdrop of the gospel. **Son of God** (*ho huios tou theou*) is meant here in its Jewish sense as a title for the Messiah, although John was not unaware of its meaning for Hellenistic readers. **Life** (*zōē*) stands here as shorthand for the entire salvific benefits of God's revelation in Christ (cf. 1:4 above). It is genuine life that emerges as a result of God's act. **In his name** (*en tō onomati autou*) means as a consequence of his life and death. If Thomas' confession (20:28) offers the Christological climax of the gospel, v. 31 provides its soteriological apex.

Quite effectively, John has drawn his conclusion from his source and adapted it to summarize the nature and purpose of his work. What is written (the "signs") has but one goal, and that is to occasion the appropriation of God's redeeming love.

■ Conclusion II: The Appendix (21:1-25)

The problem of chap. 21 must occupy our attention briefly. Nearly all contemporary students of the Fourth Gospel understand this chapter to have been a later addition by someone (perhaps even the evangelist himself) to the completed gospel. That the chapter was a later addition seems evident as one examines the relationship between chaps. 20 and 21. Chapter 20 presents a powerful and totally adequate conclusion to the gospel, with the result that the additional chapter strikes one as anticlimactic at best and to some degree spoils the finale offered in the previous unit. Particularly unharmonious is the relationship of 20:30-31 and 21:25. The latter appears to be a weak effort to imitate the former. Can we then account for the addition of chap. 21 in a way that seems feasible? (For a discussion of the literary distinctiveness of chap. 21 cf. Schnackenburg, vol. 3, pp. 341-342.)

The central issue of the final chapter seems to be the relationship of the beloved disciple and Peter. That issue is deliberately put to rest by giving each of them a significant place in the origins of the church. Peter is assigned a pastoral function and the beloved disciple a role as the authenticator of the Johannine tradition. It appears further that both figures are dead at the time of writing. The possibility presents itself that chap. 21 was relevant to the Johannine community at the time when it was in close relationship with churches which looked to Peter as their founder. This chapter addresses the relationship between the Johannine Christians and other Christians, while the main body of the gospel deals with the dialog between the Johannine church and the Jewish synagogue. If such a situation occasioned the addition of the chapter, who was its author? Similarities with the style and content of the gospel (e.g., the double "Amen" [truly] of v. 18) and differences from it (e.g., the mention of the sons of Zebedee in v. 2) are best reconciled by the suggestion that the author of chap. 21 was a Johannine Christian, a disciple of the evangelist, but not the evangelist himself. He was one who could identify with John and believed that under the guidance of the Paraclete he was empowered to continue the task of the evangelist by addressing a new and relevant issue for the community of which he was, and the evangelist had been, a member. It may be, also, that in completing his task the author of the final chapter employed some old traditions which were not included in the remainder of this gospel. We may also assume that this author was responsible for some final editorial changes and additions to the rest of the document. It is for this reason I will refer to the author of chap. 21 as the "redactor." That he was a contemporary of the author(s) of the Johannine Epistles is likely and may be none other than the writer of 1 John. (Again, I will refer to the author with the masculine pronoun, but it is entirely possible that the redactor was a woman.)

A Resurrection Appearance, a Wondrous Catch of Fish, and a Shared Meal (21:1-14)

The first segment of the chapter narrates a resurrection appearance to some of the disciples in Galilee. It combines a wondrous catch of fish with a meal on the shore. There are numerous similarities with Luke 5:1-11 and 24:13-35. They suggest the possibility that two traditions, which were associated with the ones recorded in Luke, have become interwoven to produce this narrative. Whether the redactor himself merged the two is less likely than that he found them so wedded in his tradition. The prominence of Peter in this chapter unfolds already in this first unit.

1-3—**After this** designates a sequence without any specific implications of time. **Revealed himself** (*ephanerōsen heauton*) is not an expression John uses in narrating the resurrection appearances, but it does appear elsewhere in the gospel in connection with the unveiling of the divine (e.g., 2:11; 9:3; and 17:3). It always occurs with reference to the revealing of that which might otherwise be hidden. For **Sea of Tiberias** cf. 6:1 above. Verse 2 gives the cast of characters, apparently seven in number. John frequently uses the double name **Simon Peter** (e.g., 1:40). On **Thomas** cf. 11:16 above. On **Nathanael** cf. 1:45ff. above. His origin in **Cana** is not mentioned there, however. **The sons of Zebedee** are nowhere else referred to in John. The beloved disciple who appears in v. 7 may be included in the **two others** or as one of the sons of Zebedee, although we think the former is the more likely (cf. Introduction §2). Peter's decision in v. 3 to go **fishing** seems awkward following the events of chap. 20 and demonstrates that this story was intended originally to be an initial appearance to Peter (cf. 1 Cor. 15:5 and Luke 24:34). John nowhere tells us that Peter and others of the disciples were fishermen by trade, but it is nonetheless tempting to think that Peter and the others are returning to their former way of life before becoming followers of Jesus. Their efforts are in vain (compare Luke 5:5). As in the case of the resurrection appearances of chap. 20 there is again an unpleasant human plight (this time failure) among those to whom the risen Christ appears. Nighttime fishing was common on the Sea of Galilee, since the catch could be sold fresh the next morning. The author has quickly set the stage for the arrival of Christ.

4-5—Textual variants make uncertain whether dawn had already broken or was only in process. The failure of **the disciples** to recognize **Jesus** is not surprising, in light of the use of the recognition motif in appearance stories (cf. 20:14ff. above). The use of that technique renders ineffectual the argument that the story could not have followed those of chap. 20, where the disciples have already seen the risen Christ. In v. 5 Jesus addresses the disciples **children**, the Greek word meaning "small boy" (*paidion*). It was a familiar form of address not likely to be used for strangers (cf. 4:49; 16:21; and 1 John 2:18, where it is rendered "child"). In the Johannine tradition it perhaps stood for those who were part of the new family of faith (1:12). The construction of the question in Greek implies some degree of doubt, anticipating a negative reply. **Fish** here translates *prosphagion*, one of the three different words used in the chapter for fish (the other two are *ichthys*, e.g., v. 6, and *osparion*, e.g., v. 9). The word was used originally for a dish of fish. The disciples are forced to admit their failure to this stranger on the shore.

6—Jesus' command comes before the disciples have recognized him. **The right side** was considered to be the "lucky" side in Greek parlance, but that does not seem relevant here. Luke 5:5 is found in some manuscripts after **find some**, a scribal effort to relate the similar stories. To **haul** translates *helkō* which is used in 6:44 and 12:32 of the divine "drawing" of persons to belief. This constitutes the first of the hints of symbolic meaning in the narrative. It is surely true that this story was soon read allegorically by the early church, but it is doubtful that this particular feature was meant symbolically by the redactor. The disciples are obedient to their master even before they have identified him, and therein lies one of the meanings of the narrative. Discipleship means obedi-

ence, and obedience sometimes means acting before there is recognition and thereby risks error.

7-8—The recognition is now made, thanks to the **disciple
whom Jesus loved** (cf. Introduction §2). As usual, he appears in a
narrative alongside **Peter**. His exclamation uses **Lord** as that title
has been employed in the resurrection stories of chap. 20 (vv. 2,
18, 25, and 28). It is comparable especially to 20:18, 25. Peter's
impulsive act is perplexing because of the suggestion that he **put
on his clothes** before leaping into the water to swim to shore. One
explanation proposes that Peter merely waded to shore. The distance would allow for that possibility (v. 8), although the depth of
the water might not. Another explanation is that the verb translated **put on** (*diazōnnynai*) means to "tuck in" clothing and that
Peter tucks his outer garment under his belt to make the swim. But
that leaves unexplained the fact that the author says he was naked
(or nearly so). Combined with the second explanation is the suggestion that a formal greeting between Jews necessitated that they
be properly dressed. The hasty narrative style of the story leaves
us only to speculate at this point. The thrust of the verse, however,
is Peter's eagerness to come to the Lord. So eager is he that the
Greek says he "threw" (*ebalen*) himself into the water. Strangely
enough, we are not told what transpired when Peter arrived on
shore. In v. 8 the **other disciples** are left with the work of getting
the boat and their haul to ground without the benefit of Peter's
help. The Greek states the distance to be "two hundred cubits."

9-10—One might expect the cooking of the **fish** freshly caught
by the disciples, but instead we find **fish** and **bread** already awaiting the fishermen. It may be that this is a bare "seam" in the combination of the two traditions, one having to do with the catch of
fish and the other a breakfast on the shore. **Fish** (*osparion*) and
bread are precisely what was involved in the feeding of the multitude (cf. 6:9 above), but it is not likely the author intended to exploit that fact. For the possible eucharistic meaning, cf. v. 13 below. In v. 10 **Jesus** asks for **fish** to be brought to him, and Verse 11
indicates that Peter does so. We are told nothing else about those
fish. Verse 10 seems important only as an occasion for the discussion of the size of the catch in v. 11. **Some** translates *apo*, used here
as it is nowhere in the body of the gospel.

11—Here the symbolic meaning of the incident is often found. What does the number 153 (of **large fish**) suggest? Commentators are prone to say that it is surely symbolic or else the author would not have mentioned it. Proposals abound! Presumably the fish are symbols of persons brought to faith. The 153 is taken to represent the total number of all who are brought into the church. It is sometimes thought to be a numerical symbol for completeness: 100 is the number for Gentiles and 50 for Jews, it has been argued. Gematria is proposed by some, i.e., the number is the sum of the numerical value of the letters in a name. We must be content (once again) with uncertainty! If the author intended the number to communicate an otherwise unexpressed meaning, the key is beyond our recovery. We may, however, assume that it has to do with the fullness of the mission of the church. It must be observed that this kind of numerical symbolism is not natural to the fourth evangelist, even though his work is rich with symbols. That **the net was not torn**, in spite of the abundant load, is often taken to mean the unity of the church. The verse may be suggesting, therefore, that in spite of the number and variety of persons brought into the church, its basic unity is not violated.

12—Jesus invites **the disciples** to eat. **Breakfast** translates *aristaō* which means to eat the morning meal. However, Luke uses it to mean the main meal of the day (11:37). The incomplete narrative leaves it uncertain whether the meal is comprised only of the fish and bread of v. 9 or whether fish from the grand catch are included. The reluctance of **the disciples** to ask, **"Who are you?"** is likewise not clear. The recognition has taken place as the sentence, **they knew . . . Lord**, shows. Are they awestruck, as in 4:27, or is the question a theological one, as in 8:25? It is best to understand the author to be suggesting that there is a mysterious quality about the risen Christ, in the presence of which humans are constrained by awe. Like the risen Christ resisted Mary's holding him (20:17), so he is at once with and beyond humans in his resurrected state. There is validity also to the suggestion that this verse reflects a muddled recognition scene from the second of the traditions combined in this narrative.

13—**Jesus came** is redundant and may be an emphasis on the initiative of Christ. Jesus serves the disciples as their host. The parallel with 6:11 is evident, and some manuscripts add "thanks" after **gave**, which brings the passage more closely into harmony with 6:11. This similarity with the feeding scene of chap. 6 is among the reasons for attributing eucharistic meaning to the breakfast. **Fish** was reportedly used in the eucharistic meal, and it was a common Christian symbol associated with the sacrament. The setting for the meal alongside the Sea of Galilee for some yields additional parallels to the feeding. Furthermore, the appearance of the risen Christ in the breaking of bread in Luke 24:30-31 (clearly relating the presence of the risen Christ with the Eucharist) adds support for the proposal that the author pictures a eucharistic meal here. There can be little doubt that the passage was interpreted eucharistically by the readers of the gospel, but it is less clear that such was the original meaning intended by the redactor. It is best, perhaps, to suppose that the tradition embedded in this narrative was not eucharistic, but the redactor shaped it along the lines of the feeding in order at least to hint at the sacramental presence of the risen Christ.

14—The redactor now tries to bridge the gap between the appearances in chap. 20 and vv. 10-13. He does so by referring to his narrative as **the third time** Christ has appeared to **the disciples.** Apparently he means 20:19-23 and 26-29, discounting Mary, since she was not a disciple. If such be the case, it is clear that he is using the word **disciple** in a stricter (and more institutionalized) sense than did John; for the evangelist would surely include Mary among the disciples. This may reflect the influence of other Christian churches and their thought on the redactor. For **revealed** cf. v. 1 above.

This rich, but sometimes confusing, narrative makes a number of points worth drawing together in summary. The first has to do with the necessity of obedience in discipleship. The second is the way in which the risen Christ once again transforms human depravity—in this instance turning failure into success. Third, the breadth and extent of the mission of the church to humanity is communicated somehow in the number of fish and the unbroken net. Finally, the community is nourished at the hands of Christ. He feeds them again as did the historical Jesus.

Peter's Reinstatement and Commissioning (21:15-19)

The proposal that chap. 21 was the result of a new and closer relationship between the Johannine church and other Christian communities is borne out by this brief section. Because of the prominence of Peter in other, "mainstream" Christian churches, the Johannine community is given its own statement of Peter's reinstatement and commissioning. Some subtle undertones of apologetic are heard in this narrative, as Peter's authority is reestablished.

15a—Little effort is made to link this independent piece to vv. 1-14, except for **they had finished breakfast**, where the same verb (*aristaō*) appears in v. 12. **Son of John** is the preferred reading and not "son of Jonah," which is an effort to harmonize this verse with Matt. 16:17. Only in this gospel do we have **Peter** called **son of John**. **Love me** here is *agapas me*, which is repeated in vv. 16 and 17; but *phileis me* occurs in v. 17. The verb for **love** in Peter's response in each case, however, is *phileō*. Although it is sometimes argued otherwise, it is best not to try to distinguish between different degrees of love implied in the two verbs. As the evangelist uses the two synonymously (e.g., 19:26 and 20:2), so the redactor does. **More than these** is ambiguous, since these (*toutōn*) can be either masculine or neuter. Hence, the question may compare Peter's love of Christ with that of the other disciples or his love of some *thing* else, e.g., his fishing gear. The former seems more likely, but in either case the comparison plays no further part in the conversation. It is perhaps Peter's bold claim of being able to follow Jesus anywhere (in 13:37) that occasions the use of the comparison. The prediction of Peter's martyrdom in vv. 18-19 shows the relationship of 13:36-38 to this passage.

15b—**Peter's** response uses the verb *oida* (**know**), and that verb occurs again in v. 16. In v. 17, however, *ginōskō* (**know**) is used. Again, no difference of meaning is likely. Another variation of language occurs in the command Jesus issues after each of Peter's confessions. In v. 15 the verb *boske* (**feed**) appears with the noun *arnia* for **lambs**. But in v. 16 Peter is asked to "tend" (*poimaine*) "sheep" (*probata*), and in v. 17 once again to feed (*boske*) "sheep" (*probata*). It is not necessary to seek subtle differences of meaning here, but it is important to note what emotional impact this variation of language has, namely, the inclusiveness of the task asked of Peter. In every possible way he is to care for all those who are members of Christ's flock, no matter what their character may be. Textual witnesses show that there has been an effort to overcome this stylistic variety, but it is doubtless that the author had in mind that variety. The commissioning of Peter certainly recalls 10:1-16. For the use of this image for pastors of the early church cf. Acts 20: 28-31 and 1 Peter 5:2-4. The point is that loving Christ entails caring for other human beings.

16-17—For the repetitions cf. v. 15 above. **A second time** (*palin deuteron*) is redundant in the Greek—"again a second time." It emphasizes the thoroughness of Jesus' questioning. In v. 17 the definite article occurs in the Greek translated **the third time** (*to triton*)—"still a third time." **Peter's** hurt contributes to the drama of the scene and brings to an end Jesus' questionings. We are to suppose that the questions concerning his love for Jesus remind Peter of his denial. He appropriately appeals to Jesus' wondrous knowledge of him. He cannot pretend his affection. For if what he professes is not real, Jesus already knows it; for Jesus knows his **sheep** (10:14-15). With the third question, confession, and command, Peter is restored, the blot of his denials washed away, and his mission established.

18-19—**Truly, truly** (*amēn, amēn*) is characteristic of the evangelist (cf. 1:51 above). The words attributed to Jesus here may have been a proverb describing the way the freedom of youth is lost with old age. In this context it is clear that the reference is to Peter's active ministry in contrast to his death (cf. v. 19 below). The contrast between the two stages has been seen in four different points: (1) young to old, (2) dressing oneself to being dressed, (3) going to being taken, and (4) moving freely to being moved without consent. The verb rendered **girded** (*zōnnymi*) means to tie a belt, but is sometimes used more generally for dressing. **Stretch out your hands** (*ekteneis tas cheiras sou*) has been understood both as a posture of prayer and as a reference to crucifixion. The latter is most tempting, and Barrett shows that the expression was used for crucifixion in the early church (p. 585). In either sense, the words are a declaration that Peter will lose his freedom and be led off to be put to death. Verse 19 displays that this is the meaning the author found in the words. **What death he was** . . . recalls the similar phrase used of Jesus' death (12:33 and 18:32). The martyr's death accomplishes in miniature what Jesus' death did—to **glorify God**. Christian discipleship is understood as a continuation of Jesus' ministry and death. **Follow me** (*akolouthei moi*) makes explicit the theme of discipleship in this little narrative (cf. 1:35-51 above).

Peter's reinstatement and commissioning are not to be taken so much as the authorization of a special ministry for him as it is a call to discipleship in general. The story functioned in the Johannine community to help them understand the ministry of Peter in spite of his denials, and hence it is likely to have been a later tradition. But it also expresses the mission of every Christian for the author's day. Jesus' questions, then, constitute a form of forgiveness for Peter and for later Christians, and the repetition of the questions a statement of the radical nature of devotion to Christ called for by discipleship.

The Importance and Destiny of the Beloved Disciple (21:20-24)

If vv. 15-19 clarify the ministry of Peter for the Johannine community, this section places alongside of it the role of the community's own founder. By virtue of these two sections Peter and the beloved disciple are both accepted as authorized figures with different functions.

20-21—This narrative is linked with the previous one by the utilization of the word **following**, found in v. 19. This linkage is similar to the way vv. 15-19 are tied to vv. 1-14 by "breakfast." The physical motion is not important here, and perhaps we are to think of following strictly in terms of discipleship, meaning only that the beloved disciple also follows Jesus, as does **Peter**. The rest of v. 20 repeats 13:23-25 in order to identify **the disciple whom Jesus loved**. The fact that the identification is here but not in v. 7

is evidence that the two stories were originally separate and independent of one another and have only later been brought together. Verse 21 focuses attention on the destiny of the beloved disciple, although the Greek is elliptical, i.e., lacks a specific verb. Literally it reads "and this one what?" The next verse gives the question its content.

22-23—My will (*thelō*) may imply the divine plan as it sometimes does in the main body of this gospel (e.g., 5:30; 6:38, 39). **Remain** (*menein*) may denote "continue to live," as in 1 Cor. 15:6. However, it may also carry some of its special Johannine meaning (e.g., 15:1-10 above where it is translated "abide") and imply that the beloved disciple is forever in a relationship of intimacy with Jesus. **Until I come** would seem to refer to the parousia. If so, then Jesus is saying that the beloved disciple would live until the parousia, unlike Peter, who would die a martyr's death. There was an anticipation in the earliest church that the parousia would occur before many of the original disciples died (e.g., Mark 9:1). Verse 23, then, would be the author's effort to correct the misunderstanding that the beloved disciple would not die. But it is clear that he is interpreting **until I come**, not as an allusion to the parousia, but to the "coming" of Christ in the Spirit. There is the possibility that this promise that the beloved disciple would **remain until I come** had in popular imagination been interpreted to mean that he would not die before the parousia, and now after his death the community was disappointed. Jesus' words to Peter, **Follow me**, suggest that all such imaginative gossip is not to concern the Christian. Their only task is to be faithful in their own way. In the Greek the command reads, "you follow me," with the "you" standing first, for emphasis. **Brethren** (*adelphoi*) designates Christians (cf. 20:17 and 19:26-27 above).

NB,

24—This verse concludes the section, since it finally answers the concern raised by Peter at the outset. There is some textual confusion in the first words of this verse, but it is clear that there are two participles, the first present tense, **is bearing witness** (*ho martyrōn*), and the second an aorist, **who has written** (*grapsas*). The latter suggests the completed work and the former the ongoing testimony of the work. Hence, the first does not necessarily mean the disciple is still alive. These things (*tauta*) might be the contents of chap. 21, but more probably the entire gospel. Is the author of the chapter saying that the evangelist was none other than the beloved disciple? That would seem to be the sense of the words. However, the verb has written (*grapsas*) may mean "has caused to be written," as it does at 19:19. At least the author is claiming that it is the beloved disciple who is responsible for the contents of this gospel and at most that the beloved disciple is himself the evangelist. We know (*oidamen*) is the church speaking with the redactor, thus staking their claim that the witness of the gospel is true. The last word may mean true instead of false but also true in the sense it is sometimes used elsewhere in this gospel to designate the content of the revelation in Christ (e.g., 8:26).

The function of this short passage is to establish the importance of the beloved disciple as the authority on which this gospel is based. Hence, it is not a polemic against Peter as much as it is a statement of the role of the beloved disciple, which is a different role than that of Peter. With vv. 15-19 and 20-24 the author has recognized the importance of both figures, thereby sanctioning the centrality of Peter in other Christian churches and the role of the beloved disciple in the Johannine church. Even though we find it difficult to believe that the beloved disciple is to be identified with the fourth evangelist (cf. Introduction §2), it is clear that the Johannine church laid claim to having its own tradition rooted in an eyewitness to the historical Jesus (cf. 19:35 above).

A Final Ending (21:25)

This verse appears in Codex Sinaiticus as a later addition by the hand of the same scribe who had earlier ended the gospel with v. 24. But there is no other evidence of any weight to cause doubt of the place of the verse as the final conclusion of the gospel. It intends to duplicate 20:30-31 (cf. "many other signs" in that passage), but the repetition is a bit clumsy. The point, however, is that every witness to Christ has its limitations. While 20:30-31 is a far more impressive conclusion than this, Lindars is a bit too hard on the redactor when he says it is "an exaggerated literary conceit, which is not to be taken seriously" (p. 642).

Let all of us who write and read books confess with the redactor of the gospel that each written piece about Christ is but a tiny dot in the eternal significance of God's revelation in Christ.

NOTES

1. Martin Luther, "Preface to the New Testament," in *Luther's Works*, vol. 35 (Philadelphia: Fortress, 1960) 362.
2. That such a formalized ban against Christians was ever propagated in the first century is now being seriously challenged. Cf. most recently Steven T. Katz, "Issues in the Separation of Judaism and Christianity after 70 C.E.," *JBL* 103 (1984): 43-76, and Rueven Kimmelman, *"Birkat Ha-Minim* and the Lack of Evidence for an Anti-Christian Jewish Prayer in Late Antiquity," in *Jewish and Christian Self Definition*, vol. 2, ed. E. P. Sanders (Philadelphia: Fortress, 1981) 226-244.
3. R. Alan Culpepper has proposed that the Johannine community had the character of a "school" in the sense of other ancient religious and philosophical schools; *The Johannine School* (SBLDS 29; Missoula, Mont.: Scholars Press, 1975).
4. For surveys of contemporary scholarship on the gospel, cf. in addition to the volumes in the bibliography the following: Wilbert Francis Howard, *The Fourth Gospel in Recent Criticism and Interpretation*, rev. by C. K. Barrett (London: Epworth, 1955); H. Thyen "Aus der Literatur zum Johannes-Evangelium," *Theologische Rundschau* 39 (1974): 222-252, 289-330, continued in 42 (1977): 211-270; Robert Kysar, "The Fourth Gospel: A Report on Recent Research," in *Aufstieg und Niedergang der Römischen Welt*, ed. Hildegard Temporini and Wolfgang Haase (Berlin: Walter de Gruyter) II, Band 25.3, 2389-2480; Kysar, "Community and Gospel: Vectors in Fourth Gospel Criticism," in *Interpreting the Gospels*, ed. James Luther Mays (Philadelphia: Fortress, 1981) 265-277; Kysar, "The Gospel of John in Current Research," *Religious Studies Review* 9 (1983): 314-323.
5. This structure is essentially a revision of that which I develop in *John's Story of Jesus* (Philadelphia: Fortress, 1984).

323

6. See my argument in "Christology and Controversy: The Contributions of the Prologue of the Gospel of John to New Testament Christology and Their Historical Setting," *Currents in Theology and Mission* 5 (1978): 348-364. See also the proposal of John Painter, "Christology and the History of the Johannine Community in the Prologue of the Fourth Gospel," *JBL* 30 (1984): 460-474.

7. R. Alan Culpepper argues this view on the basis of a chiastic structure he finds in the prolog; see "The Pivot of John's Prologue," *NTS* 27 (1980): 1-31.

8. But cf. Bruce Schein's effort to identify it with the scene in 2 Kings 2: 1-12, in *Following the Way* (Minneapolis: Augsburg, 1980) 18-19. Generally, Schein's arguments for the geography of the Fourth Gospel are not persuasive.

9. Cf. Foster R. McCurley's fascinating suggestion that the passage represents one instance of John's "desacralization" of the motif of the sacred mountain of the OT, in *Ancient Myths and Biblical Faith* (Philadelphia: Fortress, 1983) 179.

10. Cf. the seminal work of Wayne A. Meeks, *The Prophet-King: Moses Traditions and the Johannine Christology* (Supplements to *Novum Testamentum* 14; Leiden: Brill, 1967).

11. Cf. the argument of Joachim Jeremias, *The Lord's Prayer* (Philadelphia: Fortress, 1964) 17-21; *The Central Message of the New Testament* (New York: Scribner's, 1965) 9-30, and *The Prayers of Jesus* (London: SCM, 1967) 11-65, 108-115. However, proper reservations about Jeremias' theory are offered by Gerza Vermes, among others, in *Jesus the Jew: A Historian's Reading of the Gospels* (Philadelphia: Fortress, 1973) 210-211.

12. The problem of the relationship between chaps. 5 and 6 is most difficult and calls for some discussion. The quandary arises first of all from the matter of geography. At the conclusion of chap. 4 (v. 54) Jesus is reported to be in Galilee, and as chap. 5 begins we are told that he goes to Jerusalem for a feast (v. 1). The whole of chap. 5 seems to be set in Jerusalem; at least we are not told of any geographical movement. However, chap. 6 begins with the note that Jesus crossed the Sea of Galilee, without mentioning any resumption of the Galilean ministry. Furthermore, the reference to the signs of healing in 6:2 is not clear, unless it harks back to 4:43-54. For these reasons many suggest that chaps. 5 and 6 in the form of the gospel as we know it are in reverse order from the evangelist's original design. Such a proposed rearrangement makes for a smoother transition between the two chapters, i.e., 7:1 seems to follow 5:47; this would also afford an immediate antecedent (4:43-54) for the signs mentioned in 6:2. The problem can also be explained in at least two other ways: (1) by assuming that chap. 6 is a later addition to the gospel made without any detailed attention to the way it harmonized with the context, or (2) by

suggesting that this is another blatant instance of the evangelist's lack of concern with matters of geography (cf. 2:12 above) and consistency.

To begin rearranging portions of the gospel in order to find a more consistent and smooth order is an endless and speculative enterprise, the results of which please only the scholar who has devised the plan (cf. Bultmann's radical rearrangement as well as that of J. H. Bernard, *A Critical and Exegetical Commentary on the Gospel according to St.John* [ICC, 2 vols.; Edinburgh: T. and T. Clark, 1928] esp. 2, XVI-XXXII). There is evidence elsewhere in the gospel that either later additions have been made to the document or the evangelist was not careful in weaving connectives among bits and traditions to be included (e.g., 14:31 in relation to chaps. 15 and 16). It may be enough to say that while the evangelist was a thoughtful theologian and a skillful writer, he did not always polish transitions in his document, especially when they involved a shift between tradition and his interpretation or vice versa. In 5:31-47 it appears John has composed or reworked a discourse, and at 6:1 he begins employing a tradition. Hence, the transition is less than smooth, and the details of the piece of tradition inconsistent with the earlier narrative. The enigma remains, however: How could so skillful a writer (cf., e.g., chap. 9) be content with such glaring "seams" between his traditions and redaction?

13. E. P. Sanders, *The Tendencies of the Synoptic Traditon* (SNTSMS 9; Cambridge: University Press, 1969).

14. John Paul Heil, *Jesus Walking on the Sea* (Analecta Biblica 87; Rome: Biblical Institute, 1981).

15. James Montgomery Boice, *Witness and Revelation in the Gospel of John* (Grand Rapids, Mich.: Zondervan, 1970).

16. A. E. Harvey, *Jesus on Trial: A Study in the Fourth Gospel* (Atlanta: John Knox, 1977).

17. I would propose, as an alternative to any literary dependence on Luke and Mark, that John is here indebted to a source which has roots in traditions shared with the sources employed by the Synoptic evangelists. More specifically, it appears that two original traditions have produced three distinct stories. The first of those traditions is represented in the narrative of the anointing of the head of Jesus by an unnamed woman at Bethany in the home of Simon the leper (Mark 14:3-9 and Matt. 26:6-13). The second is reported in Luke 7:36-50, a story of the anointing of Jesus' feet by a "sinful" woman at the home of a Pharisee. The Johannine tradition appears to have coalesced these two into one narrative, resulting in the story related in 12:1-8. The Johannine anointing has some features from each of the other stories. For instance, although John preserves the story of a woman anointing the feet of Jesus and wiping them with her hair (a feature from the Lukan story), it also contains the objection from some of

those who witnessed the act that the ointment might have been sold and the money given to the poor (a feature found in the form of the story in Matthew and Mark). But the Johannine story differs at points from both of the Synoptic versions, e.g., the identification of the woman as Mary and the objector as Judas. It differs from both of the Synoptic tales as a result of the amalgamation of the two forms and the distinctive shaping of the narrative both by the Johannine tradition itself and later by the evangelist's redactional work. Our proposal may be represented in a diagram such as this:

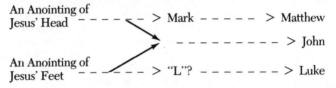

18. Robert Kysar, *The Scandal of Lent* (Minneapolis: Augsburg, 1982) 66-75.
19. Cf. the discussion of this tension in D. A. Carson, *Divine Sovereignty and Human Responsibility: Biblical Perspectives in Tension* (New Foundations Theological Library 11; Atlanta: John Knox, 1981) and, less helpful, Roland Bergmeier, *Glauben als Gabe nach Johannes* (Beiträge zur Wissenschaft vom Alten und Neuen Testament; Stuttgart: Kohlhammer, 1980).
20. This unit introduces the double problem of the unique dating of the Last Supper in John and the absence of a narrative which institutes the Eucharist. The Synoptic Gospels agree in dating the Last Supper on Passover (i.e., the evening after sundown), portraying that event as the Passover meal itself. The arrest, trial, and crucifixion, according to the Synoptic witness, all occur on Passover day (e.g., Mark 14:1, 12, and 17). John clearly dates the Last Supper and the crucifixion on the day *before* Passover (cf. 13:29; 18:28; 19:14; 31, 42). The result of John's distinctive dating is twofold: (1) He deprives the Last Supper setting of its Passover symbolism. (2) He dates the crucifixion on the afternoon before the beginning of Passover at sundown, at the very time the lambs are being slaughtered and prepared for the Passover meal.

What accounts for this difference between the dating of the event by the Synoptics and John? Two possibilities exist: (1) Either John or the Synoptic tradition (or Mark himself?) has adjusted the date for reasons of symbolic value. The Synoptics may reflect an effort to bring to bear the Passover symbolism on the Last Supper and the institution of the Eucharist. Or John may have intended to make Jesus' death correspond to the killing of the Passover lambs, since that motif was important to him. It is difficult to resolve the dilemma without resort-

ing to preconceptions of either the Eucharist or the cross. (2) The dis-
agreement arises from the use of different calendars or marking of
dates. That such is a possibility is shown by the use of a different cal-
endar of feasts by the Essenes of Qumran (cf. Brown, vol. 2, pp. 555-
556). No certainty can be attained in this matter. Whatever the reasons for the dating, however, it is clear that the symbolism of the concurrent deaths of Jesus and the Passover lambs is strongly emphasized
by the fourth evangelist.

The second problem is, if anything, even more difficult, and it is related to the first. Why is there no account of the institution of the Eucharist in John's gospel? The absence of such a narrative, combined
with the lack of Passover symbolism in the meal, has led to at least
four different positions regarding the evangelist's view of the sacraments. The first assumes that John was opposed to the sacraments and
deliberately ignored them, even removing Passover symbolism from
the account of the Last Supper. The second position is exactly the opposite. John intended to emphasize the meaning of the sacraments by
omitting their institution (the Eucharist from the Last Supper and the
absence of a narrative of Jesus' own baptism) and focusing instead on
their spiritual importance, of which the discourse in 6:35-59 and the
foot washing (13:1-11) are examples. The third position, close to the
second, understands that John attempted a significant revision of the
meaning of the sacraments, which included removing Passover symbolism from the Eucharist. The fourth position is that the Johannine
community was nonsacramental because their tradition gave them no
knowledge of the sacraments. (Cf. Kysar, *John, the Maverick Gospel*,
105-109, and *The Fourth Evangelist*, 249-259, for further discussion of
the issue.)

Here we can make only limited observations concerning this most
perplexing question. First, the interpretation of the "bread of life"
discourse is crucial to an understanding of John's view of the Eucharist. Does that discourse consist, in effect, of an institution of the Eucharist transplanted into the midst of Jesus' ministry? It can be understood without recourse to the eucharistic interpretation—with the
exception of 6:51-58 (cf. above). Those verses appear to be a later
interpretation of the bread of life theme of 6:35-50. It may be that the
eucharistic meaning of the bread of life entered the Johannine community at a point after the formulation of the discourse in vv. 35-50
and after the location of the foot washing at the Last Supper. Second,
these observations would suggest that the Johannine tradition was
nonsacramental (but not antisacramental) until a period of time after
the division of the community from the synagogue. It is plausible that
6:51-58 reflects a later, eucharistic view not found (or at least not emphasized) in the earlier tradition. If this is the case, then the absence
of Passover symbolism in the Last Supper is due to the earlier asacra-

mental view of the community and not an antisacramental polemic. Our conclusion, therefore, is that John's dating of the Last Supper was independent of any view of the Eucharist. Finally, regarding Baptism: it too suffered disuse in the community until after the expulsion of the Christians from the synagogue. In their quest for new self-identity independent of their Jewish roots, the community revived the practice of Baptism (and perhaps the words "water and" were added to 3:5, cf. above). The strange confusion about whether Jesus himself baptized (3:22 and 4:2) suggests that the community viewed with disinterest the role of Baptism until a later time. Cf. 1:33 above for John's preference for "Spirit baptism."

21. For an argument to this effect cf. Herold Weiss, "Foot-washing in the Johannine Community," *Novum Testamentum* 41 (1979): 298-325.

22. Cf. the provocative suggestion of Fernando Segovia that 13:34-35 and 15:13-17 reflect a redaction of the gospel by one in the same setting out of which 1 John was written: *Love Relationships in the Johannine Tradition* (SBLDS 58; Chico, Calif.: Scholars Press, 1982).

23. A different sort of emphasis in the first of the discourses is found by D. Bruce Woll's dissertation, *Johannine Christianity in Conflict* (SBLDS 60; Chico, Calif.: Scholars Press, 1981). Woll's case is interesting, but unconvincing. Cf. John Painter, "The Farewell Discourses and the History of the Johannine Community," *NTS* 27 (1981): 525-543. Painter's analysis of the discourses differs from mine, but proposes much the same setting.

24. For a summary of the Paraclete passages cf. Kysar, *John's Story of Jesus* 75.

25. Among the best monographs on John's soteriology is J. Terence Forestell, *The Word of the Cross* (Analecta Biblica 57; Rome: Biblical Institute, 1974). Also of considerable importance for John's view of the cross is Godfrey C. Nicholson, *Death as Departure: The Johannine Descent-Ascent Schema* (SBLDS 63; Chico, Calif.: Scholars Press, 1983).

26. Cf. the fascinating proposal of the evolution of the resurrection stories in Reginald H. Fuller, *The Formation of the Resurrection Narratives* (New York: Macmillan, 1971). Contrast Fuller's view of the empty tomb narratives with that of Rudolf Bultmann, *The History of the Synoptic Tradition* (New York: Harper and Row, 1963) 287-291. Less imaginative is Robert H. Smith, *Easter Gospels: The Resurrection of Jesus according to the Four Evangelists* (Minneapolis: Augsburg, 1983).

27. Fortunately, the study of the role of women in the Fourth Gospel has begun and promises to do justice to this long-neglected matter. Cf. esp. Raymond E. Brown, *The Community of the Beloved Disciple* (New York: Paulist, 1979) 183-198 and S. M. Schneiders, "Women in the Fourth Gospel and the Role of Women in the Contemporary Church," *Biblical Theology Bulletin* 12 (1982): 35-45.

28. Cf. Kysar, *The Scandal of Lent* 105-107.

SELECTED BIBLIOGRAPHY

The following volumes are those on which the author is most dependent and to which references are made throughout the commentary by author's name and page number.

A. Commentaries:

Barrett, C. K. *The Gospel according to St. John.* 2nd edition. Philadelphia: Westminister, 1978. The best commentary on the Greek text, strong in the area of religious-philosophical backgrounds and grammatical issues. Rather technical for the general reader.

Brown, Raymond E. *The Gospel according to John.* Anchor Bible 29 and 29a. Garden City: Doubleday, 1966 and 1970. Perhaps the best and most balanced commentary on the English text, which is the author's own translation. Noteworthy for its review of a variety of positions on controversial issues and passages.

Bultmann, Rudolf. *The Gospel of John: A Commentary.* Trans. G. R. Beasley-Murray, R. W. N. Hoare, and J. K. Riches. Philadelphia: Westminster, 1971. A modern classic. Idiosyncratic in its perspective by the standards of contemporary Johannine scholarship but the strongest theological commentary of its time.

Haenchen, Ernst. *The Gospel of John.* Trans. and ed. Robert Funk. Hermeneia Commentary. Philadelphia: Fortress, 1984. Two volumes. Significant for its redaction-critical perspective. Somewhat uneven in its treatment due to the fact that it is an edition of an uncompleted manuscript.

Lindars, Barnabas. *The Gospel of John*. New Century Bible Commentary. Grand Rapids, Mich.: Eerdmans, 1972. The best single-volume commentary in paperback. Emphasizes tradition-critical relationships with the Synoptics and the historical value of the Johannine representation of Jesus.

Schnackenburg, Rudolf. *The Gospel according to St. John*. Trans. Kevin Smyth, et al. New York: Seabury, 1968, 1980, 1982. Three volumes. The most thorough commentary in English, exhaustive in its treatment, with numerous excurses of great value.

B. Other Studies:

Borgen, Peder. *Bread from Heaven*. Supplements to *Novum Testamentum* 10. Leiden: Brill, 1965. A definitive treatment of the concept of manna in chap. 6 compared with the writings of Philo. Establishes the homiletical-exegetical nature of the Johannine discourse materials.

Culpepper, R. Alan. *Anatomy of the Fourth Gospel: A Study in Literary Design*. Foundations and Facets: New Testament. Philadlephia: Fortress, 1983. A masterful application of some of the "new literary criticism" to the Fourth Gospel with rich results for understanding the style and structure of the book. The best single-volume introduction to the literary character of this gospel.

Dodd, C. H. *The Interpretation of the Fourth Gospel*. Cambridge: University Press, 1953. A quest for the intellectual context of the gospel with reference to its major themes plus a discussion of its structure. Emphasizes the Hellenistic quality of the gospel without exclusion of its Jewish background.

_____ . *Historical Tradition in the Fourth Gospel*. Cambridge: University Press, 1963. A definitive study of the gospel from a form-critical perspective, establishing the relationship between John and the Synoptics at the stage of the oral tradition. Weakened by the claim that historical tradition is to be equated with the authentic historical Jesus.

Fortna, Robert T. *The Gospel of Signs*. SNTSMS 11. Cambridge: University Press, 1970. The most exhaustive narrative-source proposal for the gospel, isolating and reconstructing a "signs gospel" allegedly employed by the fourth evangelist.

Käsemann, Ernst. *The Testament of Jesus according to John 17.* Trans. Gerhard Krodel. Philadelphia: Fortress, 1968. A remarkable study of the passage in the light of the whole of the gospel. In effect a theology of the Gospel of John.

Kysar, Robert. *The Fourth Evangelist and His Gospel.* Minneapolis: Augsburg, 1975. A survey of contemporary scholarship on the gospel for the decade 1963-73.

——————— . *John, the Maverick Gospel.* Atlanta: John Knox, 1976. An introduction to the thought of the gospel.

Martyn, J. Louis. *History and Theology in the Fourth Gospel.* Rev. ed. Nashville: Abingdon, 1979. The epoch-making argument for the setting of the gospel understood in terms of the experience of expulsion from the synagogue.

ABOUT THE AUTHOR

Robert Kysar earned his Ph.D. in New Testament from Northwestern University, Evanston, Illinois, after an undergraduate education at the College of Idaho. He was a postdoctoral fellow in the Department of Religious Studies of Yale University, 1973–74. After 17 years of college teaching (of which 12 were spent at Hamline University, St. Paul, Minnesota), he became co-pastor of Christ United Lutheran Church, Gordon, Pennsylvania, with his wife, the Reverend Myrna C. Kysar. He is currently director of GENESIS, an educational program in the Northeastern Pennsylvania Synod of the Lutheran Church in America, and is a visiting lecturer in New Testament at the Lutheran Theological Seminary at Philadelphia and that at Gettysburg.

He is author of five previous books, four of which are on the Gospel of John, as well as a number of articles. He is a member of the Society of Biblical Literature and the Society for New Testament Studies.